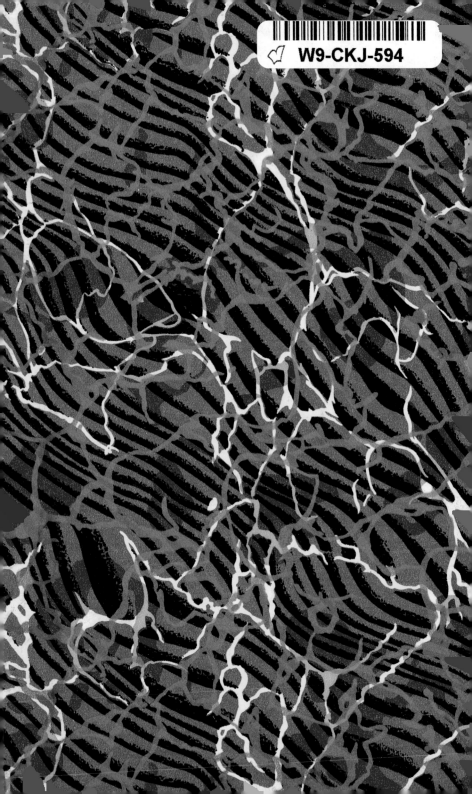

THE
HARVARD CLASSICS

Registered Edition

◆

The Five-Foot Shelf of Books

Moliere in audience with Louis XIV at Versailles

THE HARVARD CLASSICS
EDITED BY CHARLES W. ELIOT, LL.D.

Continental Drama

Calderon · Corneille
Racine · Molière · Lessing
Schiller

With Introductions and Notes
Volume 26

P. F. Collier & Son Corporation
NEW YORK

MANUFACTURED IN U. S. A.

CONTENTS

LIFE IS A DREAM

BY
PEDRO CALDERON DE LA BARCA

TRANSLATED BY
EDWARD FITZGERALD

INTRODUCTORY NOTE

THE present volume aims to represent, as far as the limits of space allow, the chief dramatists of Spain, France, and Germany. To the plays included here should be added the "Faust" and "Egmont" of Goethe, printed in another volume of this series. These eight works, along with the specimens of the Elizabethan and modern English drama given in the Harvard Classics, indicate the high-water mark of dramatic production in modern times, and afford a basis for comparison with the masterpieces of the drama of antiquity as represented in the volume of "Nine Greek Dramas."

Pedro Calderon de la Barca was born in Madrid, January 17, 1600, of good family. He was educated at the Jesuit College in Madrid and at the University of Salamanca; and a doubtful tradition says that he began to write plays at the age of thirteen. His literary activity was interrupted for ten years, 1625–1635, by military service in Italy and the Low Countries, and again for a year or more in Catalonia. In 1637 he became a Knight of the Order of Santiago, and in 1651 he entered the priesthood, rising to the dignity of Superior of the Brotherhood of San Pedro in Madrid. He held various offices in the court of Philip IV, who rewarded his services with pensions, and had his plays produced with great splendor. He died May 5, 1681.

At the time when Calderon began to compose for the stage, the Spanish drama was at its height. Lope de Vega, the most prolific and, with Calderon, the greatest, of Spanish dramatists, was still alive; and by his applause gave encouragement to the beginner whose fame was to rival his own. The national type of drama which Lope had established was maintained in its essential characteristics by Calderon, and he produced abundant specimens of all its varieties. Of regular plays he has left a hundred and twenty; of "Autos Sacramentales," the peculiar Spanish allegorical development of the medieval mystery, we have seventy-three; besides a considerable number of farces.

The dominant motives in Calderon's dramas are characteristically national: fervid loyalty to Church and King, and a sense of honor heightened almost to the point of the fantastic. Though his plays are laid in a great variety of scenes and ages, the sentiment and the characters remain essentially Spanish; and this intensely local quality has probably lessened the vogue of Calderon in other countries. In the construction and conduct

5

of his plots he showed great skill, yet the ingenuity expended in the management of the story did not restrain the fiery emotion and opulent imagination which mark his finest speeches and give them a lyric quality which some critics regard as his greatest distinction.

Of all Calderon's works, "Life is a Dream" may be regarded as the most universal in its theme. It seeks to teach a lesson that may be learned from the philosophers and religious thinkers of many ages—that the world of our senses is a mere shadow, and that the only reality is to be found in the invisible and eternal. The story which forms its basis is Oriental in origin, and in the form of the legend of "Barlaam and Josaphat" was familiar in all the literatures of the Middle Ages. Combined with this in the plot is the tale of Abou Hassan from the "Arabian Nights," the main situations in which are turned to farcical purposes in the Induction to the Shakespearean "Taming of the Shrew." But with Calderon the theme is lifted altogether out of the atmosphere of comedy, and is worked up with poetic sentiment and a touch of mysticism into a symbolic drama of profound and universal philosophical significance.

LIFE IS A DREAM

DRAMATIS PERSONÆ

BASILIO	. .	*King of Poland.*
SEGISMUND	. .	*his Son.*
ASTOLFO	. .	*his Nephew.*
ESTRELLA	. .	*his Niece.*
CLOTALDO	. .	*a General in Basilio's Service.*
ROSAURA	. .	*a Muscovite Lady.*
FIFE	. .	*her Attendant.*

CHAMBERLAIN, LORDS IN WAITING, OFFICERS, SOLDIERS,
ETC., IN BASILIO'S SERVICE.

———————

*The Scene of the first and third Acts lies on the Polish
frontier: of the second Act, in Warsaw.*

ACT I

SCENE I.—*A pass of rocks, over which a storm is rolling away, and the
sun setting: in the foreground, half-way down, a fortress.*

Enter first from the topmost rock ROSAURA, *as from
horseback, in man's attire; and, after her,* FIFE[1]

Rosaura

THERE, four-footed Fury, blast-
engender'd brute, without the wit
Of brute, or mouth to match the bit
Of man—art satisfied at last?
Who, when thunder roll'd aloof,

———

[1] As this version of Calderon's drama is not for acting, a higher and wider
mountain-scene than practicable may be imagined for Rosaura's descent in the first
Act and the soldiers' ascent in the last. The bad watch kept by the sentinels who
guarded their state-prisoner, together with much else (not all!) that defies sober sense
in this wild drama, I must leave Calderon to answer for; whose audience were not
critical of detail and probability, so long as a good story, with strong, rapid, and
picturesque action and situation, was set before them.

Tow'rd the spheres of fire your ears
Pricking, and the granite kicking
Into lightning with your hoof,
Among the tempest-shatter'd crags
Shattering your luckless rider
Back into the tempest pass'd?
There then lie to starve and die,
Or find another Phaeton
Mad-mettled as yourself; for I,
Wearied, worried, and for-done,
Alone will down the mountain try,
That knits his brows against the sun.

    Fife (*as to his mule*). There, thou mis-begotten thing,
Long-ear'd lightning, tail'd tornado,
Griffin-hoof-in hurricano,—
(I might swear till I were almost
Hoarse with roaring Asonante)
Who forsooth because our betters
Would begin to kick and fling—
You forthwith your noble mind
Must prove, and kick me off behind,
Tow'rd the very centre whither
Gravity was most inclined.
There where you have made your bed
In it lie; for, wet or dry,
Let what will for me betide you,
Burning, blowing, freezing, hailing;
Famine waste you: devil ride you:
Tempest baste you black and blue:—

    (*To* Rosaura.) There! I think in downright railing
I can hold my own with you.

    Ros. Ah, my good Fife, whose merry loyal pipe,
Come weal, come woe, is never out of tune—
What, you in the same plight too?

    Fife.   Ay;
And madam—sir—hereby desire,
When you your own adventures sing

Another time in lofty rhyme,
You don't forget the trusty squire
Who went with you Don-quixoting.

   Ros. Well, my good fellow—to leave Pegasus
Who scarce can serve us than our horses worse—
They say no one should rob another of
The single satisfaction he has left
Of singing his own sorrows; one so great,
So says some great philosopher, that trouble
Were worth encount'ring only for the sake
Of weeping over—what perhaps you know
Some poet calls the 'luxury of woe.'

   Fife. Had I the poet or philosopher
In the place of her that kick'd me off to ride,
I'd test his theory upon his hide.
But no bones broken, madam—sir, I mean?—

   Ros. A scratch here that a handkerchief will heal—
And you?—

   Fife.   A scratch in *quiddity,* or kind:
But not in '*quo*'—my wounds are all behind.
But, as you say, to stop this strain,
Which, somehow, once one's in the vein,
Comes clattering after—there again!—
What are we twain—deuce take't!—we two,
I mean, to do—drench'd through and through—
Oh, I shall choke of rhymes, which I believe
Are all that we shall have to live on here.

   Ros. What, is our victual gone too?—

   Fife.   Ay, that brute
Has carried all we had away with her,
Clothing, and cate, and all.

   Ros.   And now the sun,
Our only friend and guide, about to sink
Under the stage of earth.

   Fife.   And enter Night,
With Capa y Espada—and—pray heaven!—
With but her lanthorn also.

Ros.   Ah, I doubt
To-night, if any, with a dark one—or
Almost burnt out after a month's consumption.
Well! well or ill, on horseback or afoot,
This is the gate that lets me into Poland;
And, sorry welcome as she gives a guest
Who writes his own arrival on her rocks
In his own blood—
Yet better on her stony threshold die,
Than live on unrevenged in Muscovy.

Fife. Oh, what a soul some women have—I mean
Some men—

Ros.   Oh, Fife, Fife, as you love me, Fife,
Make yourself perfect in that little part,
Or all will go to ruin!

Fife.   Oh, I will,
Please God we find some one to try it on.
But, truly, would not any one believe
Some fairy had exchanged us as we lay
Two tiny foster-children in one cradle?

Ros. Well, be that as it may, Fife, it reminds me
Of what perhaps I should have thought before,
But better late than never—You know I love you,
As you, I know, love me, and loyally
Have follow'd me thus far in my wild venture.
Well! now then—having seen me safe thus far—
Safe if not wholly sound—over the rocks
Into the country where my business lies—
Why should not you return the way we came,
The storm all clear'd away, and, leaving me
(Who now shall want you, though not thank you, less
Now that our horses gone) this side the ridge,
Find your way back to dear old home again;
While I—Come, come!—
What, weeping my poor fellow?—

Fife.   Leave you here
Alone—my Lady—Lord! I mean my Lord—

In a strange country—among savages—
Oh, now I know—you would be rid of me
For fear my stumbling speech—
 Ros.   Oh, no, no, no!—
I want you with me for a thousand sakes
To which that is as nothing—I myself
More apt to let the secret out myself
Without your help at all—Come, come, cheer up!
And if you sing again, 'Come weal, come woe,'
Let it be that; for we will never part
Until you give the signal.
 Fife.   'Tis a bargain.
 Ros. Now to begin, then. 'Follow, follow me,
'You fairy elves that be.'
 Fife.   Ay, and go on—
Something of 'following darkness like a dream,'
For that we're after.
 Ros.   No, after the sun;
Trying to catch hold of his glittering skirts
That hang upon the mountain as he goes.
 Fife. Ah, he's himself past catching—as you spoke
He heard what you were saying, and—just so—
Like some scared water-bird,
As we say in my country, *dōve* below.
 Ros. Well, we must follow him as best we may
Poland is no great country, and, as rich
In men and means, will but few acres spare
To lie beneath her barrier mountains bare.
We cannot, I believe, be very far
From mankind or their dwellings.
 Fife.   Send it so!
And well provided for man, woman, and beast.
No, not for beast. Ah, but my heart begins
To yearn for her—
 Ros.   Keep close, and keep your feet
From serving you as hers did.
 Fife.   As for beasts.

If in default of other entertainment,
We should provide them with ourselves to eat—
Bears, lions, wolves—

Ros.   Oh, never fear.

Fife.   Or else
Default of other beasts, beastlier men,
Cannibals, Anthropophagi, bare Poles
Who never knew a tailor but by taste.

Ros. Look, look!   Unless my fancy misconceive
With twilight—down among the rocks there, Fife—
Some human dwelling, surely—
Or think you but a rock torn from the rocks
In some convulsion like to-day's, and perch'd
Quaintly among them in mock-masonry?

Fife. Most likely that, I doubt.

Ros.   No, no—for look!
A square of darkness opening in it—

Fife.   Oh,
I don't half like such openings!—

Ros.   Like the loom
Of night from which she spins her outer gloom—

Fife. Lord, Madam, pray forbear this tragic vein
In such a time and place—

Ros.   And now again
Within that square of darkness, look! a light
That feels its way with hesitating pulse,
As we do, through the darkness that it drives
To blacken into deeper night beyond.

Fife. In which could we follow that light's example,
As might some English Bardolph with his nose,
We might defy the sunset—Hark, a chain!

Ros. And now a lamp, a lamp!   And now the hand
That carries it.

Fife.   Oh, Lord! that dreadful chain!

Ros. And now the bearer of the lamp; indeed
As strange as any in Arabian tale,
So giant-like, and terrible, and grand,

Spite of the skin he's wrapt in.

Fife.　　　　　　　　　Why, 'tis his own:
Oh, 'tis some wild man of the woods; I've heard
They build and carry torches—

Ros.　　　　　　　　　Never Ape
Bore such a brow before the heavens as that—
Chain'd as you say too!—

Fife.　　　　　　　　　Oh, that dreadful chain!

Ros. And now he sets the lamp down by his side,
And with one hand clench'd in his tangled hair
And with a sigh as if his heart would break—

> [*During this* Segismund *has entered from the
> fortress, with a torch.*

Segismund. Once more the storm has roar'd itself away,
Splitting the crags of God as it retires;
But sparing still what it should only blast,
This guilty piece of human handiwork,
And all that are within it. Oh, how oft,
How oft, within or here abroad, have I
Waited, and in the whisper of my heart
Pray'd for the slanting hand of heaven to strike
The blow myself I dared not, out of fear
Of that Hereafter, worse, they say, than here,
Plunged headlong in, but, till dismissal waited,
To wipe at last all sorrow from men's eyes,
And make this heavy dispensation clear.
Thus have I borne till now, and still endure,
Crouching in sullen impotence day by day,
Till some such out-burst of the elements
Like this rouses the sleeping fire within;
And standing thus upon the threshold of
Another night about to close the door
Upon one wretched day to open it
On one yet wretcheder because one more;—
Once more, you savage heavens, I ask of you—
I, looking up to those relentless eyes
That, now the greater lamp is gone below,

Begin to muster in the listening skies;
In all the shining circuits you have gone
About this theatre of human woe,
What greater sorrow have you gazed upon
Than down this narrow chink you witness still;
And which, did you yourselves not fore-devise,
You registered for others to fulfil!

    Fife. This is some Laureate at a birthday ode;
No wonder we went rhyming.

    Ros.   Hush! And now
See, starting to his feet, he strides about
Far as his tether'd steps—

    Seg.   And if the chain
You help'd to rivet round me did contract
Since guiltless infancy from guilt in act;
Of what in aspiration or in thought
Guilty, but in resentment of the wrong
That wreaks revenge on wrong I never wrought
By excommunication from the free
Inheritance that all created life,
Beside myself, is born to—from the wings
That range your own immeasurable blue,
Down to the poor, mute, scale-imprison'd things,
That yet are free to wander, glide, and pass
About that under-sapphire, whereinto
Yourselves transfusing you yourselves englass!

    Ros. What mystery is this?

    Fife.   Why, the man's mad:
That's all the mystery. That's why he's chain'd—
And why—

    Seg.   Nor Nature's guiltless life alone—
But that which lives on blood and rapine; nay,
Charter'd with larger liberty to slay
Their guiltless kind, the tyrants of the air
Soar zenith-upward with their screaming prey,
Making pure heaven drop blood upon the stage
Of under earth, where lion, wolf, and bear,

And they that on their treacherous velvet wear
Figure and constellation like your own,[2]
With their still living slaughter bound away
Over the barriers of the mountain cage,
Against which one, blood-guiltless, and endued
With aspiration and with aptitude
Transcending other creatures, day by day
Beats himself mad with unavailing rage!

Fife. Why, that must be the meaning of my mule's
Rebellion—

Ros.   Hush!

Seg.   But then if murder be
The law by which not only conscience-blind
Creatures, but man too prospers with his kind;
Who leaving all his guilty fellows free,
Under your fatal auspice and divine
Compulsion, leagued in some mysterious ban
Against one innocent and helpless man,
Abuse their liberty to murder mine:
And sworn to silence, like their masters mute
In heaven, and like them twirling through the mask
Of darkness, answering to all I ask,
Point up to them whose work they execute!

Ros. Ev'n as I thought, some poor unhappy wretch,
By man wrong'd, wretched, unrevenged, as I!
Nay, so much worse than I, as by those chains
Clipt of the means of self-revenge on those
Who lay on him what they deserve. And I,
Who taunted Heaven a little while ago
With pouring all its wrath upon my head—
Alas! like him who caught the cast-off husk
Of what another bragg'd of feeding on,
Here's one that from the refuse of my sorrows
Could gather all the banquet he desires!

[2] 'Some report that they'—(panthers)—'have one marke on the shoulders resembling
the moone, growing and decreasing as she doth, sometimes showing a full compasse,
and otherwhiles hollowed and pointed with tips like the hornes.'—*Philemon Holland's
Pliny,* b. viii. c. 17.

Poor soul, poor soul!

Fife. Speak lower—he will hear you.

Ros. And if he should, what then? Why, if he would,
He could not harm me—Nay, and if he could,
Methinks I'd venture something of a life
I care so little for—

Seg. Who's that? Clotaldo? Who are you, I say,
That, venturing in these forbidden rocks,
Have lighted on my miserable life,
And your own death?

Ros. You would not hurt me, surely?

Seg. Not I; but those that, iron as the chain
In which they slay me with a lingering death,
Will slay you with a sudden—Who are you?

Ros. A stranger from across the mountain there,
Who, having lost his way in this strange land
And coming night, drew hither to what seem'd
A human dwelling hidden in these rocks,
And where the voice of human sorrow soon
Told him it was so.

Seg. Ay? But nearer—nearer—
That by this smoky supplement of day
But for a moment I may see who speaks
So pitifully sweet.

Fife. Take care! take care!

Ros. Alas, poor man, that I, myself so helpless,
Could better help you than by barren pity,
And my poor presence—

Seg. Oh, might that be all!
But that—a few poor moments—and, alas!
The very bliss of having, and the dread
Of losing, under such a penalty
As every moment's having runs more near,
Stifles the very utterance and resource
They cry for quickest; till from sheer despair
Of holding thee, methinks myself would tear
To pieces—

Fife.   There, his word's enough for it.

Seg. Oh, think, if you who move about at will,
And live in sweet communion with your kind,
After an hour lost in these lonely rocks
Hunger and thirst after some human voice
To drink, and human face to feed upon;
What must one do where all is mute, or harsh,
And ev'n the naked face of cruelty
Were better than the mask it works beneath?—
Across the mountain then! Across the mountain!
What if the next world which they tell one of
Be only next across the mountain then,
Though I must never see it till I die,
And you one of its angels?

Ros.   Alas; alas!
No angel! And the face you think so fair,
'Tis but the dismal frame-work of these rocks
That makes it seem so; and the world I come from—
Alas, alas, too many faces there
Are but fair vizors to black hearts below,
Or only serve to bring the wearer woe!
But to yourself—If haply the redress
That I am here upon may help to yours.
I heard you tax the heavens with ordering,
And men for executing, what, alas!
I now behold. But why, and who they are
Who do, and you who suffer—

Seg. (*pointing upwards*).   Ask of them,
Whom, as to-night, I have so often ask'd,
And ask'd in vain.

Ros.   But surely, surely—

Seg.   Hark!
The trumpet of the watch to shut us in.
Oh, should they find you!—Quick! Behind the rocks!
To-morrow—if to-morrow—

Ros. (*flinging her sword toward him*). Take my sword!

ROSAURA *and* FIFE *hide in the rocks;*
Enter CLOTALDO

Clotaldo. These stormy days you like to see the last of
Are but ill opiates, Segismund, I think,
For night to follow: and to-night you seem
More than your wont disorder'd. What! A sword?
Within there!

Enter SOLDIERS *with black vizors and torches*

Fife.   Here's a pleasant masquerade!
Clo. Whosever watch this was
Will have to pay head-reckoning. Meanwhile,
This weapon had a wearer. Bring him here,
Alive or dead.
  Seg.   Clotaldo! good Clotaldo!—
  Clo. (*to Soldiers who enclose Segismund; others
        searching the rocks*).   You know your duty.
  Soldiers (*bringing in Rosaura and Fife*). Here are
        two of them,
Whoever more to follow—
  Clo.   Who are you,
That in defiance of known proclamation
Are found, at night-fall too, about this place?
  Fife. Oh, my Lord, she—I mean he—
  Ros.   Silence, Fife,
And let me speak for both.—Two foreign men,
To whom your country and its proclamations
Are equally unknown; and had we known,
Ourselves not masters of our lawless beasts
That, terrified by the storm among your rocks,
Flung us upon them to our cost.
  Fife.   My mule—
  Clo. Foreigners? Of what country?
  Ros.   Muscovy.
  Clo. And whither bound?
  Ros.   Hither—if this be Poland;

But with no ill design on her, and therefore
Taking it ill that we should thus be stopt
Upon her threshold so uncivilly.

Clo. Whither in Poland?

Ros.   To the capital.

Clo. And on what errand?

Ros.   Set me on the road,
And you shall be the nearer to my answer.

Clo. (*aside*). So resolute and ready to reply,
And yet so young—and— (*Aloud.*) Well,—
Your business was not surely with the man
We found you with?

Ros.   He was the first we saw,—
And strangers and benighted, as we were,
As you too would have done in a like case,
Accosted him at once.

Clo.   Ay, but this sword?

Ros. I flung it toward him.

Clo.   Well, and why?

Ros.   And why?
But to revenge himself on those who thus
Injuriously misuse him.

Clo.   So—so—so!
'Tis well such resolution wants a beard—
And, I suppose, is never to attain one.
Well, I must take you both, you and your sword,
Prisoners.

Fife. (*offering a cudgel*). Pray take mine, and welcome, sir;
I'm sure I gave it to that mule of mine
To mighty little purpose.

Ros.   Mine you have;
And may it win us some more kindliness
Than we have met with yet.

Clo. (*examining the sword*). More mystery!
How came you by this weapon?

Ros.   From my father.

Clo. And do you know whence he?

Ros.   Oh, very well:
From one of this same Polish realm of yours,
Who promised a return, should come the chance,
Of courtesies that he received himself
In Muscovy, and left this pledge of it—
Not likely yet, it seems, to be redeem'd.
   Clo. (*aside*). Oh, wondrous chance—or wondrous
     Providence!
The sword that I myself in Muscovy,
When these white hairs were black, for keepsake left
Of obligation for a like return
To him who saved me wounded as I lay
Fighting against his country; took me home;
Tended me like a brother till recover'd,
Perchance to fight against him once again—
And now my sword put back into my hand
By his—if not his son—still, as so seeming,
By me, as first devoir of gratitude,
To seem believing, till the wearer's self
See fit to drop the ill-dissembling mask.
(*Aloud.*) Well, a strange turn of fortune has arrested
The sharp and sudden penalty that else
Had visited your rashness or mischance:
In part, your tender youth too—pardon me,
And touch not where your sword is not to answer—
Commends you to my care; not your life only,
Else by this misadventure forfeited;
But ev'n your errand, which, by happy chance,
Chimes with the very business I am on,
And calls me to the very point you aim at.
   Ros. The capital?
   Clo.   Ay, the capital; and ev'n
That capital of capitals, the Court:
Where you may plead, and, I may promise, win
Pardon for this, you say unwilling, trespass,
And prosecute what else you have at heart,
With me to help you forward all I can:

Provided all in loyalty to those
To whom by natural allegiance
I first am bound to.

Ros.　　　　　As you make, I take
Your offer: with like promise on my side
Of loyalty to you and those you serve,
Under like reservation for regards
Nearer and dearer still.

Clo.　　　　　Enough, enough;
Your hand; a bargain on both sides. Meanwhile,
Here shall you rest to-night. The break of day
Shall see us both together on the way.

Ros. Thus then what I for misadventure blamed,
Directly draws me where my wishes aim'd. [*Exeunt.*

Scene II.—*The Palace at Warsaw*

Enter on one side Astolfo, *Duke of Muscovy, with his train: and, on the other, the* Princess Estrella, *with hers.*

Astolfo. My royal cousin, if so near in blood,
Till this auspicious meeting scarcely known,
Till all that beauty promised in the bud
Is now to its consummate blossom blown,
Well met at last; and may—

Estrella.　　　　　Enough, my Lord,
Of compliment devised for you by some
Court tailor, and, believe me, still too short
To cover the designful heart below.

Ast. Nay, but indeed, fair cousin—

Est.　　　　　Ay, let Deed
Measure your words, indeed your flowers of speech
Ill with your iron equipage atone;
Irony indeed, and wordy compliment.

Ast. Indeed, indeed, you wrong me, royal cousin,
And fair as royal, misinterpreting
What, even for the end you think I aim at,
If false to you, were fatal to myself.

Est. Why, what else means the glittering steel, my Lord,
That bristles in the rear of these fine words?
What can it mean, but, failing to cajole,
To fight or force me from my just pretension?

Ast. Nay, might I not ask ev'n the same of you,
The nodding helmets of whose men-at-arms
Out-crest the plumage of your lady court?

Est. But to defend what yours would force from me.

Ast. Might not I, lady, say the same of mine?
But not to come to battle, ev'n of words,
With a fair lady, and my kinswoman;
And as averse to stand before your face,
Defenceless, and condemn'd in your disgrace,
Till the good king be here to clear it all—
Will you vouchsafe to hear me?

Est.   As you will.

Ast. You know that, when about to leave this world,
Our royal grandsire, King Alfonso, left
Three children; one a son, Basilio,
Who wears—long may he wear!—the crown of Poland;
And daughters twain: of whom the elder was
Your mother, Clorileña, now some while
Exalted to a more than mortal throne;
And Recisunda, mine, the younger sister,
Who, married to the Prince of Muscovy,
Gave me the light which may she live to see
Herself for many, many years to come.
Meanwhile, good King Basilio, as you know,
Deep in abstruser studies than this world,
And busier with the stars than lady's eyes,
Has never by a second marriage yet
Replaced, as Poland ask'd of him, the heir
An early marriage brought and took away;
His young queen dying with the son she bore him;
And in such alienation grown so old
As leaves no other hope of heir to Poland
Than his two sisters' children; you, fair cousin,

And me; for whom the Commons of the realm
Divide themselves into two several factions;
Whether for you, the elder sister's child;
Or me, born of the younger, but, they say,
My natural prerogative of man
Outweighing your priority of birth.
Which discord growing loud and dangerous,
Our uncle, King Basilio, doubly sage
In prophesying and providing for
The future, as to deal with it when come,
Bids us here meet to-day in solemn council
Our several pretensions to compose.
And, but the martial out-burst that proclaims
His coming, makes all further parley vain,
Unless my bosom, by which only wise
I prophesy, now wrongly prophesies,
By such a happy compact as I dare
But glance at till the Royal Sage declare.

    Trumpets, etc. Enter KING BASILIO *with his Council*

All. The King! God save the King!
  Estrella⎱ (*Kneeling.*)   Oh, Royal Sir!—
  Astolfo⎰   God save your Majesty!—
  King.   Rise, both of you,
Rise to my arms, Astolfo and Estrella;
As my two sisters' children always mine,
Now more than ever, since myself and Poland
Solely to you for our succession look'd.
And now give ear, you and your several factions,
And you, the Peers and Princes of this realm,
While I reveal the purport of this meeting
In words whose necessary length I trust
No unsuccessful issue shall excuse.
You and the world who have surnamed me "Sage"
Know that I owe that title, if my due,
To my long meditation on the book
Which ever lying open overhead—

The book of heaven, I mean—so few have read;
Whose golden letters on whose sapphire leaf,
Distinguishing the page of day and night,
And all the revolution of the year;
So with the turning volume where they lie
Still changing their prophetic syllables,
They register the destinies of men:
Until with eyes that, dim with years indeed,
Are quicker to pursue the stars than rule them,
I get the start of Time, and from his hand
The wand of tardy revelation draw.
Oh, had the self-same heaven upon his page
Inscribed my death ere I should read my life
And, by fore-casting of my own mischance,
Play not the victim but the suicide
In my own tragedy!—But you shall hear.
You know how once, as kings must for their people,
And only once, as wise men for themselves,
I woo'd and wedded: know too that my Queen
In childing died; but not, as you believe,
With her, the son she died in giving life to.
For, as the hour of birth was on the stroke,
Her brain conceiving with her womb, she dream'd
A serpent tore her entrail. And too surely
(For evil omen seldom speaks in vain)
The man-child breaking from that living tomb
That makes our birth the antitype of death,
Man-grateful, for the life she gave him paid
By killing her: and with such circumstance
As suited such unnatural tragedy;
He coming into light, if light it were
That darken'd at his very horoscope,
When heaven's two champions—sun and moon I mean—
Suffused in blood upon each other fell
In such a raging duel of eclipse
As hath not terrified the universe
Since that which wept in blood the death of Christ:

When the dead walk'd, the waters turn'd to blood,
Earth and her cities totter'd, and the world
Seem'd shaken to its last paralysis.
In such a paroxysm of dissolution
That son of mine was born; by that first act
Heading the monstrous catalogue of crime,
I found fore-written in his horoscope;
As great a monster in man's history
As was in nature his nativity;
So savage, bloody, terrible, and impious,
Who, should he live, would tear his country's entrails
As by his birth his mother's; with which crime
Beginning, he should clench the dreadful tale
By trampling on his father's silver head.
All which fore-reading, and his act of birth
Fate's warrant that I read his life aright;
To save his country from his mother's fate,
I gave abroad that he had died with her
His being slew; with midnight secrecy
I had him carried to a lonely tower
Hewn from the mountain-barriers of the realm,
And under strict anathema of death
Guarded from men's inquisitive approach,
Save from the trusty few one needs must trust;
Who while his fasten'd body they provide
With salutary garb and nourishment,
Instruct his soul in what no soul may miss
Of holy faith, and in such other lore
As may solace his life-imprisonment,
And tame perhaps the Savage prophesied
Toward such a trial as I aim at now,
And now demand your special hearing to.
What in this fearful business I have done,
Judge whether lightly or maliciously,—
I, with my own and only flesh and blood,
And proper lineal inheritor!
I swear, had his foretold atrocities

Touch'd me alone, I had not saved myself
At such a cost to him; but as a king,—
A Christian king,—I say, advisedly,
Who would devote his people to a tyrant
Worse than Caligula fore-chronicled?
But even this not without grave mis-giving,
Lest by some chance mis-reading of the stars,
Or mis-direction of what rightly read,
I wrong my son of his prerogative,
And Poland of her rightful sovereign.
For, sure and certain prophets as the stars,
Although they err not, he who reads them may;
Or rightly reading—seeing there is One
Who governs them, as, under Him, they us,
We are not sure if the rough diagram
They draw in heaven and we interpret here,
Be sure of operation, if the Will
Supreme, that sometimes for some special end
The course of providential nature breaks
By miracle, may not of these same stars
Cancel his own first draft, or overrule
What else fore-written all else overrules.
As, for example, should the Will Almighty
Permit the Free-will of particular man
To break the meshes of else strangling fate—
Which Free-will, fearful of foretold abuse,
I have myself from my own son fore-closed
From ever possible self-extrication;
A terrible responsibility,
Not to the conscience to be reconciled
Unless opposing almost certain evil
Against so slight contingency of good.
Well—thus perplex'd, I have resolved at last
To bring the thing to trial: whereunto
Here have I summon'd you, my Peers, and you
Whom I more dearly look to, failing him,
As witnesses to that which I propose;

And thus propose the doing it. Clotaldo,
Who guards my son with old fidelity,
Shall bring him hither from his tower by night
Lockt in a sleep so fast as by my art
I rivet to within a link of death,
But yet from death so far, that next day's dawn
Shall wake him up upon the royal bed,
Complete in consciousness and faculty,
When with all princely pomp and retinue
My loyal Peers with due obeisance
Shall hail him Segismund, the Prince of Poland.
Then if with any show of human kindness
He fling discredit, not upon the stars,
But upon me, their misinterpreter,
With all apology mistaken age
Can make to youth it never meant to harm,
To my son's forehead will I shift the crown
I long have wish'd upon a younger brow;
And in religious humiliation,
For what of worn-out age remains to me,
Entreat my pardon both of Heaven and him
For tempting destinies beyond my reach.
But if, as I misdoubt, at his first step
The hoof of the predicted savage shows;
Before predicted mischief can be done,
The self-same sleep that loosed him from the chain
Shall re-consign him, not to loose again.
Then shall I, having lost that heir direct,
Look solely to my sisters' children twain
Each of a claim so equal as divides
The voice of Poland to their several sides,
But, as I trust, to be entwined ere long
Into one single wreath so fair and strong
As shall at once all difference atone,
And cease the realm's division with their own.
Cousins and Princes, Peers and Councillors,
Such is the purport of this invitation,

And such is my design. Whose furtherance
If not as Sovereign, if not as Seer,
Yet one whom these white locks, if nothing else,
To patient acquiescence consecrate,
I now demand and even supplicate.

    Ast. Such news, and from such lips, may well sus-
pend
The tongue to loyal answer most attuned;
But if to me as spokesman of my faction
Your Highness looks for answer; I reply
For one and all—Let Segismund, whom now
We first hear tell of as your living heir,
Appear, and but in your sufficient eye
Approve himself worthy to be your son,
Then we will hail him Poland's rightful heir.
What says my cousin?

    Est.   Ay, with all my heart.
But if my youth and sex upbraid me not
That I should dare ask of so wise a king—

    King. Ask, ask, fair cousin! Nothing, I am sure,
Not well consider'd; nay, if 'twere, yet nothing
But pardonable from such lips as those.

    Est. Then, with your pardon, Sir—if Segismund,
My cousin, whom I shall rejoice to hail
As Prince of Poland too, as you propose,
Be to a trial coming upon which
More, as I think, than life itself depends,
Why, Sir, with sleep-disorder'd senses brought
To this uncertain contest with his stars?

    King. Well ask'd indeed! As wisely be it answer'd!—
Because it is uncertain, see you not?
For as I think I can discern between
The sudden flaws of a sleep-startled man,
And of the savage thing we have to dread;
If but bewilder'd, dazzled, and uncouth,
As might the sanest and the civilest
In circumstance so strange—nay, more than that,
If moved to any out-break short of blood,

All shall be well with him; and how much more,
If 'mid the magic turmoil of the change,
He shall so calm a resolution show
As scarce to reel beneath so great a blow!
But if with savage passion uncontroll'd
He lay about him like the brute foretold,
And must as suddenly be caged again;
Then what redoubled anguish and despair,
From that brief flash of blissful liberty
Remitted—and for ever—to his chain!
Which so much less, if on the stage of glory
Enter'd and exited through such a door
Of sleep as makes a dream of all between.

   Est. Oh kindly answer, Sir, to question that
To charitable courtesy less wise
Might call for pardon rather! I shall now
Gladly, what, uninstructed, loyally
I should have waited.

   Ast.   Your Highness doubts not me,
Nor how my heart follows my cousin's lips,
Whatever way the doubtful balance fall,
Still loyal to your bidding.

   Omnes.   So say all.

   King. I hoped, and did expect, of all no less—
And sure no sovereign ever needed more
From all who owe him love or loyalty.
For what a strait of time I stand upon,
When to this issue not alone I bring
My son your Prince, but e'en myself your King:
And, whichsoever way for him it turn,
Of less than little honour to myself.
For if this coming trial justify
My thus withholding from my son his right,
Is not the judge himself justified in
The father's shame? And if the judge proved wrong,
My son withholding from his right thus long,
Shame and remorse to judge and father both:
Unless remorse and shame together drown'd

In having what I flung for worthless found.
But come—already weary with your travel,
And ill refresh'd by this strange history,
Until the hours that draw the sun from heaven
Unite us at the customary board,
Each to his several chamber: you to rest;
I to contrive with old Clotaldo best
The method of a stranger thing than old
Time has as yet among his records told.   [*Exeunt.*

ACT II

Scene I.—*A Throne-room in the Palace, Music within.*

Enter King *and* Clotaldo, *meeting a Lord in waiting*

King. You, for a moment beckon'd from your office,
Tell me thus far how goes it. In due time
The potion left him?
    Lord.   At the very hour
To which your Highness temper'd it. Yet not
So wholly but some lingering mist still hung
About his dawning senses—which to clear,
We fill'd and handed him a morning drink
With sleep's specific antidote suffused;
And while with princely raiment we invested
What nature surely modell'd for a Prince—
All but the sword—as you directed—
    King.   Ay—
    Lord. If not too loudly, yet emphatically
Still with the title of a Prince address'd him.
    King. How bore he that?
    Lord.   With all the rest, my liege,
I will not say so like one in a dream
As one himself misdoubting that he dream'd.
    King. So far so well, Clotaldo, either way,
And best of all if tow'rd the worse I dread.
But yet no violence?—

 Lord.   At most, impatience;
Wearied perhaps with importunities
We yet were bound to offer.
 King.   Oh, Clotaldo!
Though thus far well, yet would myself had drunk
The potion he revives from! such suspense
Crowds all the pulses of life's residue
Into the present moment; and, I think,
Whichever way the trembling scale may turn,
Will leave the crown of Poland for some one
To wait no longer than the setting sun!
 Clo. Courage, my liege! The curtain is undrawn,
And each must play his part out manfully,
Leaving the rest to heaven.
 King.   Whose written words
If I should misinterpret or transgress!
But as you say—
 (*To the Lord, who exit.*) You, back to him at once;
Clotaldo, you, when he is somewhat used
To the new world of which they call him Prince,
Where place and face, and all, is strange to him,
With your known features and familiar garb
Shall then, as chorus to the scene, accost him,
And by such earnest of that old and too
Familiar world, assure him of the new.
Last in the strange procession, I myself
Will by one full and last development
Complete the plot for that catastrophe
That he must put to all; God grant it be
The crown of Poland on his brows!—Hark! hark!—
Was that his voice within?—Now louder—Oh,
Clotaldo, what! so soon begun to roar!—
Again! above the music— But betide
What may, until the moment, we must hide.
       [*Exeunt* KING *and* CLOTALDO.
 Segismund (*within*). Forbear! I stifle with your per-
  fume! cease

Your crazy salutations! peace, I say—
Begone, or let me go, ere I go mad
With all this babble, mummery, and glare,
For I am growing dangerous—Air! room! air!—

　　　　　　　　　[He rushes in. Music ceases.

Oh but to save the reeling brain from wreck
With its bewilder'd senses!—

　　　　　　　[He covers his eyes for a while.

　　　　　　　　　　　What! E'en now
That Babel left behind me, but my eyes
Pursued by the same glamour, that—unless
Alike bewitch'd too—the confederate sense
Vouches for palpable: bright-shining floors
That ring hard answer back to the stamp'd heel,
And shoot up airy columns marble-cold,
That, as they climb, break into golden leaf
And capital, till they embrace aloft
In clustering flower and fruitage over walls
Hung with such purple curtain as the West
Fringes with such a gold; or over-laid
With sanguine-glowing semblances of men,
Each in his all but living action busied,
Or from the wall they look from, with fix'd eyes
Pursuing me; and one most strange of all
That, as I pass'd the crystal on the wall,
Look'd from it—left it—and as I return,
Returns, and looks me face to face again—
Unless some false reflection of my brain,
The outward semblance of myself—Myself?
How know that tawdry shadow for myself,
But that it moves as I move; lifts his hand
With mine; each motion echoing so close
The immediate suggestion of the will
In which myself I recognize—Myself!—
What, this fantastic Segismund the same
Who last night, as for all his nights before,
Lay down to sleep in wolf-skin on the ground

In a black turret which the wolf howl'd round,
And woke again upon a golden bed,
Round which as clouds about a rising sun,
In scarce less glittering caparison,
Gather'd gay shapes that, underneath a breeze
Of music, handed him upon their knees
The wine of heaven in a cup of gold,
And still in soft melodious under-song
Hailing me Prince of Poland!—'Segismund,'
They said, 'Our Prince! The Prince of Poland!' and
Again, 'Oh, welcome, welcome, to his own,
'Our own Prince Segismund—'
                                        Oh, but a blast—
One blast of the rough mountain air! one look
At the grim features—   [*He goes to the window.*
What they disvizor'd also! shatter'd chaos
Cast into stately shape and masonry,
Between whose channel'd and perspective sides
Compact with rooted towers, and flourishing
To heaven with gilded pinnacle and spire,
Flows the live current ever to and fro
With open aspect and free step!—Clotaldo!
Clotaldo!—calling as one scarce dares call
For him who suddenly might break the spell
One fears to walk without him—Why, that I,
With unencumber'd step as any there,
Go stumbling through my glory—feeling for
That iron leading-string—ay, for myself—
For that fast-anchor'd self of yesterday,
Of yesterday, and all my life before,
Ere drifted clean from self-identity
Upon the fluctuation of to-day's
Mad whirling circumstance!—And, fool, why not?
If reason, sense, and self-identity
Obliterated from a worn-out brain,
Art thou not maddest striving to be sane,
And catching at that Self of yesterday

That, like a leper's rags, best flung away!
Or if not mad, then dreaming—dreaming?—well—
Dreaming then—Or, if self to self be true,
Not mock'd by that, but as poor souls have been
By those who wrong'd them, to give wrong new relish?
Or have those stars indeed they told me of
As masters of my wretched life of old,
Into some happier constellation roll'd,
And brought my better fortune out on earth
Clear as themselves in heaven!—Prince Segismund
They call'd me—and at will I shook them off—
Will they return again at my command
Again to call me so?—Within there! You!
Segismund calls—Prince Segismund—

> (*He has seated himself on the throne.*
> *Enter* CHAMBERLAIN, *with lords in waiting.*)

    Chamb.   I rejoice
That unadvised of any but the voice
Of royal instinct in the blood, your Highness
Has ta'en the chair that you were born to fill.
    Seg. The chair?
    Chamb.   The royal throne of Poland, Sir,
Which may your Royal Highness keep as long
As he that now rules from it shall have ruled
When heaven has call'd him to itself.
    Seg.   When he?—
    Chamb. Your royal father, King Basilio, Sir.
    Seg. My royal father—King Basilio.
You see I answer but as Echo does,
Not knowing what she listens or repeats.
This is my throne—this is my palace—Oh,
But this out of the window?—
    Chamb.   Warsaw, Sir,
Your capital—
    Seg.   And all the moving people?
    Chamb. Your subjects and your vassals like ourselves.

Seg. Ay, ay—my subjects—in my capital—
Warsaw—and I am Prince of it—You see
It needs much iteration to strike sense
Into the human echo.
    Chamb.   Left awhile
In the quick brain, the word will quickly to
Full meaning blow.
    Seg.   You think so?
    Chamb.   And meanwhile
Lest our obsequiousness, which means no worse
Than customary honour to the Prince
We most rejoice to welcome, trouble you,
Should we retire again? or stand apart?
Or would your Highness have the music play
Again, which meditation, as they say,
So often loves to float upon?
    Seg.   The music?
No—yes—perhaps the trumpet—(*Aside*) Yet if that
Brought back the troop!
    A Lord.   The trumpet! There again
How trumpet-like spoke out the blood of Poland!
    Chamb. Before the morning is far up, your Highness
Will have the trumpet marshalling your soldiers
Under the Palace windows.
    Seg.   Ah, my soldiers—
My soldiers—not black-vizor'd?—
    Chamb.   Sir?
    Seg.   No matter.
But—one thing—for a moment—in your ear—
Do you know one Clotaldo?
    Chamb.   Oh, my Lord,
He and myself together, I may say,
Although in different vocations,
Have silver'd in your royal father's service;
And, as I trust, with both of us a few
White hairs to fall in yours.
    Seg.   Well said, well said!

Basilio, my father—well—Clotaldo—
Is he my kinsman too?
    Chamb.   Oh, my good Lord,
A General simply in your Highness' service,
Than whom your Highness has no trustier.
    Seg. Ay, so you said before, I think. And you
With that white wand of yours—
Why, now I think on't, I have read of such
A silver-hair'd magician with a wand,
Who in a moment, with a wave of it,
Turn'd rags to jewels, clowns to emperors,
By some benigner magic than the stars
Spirited poor good people out of hand
From all their woes; in some enchanted sleep
Carried them off on cloud or dragon-back
Over the mountains, over the wide Deep,
And set them down to wake in Fairyland.
    Chamb. Oh, my good Lord, you laugh at me—and I
Right glad to make you laugh at such a price:
You know me no enchanter: if I were,
I and my wand as much as your Highness',
As now your chamberlain—
    Seg.   My chamberlain?—
And these that follow you?—
    Chamb.   On you, my Lord,
Your Highness' lords in waiting.
    Seg.   Lords in waiting.
Well, I have now learn'd to repeat, I think,
If only but by rote—This is my palace,
And this my throne—which unadvised—And that
Out of the window there my Capital;
And all the people moving up and down
My subjects and my vassals like yourselves,
My chamberlain—and lords in waiting—and
Clotaldo—and Clotaldo?—
You are an aged, and seem a reverend man—
You do not—though his fellow-officer—

You do not mean to mock me?

 Chamb.   Oh, my Lord!

 Seg. Well then—If no magician, as you say,
Yet setting me a riddle, that my brain,
With all its senses whirling, cannot solve,
Yourself or one of these with you must answer—
How I—that only last night fell asleep
Not knowing that the very soil of earth
I lay down—chain'd—to sleep upon was Poland—
Awake to find myself the Lord of it,
With Lords, and Generals, and Chamberlains,
And ev'n my very Gaoler, for my vassals!

Enter suddenly CLOTALDO

 Clotaldo. Stand all aside
That I may put into his hand the clue
To lead him out of this amazement. Sir,
Vouchsafe your Highness from my bended knee
Receive my homage first.

 Seg.   Clotaldo! What,
At last—his old self—undisguised where all
Is masquerade—to end it!—You kneeling too!
What! have the stars you told me long ago
Laid that old work upon you, added this,
That, having chain'd your prisoner so long,
You loose his body now to slay his wits,
Dragging him—how I know not—whither scarce
I understand—dressing him up in all
This frippery, with your dumb familiars
Disvizor'd, and their lips unlock'd to lie,
Calling him Prince and King, and, madman-like,
Setting a crown of straw upon his head?

 Clo. Would but your Highness, as indeed I now
Must call you—and upon his bended knee
Never bent Subject more devotedly—
However all about you, and perhaps
You to yourself incomprehensiblest,

But rest in the assurance of your own
Sane waking senses, by these witnesses
Attested, till the story of it all,
Of which I bring a chapter, be reveal'd,
Assured of all you see and hear as neither
Madness nor mockery—

    Seg.   What then?

    Clo.   All it seems:

This palace with its royal garniture;
This capital of which it is the eye,
With all its temples, marts, and arsenals;
This realm of which this city is the head,
With all its cities, villages, and tilth,
Its armies, fleets, and commerce; all your own;
And all the living souls that make them up,
From those who now, and those who shall, salute you,
Down to the poorest peasant of the realm,
Your subjects—Who, though now their mighty voice
Sleeps in the general body unapprized,
Wait but a word from those about you now
To hail you Prince of Poland, Segismund.

    Seg. All this is so?

    Clo.   As sure as anything
Is, or can be.

    Seg.   You swear it on the faith
You taught me—elsewhere?—

    Clo. (*kissing the hilt of his sword*). Swear it upon this
Symbol, and champion of the holy faith
I wear it to defend.

    Seg. (*to himself*). My eyes have not deceived me, nor
      my ears,
With this transfiguration, nor the strain
Of royal welcome that arose and blew,
Breathed from no lying lips, along with it.
For here Clotaldo comes, his own old self,
Who, if not Lie and phantom with the rest—
(*Aloud*) Well, then, all this is thus.

For have not these fine people told me so,
And you, Clotaldo, sworn it? And the Why
And Wherefore are to follow by and bye!
And yet—and yet—why wait for that which you
Who take your oath on it can answer—and
Indeed it presses hard upon my brain—
What I was asking of these gentlemen
When you came in upon us; how it is
That I—the Segismund you know so long—
No longer than the sun that rose to-day
Rose—and from what you know—
Rose to be Prince of Poland?

    Clo.   So to be
Acknowledged and entreated, Sir.

    Seg.   So be
Acknowledged and entreated—
Well—But if now by all, by some at least
So known—if not entreated—heretofore—
Though not by you—For, now I think again,
Of what should be your attestation worth,
You that of all my questionable subjects
Who knowing what, yet left me where I was,
You least of all, Clotaldo, till the dawn
Of this first day that told it to myself?

    Clo. Oh, let your Highness draw the line across
Fore-written sorrow, and in this new dawn
Bury that long sad night.

    Seg.   Not ev'n the Dead,
Call'd to the resurrection of the blest,
Shall so directly drop all memory
Of woes and wrongs foregone!

    Clo.   But not resent—
Purged by the trial of that sorrow past
For full fruition of their present bliss.

    Seg. But leaving with the Judge what, till this earth
Be cancell'd in the burning heavens, He leaves
His earthly delegates to execute,

Of retribution in reward to them
And woe to those who wrong'd them—Not as you,
Not you, Clotaldo, knowing not—And yet
Ev'n to the guiltiest wretch in all the realm,
Of any treason guilty short of that,
Stern usage—but assuredly not knowing,
Not knowing 'twas your sovereign lord, Clotaldo,
You used so sternly.

  Clo.   Ay, sir; with the same
Devotion and fidelity that now
Does homage to him for my sovereign.

  Seg. Fidelity that held his Prince in chains!

  Clo. Fidelity more fast than had it loosed him—

  Seg. Ev'n from the very dawn of consciousness
Down at the bottom of the barren rocks,
Where scarce a ray of sunshine found him out,
In which the poorest beggar of my realm
At least to human-full proportion grows—
Me! Me—whose station was the kingdom's top
To flourish in, reaching my head to heaven,
And with my branches overshadowing
The meaner growth below!

  Clo.   Still with the same
Fidelity—

  Seg. To me!—

  Clo.   Ay, sir, to you,
Through that divine allegiance upon which
All Order and Authority is based;
Which to revolt against—

  Seg.   Were to revolt
Against the stars, belike!

  Clo.   And him who reads them;
And by that right, and by the sovereignty
He wears as you shall wear it after him;
Ay, one to whom yourself—
Yourself, ev'n more than any subject here,
Are bound by yet another and more strong

Allegiance—King Basilio—your Father—

Seg. Basilio—King—my father!—

Clo.   Oh, my Lord,
Let me beseech you on my bended knee,
For your own sake—for Poland's—and for his,
Who, looking up for counsel to the skies,
Did what he did under authority
To which the kings of earth themselves are subject,
And whose behest not only he that suffers,
But he that executes, not comprehends,
But only He that orders it—

Seg.   The King—
My father!—Either I am mad already,
Or that way driving fast—or I should know
That fathers do not use their children so,
Or men were loosed from all allegiance
To fathers, kings, and heaven that order'd all.
But, mad or not, my hour is come, and I
Will have my reckoning—Either you lie,
Under the skirt of sinless majesty
Shrouding your treason; or if *that* indeed,
Guilty itself, take refuge in the stars
That cannot hear the charge, or disavow—
You, whether doer or deviser, who
Come first to hand, shall pay the penalty
By the same hand you owe it to—
(*Seizing* CLOTALDO's *sword and about to strike him.*)

Enter ROSAURA *suddenly*

Rosaura. Fie, my Lord—forbear,
What! a young hand raised against silver hair!—
                        (*She retreats through the crowd.*)

Seg. Stay! stay! What come and vanish'd as before—
I scarce remember how—but—

Voices within. Room for Astolfo, Duke of Muscovy!

Enter ASTOLFO

Astolfo. Welcome, thrice welcome, the auspicious day,

When from the mountain where he darkling lay,
The Polish sun into the firmament
Sprung all the brighter for his late ascent,
And in meridian glory—
  Seg.   Where is he?
Why must I ask this twice?—
  A Lord.   The Page, my Lord?   .   .
I wonder at his boldness—
  Seg.   But I tell you
He came with Angel written in his face
As now it is, when all was black as hell
About, and none of you who now—he came,
And Angel-like flung me a shining sword
To cut my way through darkness; and again
Angel-like wrests it from me in behalf
Of one—whom I will spare for sparing him:
But he must come and plead with that same voice
That pray'd for me—in vain.
  Chamb.   He is gone for,
And shall attend your pleasure, sir. Meanwhile,
Will not your Highness, as in courtesy,
Return your royal cousin's greeting?
  Seg.   Whose?
  Chamb. Astolfo, Duke of Muscovy, my Lord,
Saluted, and with gallant compliment
Welcomed you to your royal title.
  Seg. (*to Astolfo*).   Oh—
You knew of this then?
  Ast.   Knew of what, my Lord?
  Seg. That I was Prince of Poland all the while,
And you my subject?
  Ast.   Pardon me, my Lord,
But some few hours ago myself I learn'd
Your dignity; but, knowing it, no more
Than when I knew it not, your subject.
  Seg.   What then?
  Ast. Your Highness' chamberlain ev'n now has told you;

Astolfo, Duke of Muscovy,
Your father's sister's son; your cousin, sir:
And who as such, and in his own right Prince,
Expects from you the courtesy he shows.

   Chamb. His Highness is as yet unused to Court,
And to the ceremonious interchange
Of compliment, especially to those
Who draw their blood from the same royal fountain.

   Seg. Where is the lad? I weary of all this—
Prince, cousins, chamberlains, and compliments—
Where are my soldiers? Blow the trumpet, and
With one sharp blast scatter these butterflies
And bring the men of iron to my side,
With whom a king feels like a king indeed!

   Voices within. Within there! room for the Princess
     Estrella!

Enter ESTRELLA *with Ladies*

   Estrella. Welcome, my Lord, right welcome to the throne
That much too long has waited for your coming:
And, in the general voice of Poland, hear
A kinswoman and cousin's no less sincere.

   Seg. Ay, this is welcome-worth indeed,
And cousin cousin-worth! Oh, I have thus
Over the threshold of the mountain seen,
Leading a bevy of fair stars, the moon
Enter the court of heaven—My kinswoman!
My cousin! But my subject?—

   Est.   If you please
To count your cousin for your subject, sir,
You shall not find her a disloyal.

   Seg.   Oh,
But there are twin stars in that heavenly face,
That now I know for having over-ruled
Those evil ones that darken'd all my past
And brought me forth from that captivity
To be the slave of her who set me free.

Est. Indeed, my Lord, these eyes have no such power
Over the past or present: but perhaps
They brighten at your welcome to supply
The little that a lady's speech commends;
And in the hope that, let whichever be
The other's subject, we may both be friends.

Seg. Your hand to that—But why does this warm hand
Shoot a cold shudder through me?

Est.   In revenge
For likening me to that cold moon, perhaps.

Seg. Oh, but the lip whose music tells me so
Breathes of a warmer planet, and that lip
Shall remedy the treason of the hand!

                                    (He catches to embrace her.)

Est. Release me, sir!

Chamb.   And pardon me, my Lord.
This lady is a Princess absolute,
As Prince he is who just saluted you,
And claims her by affiance.

Seg.   Hence, old fool,
For ever thrusting that white stick of yours
Between me and my pleasure!

Ast.   This cause is mine.
Forbear, sir—

Seg.   What, sir mouth-piece, you again?

Ast. My Lord, I waive your insult to myself
In recognition of the dignity
You yet are new to, and that greater still
You look in time to wear. But for this lady—
Whom, if my cousin now, I hope to claim
Henceforth by yet a nearer, dearer name—

Seg. And what care I? She is my cousin too:
And if you be a Prince—well, am not I
Lord of the very soil you stand upon?
By that, and by that right beside of blood
That like a fiery fountain hitherto
Pent in the rock leaps toward her at her touch,

Mine, before all the cousins in Muscovy!
You call me Prince of Poland, and yourselves
My subjects—traitors therefore to this hour,
Who let me perish all my youth away
Chain'd there among the mountains; till, forsooth,
Terrified at your treachery foregone,
You spirit me up here, I know not how,
Popinjay-like invest me like yourselves,
Choke me with scent and music that I loathe,
And, worse than all the music and the scent,
With false, long-winded, fulsome compliment,
That 'Oh, you are my subjects!' and in word
Reiterating still obedience,
Thwart me in deed at every step I take:
When just about to wreak a just revenge
Upon that old arch-traitor of you all,
Filch from my vengeance him I hate; and him
I loved—the first and only face—till this—
I cared to look on in your ugly court—
And now when palpably I grasp at last
What hitherto but shadow'd in my dreams—
Affiances and interferences,
The first who dares to meddle with me more—
Princes and chamberlains and counsellors,
Touch her who dares!—

    Ast.   That dare I—
Seg. (seizing him by the throat).   You dare!
Chamb. My Lord!—
A Lord.   His strength's a lion's—
Voices within.   The King! The King!—

Enter KING

    A Lord. And on a sudden how he stands at gaze
As might a wolf just fasten'd on his prey,
Glaring at a suddenly encounter'd lion.
    King. And I that hither flew with open arms
To fold them round my son, must now return

To press them to an empty heart again!

                          [*He sits on the throne.*

    Seg. That is the King?—My father?—

    (*After a long pause.*)   I have heard
That sometimes some blind instinct has been known
To draw to mutual recognition those
Of the same blood, beyond all memory
Divided, or ev'n never met before.
I know not how this is—perhaps in brutes
That live by kindlier instincts—but I know
That looking now upon that head whose crown
Pronounces him a sovereign king, I feel
No setting of the current in my blood
Tow'rd him as sire. How is't with you, old man,
Tow'rd him they call your son?—

    King   Alas! Alas!

    Seg. Your sorrow, then?

    King.   Beholding what I do.

    Seg. Ay, but how know this sorrow that has grown
And moulded to this present shape of man,
As of your own creation?

    King.   Ev'n from birth.

    Seg. But from that hour to this, near, as I think,
Some twenty such renewals of the year
As trace themselves upon the barren rocks,
I never saw you, nor you me—unless,
Unless, indeed, through one of those dark masks
Through which a son might fail to recognize
The best of fathers.

    King.   Be that as you will:
But, now we see each other face to face,
Know me as you I know; which did I not,
By whatsoever signs, assuredly
You were not here to prove it at my risk.

    Seg. You are my father.
And is it true then, as Clotaldo swears,
'Twas you that from the dawning birth of one

Yourself brought into being,—you, I say,
Who stole his very birthright; not alone
That secondary and peculiar right
Of sovereignty, but even that prime
Inheritance that all men share alike,
And chain'd him—chain'd him!—like a wild beast's whelp.
Among as savage mountains, to this hour?
Answer if this be thus.

  King.   Oh, Segismund,
In all that I have done that seems to you,
And, without further hearing, fairly seems,
Unnatural and cruel—'twas not I,
But One who writes His order in the sky
I dared not misinterpret nor neglect,
Who knows with what reluctance—

  Seg.   Oh, those stars,
Those stars, that too far up from human blame
To clear themselves, or careless of the charge,
Still bear upon their shining shoulders all
The guilt men shift upon them!

  King.   Nay, but think:
Not only on the common score of kind,
But that peculiar count of sovereignty—
If not behind the beast in brain as heart,
How should I thus deal with my innocent child,
Doubly desired, and doubly dear when come,
As that sweet second-self that all desire,
And princes more than all, to root themselves
By that succession in their people's hearts,
Unless at that superior Will, to which
Not kings alone, but sovereign nature bows?

  Seg. And what had those same stars to tell of me
That should compel a father and a king
So much against that double instinct?

  King   That,
Which I have brought you hither, at my peril,
Against their written warning, to disprove.

By justice, mercy, human kindliness.

    Seg. And therefore made yourself their instrument
To make your son the savage and the brute
They only prophesied?—Are you not afear'd,
Lest, irrespective as such creatures are
Of such relationship, the brute you made
Revenge the man you marr'd—like sire, like son,
To do by you as you by me have done?

    King. You never had a savage heart from me;
I may appeal to Poland.

    Seg.   Then from whom?
If pure in fountain, poison'd by yourself
When scarce begun to flow.—To make a man
Not, as I see, degraded from the mould
I came from, nor compared to those about,
And then to throw your own flesh to the dogs!—
Why not at once, I say, if terrified
At the prophetic omens of my birth,
Have drown'd or stifled me, as they do whelps
Too costly or too dangerous to keep?

    King. That, living, you might learn to live, and rule
Yourself and Poland.

    Seg.   By the means you took
To spoil for either?

    King.   Nay, but, Segismund!
You know not—cannot know—happily wanting
The sad experience on which knowledge grows,
How the too early consciousness of power
Spoils the best blood; nor whether for your long-
Constrain'd disheritance (which, but for me,
Remember, and for my relenting love
Bursting the bond of fate, had been eternal)
You have not now a full indemnity;
Wearing the blossom of your youth unspent
In the voluptuous sunshine of a court,
That often, by too early blossoming,
Too soon deflowers the rose of royalty.

Seg. Ay, but what some precocious warmth may spill,
May not an early frost as surely kill?
    King. But, Segismund, my son, whose quick discourse
Proves I have not extinguish'd and destroy'd
The Man you charge me with extinguishing,
However it condemn me for the fault
Of keeping a good light so long eclipsed,
Reflect! This is the moment upon which
Those stars, whose eyes, although we see them not,
By day as well as night are on us still,
Hang watching up in the meridian heaven
Which way the balance turns; and if to you—
As by your dealing God decide it may,
To my confusion!—let me answer it
Unto yourself alone, who shall at once
Approve yourself to be your father's judge,
And sovereign of Poland in his stead,
By justice, mercy, self-sobriety,
And all the reasonable attributes
Without which, impotent to rule himself,
Others one cannot, and one must not rule;
But which if you but show the blossom of—
All that is past we shall but look upon
As the first out-fling of a generous nature
Rioting in first liberty; and if
This blossom do but promise such a flower
As promises in turn its kindly fruit:
Forthwith upon your brows the royal crown,
That now weighs heavy on my agèd brows,
I will devolve; and while I pass away
Into some cloister, with my Maker there
To make my peace in penitence and prayer,
Happily settle the disorder'd realm
That now cries loudly for a lineal heir.
    Seg. And so—
When the crown falters on your shaking head,
And slips the sceptre from your palsied hand,

And Poland for her rightful heir cries out;
When not only your stol'n monopoly
Fails you of earthly power, but 'cross the grave
The judgment-trumpet of another world
Calls you to count for your abuse of this;
Then, oh then, terrified by the double danger,
You drag me from my den—
Boast not of giving up at last the power
You can no longer hold, and never rightly
Held, but in fee for him you robb'd it from;
And be assured your Savage, once let loose,
Will not be caged again so quickly; not
By threat or adulation to be tamed,
Till he have had his quarrel out with those
Who made him what he is.

   King.   Beware! Beware!
Subdue the kindled Tiger in your eye,
Nor dream that it was sheer necessity
Made me thus far relax the bond of fate,
And, with far more of terror than of hope
Threaten myself, my people, and the State.
Know that, if old, I yet have vigour left
To wield the sword as well as wear the crown;
And if my more immediate issue fail,
Not wanting scions of collateral blood,
Whose wholesome growth shall more than compensate
For all the loss of a distorted stem.

   Seg. That will I straightway bring to trial—Oh,
After a revelation such as this,
The Last Day shall have little left to show
Of righted wrong and villainy requited!
Nay, Judgment now beginning upon earth,
Myself, methinks, in sight of all my wrongs,
Appointed heaven's avenging minister,
Accuser, judge, and executioner,
Sword in hand, cite the guilty—First, as worst,
The usurper of his son's inheritance;

Him and his old accomplice, time and crime
Inveterate, and unable to repay
The golden years of life they stole away.
What, does he yet maintain his state, and keep
The throne he should be judged from? Down with him,
That I may trample on the false white head
So long has worn my crown! Where are my soldiers?
Of all my subjects and my vassals here
Not one to do my bidding? Hark! A trumpet!
The trumpet—

> *(He pauses as the trumpet sounds as in* ACT I.,
> *and masked Soldiers gradually fill in behind
> the Throne.)*

  King (rising before his throne). Ay, indeed, the trumpet
    blows
A memorable note, to summon those
Who, if forthwith you fall not at the feet
Of him whose head you threaten with the dust,
Forthwith shall draw the curtain of the Past
About you; and this momentary gleam
Of glory that you think to hold life-fast,
So coming, so shall vanish, as a dream.
  Seg. He prophesies; the old man prophesies;
And, at his trumpet's summons, from the tower
The leash-bound shadows loosen'd after me
My rising glory reach and over-lour—
But, reach not I my height, he shall not hold,
But with me back to his own darkness!

> *(He dashes toward the throne and is enclosed
> by the soldiers.)*

                          Traitors!
Hold off! Unhand me!—Am not I your king?
And you would strangle him!—
But I am breaking with an inward Fire
Shall scorch you off, and wrap me on the wings
Of conflagration from a kindled pyre
Of lying prophecies and prophet-kings

Above the extinguish'd stars—Reach me the sword
He flung me—Fill me such a bowl of wine
As that you woke the day with—
  King.   And shall close,—
But of the vintage that Clotaldo knows.   [*Exeunt.*

ACT III

Scene I.—*The Tower, etc., as in* Act I. Scene I.

Segismund, *as at first, and* Clotaldo

 Clotaldo. Princes and princesses, and counsellors
Fluster'd to right and left—my life made at—
But that was nothing—
Even the white-hair'd, venerable King
Seized on—Indeed, you made wild work of it;
And so discover'd in your outward action,
Flinging your arms about you in your sleep,
Grinding your teeth—and, as I now remember,
Woke mouthing out judgment and execution,
On those about you.
  Seg.   Ay, I did indeed.
  Clo. Ev'n now your eyes stare wild; your hair stands up—
Your pulses throb and flutter, reeling still
Under the storm of such a dream—
  Seg.   A dream!
That seem'd as swearable reality
As what I wake in now.
  Clo.   Ay—wondrous how
Imagination in a sleeping brain
Out of the uncontingent senses draws
Sensations strong as from the real touch;
That we not only laugh aloud, and drench
With tears our pillow; but in the agony
Of some imaginary conflict, fight
And struggle—ev'n as you did; some, 'tis thought,
Under the dreamt-of stroke of death have died.

Seg. And what so very strange too—In that world
Where place as well as people all was strange,
Ev'n I almost as strange unto myself,
You only, you, Clotaldo—you, as much
And palpably yourself as now you are,
Came in this very garb you ever wore,
By such a token of the past, you said,
To assure me of that seeming present.
   Clo.   Ay?
   Seg. Ay; and even told me of the very stars
You tell me here of—how in spite of them,
I was enlarged to all that glory.
   Clo.   Ay,
By the false spirits' nice contrivance thus
A little truth oft leavens all the false,
The better to delude us.
   Seg.   For you know
'Tis nothing but a dream?
   Clo.   Nay, you yourself
Know best how lately you awoke from that
You know you went to sleep on?—
Why, have you never dreamt the like before?
   Seg. Never, to such reality.
   Clo.   Such dreams
Are oftentimes the sleeping exhalations
Of that ambition that lies smouldering
Under the ashes of the lowest fortune;
By which, when reason slumbers, or has lost
The reins of sensible comparison,
We fly at something higher than we are—
Scarce ever dive to lower—to be kings,
Or conquerors, crown'd with laurel or with gold,
Nay, mounting heaven itself on eagle wings.
Which, by the way, now that I think of it,
May furnish us the key to this high flight—
That royal Eagle we were watching, and
Talking of as you went to sleep last night.

Seg. Last night? Last night?

Clo.   Ay, do you not remember
Envying his immunity of flight,
As, rising from his throne of rock, he sail'd
Above the mountains far into the West,
That burn'd about him, while with poising wings
He darkled in it as a burning brand
Is seen to smoulder in the fire it feeds?

Seg. Last night—last night—Oh, what a day was that
Between that last night and this sad To-day!

Clo. And yet, perhaps,
Only some few dark moments, into which
Imagination, once lit up within
And unconditional of time and space,
Can pour infinities.

Seg.   And I remember
How the old man they call'd the King, who wore
The crown of gold about his silver hair,
And a mysterious girdle round his waist,
Just when my rage was roaring at its height,
And after which it all was dark again,
Bid me beware lest all should be a dream.

Clo. Ay—there another specialty of dreams,
That once the dreamer 'gins to dream he dreams,
His foot is on the very verge of waking.

Seg. Would it had been upon the verge of death
That knows no waking—
Lifting me up to glory, to fall back,
Stunn'd, crippled—wretcheder than ev'n before.

Clo. Yet not so glorious, Segismund, if you
Your visionary honour wore so ill
As to work murder and revenge on those
Who meant you well.

Seg.   Who meant me!—me! their Prince
Chain'd like a felon—

Clo.   Stay, stay—Not so fast,
You dream'd the Prince, remember.

Seg.   Then in dream
Revenged it only.
    Clo.   True. But as they say
Dreams are rough copies of the waking soul
Yet uncorrected of the higher Will,
So that men sometimes in their dreams confess
An unsuspected, or forgotten, self;
One must beware to check—ay, if one may,
Stifle ere born, such passion in ourselves
As makes, we see, such havoc with our sleep,
And ill reacts upon the waking day.
And, by the bye, for one test, Segismund,
Between such swearable realities—
Since Dreaming, Madness, Passion, are akin
In missing each that salutary rein
Of reason, and the guiding will of man:
One test, I think, of waking sanity
Shall be that conscious power of self-control,
To curb all passion, but much most of all
That evil and vindictive, that ill squares
With human, and with holy canon less,
Which bids us pardon ev'n our enemies,
And much more those who, out of no ill will,
Mistakenly have taken up the rod
Which heaven, they think, has put into their hands.
    Seg. I think I soon shall have to try again—
Sleep has not yet done with me.
    Clo.   Such a sleep.
Take my advice—'tis early yet—the sun
Scarce up above the mountain; go within,
And if the night deceived you, try anew
With morning; morning dreams they say come true.
    Seg. Oh, rather pray for me a sleep so fast
As shall obliterate dream and waking too.
                            [Exit into the tower.
    Clo. So sleep; sleep fast: and sleep away those two
Night-potions, and the waking dream between

Which dream thou must believe; and, if to see
Again, poor Segismund! that dream must be.—
And yet, and yet, in these our ghostly lives,
Half night, half day, half sleeping, half awake,
How if our waking life, like that of sleep,
Be all a dream in that eternal life
To which we wake not till we sleep in death?
How if, I say, the senses we now trust
For date of sensible comparison,—
Ay, ev'n the Reason's self that dates with them,
Should be in essence or intensity
Hereafter so transcended, and awake
To a perceptive subtlety so keen
As to confess themselves befool'd before,
In all that now they will avouch for most?
One man—like this—but only so much longer
As life is longer than a summer's day,
Believed himself a king upon his throne,
And play'd at hazard with his fellows' lives,
Who cheaply dream'd away their lives to him.
The sailor dream'd of tossing on the flood:
The soldier of his laurels grown in blood:
The lover of the beauty that he knew
Must yet dissolve to dusty residue:
The merchant and the miser of his bags
Of finger'd gold; the beggar of his rags:
And all this stage of earth on which we seem
Such busy actors, and the parts we play'd,
Substantial as the shadow of a shade,
And Dreaming but a dream within a dream!
    Fife. Was it not said, sir,
By some philosopher as yet unborn,
That any chimney-sweep who for twelve hours
Dreams himself king is happy as the king
Who dreams himself twelve hours a chimney-sweep?
    Clo. A theme indeed for wiser heads than yours
To moralize upon—How came you here?—

Fife. Not of my own will, I assure you, sir.
No matter for myself: but I would know
About my mistress—I mean, master—
   Clo.   Oh,
Now I remember—Well, your master-mistress
Is well, and deftly on its errand speeds,
As you shall—if you can but hold your tongue.
Can you?
   Fife.   I'd rather be at home again.
   Clo. Where you shall be the quicker if while here
You can keep silence.
   Fife.   I may whistle, then?
Which by the virtue of my name I do,
And also as a reasonable test
Of waking sanity—
   Clo.   Well, whistle then;
And for another reason you forgot,
That while you whistle, you can chatter not.
Only remember—if you quit this pass—
   Fife. (His rhymes are out, or he had call'd it spot)—
   Clo. A bullet brings you to.
I must forthwith to court to tell the King
The issue of this lamentable day,
That buries all his hope in night. (*To Fife.*) Farewell.
Remember.
   Fife.   But a moment—but a word!
When shall I see my mis—mas—
   Clo.   Be content:
All in good time; and then, and not before,
Never to miss your master any more.   [*Exit.*
   Fife. Such talk of dreaming—dreaming—I begin
To doubt if I be dreaming I am Fife,
Who with a lad who call'd herself a boy
Because—I doubt there's some confusion here—
He wore no petticoat, came on a time
Riding from Muscovy on half a horse,
Who must have dreamt she was a horse entire,

To cant me off upon my hinder face
Under this tower, wall-eyed and musket-tongued,
With sentinels a-pacing up and down,
Crying All's well when all is far from well,
All the day long, and all the night, until
I dream—if what is dreaming be not waking—
Of bells a-tolling and processions rolling
With candles, crosses, banners, San-benitos,
Of which I wear the flamy-finingest,
Through streets and places throng'd with fiery faces
To some back platform—
Oh, I shall take a fire into my hand
With thinking of my own dear Muscovy—
Only just over that Sierra there,
By which we tumbled headlong into—No-land.
Now, if without a bullet after me,
I could but get a peep of my old home—
Perhaps of my own mule to take me there—
All's still—perhaps the gentlemen within
Are dreaming it is night behind their masks—
God send 'em a good nightmare!—Now then—Hark!
Voices—and up the rocks—and armed men
Climbing like cats—Puss in the corner then.   [*He hides.*

Enter SOLDIERS *cautiously up the rocks*

Captain. This is the frontier pass, at any rate,
Where Poland ends and Muscovy begins.
    Soldier. We must be close upon the tower, I know,
That half way up the mountain lies ensconced.
    Capt. How know you that?
    Sol.   He told me so—the Page
Who put us on the scent.
    Sol. 2.   And, as I think,
Will soon be here to run it down with us.
    Capt. Meantime, our horses on these ugly rocks
Useless, and worse than useless with their clatter—

Leave them behind, with one or two in charge,
And softly, softly, softly.

SOLDIERS

⎧—   There it is!
⎪— There what?—
⎪—   The tower—the fortress—
⎪—   That the tower!—
⎪— That mouse-trap! We could pitch it down the rocks
⎪With our own hands.
⎨—   The rocks it hangs among
⎪Dwarf its proportions and conceal its strength;
⎪Larger and stronger than you think.
⎪—   No matter;
⎪No place for Poland's Prince to be shut up in.
⎩At it at once!

    Capt.   No—no—I tell you wait—
Till those within give signal. For as yet
We know not who side with us, and the fort
Is strong in man and musket.

    Sol.   Shame to wait
For odds with such a cause at stake.

    Capt.   Because
Of such a cause at stake we wait for odds—
For if not won at once, for ever lost:
For any long resistance on their part
Would bring Basilio's force to succour them
Ere we had rescued him we come to rescue.
So softly, softly, softly, still—

    A Soldier (*discovering* FIFE). Hilloa!

SOLDIERS

⎧— Hilloa! Here's some one skulking—
⎪—   Seize and gag him!
⎨— Stab him at once, say I: the only way
⎪To make all sure.
⎪—   Hold, every man of you!
⎩And down upon your knees!—Why, 'tis the Prince!

— The Prince!—
—   Oh, I should know him anywhere,
And anyhow disguised.
—   But the Prince is chain'd.
— And of a loftier presence—
—   'Tis he, I tell you;
Only bewilder'd as he was before.
God save your Royal Highness! On our knees
Beseech you answer us!

Fife.   Just as you please.
Well—'tis this country's custom, I suppose,
To take a poor man every now and then
And set him on the throne; just for the fun
Of tumbling him again into the dirt.
And now my turn is come. 'Tis very pretty.

Sol. His wits have been distemper'd with their drugs.
But do you ask him, Captain.

Capt.   On my knees,
And in the name of all who kneel with me,
I do beseech your Highness answer to
Your royal title.

Fife.   Still, just as you please.
In my own poor opinion of myself—
But that may all be dreaming, which it seems
Is very much the fashion in this country—
No Polish prince at all, but a poor lad
From Muscovy; where only help me back,
I promise never to contest the crown
Of Poland with whatever gentleman
You fancy to set up.

SOLDIERS

—   From Muscovy?
— A spy then—
—   Of Astolfo's—
—   Spy! a spy!
— Hang him at once!

Fife. No, pray don't dream of that!

Sol. How dared you then set yourself up for our
Prince Segismund?

Fife. *I* set up!—I like that—
When 'twas yourselves be-siegesmunded me.

Capt. No matter—Look!—The signal from the tower.
Prince Segismund!

Sol. (*from the tower*). Prince Segismund!

Capt. All's well.
Clotaldo safe secured?—

Sol. (*from the tower*). No—by ill luck,
Instead of coming in, as we had look'd for,
He sprang on horse at once, and off at gallop.

Capt. To Court, no doubt—a blunder that—And yet
Perchance a blunder that may work as well
As better forethought. Having no suspicion
So will he carry none where his not going
Were of itself suspicious. But of those
Within, who side with us?

Sol. Oh, one and all
To the last man, persuaded or compell'd.

Capt. Enough: whatever be to be retrieved
No moment to be lost. For though Clotaldo
Have no revolt to tell of in the tower,
The capital will soon awake to ours,
And the King's force come blazing after us.
Where is the Prince?

Sol. Within; so fast asleep
We woke him not ev'n striking off the chain
We had so cursedly holp bind him with,
Not knowing what we did; but too ashamed
Not to undo ourselves what we had done.

Capt. No matter, nor by whosesoever hands,
Provided done. Come; we will bring him forth
Out of that stony darkness here abroad,
Where air and sunshine sooner shall disperse
The sleepy fume which they have drugg'd him with.

(They enter the tower, and thence bring out
SEGISMUND *asleep on a pallet, and set him*
in the middle of the stage.)

Capt. Still, still so dead asleep, the very noise
And motion that we make in carrying him
Stirs not a leaf in all the living tree.

SOLDIERS

If living—But if by some inward blow
For ever and irrevocably fell'd
By what strikes deeper to the root than sleep?
  — He's dead! He's dead! They've kill'd him—
  —   No—he breathes—
And the heart beats—and now he breathes again
Deeply, as one about to shake away
The load of sleep.

Capt.   Come, let us all kneel round,
And with a blast of warlike instruments,
And acclamation of all loyal hearts,
Rouse and restore him to his royal right,
From which no royal wrong shall drive him more.

(They all kneel round his bed: trumpets,
drums, etc.)

SOLDIERS

  — Segismund! Segismund! Prince Segismund!
  — King Segismund! Down with Basilio!
  — Down with Astolfo! Segismund our King! etc.
Soldier 1. He stares upon us wildly. He cannot speak.
Soldier 2. I said so—driv'n him mad.
Soldier 3.   Speak to him, Captain.
Captain. Oh Royal Segismund, our Prince and King,
Look on us—listen to us—answer us,
Your faithful soldiery and subjects, now
About you kneeling, but on fire to rise
And cleave a passage through your enemies,
Until we seat you on your lawful throne.

For though your father, King Basilio,
Now King of Poland, jealous of the stars
That prophesy his setting with your rise,
Here holds you ignominiously eclipsed,
And would Astolfo, Duke of Muscovy,
Mount to the throne of Poland after him;
So will not we, your loyal soldiery
And subjects; neither those of us now first
Apprised of your existence and your right:
Nor those that hitherto deluded by
Allegiance false, their vizors now fling down,
And craving pardon on their knees with us
For that unconscious disloyalty,
Offer with us the service of their blood;
Not only we and they; but at our heels
The heart, if not the bulk, of Poland follows
To join their voices and their arms with ours,
In vindicating with our lives our own
Prince Segismund to Poland and her throne.

SOLDIERS

{— Segismund, Segismund, Prince Segismund!
{— Our own King Segismund, etc. (*They all rise.*)
   Seg. Again? So soon?—What, not yet done with me?
The sun is little higher up, I think,
Than when I last lay down,
To bury in the depth of your own sea
You that infest its shallows.
   Capt.   Sir!
   Seg.   And now,
Not in a palace, not in the fine clothes
We all were in; but here, in the old place,
And in our old accoutrement—
Only your vizors off, and lips unlock'd
To mock me with that idle title—
   Capt.   Nay,
Indeed no idle title, but your own,

Then, now, and now for ever. For, behold,
Ev'n as I speak, the mountain passes fill
And bristle with the advancing soldiery
That glitters in your rising glory, sir;
And, at our signal, echo to our cry,
'Segismund, King of Poland!' etc.

                                     (Shouts, trumpets, etc.)

   Seg.   Oh, how cheap
The muster of a countless host of shadows,
As impotent to do with as to keep!
All this they said before—to softer music.

   Capt. Soft music, sir, to what indeed were shadows,
That, following the sunshine of a Court,
Shall back be brought with it—if shadows still,
Yet to substantial reckoning.

   Seg.   They shall?
The white-hair'd and white-wanded chamberlain,
So busy with his wand too—the old King
That I was somewhat hard on—he had been
Hard upon me—and the fine feather'd Prince
Who crow'd so loud—my cousin,—and another,
Another cousin, we will not bear hard on—
And—But Clotaldo?

   Capt.   Fled, my lord, but close
Pursued; and then—

   Seg.   Then, as he fled before,
And after he had sworn it on his knees,
Came back to take me—where I am!—No more,
No more of this! Away with you! Begone!
Whether but visions of ambitious night
That morning ought to scatter, or grown out
Of night's proportions you invade the day
To scare me from my little wits yet left,
Begone! I know I must be near awake,
Knowing I dream; or, if not at my voice,
Then vanish at the clapping of my hands,
Or take this foolish fellow for your sport:

Dressing me up in visionary glories,
Which the first air of waking consciousness
Scatters as fast as from the almander[3]—
That, waking one fine morning in full flower,
One rougher insurrection of the breeze
Of all her sudden honour disadorns
To the last blossom, and she stands again
The winter-naked scare-crow that she was!

    Capt. I know not what to do, nor what to say,
With all this dreaming; I begin to doubt
They have driv'n him mad indeed, and he and we
Are lost together.

    A Soldier (*to* CAPTAIN). Stay, stay; I remember—
Hark in your ear a moment. (*Whispers.*)

    Capt.   So—so—so?—
Oh, now indeed I do not wonder, sir,
Your senses dazzle under practices
Which treason, shrinking from its own device,
Would now persuade you only was a dream;
But waking was as absolute as this
You wake in now, as some who saw you then,
Prince as you were and are, can testify:
Not only saw, but under false allegiance
Laid hands upon—

    Soldier 1.   I, to my shame!

    Soldier 2.   And I!

    Capt. Who, to wipe out that shame, have been the first
To stir and lead us—Hark! (*Shouts, trumpets, etc.*)

    A Soldier.   Our forces, sir,
Challenging King Basilio's, now in sight,
And bearing down upon us.

    Capt.   Sir, you hear;
A little hesitation and delay,
And all is lost—your own right, and the lives
Of those who now maintain it at that cost;
With you all saved and won; without, all lost.

---

[3] Almander, or almandre, Chaucer's word for *almond-tree,* Rom. Rose, 1363.

That former recognition of your right
Grant but a dream, if you will have it so;
Great things forecast themselves by shadows great:
Or will you have it, this like that dream too,
People, and place, and time itself, all dream—
Yet, being in't, and as the shadows come
Quicker and thicker than you can escape,
Adopt your visionary soldiery,
Who, having struck a solid chain away,
Now put an airy sword into your hand,
And harnessing you piece-meal till you stand
Amidst us all complete in glittering,
If unsubstantial, steel—

 Rosaura (*without*). The Prince! The Prince!
 Capt. Who calls for him?
 Sol.   The Page who spurr'd us hither,
And now, dismounted from a foaming horse—

Enter Rosaura

 Rosaura. Where is—but where I need no further ask
Where the majestic presence, all in arms,
Mutely proclaims and vindicates himself.
 Fife. My darling Lady-lord—
 Ros.   My own good Fife,
Keep to my side—and silence!—Oh, my Lord,
For the third time behold me here where first
You saw me, by a happy misadventure
Losing my own way here to find it out
For you to follow with these loyal men,
Adding the moment of my little cause
To yours; which, so much mightier as it is,
By a strange chance runs hand in hand with mine;
The self-same foe who now pretends your right,
Withholding mine—that, of itself alone,
I know the royal blood that runs in you
Would vindicate, regardless of your own:
The right of injured innocence; and, more,

Spite of this epicene attire, a woman's;
And of a noble stock I will not name
Till I, who brought it, have retrieved the shame.
Whom Duke Astolfo, Prince of Muscovy,
With all the solemn vows of wedlock won,
And would have wedded, as I do believe,
Had not the cry of Poland for a Prince
Call'd him from Muscovy to join the prize
Of Poland with the fair Estrella's eyes.
I, following him hither, as you saw,
Was cast upon these rocks; arrested by
Clotaldo: who, for an old debt of love
He owes my family, with all his might
Served, and had served me further, till my cause
Clash'd with his duty to his sovereign,
Which, as became a loyal subject, sir,
(And never sovereign had a loyaller,)
Was still his first. He carried me to Court,
Where, for the second time, I cross'd your path;
Where, as I watch'd my opportunity,
Suddenly broke this public passion out;
Which, drowning private into public wrong,
Yet swiftlier sweeps it to revenge along.
    Seg. Oh God, if this be dreaming, charge it not
To burst the channel of enclosing sleep
And drown the waking reason! Not to dream
Only what dreamt shall once or twice again
Return to buzz about the sleeping brain
Till shaken off for ever—
But reassailing one so quick, so thick—
The very figure and the circumstance
Of sense-confess'd reality foregone
In so-call'd dream so palpably repeated,
The copy so like the original,
We know not which is which; and dream so-call'd
Itself inweaving so inextricably
Into the tissue of acknowledged truth;

The very figures that empeople it
Returning to assert themselves no phantoms
In something so much like meridian day,
And in the very place that not my worst
And veriest disenchanter shall deny
For the too well-remember'd theatre
Of my long tragedy—Strike up the drums!
If this be Truth, and all of us awake,
Indeed a famous quarrel is at stake:
If but a Vision I will see it out,
And, drive the Dream, I can but join the rout.

   Capt. And in good time, sir, for a palpable
Touchstone of truth and rightful vengeance too,
Here is Clotaldo taken.

   Soldiers.   In with him!
In with the traitor!   (*Clotaldo brought in.*)

   Seg.   Ay, Clotaldo, indeed—
Himself—in his old habit—his old self—
What! back again, Clotaldo, for a while
To swear me this for truth, and afterwards
All for a dreaming lie?

   Clo.   Awake or dreaming,
Down with that sword, and down these traitors theirs,
Drawn in rebellion 'gainst their Sovereign.

   Seg. (*about to strike*). Traitor! Traitor yourself!—
But soft—soft—soft!—
You told me, not so very long ago,
Awake or dreaming—I forget—my brain
Is not so clear about it—but I know
One test you gave me to discern between,
Which mad and dreaming people cannot master;
Or if the dreamer could, so best secure
A comfortable waking—Was't not so?—
(*To* ROSAURA). Needs not your intercession now, you see,
As in the dream before—
Clotaldo, rough old nurse and tutor too
That only traitor wert, to me if true—

Give him his sword; set him on a fresh horse;
Conduct him safely through my rebel force;
And so God speed him to his sovereign's side!
Give me your hand; and whether all awake
Or all a-dreaming, ride, Clotaldo, ride—
Dream-swift—for fear we dreams should overtake.

(*A Battle may be supposed to take place; after which*)

Scene II.—*A wooded pass near the field of battle: drums, trumpets,
firing, etc. Cries of 'God save Basilio! Segismund,' etc.*

Enter Fife, *running*

Fife. God save them both, and save them all! say I!—
Oh—what hot work!—Whichever way one turns
The whistling bullet at one's ears—I've drifted
Far from my mad young—master—whom I saw
Tossing upon the very crest of battle,
Beside the Prince—God save her first of all!
With all my heart I say and pray—and so
Commend her to His keeping—bang!—bang!—bang!—
And for myself—scarce worth His thinking of—
I'll see what I can do to save myself
Behind this rock, until the storm blows over.

(*Skirmishes, shouts, firing, etc. After some time enter* King
Basilio, Astolfo, *and* Clotaldo.)

King. The day is lost!
Ast.   Do not despair—the rebels—
King. Alas! the vanquish'd only are the rebels.
Clotaldo. Ev'n if this battle lost us, 'tis but one
Gain'd on their side, if you not lost in it;
Another moment and too late: at once
Take horse, and to the capital, my liege,
Where in some safe and holy sanctuary
Save Poland in your person.
Ast.   Be persuaded:
You know your son: have tasted of his temper;

At his first onset threatening unprovoked
The crime predicted for his last and worst.
How whetted now with such a taste of blood,
And thus far conquest!

King.   Ay, and how he fought!
Oh how he fought, Astolfo; ranks of men
Falling as swathes of grass before the mower;
I could but pause to gaze at him, although,
Like the pale horseman of the Apocalypse,
Each moment brought him nearer—Yet I say,
I could but pause and gaze on him, and pray
Poland had such a warrior for her king.

Ast. The cry of triumph on the other side
Gains ground upon us here—there's but a moment
For you, my liege, to do, for me to speak,
Who back must to the field, and what man may
Do, to retrieve the fortune of the day.   (*Firing.*)

Fife (*falling forward, shot*). Oh, Lord, have mercy on me.

King.   What a shriek—
Oh, some poor creature wounded in a cause
Perhaps not worth the loss of one poor life!—
So young too—and no soldier—

Fife.   A poor lad,
Who choosing play at hide and seek with death,
Just hid where death just came to look for him;
For there's no place, I think, can keep him out,
Once he's his eye upon you. All grows dark—
You glitter finely too—Well—we are dreaming—
But when the bullet's off—Heaven save the mark!
So tell my mister—mastress—   (*Dies.*)

King. Oh God! How this poor creature's ignorance
Confounds our so-call'd wisdom! Even now
When death has stopt his lips, the wound through which
His soul went out, still with its bloody tongue
Preaching how vain our struggle against fate!

(VOICES *within*). After them! After them! This way!
       This way!

The day is ours—Down with Basilio, etc.
  Ast. Fly, sir—
  King.   And slave-like flying not out-ride
The fate which better like a King abide!

Enter SEGISMUND, ROSAURA, SOLDIERS, *etc.*

  Seg. Where is the King?
  King (*prostrating himself*). Behold him,—by this late
Anticipation of resistless fate,
Thus underneath your feet his golden crown,
And the white head that wears it, laying down,
His fond resistance hope to expiate.
  Seg. Princes and warriors of Poland—you
That stare on this unnatural sight aghast,
Listen to one who, Heaven-inspired to do
What in its secret wisdom Heaven forecast,
By that same Heaven instructed prophet-wise
To justify the present in the past.
What in the sapphire volume of the skies
Is writ by God's own finger misleads none,
But him whose vain and misinstructed eyes,
They mock with misinterpretation,
Or who, mistaking what he rightly read,
Ill commentary makes, or misapplies
Thinking to shirk or thwart it. Which has done
The wisdom of this venerable head;
Who, well provided with the secret key
To that gold alphabet, himself made me,
Himself, I say, the savage he fore-read
Fate somehow should be charged with; nipp'd the growth
Of better nature in constraint and sloth,
That only bring to bear the seed of wrong
And turn'd the stream to fury whose out-burst
Had kept his lawful channel uncoerced,
And fertilized the land he flow'd along.
Then like to some unskilful duellist,
Who having over-reached himself pushing too hard

His foe, or but a moment off his guard—
What odds, when Fate is one's antagonist!—
Nay, more, this royal father, self-dismay'd
At having Fate against himself array'd,
Upon himself the very sword he knew
Should wound him, down upon his bosom drew,
That might well handled, well have wrought; or, kept
Undrawn, have harmless in the scabbard slept.
But Fate shall not by human force be broke,
Nor foil'd by human feint; the Secret learn'd
Against the scholar by that master turn'd
Who to himself reserves the master-stroke.
Witness whereof this venerable Age,
Thrice crown'd as Sire, and Sovereign, and Sage,
Down to the very dust dishonour'd by
The very means he tempted to defy
The irresistible. And shall not I,
Till now the mere dumb instrument that wrought
The battle Fate has with my father fought,
Now the mere mouth-piece of its victory—
Oh, shall not I, the champion's sword laid down,
Be yet more shamed to wear the teacher's gown,
And, blushing at the part I had to play,
Down where that honour'd head I was to lay
By this more just submission of my own,
The treason Fate has forced on me atone?
   King. Oh, Segismund, in whom I see indeed,
Out of the ashes of my self-extinction
A better self revive; if not beneath
Your feet, beneath your better wisdom bow'd,
The Sovereignty of Poland I resign,
With this its golden symbol; which if thus
Saved with its silver head inviolate,
Shall nevermore be subject to decline;
But when the head that it alights on now
Falls honour'd by the very foe that must,
As all things mortal, lay it in the dust,

Shall star-like shift to his successor's brow.
    Shouts, trumpets, etc. God save King Segismund!
    Seg.   For what remains—
As for my own, so for my people's peace,
Astolfo's and Estrella's plighted hands
I disunite, and taking hers to mine,
His to one yet more dearly his resign.
    Shouts, etc. God save Estrella, Queen of Poland!
    Seg. (*to* CLOTALDO).   You
That with unflinching duty to your King,
Till countermanded by the mightier Power,
Have held your Prince a captive in the tower,
Henceforth as strictly guard him on the throne
No less my people's keeper than my own.[4]

You stare upon me all, amazed to hear
The word of civil justice from such lips
As never yet seem'd tuned to such discourse.
But listen—In that same enchanted tower,
Not long ago I learn'd it from a dream
Expounded by this ancient prophet here;
And which he told me, should it come again,
How I should bear myself beneath it; not
As then with angry passion all on fire,
Arguing and making a distemper'd soul;
But ev'n with justice, mercy, self-control,
As if the dream I walk'd in were no dream,
And conscience one day to account for it.
A dream it was in which I thought myself,

---

[4] In Calderon's drama, the Soldier who liberates Segismund meets with even worse recompense than in the version below. I suppose some such saving clause against prosperous treason was necessary in the days of Philip IV., if not later.

      CAPT. And what for him, my liege, who made you free
    To honour him who held you prisoner?
      SEG. By such self-proclamation self-betray'd
    Less to your Prince's service or your King's
    Loyal, than to the recompence it brings;
    The tower he leaves I make you keeper of
    For life—and, mark you, not to leave alive;
    For treason may, but not the traitor, thrive.

And you that hail'd me now then hail'd me King,
In a brave palace that was all my own,
Within, and all without it, mine; until,
Drunk with excess of majesty and pride,
Methought I tower'd so high and swell'd so wide,
That of myself I burst the glittering bubble,
That my ambition had about me blown,
And all again was darkness. Such a dream
As this in which I may be walking now;
Dispensing solemn justice to you shadows,
Who make believe to listen; but anon,
With all your glittering arms and equipage,
King, princes, captains, warriors, plume and steel,
Ay, ev'n with all your airy theatre,
May flit into the air you seem to rend
With acclamation, leaving me to wake
In the dark tower; or dreaming that I wake
From this that waking is; or this and that
Both waking or both dreaming; such a doubt
Confounds and clouds our mortal life about.
And, whether wake or dreaming, this I know,
How dream-wise human glories come and go;
Whose momentary tenure not to break,
Walking as one who knows he soon may wake,
So fairly carry the full cup, so well
Disorder'd insolence and passion quell,
That there be nothing after to upbraid
Dreamer or doer in the part he play'd,
Whether To-morrow's dawn shall break the spell,
Or the Last Trumpet of the eternal Day,
When Dreaming with the Night shall pass away.

[*Exeunt.*

POLYEUCTE

BY
PIERRE CORNEILLE

TRANSLATED BY
THOMAS CONSTABLE

INTRODUCTORY NOTE

PIERRE CORNEILLE was born in Rouen in 1606, the son of an official; was educated by the Jesuits, and practised unsuccessfully as a lawyer. His dramatic career began with the comedy of "Mélite," but it was by his "Médée" that he first proved his tragic genius. "The Cid" appeared in 1636, and a series of masterpieces followed—"Horace," "Cinna," "Polyeucte," "Le Menteur." After a failure in "Pertharite" he retired from the stage, deeply hurt by the disapproval of his audience. Six years later he resumed play-writing with "Œdipe" and continued till 1674, producing in all some thirty plays. Though he earned a great reputation, he was poorly paid; and a proud and sensitive nature laid him open to considerable suffering. He died in 1684.

The works of Corneille represent most fully the ideal of French so-called "classical" tragedy. The laws to which this type of tragedy sought to conform were not so much truth to nature as the principles which the critics had derived from a somewhat inadequate interpretation of Aristotle and of the practise of the Greek tragedians. These principles concentrated the interest of the play upon a single central situation, in order to emphasize which, subordinate characters and complicating under-plots were avoided as much as possible. There was little or no action upon the stage, and the events of the plot were narrated by messengers, or by the main characters in conversation with confidantes. Further, the "dramatic unities" of time and place, as well as of action, were held to be binding.

One result of these rules was to give an extraordinary importance to the speeches; and it is in the eloquence of these, in the grandeur and dignity of the versification, and in the lofty moral elevation of the characters, that Corneille excels. All of these qualities are admirably exemplified in "Polyeucte"; and in the conduct of the leading personages one may perceive the most persistent trait of this dramatist's treatment of heroic character—the conquest of the passions by the reason and the will. "Among the masterpieces of Corneille," says Paul de Saint-Victor, " 'Polyeucte' is assuredly the greatest; and nothing in all his dramas equals the extraordinary beauty of the character of 'Pauline.' "

POLYEUCTE

CHARACTERS

FELIX, *Roman senator, Governor of Armenia.*
POLYEUCTE, *an Armenian noble, son-in-law to Felix.*
SEVERUS, *a Roman Knight, favourite of the Emperor Decius.*
NEARCHUS, *an Armenian noble, friend to Polyeucte.*
PAULINE, *daughter to Felix, wife to Polyeucte.*
STRATONICE, *companion to Pauline.*
ALBIN, *friend to Felix.*
FABIAN, *servant to Severus.*
CLEON, *friend to Felix.*
THREE GUARDS.

The Scene is at Melitena, capital of Armenia.
The action takes place in the Palace of Felix.

ACT I

POLYEUCTE. NEARCHUS

Nearchus

SHALL woman's dream of terror hurl the dart?
   Oh, feeble weapon 'gainst so great a heart!
   Must courage proved a thousand times in arms
Bow to a peril forged by vain alarms?
  Poly. I know that dreams are born to fade away,
And melt in air before the light of day;
I know that misty vapours of the night
Dissolve and fly before the morning bright.
The dream is naught—but the dear dreamer—all!
She has my soul, Nearchus, fast in thrall;
Who holds the marriage torch—august, divine,
Bids me to her sweet voice my will resign.
She fears my death—tho' baseless this her fright,
Pauline is wrung with fear—by day—by night;
My road to duty hampered by her fears,
How can I go when all undried her tears?

Her terror I disown—and all alarms,
Yet pity holds me in her loving arms:
No bolts or bars imprison,—yet her sighs
My fetters are—my conquerors, her eyes!
Say, kind Nearchus, is the cause you press
Such as to make me deaf to her distress?
The bonds I slacken I would not unloose—
Nothing I yield—yet grant a timely truce.

    Near. How grant you know not what? Are you assured
Of constancy?—as one who has endured?
God claims your soul for Him!—Now! Now! To-day!
The fruit to-morrow yields—oh, who shall say?
Our God is just, but do His grace and power
Descend on recreants with equal shower?
On darkened souls His flame of light He turns,
Yet flame neglected soon but faintly burns,
And dying embers fade to ashes cold
If we the heart His spirit wooes withhold.
Great Heaven retains the fire no longer sought,
While ashes turn to dust, and dust to naught.
His holy baptism He bids thee seek,—
Neglect the call, and the desire grows weak.
Ah! whilst from woman's breast thou heedst the sighs,
The flame first flickers, then, untended—dies!

    Poly. You know me ill,—'tis mine, that holy fire,
Fed, not extinguished, by unslaked desire;
Her tears—I view them with a lover's eye;
And yet your Christ is mine—a Christian I!
The healing, cleansing flood o'er me shall flow,
I would efface the stain from birth I owe;
I would be pure—my sealéd eyes would see!
The birthright Adam lost restored to me—
This, this, the unfading crown! For this I yearn,
For that exhaustless fount I thirst, I burn.
Then, since my heart is true, Nearchus, say—
Shall I not grant to pity this delay?

    Near. So doth the ghostly foe our souls abuse,

And all beyond his force he gains by ruse;
He hates the purpose fast he cannot foil,—
Then he retreats—retreats but to recoil!
In endless barricade obstruction piles,—
To-day 'tis tears impede, to-morrow—smiles!
And this poor dream—his coinage of the night—
Gives place to other lures, all falsely bright:
All tricks he knows and uses—threats and prayers—
Attacks in parley—as the Parthian dares.
In chain unheeded weakest link must fail,
So fortress yet unwon he'll mount and scale.
O break his bonds! Let feeble woman weep!
The heart that God has touched 'tis God must keep!
Who looks behind to dally with his choice
When Heaven demands—obeys another voice!
 Poly. Who loves thy Christ—say, must he love no other?
 Near. He may—he must! 'Tis Christ says, 'Love thy brother,'
Yet on the altar of the Heavenly King
No rival place, no alien incense fling!
Through Him—by Him—for Him—all goodness know!
'Tis from the source alone each stream must flow.
To please Him, wife, and wealth, and rank, and state
Must be forsaken—strait the heavenly gate.
Poor silly sheep! afar you err and stray
From Him who is The Life, The Truth, The Way!
My grief chokes utterance! I see your fate,
As round the fold the hungry wolves of hate
Closer and fiercer rage: from sword and flame
One shelter for His flock—one only Name!
The Cross alone our victor over fears,
Not this thy strength,—thy plea—a woman's tears!
 Poly. I know thy heart! It is mine own—the tear
My pity drops hath ne'er a taint of fear!
Who dreads not torture, yet—to give relief
To her he loves, perforce must ease her grief!
If Heaven should claim my life, my death, my all,—
Then Heaven will give the strength to heed the call.

The shepherd guides me surely to the fold,
There, safe with Him, 'tis He will make me bold!
  Near. Be bold! O come!
  Poly.   Yes, let thy faith be mine!
There—at his feet—do I my life resign
If but Pauline—my love—would give consent!
Else heaven were hell, and home but banishment!
  Near. Come!—to return. Thrice welcome to her sight,
To see thee safe will double her delight:
As the pierced cloud unveils a brighter sun,—
So is her joy enhanced—thy glory won!
O come, they wait!
  Poly.   Appease her fear! Ah, this
Alone will give her rest—her lover bliss.
She comes!
  Near.   Then fly!
  Poly.   I cannot!
  Near.   To deny
Would yield thine enemy the victory!
He loves to kill, and knows his deadliest dart
Finds friend within the fort—thy traitor heart!

Enter PAULINE *and* STRATONICE

  Poly. I needs must go, Pauline! My love, good-bye!
I go but to return—for thine am I!
  Paul. Oh, why this haste to leave a loving wife?
Doth honour call?—or fear'st thou for thy life?
  Poly. For more, a thousandfold!
  Paul.   Great Gods above!
  Poly. Thou hast my heart! Let this content thy love!
  Paul. You love and yet you leave me. What am I?
Not mine to solve the dreary mystery!
  Poly. I love thee more than self—than life—than fame—
But——
  Paul. There is something that thou dar'st not name.
Oh, on my knees I supplicate, I pray,
Remove my darkness!—turn my night to day!

Poly. Oh, dreams are naught!

Paul. Yet, when they tell of thee,
I needs must listen, for I love! Ah, me!

Poly. Take courage, dear one, 'tis but for an hour,
Thy love must draw me back, for love hath power
O'er all in earth and heaven. My soul's delight,
I can no more! My only safety—flight!

[*Exeunt* POLYEUCTE *and* NEARCHUS.

Paul. Yes, go, despise my prayer—my agony;
Go, ruthless—meet thy fate—forewarned by me;
Chase thy pursuer, herald thine own doom;
Go, kiss the murderer's hand, and hail the tomb!
Ah, Stratonice! for our boasted power
As sovereigns o'er man's heart! Poor regents of an hour!
Faint, helpless, moonbeam-light was all I gave,
The sun breaks forth—his queen becomes his slave!
Wooed? Yes; as other queens I held my court—
Won—but to lose my crown, and be the sport
Of proud, absorbing and imperious man!

Strat. Ah, man does what he wills—we, what we can;
He loves thee, lady!

Paul. Love should mate with trust;
He leaves me!

Strat. Lady, 'tis because he must!
He loves thee with a love will never die,
Then, if he leave thee, reason not the why:
Give him thy trust! Oh, thou shalt have reward,
For thee he hides the secret! Let him guard
Thy life beloved—in fullest liberty.
The wife who wholly trusts alone is free!
One heart for thee and him—one purpose sure,
Yet this heart beats to dare—and to endure.
The wife's true heart must o'er the peril sigh
Which meets his heart moved but to purpose high;
Thy pain his pain, but not his terror thine:
He is Armenian, thou of Roman line.
We, of Armenia, mock thy dreams to scorn,

For they are born of night, as truth ot morn;
While Romans hold that dreams are heaven-sent,
And spring from Jove for man's admonishment.
    Paul. Though this thy faith—if thou my dream shouldst
      hear—
My grief must needs be thine, thy fear my fear,
And, that the horror thou may'st fully prove,
Know that I—his dear wife—did once another love!
Nay, start not, shrink not, 'tis no tale of shame,
For though in other years the heavenly flame
Descended, kindled, scorched—it left me pure—
With courage to resign—with strength to endure.
He touched my heart, but never stained the soul
That gained this hardest conquest—self-control.
At Rome—where I was born—a soldier's eye
Marked this poor face, from which must Polyeucte fly;
Severus was his name:—Ah! memory
May spare love linked with death a tear, a sigh!
    Strat. Say, is it he who, at the risk of life,
Saved Decius from his foes and endless strife?
Who, dying, dealt to Persia stroke of death,
And shouted 'Victory!' with his latest breath?
His whitening bones, amid the nameless brave,
Lie still unfound, unknown, without a grave;
Unburied lies his dust amid the slain,
While Decius rears an empty urn in vain!
    Paul. Alas! 'tis he; all Rome attests his worth,—
Hide not his memory, kindly Mother Earth!
'Tis but his memory that I adore—
The past is past—and I can say no more.
All gifts save one had he—yes, Fortune held her hand,
And I, as Fortune's slave, obeyed my sire's command.
    Strat. Ah! I must wish that love the day had won!
    Paul. Which duty lost—then had I been undone;
Though duty gave, yet duty healed, my pain;
Yet say not that my love was weak or vain!
Our tears fell fast, yet ne'er bore our distress

The fatal fruit of strife and bitterness.
Then, then, I left my hero, hope and Rome,
And, far from him, I found another home;
While he, in his despair, sought sure relief
In death, the only end to life's long grief!
You know the rest:—you know that Polyeucte's eye
Was caught,—his fancy pleased; his wife am I.
Once more by counsel of my father led,
To Armenia's greatest noble am I wed;
Ambition, prudence, policy his guide
Yet only duty made Pauline his bride;
Love might have bound me to Severus' heart,
Had duty not enforced a sterner part.
Yes, let these fears attest, all trembling for his life,
That I am his for aye—his faithful, loving wife.
    Strat. Thy new love true and tender as the old:—
But this thy dream? No more thy tale withhold!
    Paul. Last night I saw Severus: but his eye
With anger blazed; his port was proud and high,
No suppliant he—no feeble, formless shade,
With dim, averted eye; no sword had made
My hero lifeless ghost. Nor wound, nor scar
Marked death his only conqueror in war.
Nor spoil of death, nor memory's child was he,
His mien triumphant, full of majesty!
So might victorious Caesar near his home
To claim the key to every heart in Rome!
He spoke: in nameless awe I heard his voice,—
'Give love, that is my due, to him—thy choice,—
But know, oh faithless one, ere day expires,
All vain these tears for him thy heart desires!'
Anon a Christian band (an impious horde),
With shameful cross in hand, attest his word;
They vouch Severus' truth—and, to complete
My doom, hurl Polyeucte beneath his feet!
I cried, 'O father, timely succour bear!'
He heard, he came, my grief was now despair!

He drew his dagger—plunged it in the breast
Of him, my husband, late his honoured guest!
Relief came but from agony supreme—
I shrieked—I writhed—I woke—it was a dream!
And yet my dream is true!

    Strat.   'Tis true your dream is sad,
But now you are awake, 'tis but a dream you had!
For horror's prey in darkness of the night
Is but our reason's sport in morning light.
How can you dread a shade? How a fond father fear,
Who as a son regards the man you hold so dear?
To phantom of the night no credence yield;
For him and you he chose thy strength and shield.

    Paul. You say *his* words: at all my fears he smiles,
But I must dread these Christians and their wiles!
I dread their vengeance, wreaked upon my lord,
For Christian blood my father has outpoured!

    Strat. Their sect is impious, mad, absurd and vain,
Their rites repulsive, as their cult profane.
Deride their altar, their weak frenzy ban,
Yet do they war with gods and not with man!
Relentless wills our law that they must die:
Their joy—endurance; death—their ecstasy;
Judged—by decree, the foes of human race,
Meekly their heads they bow—to court disgrace!

    Paul. My father comes—oh, peace!

Enter FELIX and ALBIN

    Felix.   Nay, peace is flown!
Thy dream begets dull fears, till now unknown;
In part this dream is true, and for the rest——

    Paul. By what new fear, say, is thy heart opprest?

    Felix. Severus lives!

    Paul.   Ah! this no cause for fear!

    Felix. At Decius' court, he, held in honour dear,
Risked life to save his Emperor from his foes,
'Tis to his saviour Decius honour shows!

Paul. Thus fickle Fortune bows her head to fate,
And pays the honour due, though all too late!
  Felix. He comes! Is near——
  Paul.   The gods——
  Felix.   Do all things well.
  Paul. My dream fulfilled! But how? O father, tell!
  Felix. Let Albin speak, who saw him face to face
With tribe of courtiers; all to him give place;
Unscathed in battle, all extol his fame,
Unstained, undimmed, his glory, life and name!
  Albin. You know the issue of that glorious fight:
The crowning glory his—who, in despite
Of danger sore to life and liberty,
Became a slave to set his Emperor free:
Rome gave her honours to Severus' shade,
Whilst he, her ransomer, in a dungeon stayed.
His death they mourned above ten thousand slain,
While Persia held him—yes, their tears were vain,
But not in vain his noble sacrifice!
The king released him: Rome grudged not the price;
No Persian bribe could tempt him from his home.
When Decius cried—'Fight once again for Rome!'
Again he fights—he leads—all others hope resign;
But from despair's deep breast he plucks a star benign,
This—hope's fair fruit, contentment, plenty, ease,
Brings joy from grief, to crown a lasting peace.
The Emperor holds him as his dearest friend,
And doth Severus to Armenia send—
To offer up to Mars, and mighty Jove,
'Mid feast and sacrifice, his thanks and love.
  Felix. Ah, Fortune, turn thy wheel, else I misfortune meet!
  Albin. This news I learn'd from one of great Severus' suite:
Thence, swiftly here, the tale to tell I sped.
  Felix. He who once vainly wooed, hopes now to wed.
The sacrifice, the offering, all are feigned,
All but the suit, which lightly I disdained.
  Paul. Yes, this may be, for ah! he loved me well!

Felix. What room for hope? Such wrath is child of hell.
Before his righteous ire I shrink, I cower;
Revenge I dread—and vengeance linked with power
Unnerves me quite.
  Paul.   Fear not, his soul is great.
  Felix. Thy comfort, oh my daughter, comes too late.
The thought to crush me down, to turn my heart to stone,
This, that I prized not worth for worth's dear sake alone!
Too well, Pauline, thou hast thy sire obeyed;
Thy heart was fond, but duty love betrayed.
How surely thy revolt had safety won!
'Tis thine obedience leaves us all undone.
In thee, in thee alone, one hope remains,
Love held him fast, relax not thou love's chains.
O Love, my sometime foe, forgive, be mine ally,
And let the dart that slew now bring the remedy!
  Paul. Forbid it, Heaven! One good yet mine,—*my will,*
The dart that wounded has the power to kill.
One lesson woman learns—her feebleness;
Shame is the only grief without redress.
The traitor heart shall still a prisoner be;
For freedom were disgrace to thee and me!
I will not see him!
  Felix.   But one word! Be kind!
  Paul. I will not, for I love!—and love is blind.
Before his kingly eye my soul to unveil
Were shame and failure: and I will not fail:
I will not see him!
  Felix.   One word more—'Obey!'
Wouldst thou thy father and his weal betray?
  Paul. I yield! Come woe!—come shame!—come every ill!
My father thou!—and I thy daughter still!
  Felix. I know thee pure.
  Paul.   And pure I will remain,
But, crushed and bruised, the flower no guilt shall stain.
I fear the combat that I may not fly,—
Hard-won the fight, and dear the victory.

Here, love, my curse! Here, dearest friend, my foe!
Yet will I arm me! Father, I would go
To steel my heart—all weapons to embrace!
    Felix. I too will go, the conqueror's march to grace!
Restore thy strength, ere yet it be too late,
And know that in thy hands thou hold'st our fate!
    Paul. Go, broken heart, to probe thy wound; cut deep and do
      not spare!
Herself—the crowning sacrifice—the victim shall prepare!

ACT II

SEVERUS. FABIAN

    Sev. Let Felix bow to Jove and incense pour,—
I seek a dearer shrine, for I adore
Nor Jove, nor Mars, nor Fortune—but Pauline.
This fruit now ripening late my hand would glean:
You know, my friend, the god who wings my way,—
You know the only goddess I obey:
What reck the gods on high our sacrifice and prayer?
An earthly worship mine, sole refuge from despair!
    Fabian. Ah! You may see her——
    Sev.   Blesséd be thy tongue!
O magic word, that turns my grief to song!
Yet, if she now forget each fair, fond vow?
She loved me once,—but does she love me now?
On that sweet face shall I but trouble see—
Who hope for love undimmed, for ecstasy?
Great Decius gives her hand, but if her heart
Be mine no more—then let vain hope depart!
This mandate binds her father only; she
Shall give no captive hand—her heart is free:
No promise wrung, no king's command be mine to claim,
Her love the boon I crave; all else an empty name!
    Fabian. Yes,—you may—see her—*see* her—this you may—
    Sev. Thy speech is halting—odious thy delay!
She loves no more? I grope! O give me light!

Fabian. O see her not, for painful were the sight!
In Rome each matron's kind! In Rome all maids are fair!
Let lips meet other lips—seek for caresses there!
No stately Claudia will refuse—no Julia proud disdain;
A hero captures every heart, from Antioch to Spain!

    Sev. To wed a queen—an empress—were only loss and
    shame;
One heart for me—Pauline's! *One* boast—that dearest name!
Her love was virgin gold! O ne'er shall baser metal ring
From mine, who live her name to bless! her peerless praise
    to sing!
O, words are naught, till that I see her face,—
Then doubly naught till I my love embrace.
In every war my hope was placed in death,
Her name upon my lips at every breath:
My rank, my fame, now hers and hers alone,
What is not hers, hers only—I disown!

    Fabian. Once more, oh see her not, 'twere for thy peace!

    Sev. Thy meaning, knave, or let this babble cease!
Say, was she cold? My love! My only life!

    Fabian. No—but—my lord——

    Sev.   Say on!

    Fabian.   Another's wife!

    Sev. (*Reels.*) Help!—No, I will not blench—ah, say you lie!
If this be true!—ye gods—can I be I?

    Fabian. No, thou art changed. Where is thy courage fled?

    Sev. I know not, Fabian. Lost! Gone! Vanished! Dead!
I thought my strength was oak—'tis but a reed!
Pauline is wed, then am I lost indeed!
Hope hid beyond the cloud, yet still fond hope was there:
But now all hope is dead, lives only black despair!
Pauline another's wife?

    Fabian.   Yes, Polyeucte is her lord.
He came, he saw, he conquered thine adored.

    Sev. Her choice is not unworthy—his a name
Illustrious, from a line of kings he came—
Cold comfort for a wound no cure can heal!

My cause is lost, —foredoomed without appeal!
Malignant Jove, to drag me back to-day!
Relentless Fate, to quench hope's dawning ray!
Take back your gifts! One boon alone I crave,
That only boon to none denied—the grave.
Yet would I see her, breathe one last good-bye,
Would hear once more that voice before I die!
My latest breath would still my homage pay,—
That memory mine, when lost to realms of day.

   Fabian. Yet think, my lord——
   Sev.   Oh, I have thought of all;
What worser ill can dull despair befall?
She will not see me?
   Fabian.   Yes, my lord, but——
   Sev.   Cease!
   Fabian. 'Twill but enhance the grief I would appease.
   Sev. For hopeless ill, good friend, I seek no cure.
Who welcomes death can life's short pain endure!
   Fabian. O lost indeed, if round her fatal light you hover!—
The lover, losing all, speaks hardly like a lover!
While passion still is lord—the passion-swept is slave—
From this last bitterness would I Severus save!
   Sev. That word, my friend, unsay; tho' grief this bosom tear,
The hand that wounds I kiss—love vanquishes despair;
Fate only, not Pauline, the foe that I accuse,
No plighted faith she breaks who did this hand refuse.
Duty—her father—Fate—these willed, she but obeyed;
Not hers the woe, the strife that envious Até made!
Untimely, Fortune's shower must drown me, not revive;
Too lavish and too late her fatal gifts arrive.
The golden apple falls, the gold is turned to dross:
When Fate at Fortune mocks, all gain is only loss!
   Fabian. Yes, I will go to tell her thou hast drained
To the last drop the cup that Fate ordained.
She knows thee hero, but she feared that pain
Might prove thee also man—by passion slain.
She feared Despair, who gains the victory

O'er other men, might e'en thy master be!
 Sev. Peace! Peace! She comes!
 Fabian.   To thine own self be true!
 Sev. Nay! True to her! Shall I her life undo?
She loves the Armenian!

      Enter PAULINE

 Paul.   Yes, that debt I pay,
Hard-wrung, acquitted,—his my love alway!
Who has my hand, he holds—shall hold—my heart!
Truth is my guide,—let sophistry depart!
Had Fate been kind, then had Pauline been thine,
Heart, faith and duty, linked with bliss divine.
In vain had fickle Fortune barred the way,
Want had been wealth with thee, my guide, my stay,
And poverty had fallen from the wings
Of soaring love, who mocks the wealth of kings!
Not mine to choose, for he—my father's choice—
Must needs be mine; yes, when I heard his voice,
Duty must echo be: if thou couldst cast
Before my feet an emperor's crown,—a past
By worth and glory lit—beloved, adored—
Yet at my father's word, 'Not this thy lord;
Take one despised—nay, loathed—to share thy bed,'—
Him, and not thee, belovéd, would I wed.
Duty, obedience, must have been the part
Of me, who own their sway, e'en with a broken heart!
 Sev. O happy thou! O easy remedy!
One poor faint sigh cures love's infirmity!
Thy heart thy tool, o'er every passion queen,
Beyond all change and chance thou sit'st serene!
In easy flow can pass thy love new-born
From cold indifference to colder scorn;
Such resolution is the equal mate
Of god or monster, love, aversion, hate.
This fine-spun adamant Ithuriel's spear

Could never pierce: for other stuff is here!

[Points to himself.

No faint 'Alas!' no swift-repented sigh
Can heal the cureless wound from which I die.
Sure, reason finds that love his easy prey
With Lethe aye at hand to point the way;
With ordered fires like thine, I too could smother
A heart in leash, find solace in another.
Too fair, too dear—from whom the Fates me sever!
Thou hast no heart to give—thou lov'dst me never!

 Paul. Too plain, Severus, I my torture show,—
Tho' flame leap up no more, the embers glow;
Far other speech and voice, and mien were mine,
Could I forget that once thou call'dst me thine!
Tho' reason rules, yes, gains the mastery—
No queen benignant, but a tyrant she!
Oh, if I conquer—if the strife I gain,
Yet memory for aye is linked with pain!
I feel the charm that binds me still to thee;
If duty great, yet great thy worth to me:
I see thee still the same, who waked the fire
Which waked in me ineffable desire.
Begirt by crown of everlasting fame
Thou art more glorious—yet art still the same.
I know thy valour's worth,—well hast thou justified
That bounding hope of mine, though fruitage was denied,
Yet this same fate which did our union ban
Hath made me, fated—wed another man.
Let Duty still be queen! Yea, let her break
The heart she pierces, yet can never shake.
The virtue, once thy pride in days gone by—
Doth that same worth now merit blasphemy?
Bewail her bitter fruit—but praiséd be
The rights that triumph over thee and me!

 Sev. Forgive, Pauline, forgive; ah! grief hath made me blind
To all but grief's excess, and fortune most unkind.

Forgive that I mistook—nay, treated as a crime—
Thy constancy of soul, unequalled and sublime;
In pity for my life forlorn, my peace denied,
Ah! show thyself less fair,—one least perfection hide!
Let some alloy be seen, some saving weakness left,
Take pity on a heart of thee and Heaven bereft!
One faintest flaw reveal, to give my soul relief!
Else, how to bear the love that only mates with grief?

   Paul. Alas! the rents in armour donned and proved
Too well my fight proclaim; yes, I have loved;
The traitor sigh, the tear unbid, attest
The combat fierce—the warrior sore distrest.
Say, who can stanch these wounds, that armour mend?
Thou who hast pierced, thou, thou alone defend!
Ah, if thou honourest my victory—
Depart, that thou may'st still defender be!
So dry the tears that, to my shame, still flow—
So quench the fire would work my overthrow!
Yes, go, my only friend, with me combine
To end my torture, for thy pain is mine!

   Sev. This last poor drop of comfort may not be?
   Paul. The cup is poisoned both for me and thee!
   Sev. The flower is gone—I cherish but the root!
   Paul. Untimely blossom bears a fated fruit!
   Sev. My grief be mine! Let memory remain!
   Paul. That grief might hope beget, so leave a stain!
   Sev. Not mine to stain what Heaven hath made so pure!
For me one offering left: 'tis this: Endure!
Thy glory shall be mine, my load I bear,
So, spotless, thou thy peerless crown shalt wear!
Farewell, my love, farewell; I go to prove my faith,
To bless, to save thy life, so will I mate with death!
If prostrate from the blow, there yet remains of life
Enough to summon death, and end the piteous strife!

   Paul. My grief, too deep for voice, shall silent be,
There, in my chamber, will I pray for thee!
When thou art gone, great Heaven shall hear my cry;

Grief's fruit for thee be hope—death—immortality!

Sev. Now with my loss alone let Fate contented be,
May Heaven shower bliss and peace on Polyeucte and thee!

Paul. Stern Fate obeyed, end, Death, his agony,
And Jove receive my hero—to the sky!

Sev. Thou wast my heaven!

Paul.   My father I obeyed—

Sev. O victim pure, obedient, undismayed!
Pauline—too fair—too dear—I can no more!

Paul. So must I say—depart—where I adore!

                               [*Exit* SEVERUS.

Strat. Yes, it is hard—most sad—behold my tears!
But now, at least, there is no cause for fears:
Thy dream is but a dream—is naught, is vain;
Severus pardons. Gone that cause for pain!

Paul. Oh, if from pity start thy easy tear,
Add not that other woe—forgotten fear!
Ah! let me breathe, some respite give from trouble,
Those fears, half-dead, thou dost revive, redouble!

Strat. What dost thou dread?

Paul.   Heaven—hell—earth—empty air!
All, all is food for dread to my despair,
As thou unveil'st, begirt in lurid light,
The pallid ghost that slew me in the night!

Strat. Severus he by name, yet noble in his heart!

Paul. Ah, Polyeucte bathed in blood! Depart! depart!

Strat. For Polyeucte's welfare did Severus pray!

Paul. Yes, yes, his heart is great; be that my stay!
Yet, tho' his truth, his faith, well-provéd be,
Most baleful is his presence here to me;
Yea, tho' he would all ill for me undo—
Yet he hath power, he loves—he came to woo.

Enter POLYEUCTE *and* NEARCHUS

Poly. The source of tears is dry, oh, weep no more,
Thy grief lay down, thy fearful heart restore!
Let night's dark dream with superstition die,

The dream is past, for here in life am I!

Paul. The day is young, and oh, the day is long,—
And half the dream is true, and Fate is strong;
Severus have I seen, who thought him dead!

Poly. I know it! Let no tear for this be shed!
Secure with thee am I! Tho' great the knight,
Thy father will command to do me right;
The general is a man of honour,—he
Would ne'er that honour dim by treachery!
He comes in amity, our friend, our guest;
To greet his worth and valour now my quest.

Paul. Radiant he came, who left me hopeless, sad,
But he will come no more,—this grace I had.

Poly. What? Thinkest thou that I can jealous be?

Paul. An outrage this on him, on thee, on me!
He came in peace, who all my peace hath marred.
Who would run safely, every step must guard;
The wife who danger courts but courts her fall—
My husband, aid me!—I would tell thee all!
His worth, his charm, do my weak hearth enflame—
A traitor *here!* And he is aye the same!
If I should gaze, and long—'gainst virtue, honour, sense,
The citadel I yield, and mine my own defence!
I know my virtues sure, and fair my fame,
But struggle is defeat,—and combat shame!

Poly. Oh, true thy shield, thy victory is won,
He only who has lost thee is undone;
His noble grief the cost of all my bliss,
Ah, Cleopatra's pearl was naught to this!
The more my faults I see, the more thy truth I learn,
The more do I admire——

Enter CLEON

Cleon.   My lord, the altars burn
With holy fire. The victim they prepare;
On thee alone they wait, our rites to share.

Poly. Go, we do follow thee!

Paul.   I cannot go;
Severus flies my sight; to him I owe
My absence—not, alas! to him alone!
Go thou, and oh, remember he is great;
In his sole hands Severus holds thy fate!
    Poly. A foe so great, so noble, is a friend,
Oh, not from him the lance that Heaven will send!
                    [*Exeunt* PAULINE, STRATONICE *and* CLEON.
    Near. Where go'st thou?
    Poly.   To the temple is the call.
    Near. What! Wouldst thou mingle in their heathen brawl?
Thou art a Christian, and canst thou forget?
    Poly. Canst *thou,* who fore mine eyes the cross didst set?
    Near. Not mine their gods!
    Poly.   He calls me! I must go!
    Near. I fly their altars!
    Poly.   I would overthrow!
Not mine to fly a worship I disown,
By me Jehovah, King of kings, be known!
Not mine to tremble as I kiss the rod!
I conquer by the Cross, I fight for God!
Thou wouldst abstain! For me another course—
From Heaven the call, and Heaven will give the force!
What! Yield to evil! His Cross on my brow!
His freemen we! O fight, Nearchus, now!
For us our Lord was scourged, pierced, tortured, slain!
For us He bled! Say, has He died in vain?
    Near. Let timely moderation temper zeal!
    Poly. His—His alone am I! His woe my weal!
    Near. In love with death?
    Poly.   For Him I love I die!
He died for me! So death is victory!
    Near. Thy flesh is weak!
    Poly.   Yet He will make me bold!
    Near. And if thou waver?
    Poly.   He will me uphold!
    Near. To tempt the Lord thy God were an offence.

Poly. He is my shield—hence! cursed tempter, hence!
Near. In time of need the faith must be confessed.
Poly. The offering grudged is sacrifice unblessed.
Near. Seek thou the death thine own self-will prepares!
Poly. A crown I seek, which every martyr shares!
Near. A life of duty well that crown can win.
Poly. The purest life on earth is stained with sin.
Why yield to time and chance what death assures?
Death but the gate of life that aye endures.
If I be His—let me be His alone!
The faith that soars shall full fruition own;
Who trusts, yet fears and doubts, his faith is dead!
Near. Not death the Christian's prayer, but daily bread.
Live to protect the flock, so sore oppressed.
Poly. Example be their friend, most sure, most blessed!
Near. Thou woo'st thy death!
Poly.   Is this poor life so dear?
Near. Ah, I must own my heart is slave to fear.
The rack! The cross! I might my Lord disown!
Poly. From Him our help, our strength, from Him alone!
Who fears denial does at heart deny;
Who doubts the power of faith makes faith a lie!
Near. Who leans upon a reed shall find distress.
Poly. His staff will guide, support my feebleness.
Thou wert my staff, to show the Truth, the Way,
Must I now urge thee to the realms of day?
Thou fearest death?
Near.   The Christ once feared to die!
Poly. Yet drained the bitter cup of agony!
The way that thou hast shown—that way He trod;
His way be ours to lead man's soul to God—
For heathen shrine—to rear His altar fair,—
The deathless hope alone can kill despair!
Thou said'st: 'If Him thou wilt for pattern take,
Then leave wife, wealth, home, all for His dear sake!'
Alas! that love of thine, now weak and poor,
Glows yet within my breast—and shall endure;

Ah, must the dawn of this my perfect day
Find thy full light beclouded, dimmed, astray?
  Near. Baptismal waters yet bedew thy brow;
The grace that once was mine, that grace hast thou.
No worldly thought has checked the flow, no guilty act has
    stained;
Thy wings are strong, while mine are weak; thy love is
    fresh, unfeigned,—
To these, thy heights, I cannot soar, held down by sense and
    sin,
How can I storm the citadel?—the traitor lurks within!
Forsake me not, my God! Thy spirit pour!
Oh, make me true to Him whom I adore!
With Thee I rise,—the flesh, the world, defy,
Thou, who hast died for me, for Thee I die!
Yes, I will go! With heaven-born zeal I burn,
I will be free,—all Satan's lures I spurn;
Death, torture, outrage, these will I embrace,
To nerve my heart and arm, Heaven grant me grace!
  Poly. On eagle wings of faith and hope ascend!
I hail my master—recognise my friend;
The old faith wanes,—we light her funeral pyre,
Her ashes fall before our holy fire;
Come, trample under foot the gods that men have wrought;
The rotten, helpless staff is broke, is gone—is naught.
Their darkness felt they own, but let them see the light!
Their gods of stone, of clay, but vampires of the night!
Their dust shall turn to dust,—shall moulder with the sod,
Ours for His name to fight:—the issue is with God.
  Near. The cause is just, is true—O coward heart, be still!
I lived to doubt His word—I die to do His Will!

ACT III

PAULINE

  Paul. Cares—clouded and confused—oppress, obscure
In changeful forms, my eye, my heart, my mind:
My soul finds room for every guest save one;

Fair hope has flown,—no star can pierce my night:
Each tyrant rages 'gainst opposing foe
In deadly fight—yet brings to light no friend:
In travail sore hope comes not to the birth—
Fear hydra-headed terror still begets;—
All fancies grim I see, and straight embrace,
At hope I clutch, who still eludes my grasp;
Her rainbow hues adored are but a frame
That serve by contrast to make fear more dark.
Severus haunts me—oh, I know his love,
Yet hopeless love must mate with jealousy,—
While Polyeucte, who has won what he has lost,
Can meet no rival with an equal eye.
The fruit of rivalry is ever hate
And envy; both must still engender strife:
One sees that rival hand has grasped his prize,
The other yearns for prize himself has missed.
Weak reason naught, when headlong passion reigns,
For valour seeks a sword, and love—revenge.
One fears to see the prize he gained impaired,
The other would that wrested prize regain;
While patience, duty, conscience, vail their heads
'Fore obstinate defence and fierce attack.
Such steeds no charioteer controls—for they
Mistake both curb and reign for maddening whip
Ah! what a base, unworthy fear is mine!
How ill I read these fair, these noble souls,
Whose virtue must all common snares o'erleap!
Their gold unstained by dross or mean alloy!
As generous foes so will they—must they meet!
Yet are they rivals—this the thought that kills!
Not even here—at home—is Polyeucte safe,
The eagle wings of Rome reach over all.
Oh, if my father bow to Roman might,
If he repent the choice that he hath made,—
At this one thought hope's flame leaps up to die!
Or—if new-born—dies ere she see the light.

Hope but deceived,—my fear alone I trust,
Heaven grant such confidence be false—be vain!

Enter STRATONICE

Nay, let me know the worst! What, girl!—no word?
The rites are o'er? What hast thou seen—what heard?
They met in amity?—In peace they part?
   Strat. Alas! Alas!
   Paul.   Nay, soothe my aching heart!
I would have comfort,—but this face of woe—
A quarrel?
   Strat.   Polyeucte—Nearchus—go—
The Christians——
   Paul.   What of them?
   Strat.   Ah, how to speak——
   Paul. They on my father would their vengeance wreak?
   Strat. Oh, fear whate'er thou wilt—that fear too small!
   Paul. The Christians rise?
   Strat.   Oh, would that this were all!
Thy dream, Pauline, is true; Polyeucte is——
   Paul.   Dead?
   Strat. Ah, no, he lives—yet every hope is fled;
That courage once so high, that noble name
Sunk in the mire of everlasting shame!
He lives,—who once was lovely in thy sight—
As monster foul—his every breath a blight;
The foe of Heaven, of Jove, of all our race,
His kisses poison, and his love—disgrace!
Wretch, coward, miscreant, steeped in infamy,
O worse than every name!—a *Christian* he!
   Paul. Nay, that one word's enough! There needed not abuse.
   Strat. My words fit well their guilt;—with evil make no
     truce.
   Paul. If *he* be *Nazarene*—he must an outcast be!
But insult to my lord is insult unto me!
   Strat. Think only that he hails the Cross, the badge of shame.
   Paul. My plighted faith, my troth, my duty still the same!

Strat. When twined about thy breast, the hideous serpent
    slay!
Who mocks the Gods on high will his own wife betray!
    Paul. If he be false, yet I will still be true,
The ties that bind me I will ne'er undo:
Let fate—Severus—passion—all combine
Against him!—I am his, and he is mine.
Yes, mine to guide, lead, win, forgive, and save!
I seek his honour tho' he court the grave.
Let Polyeucte be Christ's slave!—For woe, for weal,
He is my lord; the bond I owe I seal;
I fear my father,—all his vengeance, dread.
    Strat. Fierce burns his rage o'er that devoted head;—
Yet embers of old love still faintly glow,
And through his wrath some weak compassion show;
'Gainst Polyeucte biting words alone he speaks—
But on Nearchus fullest vengeance wreaks!
    Paul. Nearchus lured him on?
    Strat.   The tempter he;
Such friendship leads to death, or infamy.
Oh, curséd friend, who, in dear love's despite,
Has torn him from thine arms—his neophyte!
He dragged him to the front;—baptized, annealed—
He fights for Christ!—The secret is revealed.
    Paul. Which I would know—and straightway had thy
    blame!
    Strat. Ah! I foresaw not this—their deed of shame!
    Paul. Ere dull despair o'ermaster all my fears,
Oh, let me gauge the worth of woman's tears!
For, if the daughter lose, the wife may gain,—
Or Felix may relent, if Polyeucte mock my pain;
If both are adamant unto my prayer,
Then—then alone—take counsel from despair!
How passed the temple sacrifice? Hide naught, my friend,
    tell all!
    Strat. The horror and the sacrilege must I, perforce, re-
    call?

To say the words, to think the thoughts, seems blasphemy and
 shame;
Yet will I tell their infamy,—their deed without a name.
To silence hushed, the people knelt, and turned them to the
 East;
Then impious Polyeucte and his friend mock sacrifice and
 priest.
They every holy name invoked jeer with unbridled tongue,
To laughter vile the incense rose—'tis thus our hymn was
 sung;
Both loud and deep the murmurs rang, and Felix' face grew
 pale,
Then Polyeucte mad defiance hurls, while all the people
 quail.
'Vain are your gods of wood and stone!' his voice was stern
 and high—
'Vain every rite, prayer, sacrifice,' so ran his blasphemy.
'Your Jupiter is parricide, adulterer, demon, knave,
'He cannot listen to your cry, not his to bless or save.
'One God—Jehovah—rules alone, supreme o'er earth and
 heaven,
'And ye are His—yes, only His—to Him your prayers be
 given!
'He is our source, our life, our end,—no other god adore,
'To Him alone all prayer is due, then serve Him evermore!
'Who kneels before a meaner shrine, by devils' power enticed,
'Denies his Maker and his King, denies the Saviour Christ.
'He is our source, our guide, our end, our prophet, priest and
 King;
' 'Twas He that nerved Severus' arm,—His praise let Decius
 sing.
'Jehovah rules the battle-field ye call the field of Mars,
'He only grants a glorious peace, 'tis He guides all our wars.
'He casts the mighty from his seat, He doth the proud
 abase,—
'They only peace and blessing know who love and seek His
 face.

'His sword alone is strong to strike, His shield our only guard.

'He will His bleeding saints avenge, He is their sure reward.

'In vain to Jove and feeble Mars your full libations pour—

'Oh, kneel before the might ye spurn, the God ye mock—adore!'

Then Polyeucte the shrine o'erthrows, the holy vessels breaks,

Nor wrath of Jove, nor Felix' ire, his fatal purpose shakes.

Foredoomed by Fate, the Furies' prey—they rush, they rend, they tear,

The vessels all to fragments fly—all prone the offerings fair;

And on the front of awful Jove they set their impious feet,

And order fair to chaos turn, and thus their work complete.

Our hallowed mysteries disturbed, our temple dear profaned,

Mad flight and tumult dire let loose, proclaim a God disdained.

Thus pallid fear broods over all, presaging wrath to come,

While Felix—but I mark his step!—'tis he shall speak the doom.

Paul. How threatening, how dark his mien! How lightning-fraught his eye!

Where wrath and grief, revenge and pain, do strive for mastery!

Enter Felix

Felix. O insolence undreamed!—Before my very eyes!—

Before the people's gaze! It is too much!—he dies!

Paul. O father!—on my knees! (*kneels*). Unsay that word!

Felix. Nearchus' doom I speak,—not his, thy lord.

Though all unworthy he to be my son,

Yet still he bears the name that he hath won;

Nor crime of his nor wrath of mine shall ever move

Thy father's heart to hate the man thou crown'st with love!

Paul. Ne'er vainly have I sued for pity from my sire!

Felix. And yet meet food were he for righteous ire!
To recount an act so fell my feeble words too weak,
But thou hast heard the tale my lips refuse to speak
From her, thy maiden; she hath told thee all.
 Paul. Nearchus goaded—planned—and he shall fall!
 Felix. So taught by torture of his vilest friend,
Shall Polyeucte mark of guilt the certain end,
When of the frenzied race he sees the goal,
The dread of torture shall subdue his soul!
Who mocked the thought of death, when death he views,
Will choose an easier mate—and rightly choose.
That shadowy guest, that doth his soul entice,
Once master, glues all ardour into ice,
And that proud heart, which never meekness knew,
When face to face with Death—will learn to sue!
 Paul. What! Thinkest thou his soul can ever blench?
 Felix. Death's mighty flood must every furnace quench!
 Paul. It might! It may!—I know such things can be!
A Polyeucte changed—debased—forsworn I see!
O, changeful Fortune! changeless Polyeucte move,
And grant a boon denied by father's love!
 Felix. My love too plain—myself too weakly kind,
Let him repent and he shall pardon find;
Nearchus' sin is his,—and yet the grace
He shall not win, thy Polyeucte may embrace!
My duty—to a father's love betrayed—
Hath of thy sire a fond accomplice made;
A healing balm I bring for all thy fears,
I look for thanks, and lo—thou giv'st me tears!
 Paul. I give no thanks—no cause for thanks I find;
I know the Christian temper—know their mind,
They can blaspheme, but ah, they cannot lie!
They know not how to yield—but they can die!
 Felix. As bird in hand, he holds his pardon still.
 Paul. The bird escapes, when 'tis the owner's will.
 Felix. He death escapes—if so he do elect.
 Paul. He death embraces—as doth all his sect.

Is 't thus a father pleads for his own son?
   Felix. Who wills his death is by himself undone.
   Paul. He cannot see!
   Felix.   Because he chooses night.
Who loves the darkness hateth still the light.
   Paul. O, by the Gods—
   Felix.   Nay, daughter, save thy breath;
Spurned—outraged—'tis the Gods demand his death.
   Paul. They hear our prayers—
   Felix.   Nay, then let Polyeucte pray!
   Paul. Since Decius gives thee power,—that word unsay!
   Felix. He gives me power, Pauline, to do his will
Against his foes—'gainst all who work him ill.
   Paul. Is Polyeucte his foe?
   Felix.   All Christians rebels are.
   Paul. Thy son shall plead more loud than policy or war.
For mine is thine; O father, save thine own—
   Felix. The son who is a traitor I disown!
For treason is a crime without redress,
'Gainst which all else sinks into nothingness.
   Paul. Too great thy rigour!
   Felix.   Yet more great his guilt.
   Paul. Too true my dream! Must his dear blood be spilt?
With Polyeucte, I too—thy child—shall fall!
   Felix. The Gods—the Emperor—rule over all.
   Paul. O hear our dying supplication—hear!
   Felix. Not Jove alone, but Decius I fear:—
But why anticipate a doom so sad?
Shall this—his blindness—make thy Polyeucte mad?
Fresh Christian zeal remains not always new,
The sight of death compels a saner view.
   Paul. O, if thou lov'st him still, all hope forsake!
In one day can he two conversions make?
Not this the Christians' mould: they never change;
His heart is fixed—past power of man to estrange.
This is no poison quaffed all unawares,
What martyrs do and dare—that Polyeucte dares;

He saw the lure by which he was enticed,
He thinks the universe well lost for Christ.
I know the breed; I know their courage high,
They love the cross,—so, for the cross, they die.
We see two stakes of wood, the felon's shame,
They see a halo round one matchless Name.
To powers of earth, and hell, and torture blind,
In death, for Him they love, they rapture find.
They joy in agony,—our gain their loss,
To die for Christ they count the world but dross:
Our rack their crown, our pain their highest pleasure,
And in the world's contempt they find their treasure.
Their cherished heritage is—martyrdom!

   Felix. Let then this heir into his kingdom come!
No more!——

   Paul.   O father!

Enter ALBIN

   Felix.   Albin, is it done?

   Albin. It is,—Nearchus' frantic race is run!

   Felix. And with what eye saw Polyeucte the sight?

   Albin. With envious eye,—as one who sees a light
That lures him, moth-like, to devouring flame.
His heart is fixed, his mind is still the same.

   Paul. 'Tis as I said—oh, father, yet once more—
If thou hast ever loved me,—I implore!
Let filial duty and obedience plead
For his dear life! To my last prayer give heed!

   Felix. Too much thou lovest an unworthy lord!

   Paul. Thou gavest him my hand, 'twas at thy word
I gave both love and duty; what I give
I take not back; oh, Polyeucte must live!
For his dear sake I quenched another flame
Most pure. Is he my lord alone in name?
O, by my blind and swift obedience paid
To thy command—be thy hard words unsaid!
I gave thee all a daughter had to give,

Grant, father, this one prayer—Let Polyeucte live!
By thy stern power, which now I only fear,
Make thou that power benignant, honoured, dear!
Thou gav'st that gift unsought,—that gift restore!
I claim it at the giver's hand once more!

Felix. Importunate! Although my heart is soft,
It is not wax,—and these entreaties oft
Repeated waste thy breath, and vex mine ear,
For man is deaf to what he will not hear.
I am the master! This let all men know,
And if thou force that note thou'lt find 'tis so.
Prepare to see thy curséd Christian fool,
Do thou caress when I have scourged the mule,—
Go! vex no more a loving father's ear,
From Polyeucte's self win what thou hold'st so dear.

Paul. In pity!——

Felix. Leave me, leave me here alone!——
Say more—my goaded heart will turn to stone;
Vex me no more—I will not be denied!
Go, save thy madman from his suicide!   [*Exit* PAULINE.
How met Nearchus death?

Albin. The fiend abhorred
He hailed,—embraced: 'For Christ!' his latest word;
No sigh, no tear,—he passed without amaze
Adown the narrow vale with upward gaze.

Felix. And he—his friend?

Albin. Is, as I said, unmoved
He looks on death but as a friend beloved,
He clasped the scaffold as a guide most sure,
And, in his prison, he can still endure.

Felix. Oh, wretched that I am!

Albin. All pity thee.

Felix. With reason greater than they know. Ah, me!
Thought surges upon thought, and has its will,
Care, gnawing upon care, my soul must kill;
Love—hate—fear—pain: I am of each the prey,
I grope for light, but never find the day!—

Oh, what I suffer thou canst not conceive,
Each passion rages, but can ne'er relieve;
For I have noble thoughts that die still-born,
And I have thoughts so base my soul I scorn.
I love the foolish wretch who is my son,
I hate the folly which hath all undone;
I mourn his death,—yet, if I Polyeucte save,
I see of all my hopes the cruel grave!
'Gainst Gods and Emperor too sore the strife,
For my renown I fear,—fear for my life.
I must myself undo to save my son,
For, should I spare him, then am I undone!
   Albin. Decius a father is, and must excuse
A father's love—oh, he will not refuse!
   Felix. His edict is most clear:—'All Christians are my foes.'
The higher be their rank the more the evil grows.
If birth and state be high, their crime shows more notorious,
If he who shield be great, his fall the more inglorious;
And if I give Nearchus to the flame
Yet stoop to shield my own—thrice damned my name!
   Albin. If by thy fiat he cannot escape the grave,
Implore of Decius' grace the life thou canst not save.
   Felix. So would Severus work my ruin quite—
I fear his power, his wrath,—for might is right—
If crime with punishment I do not mate.
How high soe'er, worth what it may, I fear his hate,
For he is man, and feels as man, and I
Once spurned his suit with base indignity.
Yes, he at Decius' ear would work my woe,
He loves Pauline, thus Polyeucte is his foe:
All weapons possible to love and war,
And those who let them rust but laggards are.
I fear—and fear doth give our vision scope—
E'en now he cherisheth a tender hope;
He sees his rival prostrate in the dust,
So, as a man he hopes—because he must.
Can dark despair to love and hope give place

To save the guilty from deserved disgrace?
And were his worth so matchless, so divine,
As to forbear all ill to me and mine—
Still I must own the base, the coward hope,
'Gainst which my strength is all too weak to cope,
That hope whose phœnix ashes yet enthrall
The wretch who rises but once more to fall;
Ambition is my master, iron Fate,
I feel, obey, adore thee, while I hate!
Polyeucte was once my guard, my pride, my shield,
Yet can I, by Severus, weapons wield,
Should he my daughter wed, more tried, more true:
What wills Severus—that will Decius do.
Upheld by him, e'en Fortune I defy—
And yet I shrink!—for them, thrice base were I!

   Albin. Perish the word! It ne'er was made for thee,
But wilt thou deal just meed to treachery?

   Felix. I go to Polyeucte's cell,—though my poor breath
Should there be spent in vain to avert his death;
Then, then my fated child her strength shall try.

   Albin. What wilt thou do if both he still defy?

   Felix. O, press me not in agony so great!
To thee alone I turn—resistless Fate!

ACT IV

Polyeucte. Cleon. *Three Other* Guards

   Poly. What is thy will?

   Cleon.   Pauline would see my lord.

   Poly. Ah, how my heart quails at that single word!
Thee, Felix, I o'ercame within my cell,
Laughed at thy threats of death and torture fell;
Yet hast thou still one arm to rouse my fears,
The rest I scorn, but dread thy daughter's tears!
One only talisman remains; great God, 'tis mine,
Sufficient for my every need His strength divine!

O thou, dear saint, thy scars all healed, white-robed, in glory
 crowned,
Plead that I too may victory win, thou who hast victory
 found!
Nearchus, who hast clasped in Heaven that dear, that piercéd
 hand,
Plead that thy friend, who wrestles here, may safely by thee
 stand!
Ye Guards, one last kind service, I would ask,
Well may ye grant it, 'tis an easy task:
I do not seek deliverance from these thralls,
         [*Looks at his chains.*
I do not care to scale my prison walls,
But, since three warriors armed can surely guard
One fettered man in safest watch and ward,—
Go one, and beg of great Severus' grace
That he would deign to meet me face to face;
To him would I a secret now impart,
Which much concerns his joy and peace of heart.
 Cleon. On willing foot, my lord, do I obey.
 Poly. Severus must this kindly service pay;
Ah, lose no time, time now has fleetest wings.
 Cleon. Full soon to thee thy prayer Severus brings.
   [*Exit* CLEON. GUARDSMEN *retire to background.*
 Poly. The fount is pure, yet bitter waters flow,
Sin taints—men poison what was made all fair.
They will not choose immortal streams: they go
To seek for pleasure—but find only care:
Their pleasure wed to strife—ah, death the gate of life,—
Christ's servants, none but they His crown shall wear!
     So pain
     Is gain:
     Count not the cost!
     The world well lost,
     His Heaven to share!

O Pleasure, think not that I sigh for thee,

Thy charms, that once enslaved, no more delight;
In Christ's dear name I bid the tempter flee,
His foes are mine,—unlovely in my sight.
The mighty from their seat He hurls beneath His feet,
His fan is in His hand, His vengeful sword is bright.
                    Their crown
                    Cast down.
                    All hopes most dear
                    They cherish here
                    Shall end in night.

O Decius! Tiger! Pitiless! Athirst
With quenchless rage, for blood of Christ's redeemed—
Armenia shall arise, by thee accursed,
On her at last has Light of Asia beamed,
And our Deliverer from the holy east
Shall dash the cup from thy Belshazzar feast!
                    Secure,
                    And pure,
                    Christ's saints shall reign,
                    And, purged by pain,
                    For aye endure!

Let Felix sacrifice me to thine ire,
Yea, let my rival captivate the soul
Of her who now with Decius doth conspire
To chain immortal hope to earthly goal;
Let earth-bound men pursue the world's desire,
Sense charms not him who doth to Heaven aspire!
                    Hail pain!
                    Disdain
                    All Earthly love,
                    To seek above
                    A holier fire!

Oh, Love that passeth knowledge be my stay,
And fire my heart to beat alone for thee!

Sun of my soul?—oh, flash one purest ray
In that last hour supreme—to comfort me,
So life's brief night shall merge in endless day!
                Come, Death!
                Last breath
                Shall praise thy name,
                The same, the same,
                For aye! For aye!

O heavenly fire, most pure, embracing all,
Come, shield me from Pauline, else must I fall!
I see her, but no more as once I saw—
I am encased in armour without flaw:
To eyes that gaze alone on heavenly light,
Naught else is pure, or dear, or fair, or bright!

Enter PAULINE

With what intent, Pauline, hast thou come here?
Have I a friend to aid, or foe to fear?
Is it Christ's soldier that thou com'st to greet?
Or wouldst thou sink my triumph in defeat?
If thou wouldst bid me spurn the debt I owe,
Not Decius, but Pauline, my deadliest foe!
   Paul. All, save thyself, to thee, my love, are friends:
Love but thyself, love me,—thy torment ends.
Alone thou seal'st thy doom, alone wouldst shed
That blood by all Armenia honouréd.
Yes, thou art saved, if thou for mercy plead;
Demand thy death, and thou are lost indeed.
Think of the worth of this self-hated life,
And think in pity of Pauline,—thy wife!
Think of the people that their prince adores,
Think of the honours Felix on thee pours!
Oh, I am nothing, nothing unto thee,
But, husband, think how dear thou art to me!
Think how the path of glory on thee opes,
Thou dearest lodestar of a nation's hopes!

Shall blood of kings be but the headsman's sport?
Is life a toy wherewith thy death to court?
  Poly. I think of more than this; I know what thou wouldst
    say.
Our life is ours to use, and we that debt must pay.
What life is this men love? An idle, empty dream,
Where nothing can endure,—where all things only seem.
Death ends their every joy which fickle Fortune leaves,
They gain a royal throne to learn how pomp deceives;
They gather wealth that men may envy their estate,
They clear a path by blood, so envy turns to hate.
Such vast ambition mine as Cæsar never knew,—
Death bounds it not, for death is but its servant true.
Peace that the world ne'er gave, and cannot take away,—
That peace, Pauline, is mine, mine wholly, mine for aye!
Nor time, nor fate, nor chance, nor cruel war,
Can touch this peace, or this my kingdom mar.
Is this poor life—the creature of a day—
For endless peace too great a price to pay?
  Paul. 'Out on these Christian dreams!' my reason cries;
Whene'er they speak of truth, they utter lies.
Thou say'st: 'To win such prize my life is naught!'
But is thy life thine own? How was it bought?
Our life an heirloom to our country due;
What gave thee birth, demands thy service too?
Pay, then thy debt to her who has the right!
  Poly. Ah, for my country I would gladly fight!
I know the glory of a hero's name,
I feel the thrill,—I recognise the claim.
My life I owe to whom I owe my sword—
But most to Him who gave it—to the Lord!
Oh, if to die for fatherland be sweet,
To die for Him—my God—what word is meet?
  Paul. Which God?
  Poly. Hush! hush! Pauline; the God who hears
And answers prayers,—gives hopes, assuages fears.
Thy gods are deaf and senseless, maimed and weak,

Tongues, mouths they have, and yet they cannot speak.
The Christians' God alone is mine,—is thine,
Jehovah only rules—supreme—divine!
    Paul. Adore Him in thy heart, but say no word!
    Poly. What! Can I call Jove and Jehovah—Lord?
    Paul. One moment feign. Ah, let Severus go!
Let but my father all his kindness show!
    Poly. Another Father mine! His love most dear
Removes me from a world begirt with fear.
For life's stern race too weak, too frail am I,
So, by kind death, He gives me Victory.
Pure from the holy font—(His mercies never fail!)
He brings His barque to port, when it hath scarce set sail.
Couldst thou but understand how poor this earth,
Couldst thou but grasp how great this second birth!
And yet, why speak of treasure rare concealed
From one to whom light is yet unrevealed?
    Paul. O cruel! I can strangle pain no more!
Is this the fruit of all thy heavenly lore?
They say thy Christ His enemies did bless,
Thou addest insult to my deep distress.
How is my soul so dark—which was so fair?—
Thou call'dst me 'lovely'—'dear'—'beyond compare!'—
Of my bereavement have I said no word,
I stilled my grief that I might soothe my lord!
They say that love has wings, and all they say is true,
For all thy love has flown; yet can I ne'er undo
The vows I made, the troth I plighted binds me still!
Thou fain wouldst quit thy wife, and thou shalt have thy will.
Oh, but to leave my side with rapture, ecstasy,
No jealous Christ can will: why grudge me one poor sigh?
This joy, this transport fierce, endeavour to conceal.
I do not share thy creed, but I, at least, can feel!
Why gloat o'er heavenly gain, crowns, palms, I know not
    what—
Where Polyeucte is blest, but where Pauline is not?
Soul, body, spirit, I am thy true wife, to own

That I am but a bar to happiness unknown!
  Poly. Alas!
  Paul.   O! that 'Alas!'—so faint, so tame!
Yet, if repentant from thy heart it came,
'Twould waken hope, still brief, and banish fears:
I wait the birth of thy reluctant tears.
  Poly. These tears I shed! O, might the Spirit pour
Through them the light, the light that I adore—
Then were my only grief all swept away,
For thou wouldst join me in the realms of day!
Else Heaven itself would have its bitterness,
Should I look down to witness thy distress!
O God, who lov'st the dust on which Thy breath
Hath stamped Thine image true—save her from death!
The only death that kills, and let my love
From Heaven woo her to the realms above!
Lord, hear my call! My inmost heart now see,
Who lives a Christian life must Christian be!
Her nature god-like, stamped from print divine;
She must be sealed Thine own, yes, only Thine!
Say, must she burn, condemned to depths of hell?—
Thy Will be done—Who doest all things well!
  Paul. O wretch, what words are these? Thou dost
    desire——
  Poly. To snatch thee from a never-ending fire.
  Paul. Or else?
  Poly.   O God, I trust to Thy control,
Who when we think not, canst illume the soul!
The when—the how—is His—here am I dumb,—
I wait—I wait—That blessèd hour will come!
  Paul. Oh, leave illusions! Love me!
  Poly.   Thee I love
Far more than self, but less than God above!
  Paul. For love's dear sake, ah, listen to my prayer!
  Poly. For love's dear sake—await the answer *there!*
  Paul. To leave me here is naught! Thou wouldst seduce
    my soul!

Poly. Heaven is scarce Heaven for me, if thou reach not
  the goal.

Paul. O fancy-fooled!

Poly.   Nay, led by heavenly light!

Paul. Thy faith is blindness!

Poly.   Faith is more than sight!

Paul. Ah, death, strange rival to a wife's pure love!

Poly. This world our rival with the joys above!

Paul. Go, monster! woo thy death! Thou lov'dst me
  never!

Poly. Go, seek the world! and yet I love thee ever!

Paul. Yes, I will go—if absence bring relief—

Enter SEVERUS, FABIAN *and* GUARDS

Who comes to invade, ah, not to cure my grief?
Severus! Who could guess that thou wouldst show
Revenge unworthy o'er a prostrate foe?

   Poly. Unworthy thee the thought, Pauline, for I
Severus called, and he hath heard my cry.
My importunity he will excuse,
My prayer I know that he will not refuse.
Severus—this—the treasure that was mine—
To thy most tender care I now resign:
To thee, as noblest man that I have known;—
Since earthly ties and joys I must disown.
The gift is worthy thee,—I know thy worth
Is great, but she no equal hath on earth.
My life, the bar,—my death the link shall be,—
Oh, grudge me not my dear brief ecstasy!
Oh, ease the heart that once was hers,—and guide
Her doubting footsteps to the Crucified!
This my last benison! All else is poor!
Await the promised light! Believe! Endure!
But words are vain!

     [POLYEUCTE *signs to* GUARDS *to conduct him back to prison*
        Exeunt POLYEUCTE *and* GUARDS.]

Sev. Most vain! No word have I
Such blindness must amaze! must stupefy!
Nay, this is frenzy! I cannot conceive
A mind so strange! Mine ears cannot believe
That one who loved thee—yet, who would not love
A face that must the great immortals move?—
Blessed by thy heart!—Thy sweetest lips to taste!—
Then leave, refuse, spurn—yield with clamorous haste,
To yield a girl so dear—so pure—so fair!
And of that gift to make thy rival heir—
This beggars madness! Or the Christian bliss
Beyond man's soul to grasp! To spurn thy kiss!—
We treasure barter for a just exchange,
But to buy pain for thee! Pauline, 'tis strange!
Not thus, ye Gods! Severus had been blind
To perfect bliss—had Fortune been more kind—
The only heaven for me is in thine eyes,
These are my kings, these my divinities!
To me—for thee—were death with torture dear;
But to renounce thee!
Paul. Nay, I must not hear!
Thy words bring back the dear, the bygone days,
When I, a maid, might listen to thy praise:
Severus, thou must know my inmost heart;
I hear the knell bids Polyeucte depart.
He dies,—the victim of thine Emperor's laws,
And thou, though innocent, art yet the cause.
Oh, if thy soul, to thy desires a slave,
See hope emerging from my husband's grave—
Then will I wed with pain—despair embrace,—
But wed Severus? Never! 'Twere disgrace!
To light fresh torch from that pale, flickering fire—
Oh, bliss too monstrous! Thrice abhorred desire!
Back, hope! Back, happiness! The mate for me
When Polyeucte leaves my side—is Constancy!
Were this my will, were this, ye Gods, my fate—
To shame would memory turn, as love must yield to hate!

But generous art thou—most generous be!
His pardon will my father grant to thee.
He fears thee: more, if Polyeucte's life he take,
For thee he slays him—yes, 'tis for thy sake.
Christ died for man—let pagan virtue dim
His fame: plead for thy foe! so rival him!
No easy boon I ask, there needs a soul most rare;
But when the fight is fierce—then is the victory fair.
To help a man to be what thou wouldst be
Is triumph that belongs alone to thee!
Let this suffice thee: she, whom thou hast loved,
She, who by thy great love was not unmoved,
Of thee, and of no other dares to crave
That thou, Severus, shouldst my husband save!
Farewell! of this thy labour gauge the scope:
If thou art less than I yet dare to hope,
Then tell me not! all else Pauline can bear!

[*Exit* PAULINE

  Sev. Where am I, Fabian? Has the crack of doom
Turned heaven to hell? made life a living tomb?
Nearer and dearer ever—but to go!
The prize within my grasp must I o'erthrow?
This—Fortune's brimming cup, with poison filled,
She bids me drain;—so new-born hope is killed.
Before I proffer aught, I am refused;
Thus sad, amazed, ashamed, in doubt, abused,
I see the ghost I laid, to life revive,
The more seductive still the more I strive.
Ah! must a woman, sunk in deep despair,
Teach me that shame is base, and honour fair?
And while I madly shriek, 'O love, be kind!'
Pauline, death-stricken, keeps an equal mind!
O generous, but stern! Must these dear eyes,
Because I love them, o'er love tyrannise?
'Tis not enough to lose thee, I must give
My aid—to make my faithless rival live!
'Tis not enough: his death I would not plan,

But I must save him! bless where I would ban!
 Fabian. Ah, let the whole crew light one funeral pyre;
Yes, let the daughter perish with her sire!
This curs'd Armenian is one hornet's nest—
Crush all, then sail for Rome, ah! this were best!
She loves thee not. What canst thou hope to gain?
 Sev. A glory that shall triumph over pain;
'Tis hers, and, by the Gods, it shall be mine!
Nor God nor fiend can sully such a shrine!
 Fabian. Speak low, for Jove has bolts, and Hell has ears!
The dangers of this course arouse my fears.
What? Decius implore a Nazarene to save!
'Tis death that hath thy heart; thou woo'st a grave.
His rage against the sect thou knowest well,
His power unbridled—his revenge is fell.
To plead for Christians is a task too great,
For man or God: thou rushest on thy fate.
 Sev. Yes, such advice, I know, is much approved,
Yet not thus can Severus' soul be moved.
To Fate unequal—equal to myself—
In duty's path I go. For power and pelf
I never swerve where honour leads the way;
Come weal, come woe, her call I must obey.
Let fate depress an all unequal scale,
Let Clotho hold her distaff—I'll not fail!
Yet one more word—this to thy private ear—
The fables that thou dost of Christians hear
Are fables only, coined, I know not why,
Distorted are they seen in Decius' eye.
They practise the black art,—so all men say.
I sought to learn the laws that they obey,
And to discover what the secret guilt
The which to expiate their blood is spilt.
Yet priests of Cybele dark rites pursue
At Rome—untrammelled—this is nothing new:
To thousand gods men build, unchecked, their fanes,
The Christians' God alone our state disdains.

Each foul Egyptian beast his temple rears,
Caligula a god to Roman ears—
Tiberius is enshrined—a Nero deified—
To Christ—to Christ alone—a temple is denied!
Such metamorphoses confuse the mind
As gods in cats, and saints in fiends we find;
As Ruler absolute Jehovah stands,
Alone o'er heaven and earth and hell commands,
While pagan gods each 'gainst the other strive,
And ne'er one queen is found o'er all the hive,
Now—(strike me dead, Jove's tarrying thunderbolt!)
So many masters must provoke revolt.
And ah! where Christians live—there life is pure,
Vice dies untended, virtues all endure.
We give these men to rack, and cord, and flame,
While they forgive us—in their Pardoner's name.
They no sedition raise, they ne'er rebel,
Rome makes them soldiers, and they serve her well.
They rage in battle, faithful ward they keep,
They fight like lions, but they die like sheep.
They serve the State: Rome's servant must defend
Those who to might of Rome such succour lend.
Pauline, I will obey, whate'er befall;
The man who loseth honour loseth all.

ACT V

Felix. Albin. Cleon.

Felix. Caught in Severus' net thy Felix see!
He hates and holds me—oh, the misery!
Albin. I see a generous man, who cries, 'Forgive,
Let Pauline smile once more—let Polyeucte live!'
Felix. His soul thou canst not read—tho' noble heart he
 feigns.
The father he abhors,—the daughter he disdains!
What Polyeucte won *he* sought: his suit denied,
Severus sues no more,—I know his pride.

His words, his prayers, his threats for Polyeucte plead,
His *tongue* says, 'Listen, or be lost indeed!'
Unskilled the fowler who his snare reveals:
If at the bait I snatch—my doom is sealed:
Too plain, too coarse, this web for any fly—
Shall I this spider hail in my fatuity?
His wrath is wrath arranged, his generous fire is nursed,
That I, at Decius' hand, may meet the doom accurst,
If I should pardon grant—that grace my crime would be,
For he the spoil would reap of my credulity.
No simpleton am I, each promise to believe,
Words—oaths—are but the tools wherewith all men de-
     ceive;
Too oft escaped am I to be so lightly caught;
I know that words are wind. I know that wind is naught.
The trapper shall be trapped,—the biter shall be bit,
Unravelled is the web that he, poor fool, hath knit!
   Albin. Jove! What a plague to thee is this mistrust!
   Felix. Nay, those at court must fence; their weapons
        never rust,
If once thou yield the clue to thread the maze,
The sequence is most plain—the man betrayed betrays;
Severus, and his gifts, alike I fear!
If Polyeucte still to reason close his ear,
Severus' love is hate—his peace is strife—
First law of nature this, 'Preserve thy life!'
   Albin. Ah, let Pauline at least thy grace obtain!
   Felix. If Decius grace withhold, my pardon vain!
And—far from saving this rebellious son—
Behold us all alike entrapped, undone!
   Albin. Severus' promise—
   Felix.   He can never keep!
For Decius' rage and hatred never sleep:
If for that sect abhorred Severus plead,
He trebles loss—so are we lost indeed!
One only way is ours,—that way I try:
(*To* GUARDS) Bring Polyeucte and if he still defy,
Self-doomed, insensate, this my proffered grace,

He shall the death he wooes forthwith embrace!
  Albin. Ah, this is stern!
  Felix.   'Tis stern, 'tis just—as fate;
When justice drags a halting foot, too late,
She is not justice—for the vengeful mob
(Whose hearts for Polyeucte ne'er cease to throb),
Usurps her place, and, spurning curb and rein,
The felon crowns, and all our work is vain.
My sceptre trembles, and all insecure
Totters my crown,—a prey for every boor.
Then, swift, Severus hears the welcome news,
The jaundiced mind of Decius to abuse.
Shall I, the rabble's lord, obey the rabble's will?
  Albin. Who ill in all around foresees,—but doubles ill.
Each prop thou hast is but a sword to pierce;
If Polyeucte hold their heart, the people fierce
Will gather fiercer courage from despair.
  Felix. Death settles all; they'll find no helper there,
And if—without a bead—the body should rebel,
Convulsive throes I mock, and nerveless fury quell.
Whate'er ensues the Emperor must approve,
I shall have done my part, and win his love.
Here comes the man

Enter POLYEUCTE *and* SOLDIERS

                  I still must try to save;
If he repent—'tis well! If not—the grave!
(*To* POLYEUCTE) Is life still hateful? Doth death still allure?
Is earth still naught? Do heavenly joys endure?
Doth Christ still counsel thee to hate thy wife;—
To sheathe thy sword,—to cast away thy life?
  Poly. I never hated life, or wooed a grave,
To life I am a servant—not a slave.
Here service free I give upon this earth below,—
For higher service changed when to His Home I go.
Eternal life is this: to tread the path He trod;
To Him your body yield! Then trust your soul to God!
  Felix. Yes, trust to an abyss of depth unknown!

Poly. No, trust **to Holy Cross!** That Cross my own!

Felix. The **steep** ascent, my son, I too would climb,
Yes, I would Christian be,—but—give me time,—
By Jove! I'll tread thy path! This my desire,
Else at thy hand the judge may me require!

Poly. Nay, laugh not, Felix! He thy Judge will be,
No refuge there for impious blasphemy!
Nor kings nor clowns can 'scape His righteous ire,
His slaughtered Saints of thee will He require!

Felix. I'll slay no more;—by Hercules I swear!
So I a Christian crown perchance may wear;
I will protect the flock!

Poly.   Nay, rather be
A goad, a scourge, for their felicity!
Let suffering purify each Christian soul,
Cross, rack, and flame but lead them to their goal;
What here they lose—in Heaven an hundredfold they find.
Be cruel,—persecute!—and so alone be kind!
My words thou canst not read; thine eyes are blinded here,
Wait the unveiling *There!* Then understand and fear!

Felix. Nay, nay, in truth I would a Christian be!

Poly. In thy hard heart alone a bar I see.

Felix. (*whispering*). This Roman knight——

Poly. (*aloud*).   Severus, thou wouldst say.

Felix. Once let him sail, I will no more delay,
For this I anger feign;—let him depart!

Poly. 'Tis thus thou wouldst reveal a Christian heart?
To idols dumb—to Pagans blind, thy sugared poison bear,
Christ's servants quaff another cup, sure refuge from despair.

Felix. What is this deadly draught that thou wouldst
    drain?
I'll drink thy wine.—Till then, from death refrain!

Poly. To swine no more my holy pearls I cast,
Faith,—*faith*—not reason, shall see light at last;
Soon—when I see my God—yes, face to face,
I will implore that Felix may find grace.

Felix. O dearest son, thy loss were death to me!

Poly. This loss can be repaired—the remedy
Find in Severus; he will take my place;
By Decius honoured he will not disgrace
Thy house: my death will an advantage win
For thee, for her, for me.—The work begin!

Felix. Such my reward! Yes, insult is the child
Of injury. The grace I grant, reviled,
Shall turn to swift revenge. The gods defied
May do their will and speed the suicide!

Poly. I thought the gods were dead, but they revive
With human passion; Felix, do not strive
Against thy nature; lay aside thy ruth;
Who loves a lie can never follow truth.

Felix. I humoured madness, but the mood is o'er,
I am myself again; I did implore,—
'Twas vain; the dark abyss that yawns for thee
May hold thee now, tomb to thy constancy.
The hope I cherished—fondled—now is flown
Severus will be king, and I o'erthrown;—
Shall I the gods by incense pacify?
Or by thy death? for thou, at last, must die!

Poly. Incense might but incense; I cannot tell:

Enter PAULINE

Pauline!

Paul. That word broke from thee like a knell;
Who seeks my doom to-day? Thou—or my sire?
Who fires the brand? Who lights the funeral pyre?
My father should, by nature, be my friend,
And lover's heart to love an ear should lend.
Who here is mine ally, and who my foe?
Who has a heart to feel?—this would I know.

Felix. Nay, to thy lord appeal.

[PAULINE *turns to* POLYEUCTE

Poly.   Severus wed!

Paul. Ah, this is outrage! Rather strike me dead!

Poly. Oh, dearer than myself to me thy weal!

My love would never wound, it seeks to heal.
I see thee wrestle with thy deep distress
Alone—unless Severus bring redress;
His merit, that once gained thy maiden heart,
Hath still that worth when I from thee must part,—
Once loved—and loving still—his honour grows.

Paul. Thy wife's true heart another treatment owes:
O base reproach! For this I crushed for thee
My former love: that I disdained might be?
This my reward for dearest victory won,—
I did that love undo—to be myself undone!
Resolve, faith, abnegation, all were vain,
For thy return is outrage heaped on pain.
Oh, sunk in tomb of shame, most vile, most mean,
Come back to life—to honour—to Pauline!

[*Holds out her arms.*

To learn from her that loyalty and faith
Religion are:—and all beside but death!
Once more Alcestis wrestles with the tomb,
Arise, arise from thy enthralling doom!
And if my invocation feeble be,
Regard the tears—the sighs,—shed—breathed for thee!
Love is too weak a word—I thee adore!

Poly. Once have I said—yet now I say once more—
'Live with Severus, or—with Polyeucte die!'
Thy tears are mine, and thy pure constancy
I share: But—I am soldier of the Cross!
Take up thine own, and count all gain but loss!
Pauline—no more! (*To* FELIX.) Thy slumbering wrath
    rewake!
Thy fates and furies wait! Their vengeance slake!

Paul. His life is saved! These fetters all undo!—
For justice never yet a madman slew;
And he is mad,—but, father, thou art sane,
And thou, his father, must his friend remain.
A father cannot less than father be,
Oh, be to him what thou hast been to me!

But cast upon thy child a kinder eye,—
Slay him?—Then know that *I* am doomed to die!
But even if justly done to death were he,
The sentence wrong that, with him, slayeth me.
For double death would double wrong present,
And slay the guilty with the innocent.
'Twas thou didst link us closely hand in hand,
'To live in bliss together' thy command.
Oh, shall the will that both our lives did bless
Doom both these lives to death—to nothingness?
When lips are sealed to lips, and heart to heart,
'Tis tyranny, not law, such love to part.
Oh, not a tyrant, but a father be,
Forgive,—give back—restore my love to me!
 Felix. Dear child, thy father is thy father still,
Nothing hath parted us, and nothing will.
My heart is tender, and it beats for thee:
Against this madman let us joinéd be.
O wretched man, hast thou no eyes to see, no heart to feel?
Thy guilt, thy crime, I would efface, thy pardon I would seal,
For thee my daughter cannot die—say, must she die *with*
  thee?
A victim to the only sin which ne'er can pardoned be.
O sight most strange! Here at thy knees as suppliant I sue!
         [FELIX *kneels.*
The evil that thyself hast wrought—that ill thyself undo!
 Poly. Arise, old man, from knees unused to bend,
Or to another ear petition send!
This artifice befits nor me nor thee,
To beg of one twice threatened!—Mockery!
First, by thy hand Nearchus felt the flame,
Then love, forsooth, thy plea—(profanéd name!)
The path of Christian neophyte hast thou trod,
And, in God's name, hast mocked Almighty God!
Earth, heaven, and hell in turn have been thy tool,
And him thou hast traduced thou wouldst befool!
Go,—bully—flatterer—liar!—Every part

Thou playest, while delay doth break my heart!
Enough of dallying! While thou dost dissolve
Thy feeble soul in doubt, hear my resolve:
The God who made me—Him will I adore;
He holds my plighted faith,—and evermore
He works salvation for his ransomed race—
Who gave His Son to death that we might life embrace;
And this—Christ's sacrifice—continued day by day,
The Christ reveals and pleads—The Life—The Truth—
    The Way!
No more His mysteries to self-stopped ears
Will I disclose—(he heedeth not nor hears.)

                        [*Pointing to* FELIX.
Pray then to these thy gods of wood and stone,—
To gods who every deed of crime enthrone,
Who boast their malice, and their foul incest,
Vaunt theft and murder—all that we detest.
This, their example,—Pagan—follow thou!
To Pluto bend, to Aphrodite bow!
For this I broke their altars, rased their shrine,—
Yea, for those crimes that thou dost call divine!
And what I did, that would I do once more
Before Severus—Decius,—nay, before
The eyes of all men;—so would I proclaim
One God alone adored,—one Holiest Name!
  Felix. At last my bounties yield to wrath most stern, most
    just.
Die! or the gods adore!
  Poly.   A Christian I!
  Felix.   Thou must
Adore the gods I say! Adore, or die!
  Poly. I am a Christian.
  Felix.   This is thy reply?
Ye Guards, do my behest—prepare the knife!
  Paul. Where goes he?
  Felix   To his death!
  Poly.   Ah, no to life!

(*To* PAULINE.) Remember me! Farewell, Pauline, farewell!
Paul. Nay, I will follow thee—to heaven or hell!
Felix. Begone! For all our ills this one redress!

[*Exeunt* PAULINE, POLYEUCTE *and* GUARDS.

Enter ALBIN

O task ungrateful to my gentle mind!
Well did he say, 'Be cruel to be kind!'
The people I defy, ah, let them rage!
Severus may in war of words engage.
Yes, I have saved myself—I mean *the State,*
To wilful man there comes relentless fate;
My conscience pure of all reproach,—for I
Have lied and stormed to shake his constancy.
To give his hot young blood due time to cool
I played the coward—nay, I played the fool!
Why did he thus assail the gods and me
With insult, and with horrid blasphemy?
But interest helped me, and resentment too.
Else had I found my duty hard to do!

Albin. Soon mayst thou this thy dear-bought victory rue,
For thou hast done what thou canst ne'er undo!
Unworthy deed for Roman knight! ah, me!   [*Aside.*
I would that I could add, 'unworthy *thee!*'

Felix. Manlius and Brutus both a son have slain,
And neither did thereby his glory stain;
The part that is diseased—that part we bleed,
So is the State from knaves and caitiffs freed.

Albin. Revenge and pressing peril thee unman,
Else—couldst thou bless a deed all men must ban?
When she, thy widowed daughter, comes—the air
Of heaven will echo to her deep despair!

Felix. Thou dost remind me she with Polyeucte went—
I know not with what mind, with what intent:
But her despair awakes my fond alarm,
Go, Albin, go, and guard my child from harm!
She might the execution of the law

Impede: I would not that his death she saw.
Try to console her—Go! what dost thou fear?

Enter PAULINE

Albin. I need not go, for ah—Pauline is here!
Paul. Tyrant, why leave thy butchery half done?
Come, slay thy daughter, thou hast slain thy son!
For, hear!—His villainy—or worth—is mine!
Why stay thy hand while I my neck incline?
Thy sword in me shall find a kindred food,
I too am new baptized, baptized in blood!
These drops that fell from off the murderous knife,
Have made the martyr's widow a true wife.
I see!—I feel!—I know! My darkest night
Is o'er—to break in purest heavenly light.
I too, at last, am Christ's: that word says all,
Those hands were pierced for me—I hear His call:
Death—lovely death—thy beckoning hand I hail!
Oh, help my passage, or thy schemes may fail!
Dread Decius! Fear Severus! Fear thy fall!
Oh, speed me to my lord—my love—my all!
My husband calls me to his happier land—
See!—there Nearchus at his side doth stand!
Lead me to these—the gods by thee confest,
Some shrines spared Polyeucte, I will break the rest!
There, there the gods thou fearest I will brave,
Oh, bare thy knife!—no other gift I crave.
Thou hast my master been: another Lord
Claims my obedience now; yes, raise thy sword!
Revolt is holy when for Christ we fight,—
My day has dawned, the day that knows no night!
Once more I cry—'Christ only has my heart!'
Thy bliss and mine secure! Let me depart!
Keep thou thy kingdom! Safe its treasure hold!
My kingdom *there*—with Christ—within the fold!

Enter SEVERUS

Sev. Unnatural sire, whose craft leads to the grave,

The slaves of fear themselves alone enslave.
Yes, Polyeucte is slain, and slain by thee,—
A sacrifice to greed and treachery.
I offered rescue from the opening tomb,
Base doubts enthralled thee, thou didst seal his doom;
I prayed, I threatened, thou wouldst not believe,
Deceiver thou, so must all men deceive.
Thou thoughtst me coward, liar—thou shalt see
All oaths Severus swears fulfilled shall be.
Poor moth! I might have saved thee—nay, I planned to save,
Thy perfidy the torch that marks thee for the grave.
Drench earth in blood,—for Jove pour forth malignant zeal,
The strokes that thou hast dealt redoubled shalt thou feel!
I go: the storm shall break o'er this devoted land,
From Jove the bolt?—maybe—but I direct his hand.
    Felix. Why lags that hand? A willing victim I,
I choose to suffer for my perfidy;
My doubts, my fears unworthy, all I own,
I have offended—let my death atone.
Take thou my honours, their poor lustre thine,
I kneel before another, nobler shrine.
The Power that moved me, groping through the night
Of wrong and darkness, wafts me to The Light!
I slew thee, Polyeucte, but thy pardoning hand
Shall guide thy murderer to the better land!
He prays for me, and by his sacrifice,
New-born upon his ashes I arise.
(*To* PAULINE.) Raised by his death from out the grave of
    sin,
Thou tread'st the path thy father shall begin;
By me his martyr-crown, as all my bliss
By him. His Christ is mine, and I am his;
O, blessed Christian vengeance! All my loss
Is turned to gain by the redeeming Cross!
Now, Pauline, am I thine, a Christian I,
That Death gives life by which alike we die!
(*To* SEVERUS.) Then slay us both! Behold a willing prey!

Paul. (*To* FELIX.) Yes, mine for ever now! Hail, glorious
    day,
That sees earth's loss transformed to endless gain!
    Felix. The gain, the glory, Christ's! By Him we reign.
    Sev. Now am I dumb, some miracle is here;
Their courage and their faith must I revere;
We slay them; yet, like Cadmus' seed, new-born
They sprout afresh, and laugh our scythe to scorn.
We give them cord and flame, they torture hail;
Friends fail them, but themselves they never fail.
We mow them down, fresh nurslings to unbare,
What moves the seed lies hid, but *it is there*.
They bless the world, though by the world accurst,
Their shield am I—let Decius do his worst.
I yet may own their power, though now my will
That each to his own gods be faithful still,
Let each still search for truth, and truth adore.
(*To* FELIX.) A Christian thou? Then fear my wrath no more,
Thy sect I cherish; this their awful cult
Severus will protect, but ne'er insult.
Keep thou thy power from Roman sword secure,
So long as loyalty with faith endure;
I swear it: ay, the Emperor shall learn
The guiltless from the traitor to discern;
His persecution baseless as his fear.
    Felix. Severus—thou who hast the hearing ear,—
Freeman of Rome—God's Spirit grant thee grace
To be Christ's Freeman, and behold His face:
To these—Christ's martyrs—earth's last rites be given,
Earth, guard their ashes as a trust for Heaven!
Earth hides their dust. When envious time is o'er,
That dust shall wake to life for evermore!

PHÆDRA

BY
JEAN BAPTISTE RACINE

TRANSLATED BY
ROBERT BRUCE BOSWELL

INTRODUCTORY NOTE

JEAN BAPTISTE RACINE, the younger contemporary of Corneille, and his rival for supremacy in French classical tragedy, was born at Ferté-Milon, December 21, 1639. He was educated at the College of Beauvais, at the great Jansenist school at Port Royal, and at the Collège d'Harcourt. He attracted notice by an ode written for the marriage of Louis XIV in 1660, and made his first really great dramatic success with his "Andromaque." His tragic masterpieces include "Britannicus," "Bérénice," "Bajazet," "Mithridate," "Iphigénie," and "Phèdre," all written between 1669 and 1677. Then for some years he gave up dramatic composition, disgusted by the intrigues of enemies who sought to injure his career by exalting above him an unworthy rival. In 1689 he resumed his work under the persuasion of Mme. de Maintenon, and produced "Esther" and "Athalie," the latter ranking among his finest productions, although it did not receive public recognition until some time after his death in 1699. Besides his tragedies, Racine wrote one comedy, "Les Plaideurs," four hymns of great beauty, and a history of Port Royal.

The external conventions of classical tragedy which had been established by Corneille, Racine did not attempt to modify. His study of the Greek tragedians and his own taste led him to submit willingly to the rigor and simplicity of form which were the fundamental marks of the classical ideal. It was in his treatment of character that he differed most from his predecessor; for whereas, as we have seen, Corneille represented his leading figures as heroically subduing passion by force of will, Racine represents his as driven by almost uncontrollable passion. Thus his creations appeal to the modern reader as more warmly human; their speech, if less exalted, is simpler and more natural; and he succeeds more brilliantly with his portraits of women than with those of men.

All these characteristics are exemplified in "Phèdre," the tragedy of Racine which has made an appeal to the widest audience. To the legend as treated by Euripides, Racine added the love of Hippolytus for Aricia, and thus supplied a motive for Phædra's jealousy, and at the same time he made the nurse instead of Phædra the calumniator of his son to Theseus.

PHÆDRA

CHARACTERS

THESEUS, *son of Ægeus and King of Athens.*
PHÆDRA, *wife of Theseus and Daughter of Minos and Pasiphaë.*
HIPPOLYTUS, *son of Theseus and Antiope, Queen of the Amazons.*
ARICIA, *Princess of the Blood Royal of Athens.*
ŒNONE, *nurse of Phædra.*
THERAMENES, *tutor of Hippolytus.*
ISMENE, *bosom friend of Aricia.*
PANOPE, *waiting-woman of Phædra.*
Guards

The scene is laid at Trœzen, a town of the Peloponnesus.

ACT I

SCENE I

HIPPOLYTUS, THERAMENES.

Hippolytus

MY mind is settled, dear Theramenes,
And I can stay no more in lovely Trœzen.
In doubt that racks my soul with mortal anguish,
I grow ashamed of such long idleness.
Six months and more my father has been gone,
And what may have befallen one so dear
I know not, nor what corner of the earth
Hides him.

        Theramenes

        And where, prince, will you look for him?
Already, to content your just alarm,
Have I not cross'd the seas on either side
Of Corinth, ask'd if aught were known of Theseus
Where Acheron is lost among the Shades,
Visited Elis, doubled Tœnarus,
And sail'd into the sea that saw the fall

Of Icarus? Inspired with what new hope,
Under what favour'd skies think you to trace
His footsteps? Who knows if the King, your father,
Wishes the secret of his absence known?
Perchance, while we are trembling for his life,
The hero calmly plots some fresh intrigue,
And only waits till the deluded fair—

Hippolytus

Cease, dear Theramenes, respect the name
Of Theseus. Youthful errors have been left
Behind, and no unworthy obstacle
Detains him. Phædra long has fix'd a heart
Inconstant once, nor need she fear a rival.
In seeking him I shall but do my duty,
And leave a place I dare no longer see.

Theramenes

Indeed! When, prince, did you begin to dread
These peaceful haunts, so dear to happy childhood,
Where I have seen you oft prefer to stay,
Rather than meet the tumult and the pomp
Of Athens and the court? What danger shun you,
Or shall I say what grief?

Hippolytus

                That happy time
Is gone, and all is changed, since to these shores
The gods sent Phædra.

Theramenes

                I perceive the cause
Of your distress. It is the queen whose sight
Offends you. With a step dame's spite she schemed
Your exile soon as she set eyes on you.
But if her hatred is not wholly vanish'd,
It has at least taken a milder aspect.

Besides, what danger can a dying woman,
One too who longs for death, bring on your head?
Can Phædra, sick'ning of a dire disease
Of which she will not speak, weary of life
And of herself, form any plots against you?

Hippolytus

It is not her vain enmity I fear,
Another foe alarms Hippolytus.
I fly, it must be own'd, from young Aricia,
The sole survivor of an impious race.

Theramenes

What! You become her persecutor too!
The gentle sister of the cruel sons
Of Pallas shared not in their perfidy;
Why should you hate such charming innocence?

Hippolytus

I should not need to fly, if it were hatred.

Theramenes

May I, then, learn the meaning of your flight?
Is this the proud Hippolytus I see,
Than whom there breathed no fiercer foe to love
And to that yoke which Theseus has so oft
Endured? And can it be that Venus, scorn'd
So long, will justify your sire at last?
Has she, then, setting you with other mortals,
Forced e'en Hippolytus to offer incense
Before her? Can you love?

Hippolytus

                                        Friend, ask me not.
You, who have known my heart from infancy
And all its feelings of disdainful pride,
Spare me the shame of disavowing all

That I profess'd. Born of an Amazon,
The wildness that you wonder at I suck'd
With mother's milk. When come to riper age,
Reason approved what Nature had implanted.
Sincerely bound to me by zealous service,
You told me then the story of my sire,
And know how oft, attentive to your voice,
I kindled when I heard his noble acts,
As you described him bringing consolation
To mortals for the absence of Alcides,
The highways clear'd of monsters and of robbers,
Procrustes, Cercyon, Sciro, Sinnis slain,
The Epidaurian giant's bones dispersed,
Crete reeking with the blood of Minotaur.
But when you told me of less glorious deeds,
Troth plighted here and there and everywhere,
Young Helen stolen from her home at Sparta,
And Peribœa's tears in Salamis,
With many another trusting heart deceived
Whose very names have 'scaped his memory,
Forsaken Ariadne to the rocks
Complaining, last this Phædra, bound to him
By better ties,—you know with what regret
I heard and urged you to cut short the tale,
Happy had I been able to erase
From my remembrance that unworthy part
Of such a splendid record. I, in turn,
Am I too made the slave of love, and brought
To stoop so low? The more contemptible
That no renown is mine such as exalts
The name of Theseus, that no monsters quell'd
Have given me a right to share his weakness.
And if my pride of heart must needs be humbled,
Aricia should have been the last to tame it.
Was I beside myself to have forgotten
Eternal barriers of separation
Between us? By my father's stern command

Her brethren's blood must ne'er be reinforced
By sons of hers; he dreads a single shoot
From stock so guilty, and would fain with her
Bury their name, that, even to the tomb
Content to be his ward, for her no torch
Of Hymen may be lit. Shall I espouse
Her rights against my sire, rashly provoke
His wrath, and launch upon a mad career—

Theramenes

The gods, dear prince, if once your hour is come,
Care little for the reasons that should guide us.
Wishing to shut your eyes, Theseus unseals them;
His hatred, stirring a rebellious flame
Within you, lends his enemy new charms.
And, after all, why should a guiltless passion
Alarm you? Dare you not essay its sweetness,
But follow rather a fastidious scruple?
Fear you to stray where Hercules has wander'd?
What heart so stout that Venus has not vanquish'd?
Where would you be yourself, so long her foe,
Had your own mother, constant in her scorn
Of love, ne'er glowed with tenderness for Theseus?
What boots it to affect a pride you feel not?
Confess it, all is changed; for some time past
You have been seldom seen with wild delight
Urging the rapid car along the strand,
Or, skilful in the art that Neptune taught,
Making th' unbroken steed obey the bit;
Less often have the woods return'd our shouts;
A secret burden on your spirits cast
Has dimm'd your eye. How can I doubt you love?
Vainly would you conceal the fatal wound.
Has not the fair Aricia touch'd your heart?

Hippolytus

Theramenes, I go to find my father.

Theramenes

Will you not see the queen before you start,
My prince?

Hippolytus

That is my purpose: you can tell her.
Yes, I will see her; duty bids me do it.
But what new ill vexes her dear Œnone?

Scene II

Hippolytus, Œnone, Theramenes

Œnone

Alas, my lord, what grief was e'er like mine?
The queen has almost touch'd the gates of death.
Vainly close watch I keep by day and night,
E'en in my arms a secret malady
Slays her, and all her senses are disorder'd.
Weary yet restless from her couch she rises,
Pants for the outer air, but bids me see
That no one on her misery intrudes.
She comes.

Hippolytus

Enough. She shall not be disturb'd,
Nor be confronted with a face she hates.

Scene III

Phædra, Œnone

Phædra

We have gone far enough. Stay, dear Œnone;
Strength fails me, and I needs must rest awhile.
My eyes are dazzled with this glaring light
So long unseen, my trembling knees refuse
Support. Ah me!

Œnone

Would Heaven that our tears
Might bring relief!

Phædra

Ah, how these cumbrous gauds,
These veils oppress me! What officious hand
Has tied these knots, and gather'd o'er my brow
These clustering coils? How all conspires to add
To my distress!

Œnone

What is one moment wish'd,
The next, is irksome. Did you not just now,
Sick of inaction, bid us deck you out,
And, with your former energy recall'd,
Desire to go abroad, and see the light
Of day once more? You see it, and would fain
Be hidden from the sunshine that you sought.

Phædra

Thou glorious author of a hapless race,
Whose daughter 'twas my mother's boast to be,
Who well may'st blush to see me in such plight,
For the last time I come to look on thee,
O Sun!

Œnone

What! Still are you in love with death?
Shall I ne'er see you, reconciled to life,
Forego these cruel accents of despair?

Phædra

Would I were seated in the forest's shade!
When may I follow with delighted eye,
Thro' glorious dust flying in full career,
A chariot—

Œnone
Madam?

Phædra
                         Have I lost my senses?
What said I? and where am I? Whither stray
Vain wishes? Ah! The gods have made me mad.
I blush, Œnone, and confusion covers
My face, for I have let you see too clearly
The shame of grief that, in my own despite,
O'erflows these eyes of mine.

Œnone
                              If you must blush,
Blush at a silence that inflames your woes.
Resisting all my care, deaf to my voice,
Will you have no compassion on yourself,
But let your life be ended in mid course?
What evil spell has drain'd its fountain dry?
Thrice have the shades of night obscured the heav'ns
Since sleep has enter'd thro' your eyes, and thrice
The dawn has chased the darkness thence, since food
Pass'd your wan lips, and you are faint and languid.
To what dread purpose is your heart inclined?
How dare you make attempts upon your life,
And so offend the gods who gave it you,
Prove false to Theseus and your marriage vows,
Ay, and betray your most unhappy children,
Bending their necks yourself beneath the yoke?
That day, be sure, which robs them of their mother,
Will give high hopes back to the stranger's son,
To that proud enemy of you and yours,
To whom an Amazon gave birth, I mean
Hippolytus—
                    Phædra
              Ye gods!

Œnone

                    Ah, this reproach
Moves you!

Phædra

          Unhappy woman, to what name
Gave your mouth utterance?

Œnone

                    Your wrath is just.
'Tis well that that ill-omen'd name can rouse
Such rage. Then live. Let love and duty urge
Their claims. Live, suffer not this son of Scythia,
Crushing your children 'neath his odious sway,
To rule the noble offspring of the gods,
The purest blood of Greece. Make no delay;
Each moment threatens death; quickly restore
Your shatter'd strength, while yet the torch of life
Holds out, and can be fann'd into a flame.

Phædra

Too long have I endured its guilt and shame!

Œnone

Why? What remorse gnaws at your heart? What crime
Can have disturb'd you thus? Your hands are not
Polluted with the blood of innocence?

Phædra

Thanks be to Heav'n, my hands are free from stain.
Would that my soul were innocent as they!

Œnone

What awful project have you then conceived,
Whereat your conscience should be still alarm'd?

Phædra

Have I not said enough? Spare me the rest.
I die to save myself a full confession.

Œnone

Die then, and keep a silence so inhuman;
But seek some other hand to close your eyes.
Tho' but a spark of life remains within you,
My soul shall go before you to the Shades.
A thousand roads are always open thither;
Pain'd at your want of confidence, I'll choose
The shortest. Cruel one, when has my faith
Deceived you! Think how in my arms you lay
New born. For you, my country and my children
I have forsaken. Do you thus repay
My faithful service?

Phædra

        What do you expect
From words so bitter? Were I to break silence,
Horror would freeze your blood.

Œnone

           What can you say
To horrify me more than to behold
You die before my eyes?

Phædra

         When you shall know
My crime, my death will follow none the less,
But with the added stain of guilt.

Œnone

         Dear Madam,
By all the tears that I have shed for you,
By these weak knees I clasp, relieve my mind
From torturing doubt.

Phædra

It is your wish. Then rise.

Œnone

I hear you. Speak.

Phædra

Heav'ns! How shall I begin?

Œnone

Dismiss vain fears, you wound me with distrust.

Phædra

O fatal animosity of Venus!
Into what wild distractions did she cast
My mother!

Œnone

Be they blotted from remembrance,
And for all time to come buried in silence.

Phædra

My sister Ariadne, by what love
Were you betray'd to death, on lonely shores
Forsaken!

Œnone

Madam, what deep-seated pain
Prompts these reproaches against all your kin?

Phædra

It is the will of Venus, and I perish,
Last, most unhappy of a family
Where all were wretched.

Œnone

Do you love?

Phædra

                                   I feel
All its mad fever.

Œnone
Ah! For whom?

Phædra

                                   Hear now
The crowning horror. Yes, I love—my lips
Tremble to say his name.

Œnone
        Whom?

Phædra

                        Know you him,
Son of the Amazon, whom I've oppress'd
So long?

Œnone
Hippolytus? Great gods!

Phædra

                                   'Tis you
Have named him.

Œnone
        All my blood within my veins
Seems frozen. O despair! O cursèd race!
Ill-omen'd journey! Land of misery!
Why did we ever reach thy dangerous shores?

Phædra

My wound is not so recent. Scarcely had I
Been bound to Theseus by the marriage yoke,

And happiness and peace seem'd well secured,
When Athens show'd me my proud enemy.
I look'd, alternately turn'd pale and blush'd
To see him, and my soul grew all distraught;
A mist obscured my vision, and my voice
Falter'd, my blood ran cold, then burn'd like fire;
Venus I felt in all my fever'd frame,
Whose fury had so many of my race
Pursued. With fervent vows I sought to shun
Her torments, built and deck'd for her a shrine,
And there, 'mid countless victims did I seek
The reason I had lost; but all for naught,
No remedy could cure the wounds of love!
In vain I offer'd incense on her altars;
When I invoked her name my heart adored
Hippolytus, before me constantly;
And when I made her altars smoke with victims,
'Twas for a god whose name I dared not utter.
I fled his presence everywhere, but found him—
O crowning horror!—in his father's features.
Against myself, at last, I raised revolt,
And stirr'd my courage up to persecute
The enemy I loved. To banish him
I wore a step-dame's harsh and jealous carriage,
With ceaseless cries I clamour'd for his exile,
Till I had torn him from his father's arms.
I breathed once more, Œnone; in his absence
My days flow'd on less troubled than before,
And innocent. Submissive to my husband,
I hid my grief, and of our fatal marriage
Cherish'd the fruits. Vain caution! Cruel Fate!
Brought hither by my spouse himself, I saw
Again the enemy whom I had banish'd,
And the old wound too quickly bled afresh.
No longer is it love hid in my heart,
But Venus in her might seizing her prey.
I have conceived just terror for my crime;

I hate my life, and hold my love in horror.
Dying I wish'd to keep my fame unsullied,
And bury in the grave a guilty passion;
But I have been unable to withstand
Tears and entreaties, I have told you all;
Content, if only, as my end draws near,
You do not vex me with unjust reproaches,
Nor with vain efforts seek to snatch from death
The last faint lingering sparks of vital breath.

Scene IV

Phædra, Œnone, Panope

Panope

Fain would I hide from you tidings so sad,
But 'tis my duty, Madam, to reveal them.
The hand of death has seized your peerless husband,
And you are last to hear of this disaster.

Œnone

What say you, Panope?

Panope

          The queen, deceived
By a vain trust in Heav'n, begs safe return
For Theseus, while Hippolytus his son
Learns of his death from vessels that are now
In port.

Phædra

     Ye gods!

Panope

          Divided counsels sway
The choice of Athens; some would have the prince,
Your child, for master; others, disregarding
The laws, dare to support the stranger's son.

'Tis even said that a presumptuous faction
Would crown Aricia and the house of Pallas.
I deem'd it right to warn you of this danger.
Hippolytus already is prepared
To start, and should he show himself at Athens,
'Tis to be fear'd the fickle crowd will all
Follow his lead.

Œnone

    Enough. The queen, who hears you,
By no means will neglect this timely warning.

SCENE V

PHÆDRA, ŒNONE

Œnone

Dear lady, I had almost ceased to urge
The wish that you should live, thinking to follow
My mistress to the tomb, from which my voice
Had fail'd to turn you; but this new misfortune
Alters the aspect of affairs, and prompts
Fresh measures. Madam, Theseus is no more,
You must supply his place. He leaves a son,
A slave, if you should die, but, if you live,
A King. On whom has he to lean but you?
No hand but yours will dry his tears. Then live
For him, or else the tears of innocence
Will move the gods, his ancestors, to wrath
Against his mother. Live, your guilt is gone,
No blame attaches to your passion now.
The King's decease has freed you from the bonds
That made the crime and horror of your love.
Hippolytus no longer need be dreaded,
Him you may see henceforth without reproach.
It may be, that, convinced of your aversion,
He means to head the rebels. Undeceive him,
Soften his callous heart, and bend his pride.

King of this fertile land, in Trœzen here
His portion lies; but as he knows, the laws
Give to your son the ramparts that Minerva
Built and protects. A common enemy
Threatens you both, unite them to oppose
Aricia.

Phædra

To your counsel I consent.
Yes, I will live, if life can be restored,
If my affection for a son has pow'r
To rouse my sinking heart at such a dangerous hour.

ACT II

Scene I

Aricia, Ismene

Aricia

Hippolytus request to see me here!
Hippolytus desire to bid farewell!
Is't true, Ismene? Are you not deceived?

Ismene

This is the first result of Theseus' death.
Prepare yourself to see from every side
Hearts turn towards you that were kept away
By Theseus. Mistress of her lot at last,
Aricia soon shall find all Greece fall low,
To do her homage.

Aricia

'Tis not then, Ismene,
An idle tale? Am I no more a slave?
Have I no enemies?

Ismene

The gods oppose
Your peace no longer, and the soul of Theseus
Is with your brothers.

Aricia

Does the voice of fame
Tell how he died?

Ismene

Rumours incredible
Are spread. Some say that, seizing a new bride,
The faithless husband by the waves was swallow'd.
Others affirm, and this report prevails,
That with Pirithoüs to the world below
He went, and saw the shores of dark Cocytus,
Showing himself alive to the pale ghosts;
But that he could not leave those gloomy realms,
Which whoso enters there abides for ever.

Aricia

Shall I believe that ere his destined hour
A mortal may descend into the gulf
Of Hades? What attraction could o'ercome
Its terrors?

Ismene

He is dead, and you alone
Doubt it. The men of Athens mourn his loss.
Trœzen already hails Hippolytus
As King. And Phædra, fearing for her son,
Asks counsel of the friends who share her trouble,
Here in this palace.

Aricia

Will Hippolytus,
Think you, prove kinder than his sire, make light
My chains, and pity my misfortunes?

Ismene

Yes,
I think so, Madam.

Aricia

        Ah, you know him not
Or you would never deem so hard a heart
Can pity feel, or me alone except
From the contempt in which he holds our sex.
Has he not long avoided every spot
Where we resort?

Ismene

        I know what tales are told
Of proud Hippolytus, but I have seen
Him near you, and have watch'd with curious eye
How one esteem'd so cold would bear himself.
Little did his behaviour correspond
With what I look'd for; in his face confusion
Appear'd at your first glance, he could not turn
His languid eyes away, but gazed on you.
Love is a word that may offend his pride,
But what the tongue disowns, looks can betray.

Aricia

How eagerly my heart hears what you say,
Tho' it may be delusion, dear Ismene!
Did it seem possible to you, who know me,
That I, sad sport of a relentless Fate,
Fed upon bitter tears by night and day,
Could ever taste the maddening draught of love?
The last frail offspring of a royal race,
Children of Earth, I only have survived
War's fury. Cut off in the flow'r of youth,
Mown by the sword, six brothers have I lost,
The hope of an illustrious house, whose blood
Earth drank with sorrow, near akin to his
Whom she herself produced. Since then, you know
How thro' all Greece no heart has been allow'd
To sigh for me, lest by a sister's flame

The brothers' ashes be perchance rekindled.
You know, besides, with what disdain I view'd
My conqueror's suspicions and precautions,
And how, oppos'd as I have ever been
To love, I often thank'd the King's injustice
Which happily confirm'd my inclination.
But then I never had beheld his son.
Not that, attracted merely by the eye,
I love him for his beauty and his grace,
Endowments which he owes to Nature's bounty,
Charms which he seems to know not or to scorn.
I love and prize in him riches more rare,
The virtues of his sire, without his faults.
I love, as I must own, that generous pride
Which ne'er has stoop'd beneath the amorous yoke.
Phædra reaps little glory from a lover
So lavish of his sighs; I am too proud
To share devotion with a thousand others,
Or enter where the door is always open.
But to make one who ne'er has stoop'd before
Bend his proud neck, to pierce a heart of stone,
To bind a captive whom his chains astonish,
Who vainly 'gainst a pleasing yoke rebels,—
That piques my ardour, and I long for that.
'Twas easier to disarm the god of strength
Than this Hippolytus, for Hercules
Yielded so often to the eyes of beauty,
As to make triumph cheap. But, dear Ismene,
I take too little heed of opposition
Beyond my pow'r to quell, and you may hear me,
Humbled by sore defeat, upbraid the pride
I now admire. What! Can he love? and I
Have had the happiness to bend—

Ismene

                              He comes
Yourself shall hear him.

Scene II

Hippolytus, Aricia, Ismene

Hippolytus

> Lady, ere I go
> My duty bids me tell you of your change
> Of fortune. My worst fears are realized;
> My sire is dead. Yes, his protracted absence
> Was caused as I foreboded. Death alone,
> Ending his toils, could keep him from the world
> Conceal'd so long. The gods at last have doom'd
> Alcides' friend, companion, and successor.
> I think your hatred, tender to his virtues,
> Can hear such terms of praise without resentment,
> Knowing them due. One hope have I that soothes
> My sorrow: I can free you from restraint.
> Lo, I revoke the laws whose rigour moved
> My pity; you are at your own disposal,
> Both heart and hand; here, in my heritage,
> In Trœzen, where my grandsire Pittheus reign'd
> Of yore and I am now acknowledged King,
> I leave you free, free as myself,—and more.

Aricia

> Your kindness is too great, 'tis overwhelming.
> Such generosity, that pays disgrace
> With honour, lends more force than you can think
> To those harsh laws from which you would release me.

Hippolytus

> Athens, uncertain how to fill the throne
> Of Theseus, speaks of you, anon of me,
> And then of Phædra's son.

Aricia

> Of me, my lord?

Hippolytus

I know myself excluded by strict law:
Greece turns to my reproach a foreign mother.
But if my brother were my only rival,
My rights prevail o'er his clearly enough
To make me careless of the law's caprice.
My forwardness is check'd by juster claims:
To you I yield my place, or, rather, own
That it is yours by right, and yours the sceptre,
As handed down from Earth's great son, Erechtheus.
Adoption placed it in the hands of Ægeus:
Athens, by him protected and increased,
Welcomed a king so generous as my sire,
And left your hapless brothers in oblivion.
Now she invites you back within her walls;
Protracted strife has cost her groans enough,
Her fields are glutted with your kinsmen's blood
Fatt'ning the furrows out of which it sprung
At first. I rule this Trœzen; while the son
Of Phædra has in Crete a rich domain.
Athens is yours. I will do all I can
To join for you the votes divided now
Between us.

Aricia

　　　　Stunn'd at all I hear, my lord,
I fear, I almost fear a dream deceives me.
Am I indeed awake? Can I believe
Such generosity? What god has put it
Into your heart? Well is the fame deserved
That you enjoy! That fame falls short of truth!
Would you for me prove traitor to yourself?
Was it not boon enough never to hate me,
So long to have abstain'd from harbouring
The enmity—

Hippolytus

> To hate you? I, to hate you?
However darkly my fierce pride was painted,
Do you suppose a monster gave me birth?
What savage temper, what envenom'd hatred
Would not be mollified at sight of you?
Could I resist the soul-bewitching charm—

Aricia

Why, what is this, Sir?

Hippolytus

> I have said too much
Not to say more. Prudence in vain resists
The violence of passion. I have broken
Silence at last, and I must tell you now
The secret that my heart can hold no longer.
  You see before you an unhappy instance
Of hasty pride, a prince who claims compassion
I, who, so long the enemy of Love,
Mock'd at his fetters and despised his captives,
Who, pitying poor mortals that were shipwreck'd,
In seeming safety view'd the storms from land,
Now find myself to the same fate exposed,
Toss'd to and fro upon a sea of troubles!
My boldness has been vanquish'd in a moment,
And humbled is the pride wherein I boasted.
For nearly six months past, ashamed, despairing,
Bearing where'er I go the shaft that rends
My heart, I struggle vainly to be free
From you and from myself; I shun you, present;
Absent, I find you near; I see your form
In the dark forest depths; the shades of night,
Nor less broad daylight, bring back to my view
The charms that I avoid; all things conspire
To make Hippolytus your slave. For fruit

Of all my bootless sighs, I fail to find
My former self. My bow and javelins
Please me no more, my chariot is forgotten,
With all the Sea God's lessons; and the woods
Echo my groans instead of joyous shouts
Urging my fiery steeds.
                        Hearing this tale
Of passion so uncouth, you blush perchance
At your own handiwork. With what wild words
I offer you my heart, strange captive held
By silken jess! But dearer in your eyes
Should be the offering, that this language comes
Strange to my lips; reject not vows express'd
So ill, which but for you had ne'er been form'd.

Scene III

Hippolytus, Aricia, Theramenes, Ismene

Theramenes

Prince, the Queen comes. I herald her approach.
'Tis you she seeks.

Hippolytus

                Me?

Theramenes

                        What her thought may be
I know not. But I speak on her behalf.
She would converse with you ere you go hence.

Hippolytus

What shall I say to her? Can she expect—

Aricia

You cannot, noble Prince, refuse to hear her,
Howe'er convinced she is your enemy,
Some shade of pity to her tears is due.

Hippolytus

Shall we part thus? and will you let me go,
Not knowing if my boldness has offended
The goddess I adore? Whether this heart,
Left in your hands—

Aricia

                    Go, Prince, pursue the schemes
Your generous soul dictates, make Athens own
My sceptre. All the gifts you offer me
Will I accept, but this high throne of empire
Is not the one most precious in my sight.

SCENE IV

HIPPOLYTUS, THERAMENES

Hippolytus

Friend, is all ready?
                              But the Queen approaches.
Go, see the vessel in fit trim to sail.
Haste, bid the crew aboard, and hoist the signal:
Then soon return, and so deliver me
From interview most irksome.

SCENE V

PHÆDRA, HIPPOLYTUS, ŒNONE

Phædra (to ŒNONE)

                              There I see him!
My blood forgets to flow, my tongue to speak
What I am come to say.

Œnone

                              Think of your son,
How all his hopes depend on you.

Phædra

I hear

You leave us, and in haste. I come to add
My tears to your distress, and for a son
Plead my alarm. No more has he a father,
And at no distant day my son must witness
My death. Already do a thousand foes
Threaten his youth. You only can defend him
But in my secret heart remorse awakes,
And fear lest I have shut your ears against
His cries. I tremble lest your righteous anger
Visit on him ere long the hatred earn'd
By me, his mother.

Hippolytus

No such base resentment,

Madam, is mine.

Phædra

I could not blame you, Prince,

If you should hate me. I have injured you:
So much you know, but could not read my heart.
T' incur your enmity has been mine aim.
The self-same borders could not hold us both;
In public and in private I declared
Myself your foe, and found no peace till seas
Parted us from each other. I forbade
Your very name to be pronounced before me.
And yet if punishment should be proportion'd
To the offence, if only hatred draws
Your hatred, never woman merited
More pity, less deserved your enmity

Hippolytus

A mother jealous of her children's rights
Seldom forgives the offspring of a wife

Who reign'd before her. Harassing suspicions
Are common sequels of a second marriage.
Of me would any other have been jealous
No less than you, perhaps more violent.

Phædra

Ah, Prince, how Heav'n has from the general law
Made me exempt, be that same Heav'n my witness!
Far different is the trouble that devours me!

Hippolytus

This is no time for self-reproaches, Madam.
It may be that your husband still beholds
The light, and Heav'n may grant him safe return,
In answer to our prayers. His guardian god
Is Neptune, ne'er by him invoked in vain.

Phædra

He who has seen the mansions of the dead
Returns not thence. Since to those gloomy shores
Theseus is gone, 'tis vain to hope that Heav'n
May send him back. Prince, there is no release
From Acheron's greedy maw. And yet, methinks,
He lives, and breathes in you. I see him still
Before me, and to him I seem to speak;
My heart—
        Oh! I am mad; do what I will,
I cannot hide my passion.

Hippolytus

              Yes, I see
The strange effects of love. Theseus, tho' dead,
Seems present to your eyes, for in your soul
There burns a constant flame.

Phædra

Ah, yes, for Theseus
I languish and I long, not as the Shades
Have seen him, of a thousand different forms
The fickle lover, and of Pluto's bride
The would-be ravisher, but faithful, proud
E'en to a slight disdain, with youthful charms
Attracting every heart, as gods are painted,
Or like yourself. He had your mien, your eyes,
Spoke and could blush like you, when to the isle
Of Crete, my childhood's home, he cross'd the waves,
Worthy to win the love of Minos' daughters.
What were you doing then? Why did he gather
The flow'r of Greece, and leave Hippolytus?
Oh, why were you too young to have embark'd
On board the ship that brought thy sire to Crete?
At your hands would the monster then have perish'd,
Despite the windings of his vast retreat.
To guide your doubtful steps within the maze
My sister would have arm'd you with the clue.
But no, therein would Phædra have forestall'd her,
Love would have first inspired me with the thought;
And I it would have been whose timely aid
Had taught you all the labyrinth's crooked ways.
What anxious care a life so dear had cost me!
No thread had satisfied your lover's fears:
I would myself have wish'd to lead the way,
And share the peril you were bound to face;
Phædra with you would have explored the maze,
With you emerged in safety, or have perish'd.

Hippolytus

Gods! What is this I hear? Have you forgotten
That Theseus is my father and your husband?

Phædra

Why should you fancy I have lost remembrance
Thereof, and am regardless of mine honour?

Hippolytus

Forgive me, Madam. With a blush I own
That I misconstrued words of innocence.
For very shame I cannot bear your sight
Longer. I go—

Phædra

                    Ah! cruel Prince, too well
You understood me. I have said enough
To save you from mistake. I love. But think not
That at the moment when I love you most
I do not feel my guilt; no weak compliance
Has fed the poison that infects my brain.
The ill-starr'd object of celestial vengeance,
I am not so detestable to you
As to myself. The gods will bear me witness,
Who have within my veins kindled this fire,
The gods, who take a barbarous delight
In leading a poor mortal's heart astray.
Do you yourself recall to mind the past:
'Twas not enough for me to fly, I chased you
Out of the country, wishing to appear
Inhuman, odious; to resist you better,
I sought to make you hate me. All in vain!
Hating me more I loved you none the less:
New charms were lent to you by your misfortunes.
I have been drown'd in tears, and scorch'd by fire;
Your own eyes might convince you of the truth,
If for one moment you could look at me.
What is't I say? Think you this vile confession
That I have made is what I meant to utter?
Not daring to betray a son for whom
I trembled, 'twas to beg you not to hate him
I came. Weak purpose of a heart too full
Of love for you to speak of aught besides!
Take your revenge, punish my odious passion;

Prove yourself worthy of your valiant sire,
And rid the world of an offensive monster!
Does Theseus' widow dare to love his son?
The frightful monster! Let her not escape you!
Here is my heart. This is the place to strike.
Already prompt to expiate its guilt,
I feel it leap impatiently to meet
Your arm. Strike home. Or, if it would disgrace you
To steep your hand in such polluted blood,
If that were punishment too mild to slake
Your hatred, lend me then your sword, if not
Your arm. Quick, give't.

Œnone

             What, Madam, will you do?
Just gods! But someone comes. Go, fly from shame,
You cannot 'scape if seen by any thus.

Scene VI

HIPPOLYTUS, THERAMENES

Theramenes

Is that the form of Phædra that I see
Hurried away? What mean these signs of sorrow?
Where is your sword? Why are you pale, confused?

Hippolytus

Friend, let us fly. I am, indeed, confounded
With horror and astonishment extreme.
Phædra—but no; gods, let this dreadful secret
Remain for ever buried in oblivion.

Theramenes

The ship is ready if you wish to sail.
But Athens has already giv'n her vote;
Their leaders have consulted all her tribes;
Your brother is elected, Phædra wins.

Hippolytus

Phædra?

Theramenes

A herald, charged with a commission
From Athens, has arrived to place the reins
Of power in her hands. Her son is King.

Hippolytus

Ye gods, who know her, do ye thus reward
Her virtue?

Theramenes

A faint rumour meanwhile whispers
That Theseus is not dead, but in Epirus
Has shown himself. But, after all my search,
I know too well—

Hippolytus

Let nothing be neglected.
This rumour must be traced back to its source.
If it be found unworthy of belief,
Let us set sail, and cost whate'er it may,
To hands deserving trust the sceptre's sway.

ACT III

Scene I

PHÆDRA, ŒNONE

Phædra

Ah! Let them take elsewhere the worthless honours
They bring me. Why so urgent I should see them?
What flattering balm can soothe my wounded heart?
Far rather hide me: I have said too much.
My madness has burst forth like streams in flood,
And I have utter'd what should ne'er have reach'd

His ear. Gods! How he heard me! How reluctant
To catch my meaning, dull and cold as marble,
And eager only for a quick retreat!
How oft his blushes made my shame the deeper!
Why did you turn me from the death I sought?
Ah! When his sword was pointed to my bosom,
Did he grow pale, or try to snatch it from me?
That I had touch'd it was enough for him
To render it for ever horrible,
Leaving defilement on the hand that holds it.

Œnone

Thus brooding on your bitter disappointment,
You only fan a fire that must be stifled.
Would it not be more worthy of the blood
Of Minos to find peace in nobler cares,
And, in defiance of a wretch who flies
From what he hates, reign, mount the proffer'd throne?

Phædra

I reign! Shall I the rod of empire sway,
When reason reigns no longer o'er myself?
When I have lost control of all my senses?
When 'neath a shameful yoke I scarce can breathe?
When I am dying?

Œnone

Fly.

Phædra

I cannot leave him.

Œnone

Dare you not fly from him you dared to banish?

Phædra

The time for that is past. He knows my frenzy.
I have o'erstepp'd the bounds of modesty,

And blazon'd forth my shame before his eyes.
Hope stole into my heart against my will.
Did you not rally my declining pow'rs?
Was it not you yourself recall'd my soul
When fluttering on my lips, and with your counsel,
Lent me fresh life, and told me I might love him?

Œnone

Blame me or blame me not for your misfortunes,
Of what was I incapable, to save you?
But if your indignation e'er was roused
By insult, can you pardon his contempt?
How cruelly his eyes, severely fix'd,
Survey'd you almost prostrate at his feet!
How hateful then appear'd his savage pride!
Why did not Phædra see him then as I
Beheld him?

Phædra

This proud mood that you resent
May yield to time. The rudeness of the forests
Where he was bred, inured to rigorous laws,
Clings to him still; love is a word he ne'er
Had heard before. It may be his surprise
Stunn'd him, and too much vehemence was shown
In all I said.

Œnone

Remember that his mother
Was a barbarian.

Phædra

Scythian tho' she was,
She learned to love.

Œnone

He has for all the sex
Hatred intense.

Phædra

Then in his heart no rival
Shall ever reign. Your counsel comes too late
Œnone, serve my madness, not my reason.
His heart is inaccessible to love.
Let us attack him where he has more feeling.
The charms of sovereignty appear'd to touch him;
He could not hide that he was drawn to Athens;
His vessels' prows were thither turn'd already,
All sail was set to scud before the breeze.
Go you on my behalf, to his ambition
Appeal, and let the prospect of the crown
Dazzle his eyes. The sacred diadem
Shall deck his brow, no higher honour mine
Than there to bind it. His shall be the pow'r
I cannot keep; and he shall teach my son
How to rule men. It may be he will deign
To be to him a father. Son and mother
He shall control. Try ev'ry means to move him;
Your words will find more favour than can mine.
Urge him with groans and tears; show Phædra dying.
Nor blush to use the voice of supplication.
In you is my last hope; I'll sanction all
You say; and on the issue hangs my fate.

SCENE II

Phædra (alone)

Venus implacable, who seest me shamed
And sore confounded, have I not enough
Been humbled? How can cruelty be stretch'd
Farther? Thy shafts have all gone home, and thou
Hast triumph'd. Would'st thou win a new renown?
Attack an enemy more contumacious:
Hippolytus neglects thee, braves thy wrath,
Nor ever at thine altars bow'd the knee.

Thy name offends his proud, disdainful ears.
Our interests are alike: avenge thyself,
Force him to love—

                But what is this? Œnone
Return'd already? He detests me then,
And will not hear you.

SCENE III
PHÆDRA, ŒNONE

Œnone

                  Madam, you must stifle
A fruitless love. Recall your former virtue:
The king who was thought dead will soon appear
Before your eyes, Theseus has just arrived,
Theseus is here. The people flock to see him
With eager haste. I went by your command
To find the prince, when with a thousand shouts
The air was rent—

Phædra

               My husband is alive,
That is enough, Œnone. I have own'd
A passion that dishonours him. He lives:
I ask to know no more.

Œnone
          What?

Phædra

                I foretold it,
But you refused to hear. Your tears prevail'd
Over my just remorse. Dying this morn,
I had deserved compassion; your advice
I took, and die dishonour'd.

Œnone
                Die?

Phædra

Just Heav'ns!
What have I done to-day? My husband comes,
With him his son: and I shall see the witness
Of my adulterous flame watch with what face
I greet his father, while my heart is big
With sighs he scorn'd, and tears that could not move him
Moisten mine eyes. Think you that his respect
For Theseus will induce him to conceal
My madness, nor disgrace his sire and king?
Will he be able to keep back the horror
He has for me? His silence would be vain.
I know my treason, and I lack the boldness
Of those abandon'd women who can taste
Tranquillity in crime, and show a forehead
All unabash'd. I recognize my madness,
Recall it all. These vaulted roofs, methinks,
These walls can speak, and, ready to accuse me,
Wait but my husband's presence to reveal
My perfidy. Death only can remove
This weight of horror. Is it such misfortune
To cease to live? Death causes no alarm
To misery. I only fear the name
That I shall leave behind me. For my sons
How sad a heritage! The blood of Jove
Might justly swell the pride that boasts descent
From Heav'n, but heavy weighs a mother's guilt
Upon her offspring. Yes, I dread the scorn
That will be cast on them, with too much truth,
For my disgrace. I tremble when I think
That, crush'd beneath that curse, they'll never dare
To raise their eyes.

Œnone

Doubt not I pity both;
Never was fear more just than yours. Why, then,
Expose them to this ignominy? Why

Will you accuse yourself? You thus destroy
The only hope that's left; it will be said
That Phædra, conscious of her perfidy,
Fled from her husband's sight. Hippolytus
Will be rejoiced that, dying, you should lend
His charge support. What can I answer him?
He'll find it easy to confute my tale,
And I shall hear him with an air of triumph
To every open ear repeat your shame.
Sooner than that may fire from heav'n consume me!
Deceive me not. Say, do you love him still?
How look you now on this contemptuous prince?

Phædra

As on a monster frightful to mine eyes.

Œnone

Why yield him, then, an easy victory?
You fear him? Venture to accuse him first,
As guilty of the charge which he may bring
This day against you. Who can say 'tis false?
All tells against him: in your hands his sword
Happily left behind, your present trouble,
Your past distress, your warnings to his father,
His exile which your earnest pray'rs obtain'd.

Phædra

What! Would you have me slander innocence?

Œnone

My zeal has need of naught from you but silence.
Like you I tremble, and am loath to do it;
More willingly I'd face a thousand deaths,
But since without this bitter remedy
I lose you, and to me your life outweighs

All else, I'll speak. Theseus, howe'er enraged
Will do no worse than banish him again.
A father, when he punishes, remains
A father, and his ire is satisfied
With a light sentence. But if guiltless blood
Should flow, is not your honour of more moment?
A treasure far too precious to be risk'd?
You must submit, whatever it dictates;
For, when our reputation is at stake,
All must be sacrificed, conscience itself.
But someone comes. 'Tis Theseus.

Phædra

                      And I see
Hippolytus, my ruin plainly written
In his stern eyes. Do what you will; I trust
My fate to you. I cannot help myself.

Scene IV

THESEUS, HIPPOLYTUS, PHÆDRA, ŒNONE, THERAMENES

Theseus

Fortune no longer fights against my wishes,
Madam, and to your arms restores—

Phædra

                      Stay, Theseus!
Do not profane endearments that were once
So sweet, but which I am unworthy now
To taste. You have been wrong'd. Fortune has proved
Spiteful, nor in your absence spared your wife.
I am unfit to meet your fond caress,
How I may bear my shame my only care
Henceforth.

Scene V
Theseus, Hippolytus, Theramenes

Theseus

  Strange welcome for your father, this!
What does it mean, my son?

Hippolytus

      Phædra alone
Can solve this mystery. But if my wish
Can move you, let me never see her more;
Suffer Hippolytus to disappear
For ever from the home that holds your wife.

Theseus

You, my son! Leave me?

Hippolytus

      'Twas not I who sought her:
'Twas you who led her footsteps to these shores.
At your departure you thought meet, my lord,
To trust Aricia and the Queen to this
Trœzenian land, and I myself was charged
With their protection. But what cares henceforth
Need keep me here? My youth of idleness
Has shown its skill enough o'er paltry foes
That range the woods. May I not quit a life
Of such inglorious ease, and dip my spear
In nobler blood? Ere you had reach'd my age
More than one tyrant, monster more than one
Had felt the weight of your stout arm. Already,
Successful in attacking insolence,
You had removed all dangers that infested
Our coasts to east and west. The traveller fear'd
Outrage no longer. Hearing of your deeds,
Already Hercules relied on you,
And rested from his toils. While I, unknown

Son of so brave a sire, am far behind
Even my mother's footsteps. Let my courage
Have scope to act, and if some monster yet
Has 'scaped you, let me lay the glorious spoils
Down at your feet; or let the memory
Of death faced nobly keep my name alive,
And prove to all the world I was your son.

Theseus

Why, what is this? What terror has possess'd
My family to make them fly before me?
If I return to find myself so fear'd,
So little welcome, why did Heav'n release me
From prison? My sole friend, misled by passion,
Was bent on robbing of his wife the tyrant
Who ruled Epirus. With regret I lent
The lover aid, but Fate had made us blind,
Myself as well as him. The tyrant seized me
Defenceless and unarm'd. Pirithoüs
I saw with tears cast forth to be devour'd
By savage beasts that lapp'd the blood of men.
Myself in gloomy caverns he inclosed,
Deep in the bowels of the earth, and nigh
To Pluto's realms. Six months I lay ere Heav'n
Had pity, and I 'scaped the watchful eyes
That guarded me. Then did I purge the world
Of a foul foe, and he himself has fed
His monsters. But when with expectant joy
To all that is most precious I draw near
Of what the gods have left me, when my soul
Looks for full satisfaction in a sight
So dear, my only welcome is a shudder,
Embrace rejected, and a hasty flight.
Inspiring, as I clearly do, such terror,
Would I were still a prisoner in Epirus!
Phædra complains that I have suffer'd outrage.
Who has betray'd me? Speak. Why was I not

Avenged? Has Greece, to whom mine arm so oft
Brought useful aid, shelter'd the criminal?
You make no answer. Is my son, mine own
Dear son, confederate with mine enemies?
I'll enter. This suspense is overwhelming.
I'll learn at once the culprit and the crime,
And Phædra must explain her troubled state.

Scene VI
Hippolytus, Theramenes

Hippolytus

What do these words portend, which seem'd to freeze
My very blood? Will Phædra, in her frenzy
Accuse herself, and seal her own destruction?
What will the King say? Gods! What fatal poison
Has love spread over all his house! Myself,
Full of a fire his hatred disapproves,
How changed he finds me from the son he knew!
With dark forebodings in my mind alarm'd,
But innocence has surely naught to fear.
Come, let us go, and in some other place
Consider how I best may move my sire
To tenderness, and tell him of a flame
Vex'd but not vanquish'd by a father's blame.

ACT IV

Scene I
Theseus, Œnone

Theseus

Ah! What is this I hear? Presumptuous traitor!
And would he have disgraced his father's honour?
With what relentless footsteps Fate pursues me!
Whither I go I know not, nor where know

I am. O kind affection ill repaid!
Audacious scheme! Abominable thought!
To reach the object of his foul desire
The wretch disdain'd not to use violence.
I know this sword that served him in his fury.
The sword I gave him for a nobler use.
Could not the sacred ties of blood restrain him?
And Phædra,—was she loath to have him punish'd?
She held her tongue. Was that to spare the culprit?

Œnone

Nay, but to spare a most unhappy father.
O'erwhelm'd with shame that her eyes should have
    kindled
So infamous a flame and prompted him
To crime so heinous, Phædra would have died.
I saw her raise her arm, and ran to save her.
To me alone you owe it that she lives;
And, in my pity both for her and you,
Have I against my will interpreted
Her tears.

Theseus

      The traitor! He might well turn pale.
'Twas fear that made him tremble when he saw me.
I was astonish'd that he show'd no pleasure;
His frigid greeting chill'd my tenderness.
But was this guilty passion that devours him
Declared already ere I banish'd him
From Athens?

Œnone

      Sire, remember how the Queen
Urged you. Illicit love caused all her hatred.

Theseus

And then this fire broke out again at Trœzen?

Œnone

Sire, I have told you all. Too long the Queen
Has been allow'd to bear her grief alone
Let me now leave you and attend to her.

Scene II
THESEUS, HIPPOLYTUS

Theseus

Ah! There he is. Great gods! That noble mien
Might well deceive an eye less fond than mine!
Why should the sacred stamp of virtue gleam
Upon the forehead of an impious wretch?
Ought not the blackness of a traitor's heart
To show itself by sure and certain signs?

Hippolytus

My father, may I ask what fatal cloud
Has troubled your majestic countenance?
Dare you not trust this secret to your son?

Theseus

Traitor, how dare you show yourself before me?
Monster, whom Heaven's bolts have spared too long!
Survivor of that robber crew whereof
I cleansed the earth. After your brutal lust
Scorn'd even to respect my marriage bed,
You venture—you, my hated foe—to come
Into my presence, here, where all is full
Of your foul infamy, instead of seeking
Some unknown land that never heard my name.
Fly, traitor, fly! Stay not to tempt the wrath
That I can scarce restrain, nor brave my hatred.
Disgrace enough have I incurr'd for ever
In being father of so vile a son,
Without your death staining indelibly

The glorious record of my noble deeds.
Fly, and unless you wish quick punishment
To add you to the criminals cut off
By me, take heed this sun that lights us now
Ne'er see you more set foot upon this soil.
I tell you once again,—fly, haste, return not,
Rid all my realms of your atrocious presence.

   To thee, to thee, great Neptune, I appeal;
If erst I clear'd thy shores of foul assassins,
Recall thy promise to reward those efforts,
Crown'd with success, by granting my first pray'r.
Confined for long in close captivity,
I have not yet call'd on thy pow'rful aid,
Sparing to use the valued privilege
Till at mine utmost need. The time is come,
I ask thee now. Avenge a wretched father!
I leave this traitor to thy wrath; in blood
Quench his outrageous fires, and by thy fury
Theseus will estimate thy favour tow'rds him.

Hippolytus

Phædra accuses me of lawless passion!
This crowning horror all my soul confounds;
Such unexpected blows, falling at once,
O'erwhelm me, choke my utterance, strike me dumb.

Theseus

Traitor, you reckon'd that in timid silence
Phædra would bury your brutality.
You should not have abandon'd in your flight
The sword that in her hands helps to condemn you;
Or rather, to complete your perfidy,
You should have robb'd her both of speech and life.

Hippolytus

Justly indignant at a lie so black
I might be pardon'd if I told the truth;

But it concerns your honour to conceal it.
Approve the reverence that shuts my mouth;
And, without wishing to increase your woes,
Examine closely what my life has been.
Great crimes are never single, they are link'd
To former faults. He who has once transgress'd
May violate at last all that men hold
Most sacred; vice, like virtue, has degrees
Of progress; innocence was never seen
To sink at once into the lowest depths
Of guilt. No virtuous man can in a day
Turn traitor, murderer, an incestuous wretch.
The nursling of a chaste, heroic mother,
I have not proved unworthy of my birth.
Pittheus, whose wisdom is by all esteem'd,
Deign'd to instruct me when I left her hands.
It is no wish of mine to vaunt my merits,
But, if I may lay claim to any virtue,
I think beyond all else I have display'd
Abhorrence of those sins with which I'm charged.
For this Hippolytus is known in Greece,
So continent that he is deem'd austere.
All know my abstinence inflexible:
The daylight is not purer than my heart.
How, then, could I, burning with fire profane—

Theseus

Yes, dastard, 'tis that very pride condemns you.
I see the odious reason of your coldness·
Phædra alone bewitch'd your shameless eyes;
Your soul, to others' charms indifferent,
Disdain'd the blameless fires of lawful love.

Hippolytus

No, father, I have hidden it too long,
This heart has not disdain'd a sacred flame.
Here at your feet I own my real offence:

I love, and love in truth where you forbid me;
Bound to Aricia by my heart's devotion,
The child of Pallas has subdued your son.
A rebel to your laws, her I adore,
And breathe forth ardent sighs for her alone.

Theseus

You love her? Heav'ns!

                     But no, I see the trick.
You feign a crime to justify yourself.

Hippolytus

Sir, I have shunn'd her for six months, and still
Love her. To you yourself I came to tell it,
Trembling the while. Can nothing clear your mind
Of your mistake? What oath can reassure you?
By heav'n and earth and all the pow'rs of nature—

Theseus

The wicked never shrink from perjury.
Cease, cease, and spare me irksome protestations,
If your false virtue has no other aid.

Hippolytus

Tho' it to you seem false and insincere,
Phædra has secret cause to know it true.

Theseus

Ah! how your shamelessness excites my wrath!

Hippolytus

What is my term and place of banishment?

Theseus

Were you beyond the Pillars of Alcides,
Your perjured presence were too near me yet.

Hippolytus

What friends will pity me, when you forsake
And think me guilty of a crime so vile?

Theseus

Go, look you out for friends who hold in honour
Adultery and clap their hands at incest,
Low, lawless traitors, steep'd in infamy,
The fit protectors of a knave like you.

Hippolytus

Are incest and adultery the words
You cast at me? I hold my tongue. Yet think
What mother Phædra had; too well you know
Her blood, not mine, is tainted with those horrors.

Theseus

What! Does your rage before my eyes lose all
Restraint? For the last time,—out of my sight!
Hence, traitor! Wait not till a father's wrath
Force thee away 'mid general execration.

Scene III

Theseus (alone)

Wretch! Thou must meet inevitable ruin.
Neptune has sworn by Styx—to gods themselves
A dreadful oath,—and he will execute
His promise. Thou canst not escape his vengeance.
I loved thee; and, in spite of thine offence,
My heart is troubled by anticipation
For thee. But thou hast earn'd thy doom too well.
Had father ever greater cause for rage?
Just gods, who see the grief that overwhelms me,
Why was I cursed with such a wicked son?

Scene IV

Phædra, Theseus

Phædra

My lord, I come to you, fill'd with just dread.
Your voice raised high in anger reach'd mine ears,
And much I fear that deeds have follow'd threats.
Oh, if there yet is time, spare your own offspring.
Respect your race and blood, I do beseech you.
Let me not hear that blood cry from the ground;
Save me the horror and perpetual pain
Of having caused his father's hand to shed it.

Theseus

No, Madam, from that stain my hand is free.
But, for all that, the wretch has not escaped me.
The hand of an Immortal now is charged
With his destruction. 'Tis a debt that Neptune
Owes me, and you shall be avenged.

Phædra

                                    A debt
Owed you? Pray'rs made in anger—

Theseus

                                    Never fear
That they will fail. Rather join yours to mine.
In all their blackness paint for me his crimes,
And fan my tardy passion to white heat.
But yet you know not all his infamy;
His rage against you overflows in slanders;
Your mouth, he says, is full of all deceit,
He says Aricia has his heart and soul,
That her alone he loves.

Phædra

Aricia?

Theseus

Aye,

He said it to my face! an idle pretext!
A trick that gulls me not! Let us hope Neptune
Will do him speedy justice. To his altars
I go, to urge performance of his oaths.

SCENE V

Phædra (alone)

Ah, he is gone! What tidings struck mine ears?
What fire, half smother'd, in my heart revives?
What fatal stroke falls like a thunderbolt?
Stung by remorse that would not let me rest,
I tore myself out of Œnone's arms,
And flew to help Hippolytus with all
My soul and strength. Who knows if that repentance
Might not have moved me to accuse myself?
And, if my voice had not been choked with shame,
Perhaps I had confess'd the frightful truth.
Hippolytus can feel, but not for me!
Aricia has his heart, his plighted troth.
Ye gods, when, deaf to all my sighs and tears,
He arm'd his eye with scorn, his brow with threats,
I deem'd his heart, impregnable to love,
Was fortified 'gainst all my sex alike.
And yet another has prevail'd to tame
His pride, another has secured his favour.
Perhaps he has a heart easily melted;
I am the only one he cannot bear!
And shall I charge myself with his defence?

Scene VI

Phædra, Œnone

Phædra

Know you, dear Nurse, what I have learn'd just now?

Œnone

No; but I come in truth with trembling limbs.
I dreaded with what purpose you went forth,
The fear of fatal madness made me pale.

Phædra

Who would have thought it, Nurse? I had a rival.

Œnone

A rival?

Phædra

      Yes, he loves. I cannot doubt it.
This wild untamable Hippolytus,
Who scorn'd to be admired, whom lovers' sighs
Wearied, this tiger, whom I fear'd to rouse,
Fawns on a hand that has subdued his pride:
Aricia has found entrance to his heart.

Œnone

Aricia?

Phædra

     Ah! anguish as yet untried!
For what new tortures am I still reserved?
All I have undergone, transports of passion,
Longings and fears, the horrors of remorse,
The shame of being spurn'd with contumely,
Were feeble foretastes of my present torments.
They love each other! By what secret charm
Have they deceived me? Where, and when, and how
Met they? You knew it all. Why was I cozen'd?

You never told me of those stolen hours
Of amorous converse. Have they oft been seen
Talking together? Did they seek the shades
Of thickest woods? Alas! full freedom had they
To see each other. Heav'n approved their sighs;
They loved without the consciousness of guilt;
And every morning's sun for them shone clear,
While I, an outcast from the face of Nature,
Shunn'd the bright day, and sought to hide myself.
Death was the only god whose aid I dared
To ask: I waited for the grave's release.
Water'd with tears, nourish'd with gall, my woe
Was all too closely watch'd; I did not dare
To weep without restraint. In mortal dread
Tasting this dangerous solace, I disguised
My terror 'neath a tranquil countenance,
And oft had I to check my tears, and smile.

Œnone

What fruit will they enjoy of their vain love?
They will not see each other more.

Phædra

That love
Will last for ever. Even while I speak,
Ah, fatal thought, they laugh to scorn the madness
Of my distracted heart. In spite of exile
That soon must part them, with a thousand oaths
They seal yet closer union. Can I suffer
A happiness, Œnone, which insults me?
I crave your pity. She must be destroy'd.
My husband's wrath against a hateful stock
Shall be revived, nor must the punishment
Be light: the sister's guilt passes the brothers'.
I will entreat him in my jealous rage.
  What am I saying? Have I lost my senses?
Is Phædra jealous, and will she implore

Theseus for help? My husband lives, and yet
I burn. For whom? Whose heart is this I claim
As mine? At every word I say, my hair
Stands up with horror. Guilt henceforth has pass'd
All bounds. Hypocrisy and incest breathe
At once thro' all. My murderous hands are ready
To spill the blood of guileless innocence.
Do I yet live, wretch that I am, and dare
To face this holy Sun from whom I spring?
My father's sire was king of all the gods;
My ancestors fill all the universe.
Where can I hide? In the dark realms of Pluto?
But there my father holds the fatal urn;
His hand awards th' irrevocable doom:
Minos is judge of all the ghosts in hell.
Ah! how his awful shade will start and shudder
When he shall see his daughter brought before him,
Forced to confess sins of such varied dye,
Crimes it may be unknown to hell itself!
What wilt thou say, my father, at a sight
So dire? I think I see thee drop the urn,
And, seeking some unheard-of punishment,
Thyself become my executioner.
Spare me! A cruel goddess has destroy'd
Thy race; and in my madness recognize
Her wrath. Alas! My aching heart has reap'd
No fruit of pleasure from the frightful crime
The shame of which pursues me to the grave,
And ends in torment life-long misery.

Œnone

Ah, Madam, pray dismiss a groundless dread:
Look less severely on a venial error.
You love. We cannot conquer destiny.
You were drawn on as by a fatal charm.
Is that a marvel without precedent
Among us? Has love triumph'd over you,

And o'er none else? Weakness is natural
To man. A mortal, to a mortal's lot
Submit. You chafe against a yoke that others
Have long since borne. The dwellers in Olympus,
The gods themselves, who terrify with threats
The sins of men, have burn'd with lawless fires.

Phædra

What words are these I hear? What counsel this
You dare to give me? Will you to the end
Pour poison in mine ears? You have destroy'd me.
You brought me back when I should else have quitted
The light of day, made me forget my duty
And see Hippolytus, till then avoided.
What hast thou done? Why did your wicked mouth
With blackest lies slander his blameless life?
Perhaps you've slain him, and the impious pray'r
Of an unfeeling father has been answer'd.
No, not another word! Go, hateful monster;
Away, and leave me to my piteous fate.
May Heav'n with justice pay you your deserts!
And may your punishment for ever be
A terror to all those who would, like you,
Nourish with artful wiles the weaknesses
Of princes, push them to the brink of ruin
To which their heart inclines, and smooth the path
Of guilt. Such flatterers doth the wrath of Heav'n
Bestow on kings as its most fatal gift.

Œnone (alone)

O gods! to serve her what have I not done?
This is the due reward that I have won.

ACT V

Scene I

HIPPOLYTUS, ARICIA

Aricia

Can you keep silent in this mortal peril?
Your father loves you. Will you leave him thus
Deceived? If in your cruel heart you scorn
My tears, content to see me nevermore,
Go, part from poor Aricia; but at least,
Going, secure the safety of your life.
Defend your honour from a shameful stain,
And force your father to recall his pray'rs.
There yet is time. Why out of mere caprice
Leave the field free to Phædra's calumnies?
Let Theseus know the truth.

Hippolytus

                Could I say more,
Without exposing him to dire disgrace?
How should I venture, by revealing all,
To make a father's brow grow red with shame?
The odious mystery to you alone
Is known. My heart has been outpour'd to none
Save you and Heav'n. I could not hide from you
(Judge if I love you) all I fain would hide
E'en from myself. But think under what seal
I spoke. Forget my words, if that may be;
And never let so pure a mouth disclose
This dreadful secret. Let us trust to Heav'n
My vindication, for the gods are just;
For their own honour will they clear the guiltless;
Sooner or later punish'd for her crime,
Phædra will not escape the shame she merits.
I ask no other favour than your silence;

In all besides I give my wrath free scope.
Make your escape from this captivity,
Be bold to bear me company in flight;
Linger not here on this accursèd soil,
Where virtue breathes a pestilential air.
To cover your departure take advantage
Of this confusion, caused by my disgrace.
The means of flight are ready, be assured;
You have as yet no other guards than mine.
Pow'rful defenders will maintain our quarrel;
Argos spreads open arms, and Sparta calls us.
Let us appeal for justice to our friends,
Nor suffer Phædra, in a common ruin
Joining us both, to hunt us from the throne,
And aggrandize her son by robbing us.
Embrace this happy opportunity:
What fear restrains? You seem to hesitate.
Your interest alone prompts me to urge
Boldness. When I am all on fire, how comes it
That you are ice? Fear you to follow then
A banish'd man?

Aricia

      Ah, dear to me would be
Such exile! With what joy, my fate to yours
United, could I live, by all the world
Forgotten! But not yet has that sweet tie
Bound us together. How then can I steal
Away with you? I know the strictest honour
Forbids me not out of your father's hands
To free myself; this is no parent's home,
And flight is lawful when one flies from tyrants.
But you, Sir, love me; and my virtue shrinks—

Hippolytus

No, no, your reputation is to me
As dear as to yourself. A nobler purpose

Brings me to you. Fly from your foes, and follow
A husband. Heav'n, that sends us these misfortunes,
Sets free from human instruments the pledge
Between us. Torches do not always light
The face of Hymen.

　　　　　　　　At the gates of Trœzen,
'Mid ancient tombs where princes of my race
Lie buried, stands a temple ne'er approach'd
By perjurers, where mortals dare not make
False oaths, for instant punishment befalls
The guilty. Falsehood knows no stronger check
Than what is present there—the fear of death
That cannot be avoided. Thither then
We'll go, if you consent, and swear to love
For ever, take the guardian god to witness
Our solemn vows, and his paternal care
Entreat. I will invoke the name of all
The holiest Pow'rs; chaste Dian, and the Queen
Of Heav'n, yea all the gods who know my heart
Will guarantee my sacred promises.

Aricia

The King draws near. Depart,—make no delay.
To mask my flight, I linger yet one moment.
Go you; and leave with me some trusty guide,
To lead my timid footsteps to your side.

Scene II
Theseus, Aricia, Ismene

Theseus

Ye gods, throw light upon my troubled mind,
Show me the truth which I am seeking here.

Aricia (*aside to* Ismene)

Get ready, dear Ismene, for our flight.

Scene III
Theseus, Aricia

Theseus

Your colour comes and goes, you seem confused,
Madam! What business had my son with you?

Aricia

Sire, he was bidding me farewell for ever.

Theseus

Your eyes, it seems, can tame that stubborn pride;
And the first sighs he breathes are paid to you.

Aricia

I can't deny the truth; he has not, Sire,
Inherited your hatred and injustice;
He did not treat me like a criminal.

Theseus

That is to say, he swore eternal love.
Do not rely on that inconstant heart;
To others has he sworn as much before.

Aricia

He, Sire?

Theseus

   You ought to check his roving taste.
How could you bear a partnership so vile?

Aricia

And how can you endure that vilest slanders
Should make a life so pure as black as pitch?
Have you so little knowledge of his heart?
Do you so ill distinguish between guilt
And innocence? What mist before your eyes

Blinds them to virtue so conspicuous?
Ah! 'tis too much to let false tongues defame him.
Repent; call back your murderous wishes, Sire;
Fear, fear lest Heav'n in its severity
Hate you enough to hear and grant your pray'rs.
Oft in their wrath the gods accept our victims,
And oftentimes chastise us with their gifts.

Theseus

No, vainly would you cover up his guilt.
Your love is blind to his depravity.
But I have witness irreproachable:
Tears have I seen, true tears, that may be trusted.

Aricia

Take heed, my lord. Your hands invincible
Have rid the world of monsters numberless;
But all are not destroy'd, one you have left
Alive—Your son forbids me to say more.
Knowing with what respect he still regards you,
I should too much distress him if I dared
Complete my sentence. I will imitate
His reverence, and, to keep silence, leave you.

Scene IV

Theseus (alone)

What is there in her mind? What meaning lurks
In speech begun but to be broken short?
Would both deceive me with a vain pretence?
Have they conspired to put me to the torture?
And yet, despite my stern severity,
What plaintive voice cries deep within my heart?
A secret pity troubles and alarms me.
Œnone shall be questioned once again,
I must have clearer light upon this crime.
Guards, bid Œnone come, and come alone.

Scene V

Theseus, Panope

Panope

I know not what the Queen intends to do,
But from her agitation dread the worst.
Fatal despair is painted on her features;
Death's pallor is already in her face.
Œnone, shamed and driven from her sight,
Has cast herself into the ocean depths.
None knows what prompted her to deed so rash;
And now the waves hide her from us for ever.

Theseus

What say you?

Panope

Her sad fate seems to have added
Fresh trouble to the Queen's tempestuous soul.
Sometimes, to soothe her secret pain, she clasps
Her children close, and bathes them with her tears;
Then suddenly, the mother's love forgotten,
She thrusts them from her with a look of horror.
She wanders to and fro with doubtful steps;
Her vacant eye no longer knows us. Thrice
She wrote, and thrice did she, changing her mind,
Destroy the letter ere 'twas well begun.
Vouchsafe to see her, Sire: vouchsafe to help her.

Theseus

Heav'ns! Is Œnone dead, and Phædra bent
On dying too? Oh, call me back my son!
Let him defend himself, and I am ready
To hear him. Be not hasty to bestow
Thy fatal bounty, Neptune; let my pray'rs
Rather remain ever unheard. Too soon
I lifted cruel hands, believing lips
That may have lied! Ah! What despair may follow!

Scene VI
Theseus, Theramenes

Theseus

Theramenes, is't thou? Where is my son?
I gave him to thy charge from tenderest childhood.
But whence these tears that overflow thine eyes?
How is it with my son?

Theramenes

                    Concern too late!
Affection vain! Hippolytus is dead.

Theseus

Gods!

Theramenes

      I have seen the flow'r of all mankind
Cut off, and I am bold to say that none
Deserved it less.

Theseus

             What! My son dead! When I
Was stretching out my arms to him, has Heav'n
Hasten'd his end? What was this sudden stroke?

Theramenes

Scarce had we pass'd out of the gates of Trœzen,
He silent in his chariot, and his guards,
Downcast and silent too, around him ranged;
To the Mycenian road he turn'd his steeds,
Then, lost in thought, allow'd the reins to lie
Loose on their backs. His noble chargers, erst
So full of ardour to obey his voice,
With head depress'd and melancholy eye
Seem'd now to mark his sadness and to share it.
A frightful eye, that issues from the deep,
With sudden discord rends the troubled air;

And from the bosom of the earth a groan
Is heard in answer to that voice of terror.
Our blood is frozen at our very hearts;
With bristling manes the list'ning steeds stand still
Meanwhile upon the watery plain there rises
A mountain billow with a mighty crest
Of foam, that shoreward rolls, and, as it breaks,
Before our eyes vomits a furious monster.
With formidable horns its brow is arm'd,
And all its body clothed with yellow scales,
In front a savage bull, behind a dragon
Turning and twisting in impatient rage.
Its long continued bellowings make the shore
Tremble; the sky seems horror-struck to see it;
The earth with terror quakes; its poisonous breath
Infects the air. The wave that brought it ebbs
In fear. All fly, forgetful of the courage
That cannot aid, and in a neighbouring temple
Take refuge—all save bold Hippolytus.
A hero's worthy son, he stays his steeds,
Seizes his darts, and, rushing forward, hurls
A missile with sure aim that wounds the monster
Deep in the flank. With rage and pain it springs
E'en to the horses' feet, and, roaring, falls,
Writhes in the dust, and shows a fiery throat
That covers them with flames, and blood, and smoke.
Fear lends them wings; deaf to his voice for once,
And heedless of the curb, they onward fly.
Their master wastes his strength in efforts vain;
With foam and blood each courser's bit is red.
Some say a god, amid this wild disorder,
Was seen with goads pricking their dusty flanks.
O'er jagged rocks they rush urged on by terror;
Crash! goes the axle-tree. Th' intrepid youth
Sees his car broken up, flying to pieces;
He falls himself entangled in the reins.
Pardon my grief. That cruel spectacle

Will be for me a source of endless tears.
I saw thy hapless son, I saw him, Sire,
Dragg'd by the horses that his hands had fed,
Pow'rless to check their fierce career, his voice
But adding to their fright, his body soon
One mass of wounds. Our cries of anguish fill
The plain. At last they slacken their swift pace,
Then stop, not far from those old tombs that mark
Where lie the ashes of his royal sires.
Panting I thither run, and after me
His guard, along the track stain'd with fresh blood
That reddens all the rocks; caught in the briers
Locks of his hair hang dripping, gory spoils!
I come, I call him. Stretching forth his hand,
He opes his dying eyes, soon closed again.
"The gods have robb'd me of a guiltless life,"
I hear him say: "Take care of sad Aricia
When I am dead. Dear friend, if e'er my father
Mourn, undeceived, his son's unhappy fate
Falsely accused; to give my spirit peace,
Tell him to treat his captive tenderly,
And to restore—" With that the hero's breath
Fails, and a mangled corpse lies in my arms,
A piteous object, trophy of the wrath
Of Heav'n—so changed, his father would not know him.

Theseus

Alas, my son! Dear hope for ever lost!
The ruthless gods have served me but too well.
For what a life of anguish and remorse
Am I reserved!

Theramenes

    Aricia at that instant,
Flying from you, comes timidly, to take him
For husband, there, in presence of the gods.
Thus drawing nigh, she sees the grass all red

And reeking, sees (sad sight for lover's eye!)
Hippolytus stretch'd there, pale and disfigured.
But, for a time doubtful of her misfortune,
Unrecognized the hero she adores,
She looks, and asks—"Where is Hippolytus?"
Only too sure at last that he lies there
Before her, with sad eyes that silently
Reproach the gods, she shudders, groans, and falls
Swooning and all but lifeless, at his feet.
Ismene, all in tears, kneels down beside her,
And calls her back to life—life that is naught
But sense of pain. And I, to whom this light
Is darkness now, come to discharge the duty
The hero has imposed on me, to tell thee
His last request—a melancholy task.
But hither comes his mortal enemy.

Scene VII

Theseus, Phædra, Theramenes, Panope, Guards

Theseus

Madam, you've triumph'd, and my son is kill'd!
Ah, but what room have I for fear! How justly
Suspicion racks me that in blaming him
I err'd! But he is dead; accept your victim;
Rightly or wrongly slain, let your heart leap
For joy. My eyes shall be for ever blind:
Since you accuse him, I'll believe him guilty.
His death affords me cause enough for tears,
Without a foolish search for further light
Which, pow'rless to restore him to my grief,
Might only serve to make me more unhappy.
Far from this shore and far from you I'll fly,
For here the image of my mangled son
Would haunt my memory and drive me mad.
From the whole world I fain would banish me,

For all the world seems to rise up in judgment
Against me; and my very glory weights
My punishment; for, were my name less known
'Twere easier to hide me. All the favours
The gods have granted me I mourn and hate,
Nor will I importune them with vain pray'rs
Henceforth for ever. Give me what they may,
What they have taken will all else outweigh.

Phædra

Theseus, I cannot hear you and keep silence:
I must repair the wrong that he has suffer'd—
Your son was innocent.

Theseus

       Unhappy father!
And it was on your word that I condemn'd him!
Think you such cruelty can be excused—

Phædra

Moments to me are precious; hear me, Theseus.
'Twas I who cast an eye of lawless passion
On chaste and dutiful Hippolytus.
Heav'n in my bosom kindled baleful fire,
And vile Œnone's cunning did the rest.
She fear'd Hippolytus, knowing my madness,
Would make that passion known which he regarded
With horror; so advantage of my weakness
She took, and hasten'd to accuse him first.
For that she has been punish'd, tho' too mildly;
Seeking to shun my wrath she cast herself
Beneath the waves. The sword ere now had cut
My thread of life, but slander'd innocence
Made its cry heard, and I resolved to die
In a more lingering way, confessing first
My penitence to you. A poison, brought
To Athens by Medea, runs thro' my veins.

Already in my heart the venom works,
Infusing there a strange and fatal chill;
Already as thro' thickening mists I see
The spouse to whom my presence is an outrage;
Death, from mine eyes veiling the light of heav'n,
Restores its purity that they defiled.

Panope

She dies, my lord!

Theseus

        Would that the memory
Of her disgraceful deed could perish with her!
Ah, disabused too late!   Come, let us go,
And with the blood of mine unhappy son
Mingle our tears, clasping his dear remains,
In deep repentance for a pray'r detested.
Let him be honour'd as he well deserves;
And, to appease his sore offended ghost,
Be her near kinsmen's guilt whate'er it may,
Aricia shall be held my daughter from to-day.

TARTUFFE

OR

THE HYPOCRITE

BY

JEAN BAPTISTE POQUELIN MOLIÈRE

TRANSLATED BY

CURTIS HIDDEN PAGE

INTRODUCTORY NOTE

JEAN BAPTISTE POQUELIN, better known by his stage name of Molière, stands without a rival at the head of French comedy. Born at Paris in January, 1622, where his father held a position in the royal household, he was educated at the Jesuit Collège de Clermont, and for some time studied law, which he soon abandoned for the stage. His life was spent in Paris and in the provinces, acting, directing performances, managing theaters, and writing plays. He had his share of applause from the king and from the public; but the satire in his comedies made him many enemies, and he was the object of the most venomous attacks and the most impossible slanders. Nor did he find much solace at home; for he married unfortunately, and the unhappiness that followed increased the bitterness that public hostility had brought into his life. On February 17, 1673, while acting in "La Malade Imaginaire," the last of his masterpieces, he was seized with illness and died a few hours later.

The first of the greater works of Molière was "Les Précieuses Ridicules," produced in 1659. In this brilliant piece Molière lifted French comedy to a new level and gave it a new purpose—the satirizing of contemporary manners and affectations by frank portrayal and criticism. In the great plays that followed, "The School for Husbands" and "The School for Wives," "The Misanthrope" and "The Hypocrite" (Tartuffe), "The Miser" and "The Hypochondriac," "The Learned Ladies," "The Doctor in Spite of Himself," "The Citizen Turned Gentleman," and many others, he exposed mercilessly one after another the vices and foibles of the day.

His characteristic qualities are nowhere better exhibited than in "Tartuffe." Compared with such characterization as Shakespeare's, Molière's method of portraying life may seem to be lacking in complexity; but it is precisely the simplicity with which creations like Tartuffe embody the weakness or vice they represent that has given them their place as universally recognized types of human nature.

TARTUFFE

A COMEDY

CHARACTERS	ACTORS
MADAME PERNELLE, *mother of Orgon*	LOUIS BEJART
ORGON, *husband of Elmire*	MOLIÈRE
ELMIRE, *wife of Orgon*	MLLE. MOLIÈRE
DAMIS, *son of Orgon*	HUBERT
MARIANE, *daughter of Orgon, in love with Valère*	MLLE. DEBRIE
VALÈRE, *in love with Mariane*	LA GRANGE
CLÉANTE, *brother-in-law of Orgon*	LA THORILLIERE
TARTUFFE, *a hypocrite*	DU CROISY
DORINE, *Mariane's maid*	MADELEINE BEJART
M. LOYAL, *a bailiff*	DEBRIE
A Police Officer	
FLIPOTTE, *Madame Pernelle's servant*	

The scene is at Paris

ACT I

SCENE I

MADAME PERNELLE *and* FLIPOTTE, *her servant;* ELMIRE, MARIANE, CLÉANTE, DAMIS, DORINE

Madame Pernelle

COME, come, Flipotte, and let me get away.

Elmire

You hurry so, I hardly can attend you.

Madame Pernelle

Then don't, my daughter-in-law. Stay where you are.
I can dispense with your polite attentions.

Elmire

We're only paying what is due you, mother.
Why must you go away in such a hurry?

Madame Pernelle

Because I can't endure your carryings-on,
And no one takes the slightest pains to please me.
I leave your house, I tell you, quite disgusted;
You do the opposite of my instructions;
You've no respect for anything; each one
Must have his say; it's perfect pandemonium.

Dorine

If . .

Madame Pernelle

You're a servant wench, my girl, and much
Too full of gab, and too impertinent
And free with your advice on all occasions.

Damis

But . . .

Madame Pernelle

You're a fool, my boy—f, o, o, l
Just spells your name. Let grandma tell you that
I've said a hundred times to my poor son,
Your father, that you'd never come to good
Or give him anything but plague and torment.

Mariane

I think . . .

Madame Pernelle

O dearie me, his little sister!
You're all demureness, butter wouldn't melt
In *your* mouth, one would think to look at you.

Still waters, though, they say . . . you know the proverb;
And I don't like your doings on the sly.

Elmire

But, mother . . .

Madame Pernelle

        Daughter, by your leave, your conduct
In everything is altogether wrong;
You ought to set a good example for 'em;
Their dear departed mother did much better.
You are extravagant; and it offends me,
To see you always decked out like a princess.
A woman who would please her husband's eyes
Alone, wants no such wealth of fineries.

Cléante

But, madam, after all . . .

Madame Pernelle

          Sir, as for you,
The lady's brother, I esteem you highly,
Love and respect you. But, sir, all the same,
If I were in my son's, her husband's, place,
I'd urgently entreat you not to come
Within our doors. You preach a way of living
That decent people cannot tolerate.
I'm rather frank with you; but that's my way—
I don't mince matters, when I mean a thing.

Damis

Mr. Tartuffe, your friend, is mighty lucky . . .

Madame Pernelle

He is a holy man, and must be heeded;
I can't endure, with any show of patience,
To hear a scatterbrains like you attack him.

Damis

What! Shall I let a bigot criticaster
Come and usurp a tyrant's power here?
And shall we never dare amuse ourselves
Till this fine gentleman deigns to consent?

Dorine

If we must hark to him, and heed his maxims,
There's not a thing we do but what's a crime;
He censures everything, this zealous carper.

Madame Pernelle

And all he censures is well censured, too.
He wants to guide you on the way to heaven;
My son should train you all to love him well.

Damis

No, madam, look you, nothing—not my father
Nor anything—can make me tolerate him.
I should belie my feelings not to say so.
His actions rouse my wrath at every turn;
And I foresee that there must come of it
An open rupture with this sneaking scoundrel.

Dorine

Besides, 'tis downright scandalous to see
This unknown upstart master of the house—
This vagabond, who hadn't, when he came,
Shoes to his feet, or clothing worth six farthings,
And who so far forgets his place, as now
To censure everything, and rule the roost!

Madame Pernelle

Eh! Mercy sakes alive! Things would go better
If all were governed by his pious orders.

Dorine

He passes for a saint in your opinion.
In fact, he's nothing but a hypocrite.

Madame Pernelle

Just listen to her tongue!

Dorine

                    I wouldn't trust **him,**
Nor yet his Lawrence, without bonds and surety.

Madame Pernelle

I don't know what the servant's character
May be; but I can guarantee the master
A holy man. You hate him and reject him
Because he tells home truths to all of you.
'Tis sin alone that moves his heart to anger,
And heaven's interest is his only motive.

Dorine

Of course. But why, especially of late,
Can he let nobody come near the house?
Is heaven offended at a civil call
That he should make so great a fuss about it?
I'll tell you, if you like, just what I think;
                              (*Pointing to Elmire*)
Upon my word, he's jealous of our mistress.

Madame Pernelle

You hold your tongue, and think what you are saying.
He's not alone in censuring these visits;
The turmoil that attends your sort of people,
Their carriages forever at the door,
And all their noisy footmen, flocked together,
Annoy the neighbourhood, and raise a scandal.
I'd gladly think there's nothing really wrong;
But it makes talk; and that's not as it should be.

Cléante

Eh! madam, can you hope to keep folk's tongues
From wagging? It would be a grievous thing
If, for the fear of idle talk about us,
We had to sacrifice our friends. No, no;
Even if we could bring ourselves to do it,
Think you that everyone would then be silenced?,
Against backbiting there is no defence
So let us try to live in innocence,
To silly tattle pay no heed at all,
And leave the gossips free to vent their gall.

Dorine

Our neighbour Daphne, and her little husband,
Must be the ones who slander us, I'm thinking.
Those whose own conduct's most ridiculous,
Are always quickest to speak ill of others;
They never fail to seize at once upon
The slightest hint of any love affair,
And spread the news of it with glee, and give it
The character they'd have the world believe in.
By others' actions, painted in their colours,
They hope to justify their own; they think,
In the false hope of some resemblance, either
To make their own intrigues seem innocent,
Or else to make their neighbours share the blame
Which they are loaded with by everybody.

Madame Pernelle

These arguments are nothing to the purpose.
Orante, we all know, lives a perfect life;
Her thoughts are all of heaven; and I have heard
That she condemns the company you keep.

Dorine

O admirable pattern! Virtuous dame!
She lives the model of austerity;

But age has brought this piety upon her,
And she's a prude, now she can't help herself.
As long as she could capture men's attentions
She made the most of her advantages;
But, now she sees her beauty vanishing,
She wants to leave the world, that's leaving her,
And in the specious veil of haughty virtue
She'd hide the weakness of her worn-out charms.
That is the way with all your old coquettes;
They find it hard to see their lovers leave 'em;
And thus abandoned, their forlorn estate
Can find no occupation but a prude's.
These pious dames, in their austerity,
Must carp at everything, and pardon nothing.
They loudly blame their neighbours' way of living,
Not for religion's sake, but out of envy,
Because they can't endure to see another
Enjoy the pleasures age has weaned them from.

Madame Pernelle (to ELMIRE)

There! That's the kind of rigmarole to please you,
Daughter-in-law. One never has a chance
To get a word in edgewise, at your house,
Because this lady holds the floor all day;
But none the less, I mean to have my say, too.
I tell you that my son did nothing wiser
In all his life, than take this godly man
Into his household; heaven sent him here,
In your great need, to make you all repent;
For your salvation, you must hearken to him;
He censures nothing but deserves his censure.
These visits, these assemblies, and these balls,
Are all inventions of the evil spirit.
You never hear a word of godliness
At them—but idle cackle, nonsense, flimflam.
Our neighbour often comes in for a share,
The talk flies fast, and scandal fills the air;

It makes a sober person's head go round,
At these assemblies, just to hear the sound
Of so much gab, with not a word to say;
And as a learned man remarked one day
Most aptly, 'tis the Tower of Babylon,
Where all, beyond all limit, babble on.
And just to tell you how this point came in . . .

(*To* CLÉANTE)

So! Now the gentleman must snicker, must he?
Go find fools like yourself to make you laugh
And don't . . .

(*To* ELMIRE)

Daughter, good-bye; not one word more.
As for this house, I leave the half unsaid;
But I shan't soon set foot in it again.

(*Cuffing* FLIPOTTE)

Come, you! What makes you dream and stand agape,
Hussy! I'll warm your ears in proper shape!
March, trollop, march!

SCENE II
CLÉANTE, DORINE

Cléante

I won't escort her down,
For fear she might fall foul of me again;
The good old lady . . .

Dorine

Bless us! What a pity
She shouldn't hear the way you speak of her!
She'd surely tell you you're too "good" by half,
And that she's not so "old" as all that, neither!

Cléante

How she got angry with us all for nothing!
And how she seems possessed with her Tartuffe!

Dorine

Her case is nothing, though, beside her son's!
To see him, you would say he's ten times worse!
His conduct in our late unpleasantness[1]
Had won him much esteem, and proved his courage
In service of his king; but now he's like
A man besotted, since he's been so taken
With this Tartuffe. He calls him brother, loves him
A hundred times as much as mother, son,
Daughter, and wife. He tells him all his secrets
And lets him guide his acts, and rule his conscience.
He fondles and embraces him; a sweetheart
Could not, I think, be loved more tenderly;
At table he must have the seat of honour,
While with delight our master sees him eat
As much as six men could; we must give up
The choicest tidbits to him; if he belches,

('tis a servant speaking)[2]

Master exclaims: "God bless you!"—Oh, he dotes
Upon him! he's his universe, his hero;
He's lost in constant admiration, quotes him
On all occasions, takes his trifling acts
For wonders, and his words for oracles.
The fellow knows his dupe, and makes the most on't,
He fools him with a hundred masks of virtue,
Gets money from him all the time by canting,
And takes upon himself to carp at us.
Even his silly coxcomb of a lackey
Makes it his business to instruct us too;
He comes with rolling eyes to preach at us,
And throws away our ribbons, rouge, and patches.
The wretch, the other day, tore up a kerchief

---

[1] Referring to the rebellion called La Fronde, during the minority of Louis XIV.

[2] Molière's note, inserted in the text of all the old editions. It is a curious illustration of the desire for uniformity and dignity of style in dramatic verse of the seventeenth century, that Molière feels called on to apologize for a touch of realism like this. Indeed, these lines were even omitted when the play was given.

That he had found, pressed in the *Golden Legend*,
Calling it a horrid crime for us to mingle
The devil's finery with holy things.

Scene III

Elmire, Mariane, Damis, Cléante, Dorine

Elmire, *to* Cléante

You're very lucky to have missed the speech
She gave us at the door. I see my husband
Is home again. He hasn't seen me yet,
So I'll go up and wait till he comes in.

Cléante

And I, to save time, will await him here;
I'll merely say good-morning, and be gone.

Scene IV

Cléante, Damis, Dorine

Damis

I wish you'd say a word to him about
My sister's marriage; I suspect Tartuffe
Opposes it, and puts my father up
To all these wretched shifts. You know, besides,
How nearly I'm concerned in it myself;
If love unites my sister and Valère,
I love his sister too; and if this marriage
Were to . . .

Dorine
He's coming.

Scene V

Orgon, Cléante, Dorine

Orgon
                 Ah! Good morning, brother.

Cléante

I was just going, but am glad to greet you.
Things are not far advanced yet, in the country?

Orgon

Dorine . . .

(*To* CLÉANTE)

Just wait a bit, please, brother-in-law.
Let me allay my first anxiety
By asking news about the family.

(*To* DORINE)

Has everything gone well these last two days?
What's happening? And how is everybody?

Dorine

Madam had fever, and a splitting headache
Day before yesterday, all day and evening.

Orgon

And how about Tartuffe?

Dorine

Tartuffe? He's well;
He's mighty well; stout, fat, fair, rosy-lipped.

Orgon

Poor man!

Dorine

At evening she had nausea
And could't touch a single thing for supper,
Her headache still was so severe.

Orgon

And how
About Tartuffe?

Dorine

> He supped alone, before her,
And unctuously ate up two partridges,
As well as half a leg o' mutton, deviled.

Orgon

Poor man!

Dorine

> All night she couldn't get a wink
Of sleep, the fever racked her so; and we
Had to sit up with her till daylight.

Orgon

>   How
About Tartuffe?

Dorine

> Gently inclined to slumber,
He left the table, went into his room,
Got himself straight into a good warm bed,
And slept quite undisturbed until next morning.

Orgon

Poor man!

Dorine

> At last she let us all persuade her,
And got up courage to be bled; and then
She was relieved at once.

Orgon

>   And how about
Tartuffe?

Dorine

> He plucked up courage properly,
Bravely entrenched his soul against all evils.

And, to replace the blood that she had lost,
He drank at breakfast four huge draughts of wine.

Orgon

Poor man!

Dorine

So now they both are doing well;
And I'll go straightway and inform my mistress
How pleased you are at her recovery.

Scene VI
Orgon, Cléante

Cléante

Brother, she ridicules you to your face;
And I, though I don't want to make you angry,
Must tell you candidly that she's quite right.
Was such infatuation ever heard of?
And can a man to-day have charms to make you
Forget all else, relieve his poverty,
Give him a home, and then . . . ?

Orgon

Stop there, good brother,
You do not know the man you're speaking of.

Cléante

Since you will have it so, I do not know him;
But after all, to tell what sort of man
He is . . .

Orgon

Dear brother, you'd be charmed to know him;
Your raptures over him would have no end.
He is a man . . . who . . . ah! . . . in fact . . . a man
Whoever does his will, knows perfect peace,
And counts the whole world else, as so much dung.

His converse has transformed me quite; he weans
My heart from every friendship, teaches me
To have no love for anything on earth;
And I could see my brother, children, mother,
And wife, all die, and never care—a snap.

Cléante

Your feelings are humane, I must say, brother!

Orgon

Ah! If you'd seen him, as I saw him first,
You would have loved him just as much as I
He came to church each day, with contrite mien,
Kneeled, on both knees, right opposite my place,
And drew the eyes of all the congregation,
To watch the fervour of his prayers to heaven;
With deep-drawn sighs and great ejaculations,
He humbly kissed the earth at every moment;
And when I left the church, he ran before me
To give me holy water at the door.
I learned his poverty, and who he was,
By questioning his servant, who is like him,
And gave him gifts; but in his modesty
He always wanted to return a part.
"It is too much," he'd say, "too much by half;
I am not worthy of your pity." Then,
When I refused to take it back, he'd go,
Before my eyes, and give it to the poor.
At length heaven bade me take him to my home,
And since that day, all seems to prosper here.
He censures everything, and for my sake
He even takes great interest in my wife;
He lets me know who ogles her, and seems
Six times as jealous as I am myself.
You'd not believe how far his zeal can go:
He calls himself a sinner just for trifles;
The merest nothing is enough to shock him;

So much so, that the other day I heard him
Accuse himself for having, while at prayer,
In too much anger caught and killed a flea.

Cléante

Zounds, brother, you are mad, I think! Or else
You're making sport of me, with such a speech.
What are you driving at with all this nonsense . . . ?

Orgon

Brother, your language smacks of atheism;
And I suspect your soul's a little tainted
Therewith. I've preached to you a score of times
That you'll draw down some judgment on your head.

Cléante

That is the usual strain of all your kind;
They must have every one as blind as they.
They call you atheist if you have good eyes;
And if you don't adore their vain grimaces,
You've neither faith nor care for sacred things.
No, no; such talk can't frighten me; I know
What I am saying; heaven sees my heart.
We're not the dupes of all your canting mummers;
There are false heroes—and false devotees;
And as true heroes never are the ones
Who make much noise about their deeds of honour,
Just so true devotees, whom we should follow,
Are not the ones who make so much vain show.
What! Will you find no difference between
Hypocrisy and genuine devoutness?
And will you treat them both alike, and pay
The self-same honour both to masks and faces
Set artifice beside sincerity,
Confuse the semblance with reality,
Esteem a phantom like a living person,

And counterfeit as good as honest coin?
Men, for the most part, are strange creatures, truly!
You never find them keep the golden mean;
The limits of good sense, too narrow for them,
Must always be passed by, in each direction;
They often spoil the noblest things, because
They go too far, and push them to extremes.
I merely say this by the way, good brother.

Orgon

You are the sole expounder of the doctrine;
Wisdom shall die with you, no doubt, good brother,
You are the only wise, the sole enlightened,
The oracle, the Cato, of our age.
All men, compared to you, are downright fools.

Cléante

I'm not the sole expounder of the doctrine,
And wisdom shall not die with me, good brother.
But this I know, though it be all my knowledge,
That there's a difference 'twixt false and true.
And as I find no kind of hero more
To be admired than men of true religion,
Nothing more noble or more beautiful
Than is the holy zeal of true devoutness;
Just so I think there's naught more odious
Than whited sepulchres of outward unction,
Those barefaced charlatans, those hireling zealots,
Whose sacrilegious, treacherous pretence
Deceives at will, and with impunity
Makes mockery of all that men hold sacred;
Men who, enslaved to selfish interests,
Make trade and merchandise of godliness,
And try to purchase influence and office
With false eye-rollings and affected raptures;
Those men, I say, who with uncommon zeal
Seek their own fortunes on the road to heaven;

Who, skilled in prayer, have always much to ask,
And live at court to preach retirement;
Who reconcile religion with their vices,
Are quick to anger, vengeful, faithless, tricky,
And, to destroy a man, will have the boldness
To call their private grudge the cause of heaven;
All the more dangerous, since in their anger
They use against us weapons men revere,
And since they make the world applaud their passion,
And seek to stab us with a sacred sword.
There are too many of this canting kind.
Still, the sincere are easy to distinguish;
And many splendid patterns may be found,
In our own time, before our very eyes
Look at Ariston, Périandre, Oronte,
Alcidamas, Clitandre, and Polydore;
No one denies their claim to true religion;
Yet they're no braggadocios of virtue,
They do not make insufferable display,
And their religion's human, tractable;
They are not always judging all our actions,
They'd think such judgment savoured of presumption;
And, leaving pride of words to other men,
'Tis by their deeds alone they censure ours.
Evil appearances find little credit
With them; they even incline to think the best
Of others. No caballers, no intriguers,
They mind the business of their own right living.
They don't attack a sinner tooth and nail,
For sin's the only object of their hatred;
Nor are they over-zealous to attempt
Far more in heaven's behalf than heaven would have 'em.
That is my kind of man, that is true living,
That is the pattern we should set ourselves.
Your fellow was not fashioned on this model;
You're quite sincere in boasting of his zeal;
But you're deceived, I think, by false pretences.

Orgon

My dear good brother-in-law, have you quite done?

Cléante

Yes.

Orgon

I'm your humble servant.
(*Starts to go.*)

Cléante

Just a word.
We'll drop that other subject. But you know
Valère has had the promise of your daughter.

Orgon

Yes.

Cléante

You had named the happy day.

Orgon

'Tis true.

Cléante

Then why put off the celebration of it?

Orgon

I can't say.

Cléante

Can you have some other plan
In mind?

Orgon

Perhaps.

Cléante

You mean to break your word?

Orgon

I don't say that.

Cléante

I hope no obstacle
Can keep you from performing what you've promised.

Orgon

Well, that depends.

Cléante

Why must you beat about?
Valère has sent me here to settle matters.

Orgon

Heaven be praised!

Cléante

What answer shall I take him?

Orgon

Why, anything you please.

Cléante

But we must know
Your plans. What are they?

Orgon

I shall do the will
Of Heaven.

Cléante

Come, be serious. You've given
Your promise to Valère. Now will you keep it?

Orgon

Good-bye.

Cléante (*alone*)

His love, methinks, has much to fear;
I must go let him know what's happening here.

ACT II

Scene I
Orgon, Mariane

Orgon

Now, Mariane.

Mariane

  Yes, father?

Orgon

                        Come; I'll tell you
A secret.

Mariane

    Yes . . . What are you looking for?

Orgon (looking into a small closet-room)

To see there's no one there to spy upon us;
That little closet's mighty fit to hide in.
There! We're all right now. Mariane, in you
I've always found a daughter dutiful
And gentle. So I've always loved you dearly.

Mariane

I'm grateful for your fatherly affection.

Orgon

Well spoken, daughter. Now, prove you deserve it
By doing as I wish in all respects.

Mariane

To do so is the height of my ambition.

Orgon

Excellent well. What say you of—Tartuffe?

Mariane

Who? I?

Orgon

Yes, you. Look to it how you answer.

Mariane

Why! I'll say of him—anything you please.

SCENE II

ORGON, MARIANE; DORINE (*coming in quietly and stand-ing behind* ORGON, *so that he does not see her*)

Orgon

Well spoken. A good girl. Say then, my daughter,
That all his person shines with noble merit,
That he has won your heart, and you would like
To have him, by my choice, become your husband.
Eh?

Mariane

Eh?

Orgon

What say you?

Mariane

Please, what did you say?

Orgon

What?

Mariane

Surely I mistook you, sir?

Orgon

How now?

Mariane

Who is it, father, you would have me say
Has won my heart, and I would like to have
Become my husband, by your choice?

Orgon

                                        Tartuffe.

Mariane

But, father, I protest it isn't true!
Why should you make me tell this dreadful lie?

Orgon

Because I mean to have it be the truth.
Let this suffice for you: I've settled it.

Mariane

What, father, you would . . . ?

Orgon

                              Yes, child, I'm resolved
To graft Tartuffe into my family.
So he must be your husband. That I've settled.
And since your duty . . .

(Seeing DORINE*)*

                              What are you doing there?
Your curiosity is keen, my girl,
To make you come eavesdropping on us so.

Dorine

Upon my word, I don't know how the rumour
Got started—if 'twas guess-work or mere chance—
But I had heard already of this match,
And treated it as utter stuff and nonsense.

Orgon

What! Is the thing incredible?

Dorine

So much so
I don't believe it even from yourself, sir.

Orgon

I know a way to make you credit it.

Dorine

No, no, you're telling us a fairy tale!

Orgon

I'm telling you just what will happen shortly.

Dorine

Stuff!

Orgon

Daughter, what I say is in good earnest.

Dorine

There, there, don't take your father seriously;
He's fooling.

Orgon

But I tell you . . .

Dorine

No. No use.
They won't believe you.

Orgon

If I let my anger . . .

Dorine

Well, then, we do believe you; and the worse

For you it is. What! Can a grown-up man
With that expanse of beard across his face
Be mad enough to want . . . ?

Orgon

                              You hark to me:
You've taken on yourself here in this house
A sort of free familiarity
That I don't like, I tell you frankly, girl.

Dorine

There, there, let's not get angry, sir, I beg you.
But are you making game of everybody?
Your daughter's not cut out for bigot's meat;
And he has more important things to think of.
Besides, what can you gain by such a match?
How can a man of wealth, like you, go choose
A wretched vagabond for son-in-law?

Orgon

You hold your tongue. And know, the less he has,
The better cause have we to honour him.
His poverty is honest poverty;
It should exalt him more than worldly grandeur,
For he has let himself be robbed of all,
Through careless disregard of temporal things
And fixed attachment to the things eternal.
My help may set him on his feet again,
Win back his property—a fair estate
He has at home, so I'm informed—and prove him
For what he is, a true-born gentleman.

Dorine

Yes, so he says himself. Such vanity
But ill accords with pious living, sir.
The man who cares for holiness alone
Should not so loudly boast his name and birth;

The humble ways of genuine devoutness
Brook not so much display of earthly pride.
Why should he be so vain? . . . But I offend you:
Let's leave his rank, then,—take the man himself:
Can you without compunction give a man
Like him possession of a girl like her?
Think what a scandal's sure to come of it!
Virtue is at the mercy of the fates,
When a girl's married to a man she hates;
The best intent to live an honest woman
Depends upon the husband's being human,
And men whose brows are pointed at afar
May thank themselves their wives are what they **are.**
For to be true is more than woman can,
With husbands built upon a certain plan;
And he who weds his child against her will
Owes heaven account for it, if she do ill.
Think then what perils wait on your design.

Orgon (*to* MARIANE)

So! I must learn what's what from her, you see!

Dorine

You might do worse than follow my advice.

Orgon

Daughter, we can't waste time upon this nonsense;
I know what's good for you, and I'm your father.
True, I had promised you to young Valère;
But, first, they tell me he's inclined to gamble,
And then, I fear his faith is not quite sound.
I haven't noticed that he's regular
At church.

Dorine

       You'd have him run there just when **you do.**
Like those who go on purpose to be seen?

Orgon

I don't ask your opinion on the matter.
In short, the other is in Heaven's best graces,
And that is riches quite beyond compare.
This match will bring you every joy you long for;
'Twill be all steeped in sweetness and delight.
You'll live together, in your faithful loves,
Like two sweet children, like two turtle-doves;
You'll never fail to quarrel, scold, or tease,
And you may do with him whate'er you please.

Dorine

With him? Do naught but give him horns, I'll warrant.

Orgon

Out on thee, wench!

Dorine

           I tell you he's cut out for't;
However great your daughter's virtue, sir,
His destiny is sure to prove the stronger.

Orgon

Have done with interrupting. Hold your tongue.
Don't poke your nose in other people's business.

Dorine (*She keeps interrupting him, just as he turns and starts to speak to his daughter*).

If I make bold, sir, 'tis for your own good.

Orgon

You're too officious; pray you, hold your tongue.

Dorine

'Tis love of you . . .

Orgon

           I want none of your love.

Dorine

Then I will love you in your own despite.

Orgon

You will, eh?

Dorine

Yes, your honour's dear to me;
I can't endure to see you made the butt
Of all men's ridicule.

Orgon

Won't you be still?

Dorine

'Twould be a sin to let you make this match.

Orgon

Won't you be still, I say, you impudent viper!

Dorine

What! you are pious, and you lose your temper?

Orgon

I'm all wrought up, with your confounded nonsense;
Now, once for all, I tell you hold your tongue.

Dorine

Then mum's the word; I'll take it out in thinking.

Orgon

Think all you please; but not a syllable
To me about it, or . . . you understand!

(*Turning to his daughter.*)
As a wise father, I've considered all
With due deliberation.

Dorine

I'll go mad

If I can't speak.

(*She stops the instant he turns his head.*)

Orgon

Though he's no lady's man,

Tartuffe is well enough . . .

Dorine

A pretty phiz!

Orgon

So that, although you may not care at all

For his best qualities . . .

Dorine

A handsome dowry!

(*Orgon turns and stands in front of her, with
arms folded, eyeing her.*)

Were I in her place, any man should rue it

Who married me by force, that's mighty certain;

I'd let him know, and that within a week,

A woman's vengeance isn't far to seek.

Orgon (*to* Dorine)

So—nothing that I say has any weight?

Dorine

Eh? What's wrong now? I didn't speak to you.

Orgon

What were you doing?

Dorine

Talking to myself.

Orgon

Oh! Very well. (*Aside.*) Her monstrous impudence
Must be chastised with one good slap in the face.

(*He stands ready to strike her, and, each time he speaks
to his daughter, he glances toward her; but she stands
still and says not a word.*)[3]

Orgon

Daughter, you must approve of my design. . . .
Think of this husband . . . I have chosen for you. . .

(*To* Dorine)

Why don't you talk to yourself?

Dorine

Nothing to say.

Orgon

One little word more.

Dorine

Oh, no, thanks. Not now.

Orgon

Sure, I'd have caught you.

Dorine

Faith, I'm no such fool.

[3] As given at the Comédie française, the action is as follows: While Orgon says,
"You must approve of my design," Dorine is making signs to Mariane to resist his
orders; Orgon turns around suddenly; but Dorine quickly changes her gesture and
with the hand which she had lifted calmly arranges her hair and her cap. Orgon
goes on, "Think of the husband . . ." and stops before the middle of his sentence
to turn and catch the beginning of Dorine's gesture; but he is too quick this time,
and Dorine stands looking at his furious countenance with a sweet and gentle expression. He turns and goes on, and the obstinate Dorine again lifts her hand behind his
shoulder to urge Mariane to resistance: this time he catches her; but just as he swings
his shoulder to give her the promised blow, she stops him by changing the intent of
her gesture, and carefully picking from the top of his sleeve a bit of fluff which she
holds carefully between her fingers, then blows into the air, and watches intently as it
floats away. Orgon is paralysed by her innocence of expression, and compelled to hide
his rage.—Régnier, *Le Tartuffe des Comédiens.*

Orgon

So, daughter, now obedience is the word;
You must accept my choice with reverence.

Dorine (*running away*)

You'd never catch me marrying such a creature.

Orgon (*swinging his hand at her and missing her*)

Daughter, you've such a pestilent hussy there
I can't live with her longer, without sin.
I can't discuss things in the state I'm in.
My mind's so flustered by her insolent talk,
To calm myself, I must go take a walk.

Scene III

Mariane, Dorine

Dorine

Say, have you lost the tongue from out your head?
And must I speak your rôle from A to Zed?
You let them broach a project that's absurd,
And don't oppose it with a single word!

Mariane

What can I do? My father is the master.

Dorine

Do? Everything, to ward off such disaster.

Mariane

But what?

Dorine

Tell him one doesn't love by proxy;
Tell him you'll marry for yourself, not him;
Since you're the one for whom the thing is done,
You are the one, not he, the man must please;

If his Tartuffe has charmed him so, why let him
Just marry him himself—no one will hinder.

Mariane

A father's rights are such, it seems to me,
That I could never dare to say a word.

Dorine

Come, talk it out. Valère has asked your hand:
Now do you love him, pray, or do you not?

Mariane

Dorine! How can you wrong my love so much,
And ask me such a question? Have I not
A hundred times laid bare my heart to you?
Do you not know how ardently I love him?

Dorine

How do I know if heart and words agree,
And if in honest truth you really love him?

Mariane

Dorine, you wrong me greatly if you doubt it;
I've shown my inmost feelings, all too plainly.

Dorine

So then, you love him?

Mariane

Yes, devotedly.

Dorine

And he returns your love, apparently?

Mariane

I think so.

Dorine

And you both alike are eager
To be well married to each other?

Mariane

Surely.

Dorine

Then what's your plan about this other match?

Mariane

To kill myself, if it is forced upon **me.**

Dorine

Good! That's a remedy I hadn't thought of.
Just die, and everything will be all right.
This medicine is marvellous, indeed!
It drives me mad to hear folk talk such nonsense.

Mariane

Oh dear, Dorine, you get in such a temper!
You have no sympathy for people's troubles.

Dorine

I have no sympathy when folk talk nonsense,
And flatten out as you do, at a pinch.

Mariane

But what can you expect?—if one is timid?—

Dorine

But what is love worth, if it has no courage?

Mariane

Am I not constant in my love for him?
Is't not his place to win me from my father?

Dorine

But if your father is a crazy fool,
And quite bewitched with his Tartuffe? And breaks
His bounden word? Is that your lover's fault?

Mariane

But shall I publicly refuse and scorn
This match, and make it plain that I'm in love?
Shall I cast off for him, whate'er he be,
Womanly modesty and filial duty?
You ask me to display my love in public . . . ?

Dorine

No, no, I ask you nothing. You shall be
Mister Tartuffe's; why, now I think of it,
I should be wrong to turn you from this marriage.
What cause can I have to oppose your wishes?
So fine a match! An excellent good match!
Mister Tartuffe! Oh ho! No mean proposal!
Mister Tartuffe, sure, take it all in all,
Is not a man to sneeze at—oh, by no means!
'Tis no small luck to be his happy spouse.
The whole world joins to sing his praise already;
He's noble—in his parish; handsome too;
Red ears and high complexion—oh, my lud!
You'll be too happy, sure, with him for husband.

Mariane

Oh dear! . . .

Dorine

What joy and pride will fill your heart
To be the bride of such a handsome fellow!

Mariane

Oh, stop, I beg you; try to find some way
To help break off the match. I quite give in,
I'm ready to do anything you say.

Dorine

No, no, a daughter must obey her father,
Though he should want to make her wed a monkey.
Besides, your fate is fine. What could be better!
You'll take the stage-coach to his little village,
And find it full of uncles and of cousins,
Whose conversation will delight you. Then
You'll be presented in their best society.
You'll even go to call, by way of welcome,
On Mrs. Bailiff, Mrs. Tax-Collector,
Who'll patronise you with a folding-stool.
There, once a year, at carnival, you'll have—
Perhaps—a ball; with orchestra—two bag-pipes;
And sometimes a trained ape, and Punch and Judy;
Though if your husband . . .

Mariane

Oh, you'll kill me. Please
Contrive to help me out with your advice.

Dorine

I thank you kindly.

Mariane

Oh! Dorine, I beg you . . .

Dorine

To serve you right, this marriage must go through.

Mariane

Dear girl!

Dorine

No.

Mariane

If I say I love Valère . . .

Dorine

No, no. Tartuffe's your man, and you shall taste him.

Mariane

You know I've always trusted you; now help me . . .

Dorine

No, you shall be, my faith! Tartuffified.

Mariane

Well, then, since you've no pity for my fate
Let me take counsel only of despair;
It will advise and help and give me courage;
There's one sure cure, I know, for all my troubles.

(*She starts to go.*)

Dorine

There, there! Come back. I can't be angry long.
I must take pity on you, after all.

Mariane

Oh, don't you see, Dorine, if I must bear
This martyrdom, I certainly shall die.

Dorine

Now don't you fret. We'll surely find some way.
To hinder this . . . But here's Valère, your lover.

SCENE IV
VALÈRE, MARIANE, DORINE

Valère

Madam, a piece of news—quite new to me—
Has just come out, and very fine it is.

Mariane

What piece of news?

Valère

Your marriage with Tartuffe.

Mariane

'Tis true my father has this plan in mind.

Valère

Your father, madam . . .

Mariane

Yes, he's changed his plans,
And did but now propose it to me.

Valère

What!

Seriously?

Mariane

Yes, he was serious,
And openly insisted on the match.

Valère

And what's your resolution in the matter,
Madam?

Mariane

I don't know.

Valère

That's a pretty answer.

You don't know?

Mariane

No.

Valère

No?

Mariane

What do you advise?

Valère

I? My advice is, marry him, by all means.

Mariane

That's your advice?

Valère

Yes.

Mariane

Do you mean it?

Valère

Surely.

A splendid choice, and worthy your acceptance.

Mariane

Oh, very well, sir! I shall take your counsel.

Valère

You'll find no trouble taking it, I warrant.

Mariane

No more than you did giving it, be sure.

Valère

I gave it, truly, to oblige you, madam.

Mariane

And I shall take it to oblige you, sir.

Dorine (withdrawing to the back of the stage)

Let's see what this affair will come to.

Valère

So,

That is your love? And it was all deceit
When you . . .

Mariane

                I beg you, say no more of that.
You told me, squarely, sir, I should accept
The husband that is offered me; and I
Will tell you squarely that I mean to do so,
Since you have given me this good advice.

Valère

Don't shield yourself with talk of my advice.
You had your mind made up, that's evident;
And now you're snatching at a trifling pretext
To justify the breaking of your word.

Mariane

Exactly so.

Valère

           Of course it is; your heart
Has never known true love for me.

Mariane

                        Alas!
You're free to think so, if you please.

Valère

                        Yes, yes,
I'm free to think so; and my outraged love
May yet forestall you in your perfidy,
And offer elsewhere both my heart and hand.

Mariane

No doubt of it; the love your high deserts
May win . . .

Valère

              Good Lord, have done with my deserts!
I know I have but few, and you have proved it.
But I may find more kindness in another;

I know of someone, who'll not be ashamed
To take your leavings, and make up my loss.

Mariane

The loss is not so great; you'll easily
Console yourself completely for this change.

Valère

I'll try my best, that you may well believe.
When we're forgotten by a woman's heart,
Our pride is challenged; we, too, must forget;
Or if we cannot, must at least pretend to.
No other way can man such baseness prove,
As be a lover scorned, and still in love.

Mariane

In faith, a high and noble sentiment.

Valère

Yes; and it's one that all men must approve.
What! Would you have me keep my love alive,
And see you fly into another's arms
Before my very eyes; and never offer
To someone else the heart that you had scorned?

Mariane

Oh, no, indeed! For my part, I could wish
That it were done already.

Valère

What! You wish it?

Mariane

Yes.

Valère

This is insult heaped on injury;
I'll go at once and do as you desire.
(*He takes a step or two as if to go away.*)

Mariane

Oh, very well then.

Valère (turning back)
                But remember this.
'Twas you that drove me to this desperate pass.

Mariane

Of course.

Valère (turning back again)
                And in the plan that I have formed
I only follow your example.

Mariane

                                Yes.

Valère (at the door)
Enough; you shall be punctually obeyed.

Mariane

So much the better.

Valère (coming back again)
                This is once for all.

Mariane

So be it, then.

*Valère (He goes toward the door, but just as he reaches
            it, turns around)*
    Eh?

Mariane
        What?

Valère
            You didn't call me?

Mariane
I? You are dreaming.

Valère

Very well, I'm gone.
Madam, farewell.

(*He walks slowly away.*)

Mariane

Farewell, sir.

Dorine

I must say
You've lost your senses and both gone clean daft!
I've let you fight it out to the end o' the chapter
To see how far the thing could go. Oho, there,
Mister Valère!

(*She goes and seizes him by the arm, to stop him. He makes a great show of resistance.*)

Valère

What do you want, Dorine?

Dorine

Come here.

Valère

No, no, I'm quite beside myself.
Don't hinder me from doing as she wishes.

Dorine

Stop!

Valère

No. You see, I'm fixed, resolved, determined.

Dorine

So!

Mariane (*aside*)

Since my presence pains him, makes him go,
I'd better go myself, and leave him free.

Dorine (*leaving* VALÈRE, *and running after* MARIANE)
Now t'other! Where are you going?

Mariane

Let me be.

Dorine

Come back.

Mariane
No, no, it isn't any use.

Valère (*aside*)
'Tis clear the sight of me is torture to her;
No doubt, t'were better I should free her from it.

Dorine (*leaving* MARIANE *and running after* VALÈRE)
Same thing again! Deuce take you both, I say.
Now stop your fooling; come here, you; and you.

(*She pulls first one, then the other, toward the middle
  of the stage.*)

Valère (*to* DORINE)
What's your idea?

Mariane (*to* DORINE)
What can you mean to do?

Dorine
Set you to rights, and pull you out o' the scrape.

(*To* VALÈRE)
Are you quite mad, to quarrel with her now?

Valère
Didn't you hear the things she said to me?

Dorine (*to* MARIANE)
Are you quite mad, to get in such a passion?

Mariane

Didn't you see the way he treated me?

Dorine

Fools, both of you.

(*To* VALÈRE)

She thinks of nothing else
But to keep faith with you, I vouch for it.

(*To* MARIANE)

And he loves none but you, and longs for nothing
But just to marry you, I stake my life on't.

Mariane (*to* VALÈRE)

Why did you give me such advice then, pray?

Valère (*to* MARIANE)

Why ask for my advice on such a matter?

Dorine

You both are daft, I tell you. Here, your hands.

(*To* VALÈRE)

Come, yours.

Valère (*giving* DORINE *his hand*)

What for?

Dorine (*to* MARIANE)

Now, yours.

Mariane (*giving* DORINE *her hand*)

But what's the use?

Dorine

Oh, quick now, come along. There, both of you—
You love each other better than you think.

(VALÈRE *and* MARIANE *hold each other's hands some
time without looking at each other.*)

Valère (*at last turning toward* MARIANE)

Come, don't be so ungracious now about it;
Look at a man as if you didn't hate him.

(MARIANE *looks sideways toward* VALÈRE, *with just a bit of a smile.*)

Dorine

My faith and troth, what fools these lovers be!

Valère (*to* MARIANE)

But come now, have I not a just complaint?
And truly, are you not a wicked creature
To take delight in saying what would pain me?

Mariane

And are you not yourself the most ungrateful . . . ?

Dorine

Leave this discussion till another time;
Now, think how you'll stave off this plaguey marriage.

Mariane

Then tell us how to go about it.

Dorine

Well,
We'll try all sorts of ways.

(*To* MARIANE)

Your father's daft;

(*To* VALÈRE)

This plan is nonsense.

(*To* MARIANE)

You had better humour
His notions by a semblance of consent,

So that in case of danger, you can still
Find means to block the marriage by delay.
If you gain time, the rest is easy, trust me.
One day you'll fool them with a sudden illness,
Causing delay; another day, ill omens:
You've met a funeral, or broke a mirror,
Or dreamed of muddy water. Best of all,
They cannot marry you to anyone
Without your saying yes. But now, methinks,
They mustn't find you chattering together.

(*To* VALÈRE)

You, go at once and set your friends at work
To make him keep his word to you; while we
Will bring the brother's influence to bear,
And get the step-mother on our side, too.
Good-bye.

Valère (*to* MARIANE)
Whatever efforts we may make,
My greatest hope, be sure, must rest on you.

Mariane (*to* VALÈRE)
I cannot answer for my father's whims;
But no one save Valère shall ever have me.

Valère
You thrill me through with joy! Whatever comes . . .

Dorine
Oho! These lovers! Never done with prattling!
Now go.

Valère (*starting to go, and coming back again*)
One last word . . .

Dorine
What a gabble and pother!
Be off! By this door, you. And you, by t'other.
(*She pushes them off, by the shoulders, in opposite
directions.*)

ACT III

Scene I
Damis, Dorine

Damis

May lightning strike me dead this very instant,
May I be everywhere proclaimed a scoundrel,
If any reverence or power shall stop me,
And if I don't do straightway something desperate!

Dorine

I beg you, moderate this towering passion;
Your father did but merely mention it.
Not all things that are talked of turn to facts;
The road is long, sometimes, from plans to acts.

Damis

No, I must end this paltry fellow's plots,
And he shall hear from me a truth or two.

Dorine

So ho! Go slow now. Just you leave the fellow—
Your father too—in your step-mother's hands.
She has some influence with this Tartuffe,
He makes a point of heeding all she says,
And I suspect that he is fond of her.
Would God 'twere true!—'Twould be the height of
        humour
Now, she has sent for him, in your behalf,
To sound him on this marriage, to find out
What his ideas are, and to show him plainly
What troubles he may cause, if he persists
In giving countenance to this design.
His man says, he's at prayers, I mustn't see him,
But likewise says, he'll presently be down.
So off with you, and let me wait for him.

Damis

I may be present at this interview.

Dorine

No, no! They must be left alone.

Damis

                     I won't

So much as speak to him.

Dorine

              Go on! We know you
And your high tantrums. Just the way to spoil things!
Be off.

Damis

    No, I must see—I'll keep my temper.

Dorine

Out on you, what a plague! He's coming. Hide!
   (DAMIS *goes and hides in the closet at the back
     of the stage.*)

SCENE II

TARTUFFE, DORINE

*Tartuffe (speaking to his valet, off the stage, as soon as
he sees* DORINE *is there*)

Lawrence, put up my hair-cloth shirt and scourge,
And pray that Heaven may shed its light upon you.
If any come to see me, say I'm gone
To share my alms among the prisoners.

Dorine (aside)

What affectation and what showing off!

Tartuffe

What do you want with me?

Dorine

To tell you . . .

Tartuffe (*taking a handkerchief from his pocket*)

Ah!

Before you speak, pray take this handkerchief.

Dorine

What?

Tartuffe

Cover up that bosom, which I can't
Endure to look on. Things like that offend
Our souls, and fill our minds with sinful thoughts.

Dorine

Are you so tender to temptation, then,
And has the flesh such power upon your senses?
I don't know how you get in such a heat;
For my part, I am not so prone to lust,
And I could see you stripped from head to foot,
And all your hide not tempt me in the least.

Tartuffe

Show in your speech some little modesty,
Or I must instantly take leave of you.

Dorine

No, no, I'll leave you to yourself; I've only
One thing to say: Madam will soon be down,
And begs the favour of a word with you.

Tartuffe

Ah! Willingly.

Dorine (*aside*)

How gentle all at once!
My faith, I still believe I've hit upon it.

Tartuffe

Will she come soon?

Dorine

            I think I hear her now.
Yes, here she is herself; I'll leave you with her.

Scene III
Elmire, Tartuffe

Tartuffe

May Heaven's overflowing kindness ever
Give you good health of body and of soul,
And bless your days according to the wishes
And prayers of its most humble votary!

Elmire

I'm very grateful for your pious wishes.
But let's sit down, so we may talk at ease.

Tartuffe (*after sitting down*)

And how are you recovered from your illness?

Elmire (*sitting down also*)

Quite well; the fever soon let go its hold.

Tartuffe

My prayers, I fear, have not sufficient merit
To have drawn down this favour from on high;
But each entreaty that I made to Heaven
Had for its object your recovery.

Elmire

You're too solicitous on my behalf.

Tartuffe

We could not cherish your dear health too much;
I would have given mine, to help restore it.

Elmire

That's pushing Christian charity too far;
I owe you many thanks for so much kindness.

Tartuffe

I do far less for you than you deserve.

Elmire

There is a matter that I wished to speak of
In private; I am glad there's no one here
To listen.

Tartuffe

      Madam, I am overjoyed.
'Tis sweet to find myself alone with you.
This is an opportunity I've asked
Of Heaven, many a time; till now, in vain.

Elmire

All that I wish, is just a word from you,
Quite frank and open, hiding nothing from me.

    (DAMIS, *without their seeing him, opens the closet door*
      halfway.)

Tartuffe

I too could wish, as Heaven's especial favour,
To lay my soul quite open to your eyes,
And swear to you, the trouble that I made
About those visits which your charms attract,
Does not result from any hatred toward you,
But rather from a passionate devotion,
And purest motives . . .

Elmire

        That is how I take it,
I think 'tis my salvation that concerns you.

Tartuffe (*pressing her finger tips*)

Madam, 'tis so; and such is my devotion . . .

Elmire

Ouch! but you squeeze too hard.

Tartuffe

Excess of zeal.
In no way could I ever mean to hurt you,
And I'd as soon . . .

(*He puts his hand on her knee.*)

Elmire

What's your hand doing there?

Tartuffe

Feeling your gown; the stuff is very soft.

Elmire

Let be, I beg you; I am very ticklish.

(*She moves her chair away, and* TARTUFFE *brings his
nearer.*)

Tartuffe (*handling the lace yoke of* ELMIRE's *dress*)

Dear me how wonderful in workmanship
This lace is! They do marvels, nowadays;
Things of all kinds were never better made.

Elmire

Yes, very true. But let us come to business.
They say my husband means to break his word.
And marry Mariane to you. Is't so?

Tartuffe

He did hint some such thing; but truly, madam,
That's not the happiness I'm yearning after;
I see elsewhere the sweet compelling charms
Of such a joy as fills my every wish.

Elmire

You mean you cannot love terrestrial things.

Tartuffe

The heart within my bosom is not stone.

Elmire

I well believe your sighs all tend to Heaven,
And nothing here below can stay your thoughts.

Tartuffe

Love for the beauty of eternal things
Cannot destroy our love for earthly beauty;
Our mortal senses well may be entranced
By perfect works that Heaven has fashioned here.
Its charms reflected shine in such as you,
And in yourself, its rarest miracles;
It has displayed such marvels in your face,
That eyes are dazed, and hearts are rapt away;
I could not look on you, the perfect creature,
Without admiring Nature's great Creator,
And feeling all my heart inflamed with love
For you, His fairest image of Himself.
At first I trembled lest this secret love
Might be the Evil Spirit's artful snare;
I even schooled my heart to flee your beauty,
Thinking it was a bar to my salvation.
But soon, enlightened, O all lovely one,
I saw how this my passion may be blameless,
How I may make it fit with modesty,
And thus completely yield my heart to it.
'Tis, I must own, a great presumption in me
To dare make you the offer of my heart;
My love hopes all things from your perfect goodness,
And nothing from my own poor weak endeavour.
You are my hope, my stay, my peace of heart;
On you depends my torment or my bliss;

And by your doom of judgment, I shall be
Blest, if you will; or damned, by your decree.

Elmire

Your declaration's turned most gallantly;
But truly, it is just a bit surprising.
You should have better armed your heart, methinks,
And taken thought somewhat on such a matter.
A pious man like you, known everywhere . . .

Tartuffe

Though pious, I am none the less a man;
And when a man beholds your heavenly charms,
The heart surrenders, and can think no more.
I know such words seem strange, coming from me;
But, madam, I'm no angel, after all;
If you condemn my frankly made avowal
You only have your charming self to blame.
Soon as I saw your more than human beauty,
You were thenceforth the sovereign of my soul;
Sweetness ineffable was in your eyes,
That took by storm my still resisting heart,
And conquered everything, fasts, prayers, and tears,
And turned my worship wholly to yourself.
My looks, my sighs, have spoke a thousand times;
Now, to express it all, my voice must speak.
If but you will look down with gracious favour
Upon the sorrows of your worthless slave,
If in your goodness you will give me comfort
And condescend unto my nothingness,
I'll ever pay you, O sweet miracle,
An unexampled worship and devotion.
Then too, with me your honour runs no risk;
With me you need not fear a public scandal.
These court gallants, that women are so fond of,
Are boastful of their acts, and vain in speech;

They always brag in public of their progress;
Soon as a favour's granted, they'll divulge it;
Their tattling tongues, if you but trust to them,
Will foul the altar where their hearts have worshipped.
But men like me are so discreet in love,
That you may trust their lasting secrecy.
The care we take to guard our own good name
May fully guarantee the one we love;
So you may find, with hearts like ours sincere,
Love without scandal, pleasure without fear.

Elmire

I've heard you through—your speech is clear, at least.
But don't you fear that I may take a fancy
To tell my husband of your gallant passion,
And that a prompt report of this affair
May somewhat change the friendship which he bears you?

Tartuffe

I know that you're too good and generous,
That you will pardon my temerity,
Excuse, upon the score of human frailty,
The violence of passion that offends you,
And not forget, when you consult your mirror,
That I'm not blind, and man is made of flesh.

Elmire

Some women might do otherwise, perhaps,
But I am willing to employ discretion,
And not repeat the matter to my husband;
But in return, I'll ask one thing of you:
That you urge forward, frankly and sincerely,
The marriage of Valère to Mariane;
That you give up the unjust influence
By which you hope to win another's rights;
And . . .

Scene IV

Elmire, Damis, Tartuffe

Damis (coming out of the closet-room where he had been hiding)

No, I say! This thing must be made public.
I was just there, and overheard it all;
And Heaven's goodness must have brought me there
On purpose to confound this scoundrel's pride
And grant me means to take a signal vengeance
On his hypocrisy and arrogance,
And undeceive my father, showing up
The rascal caught at making love to you.

Elmire

No, no; it is enough if he reforms,
Endeavouring to deserve the favour shown him.
And since I've promised, do not you belie me.
'Tis not my way to make a public scandal;
An honest wife will scorn to heed such follies,
And never fret her husband's ears with them.

Damis

You've reasons of your own for acting thus;
And I have mine for doing otherwise.
To spare him now would be a mockery;
His bigot's pride has triumphed all too long
Over my righteous anger, and has caused
Far too much trouble in our family.
The rascal all too long has ruled my father,
And crossed my sister's love, and mine as well.
The traitor now must be unmasked before him:
And Providence has given me means to do it.
To Heaven I owe the opportunity,
And if I did not use it now I have it,
I should deserve to lose it once for all.

Elmire

Damis . . .

Damis

       No, by your leave; I'll not be counselled.
I'm overjoyed. You needn't try to tell me
I must give up the pleasure of revenge.
I'll make an end of this affair at once;
And, to content me, here's my father now.

Scene V

Orgon, Elmire, Damis, Tartuffe

Damis

Father, we've news to welcome your arrival,
That's altogether novel, and surprising.
You are well paid for your caressing care,
And this fine gentleman rewards your love
Most handsomely, with zeal that seeks no less
Than your dishonour, as has now been proven.
I've just surprised him making to your wife
The shameful offer of a guilty love.
She, somewhat over gentle and discreet,
Insisted that the thing should be concealed;
But I will not condone such shamelessness,
Nor so far wrong you as to keep it secret.

Elmire

Yes, I believe a wife should never trouble
Her husband's peace of mind with such vain gossip;
A woman's honour does not hang on telling;
It is enough if she defend herself;
Or so I think; Damis, you'd not have spoken,
If you would but have heeded my advice.

Scene VI
Orgon, Damis, Tartuffe

Orgon

Just Heaven! Can what I hear be credited?

Tartuffe

Yes, brother, I am wicked, I am guilty,
A miserable sinner, steeped in evil,
The greatest criminal that ever lived.
Each moment of my life is stained with soilures;
And all is but a mass of crime and filth;
Heaven, for my punishment, I see it plainly,
Would mortify me now. Whatever wrong
They find to charge me with, I'll not deny it
But guard against the pride of self-defence.
Believe their stories, arm your wrath against me,
And drive me like a villain from your house;
I cannot have so great a share of shame
But what I have deserved a greater still.

Orgon (*to his son*)

You miscreant, can you dare, with such a falsehood,
To try to stain the whiteness of his virtue?

Damis

What! The feigned meekness of this hypocrite
Makes you discredit . . .

Orgon

                Silence, cursèd plague!

Tartuffe

Ah! Let him speak; you chide him wrongfully;
You'd do far better to believe his tales.
Why favour me so much in such a matter?

How can you know of what I'm capable?
And should you trust my outward semblance, brother,
Or judge therefrom that I'm the better man?
No, no; you let appearances deceive you;
I'm anything but what I'm thought to be,
Alas! and though all men believe me godly,
The simple truth is, I'm a worthless creature.

(*To* DAMIS)

Yes, my dear son, say on, and call me traitor,
Abandoned scoundrel, thief, and murderer;
Heap on me names yet more detestable,
And I shall not gainsay you; I've deserved them;
I'll bear this ignominy on my knees,
To expiate in shame the crimes I've done.

Orgon (*to* TARTUFFE)

Ah, brother, 'tis too much!

(*To his son*)

You'll not relent,
You blackguard?

Damis

What! His talk can so deceive you . . .

Orgon

Silence, you scoundrel!

(*To* TARTUFFE)

Brother, rise, I beg you.

(*To his son*)

Infamous villain!

Damis

Can he . . .

Orgon

Silence!

Damis

What . . .

Orgon

Another word, I'll break your every bone.

Tartuffe

Brother, in God's name, don't be angry with him!
I'd rather bear myself the bitterest torture
Than have him get a scratch on my account.

Orgon (*to his son*)

Ungrateful monster!

Tartuffe

Stop. Upon my knees
I beg you pardon him . . .

Orgon (*throwing himself on his knees too, and embracing* Tartuffe)

Alas! How can you?

(*To his son*)

Villain! Behold his goodness!

Damis

So . . .

Orgon

Be still.

Damis

What! I . . .

Orgon

Be still, I say. I know your motives
For this attack. You hate him, all of you;
Wife, children, servants, all let loose upon him,
You have recourse to every shameful trick
To drive this godly man out of my house;
The more you strive to rid yourselves of him,
The more I'll strive to make him stay with me;
I'll have him straightway married to my daughter,
Just to confound the pride of all of you.

Damis

What! Will you force her to accept his hand?

Orgon

Yes, and this very evening, to enrage you,
Young rascal! Ah! I'll brave you all, and show you
That I'm the master, and must be obeyed.
Now, down upon your knees this instant, rogue,
And take back what you said, and ask his pardon.

Damis

Who? I? Ask pardon of that cheating scoundrel . . . ?

Orgon

Do you resist, you beggar, and insult him?
A cudgel, here! a cudgel!

(*To* TARTUFFE)

Don't restrain me.

(*To his son*)

Off with you! Leave my house this instant, sirrah,
And never dare set foot in it again.

Damis

Yes, I will leave your house, but . . .

Orgon

                                        Leave it quickly.

You reprobate, I disinherit you,
And give you, too, my curse into the bargain.

SCENE VII

ORGON, TARTUFFE

Orgon

What! So insult a saintly man of God!

Tartuffe

Heaven, forgive him all the pain he gives me![4]

(*To* ORGON)

Could you but know with what distress I see
Them try to vilify me to my brother!

Orgon

Ah!

Tartuffe

            The mere thought of such ingratitude
Makes my soul suffer torture, bitterly . . .
My horror at it . . . Ah! my heart's so full
I cannot speak . . . I think I'll die of it.

Orgon (*in tears, running to the door through
        which he drove away his son*)

Scoundrel! I wish I'd never let you go,
But slain you on the spot with my own hand.

---

[4] Some modern editions have adopted the reading, preserved by tradition as that
of the earliest stage version:

            Heaven, forgive him even as I forgive him!

Voltaire gives still another reading:

            Heaven, forgive me even as I forgive him!

Whichever was the original version, it appears in none of the early editions, and
Molière probably felt forced to change it on account of its too close resemblance to
the Biblical phrase.

(*To* Tartuffe)

Brother, compose yourself, and don't be angry.

Tartuffe

Nay, brother, let us end these painful quarrels.
I see what troublous times I bring upon you,
And think 'tis needful that I leave this house.

Orgon

What! You can't mean it?

Tartuffe

                          Yes, they hate me here,
And try, I find, to make you doubt my faith.

Orgon

What of it? Do you find I listen to them?

Tartuffe

No doubt they won't stop there. These same reports
You now reject, may some day win a hearing.

Orgon

No, brother, never.

Tartuffe

               Ah! my friend, a woman
May easily mislead her husband's mind.

Orgon

No, no.

Tartuffe

            So let me quickly go away
And thus remove all cause for such attacks.

Orgon

No, you shall stay; my life depends upon it.

Tartuffe

Then I must mortify myself. And yet,
If you should wish . . .

Orgon

No, never!

Tartuffe

Very well, then;
No more of that. But I shall rule my conduct
To fit the case. Honour is delicate,
And friendship binds me to forestall suspicion,
Prevent all scandal, and avoid your wife.

Orgon

No, you shall haunt her, just to spite them all.
'Tis my delight to set them in a rage;
You shall be seen together at all hours
And what is more, the better to defy them,
I'll have no other heir but you; and straightway
I'll go and make a deed of gift to you,
Drawn in due form, of all my property.
A good true friend, my son-in-law to be,
Is more to me than son, and wife, and kindred.
You will accept my offer, will you not?

Tartuffe

Heaven's will be done in everything!

Orgon

Poor man!
We'll go make haste to draw the deed aright,
And then let envy burst itself with spite!

ACT IV

Scene I

Cléante, Tartuffe

Cléante

Yes, it's become the talk of all the town,
And make a stir that's scarcely to your credit;
And I have met you, sir, most opportunely,
To tell you in a word my frank opinion.
Not to sift out this scandal to the bottom,
Suppose the worst for us—suppose Damis
Acted the traitor, and accused you falsely;
Should not a Christian pardon this offence,
And stifle in his heart all wish for vengeance?
Should you permit that, for your petty quarrel,
A son be driven from his father's house?
I tell you yet again, and tell you frankly,
Everyone, high or low, is scandalised;
If you'll take my advice, you'll make it up,
And not push matters to extremities.
Make sacrifice to God of your resentment;
Restore the son to favour with his father.

Tartuffe

Alas! So far as I'm concerned, how gladly
Would I do so! I bear him no ill will;
I pardon all, lay nothing to his charge,
And wish with all my heart that I might serve him;
But Heaven's interests cannot allow it;
If he returns, then I must leave the house.
After his conduct, quite unparalleled,
All intercourse between us would bring scandal;
God knows what everyone's first thought would be!
They would attribute it to merest scheming
On my part—say that conscious of my guilt

I feigned a Christian love for my accuser,
But feared him in my heart, and hoped to win him
And underhandedly secure his silence.

Cléante

You try to put us off with specious phrases;
But all your arguments are too far-fetched.
Why take upon yourself the cause of Heaven?
Does Heaven need our help to punish sinners?
Leave to itself the care of its own vengeance,
And keep in mind the pardon it commands us;
Besides, think somewhat less of men's opinions,
When you are following the will of Heaven.
Shall petty fear of what the world may think
Prevent the doing of a noble deed?
No!—let us always do as Heaven commands,
And not perplex our brains with further questions.

Tartuffe

Already I have told you I forgive him;
And that is doing, sir, as Heaven commands.
But after this day's scandal and affront
Heaven does not order me to live with him.

Cléante

And does it order you to lend your ear
To what mere whim suggested to his father,
And to accept the gift of his estates,
On which, in justice, you can make no claim?

Tartuffe

No one who knows me, sir, can have the thought
That I am acting from a selfish motive.
The goods of this world have no charms for me;
I am not dazzled by their treacherous glamour;
And if I bring myself to take the gift
Which he insists on giving me, I do so,
To tell the truth, only because I fear

This whole estate may fall into bad hands,
And those to whom it comes may use it ill
And not employ it, as is my design,
For Heaven's glory and my neighbours' good.

Cléante

Eh, sir, give up these conscientious scruples
That well may cause a rightful heir's complaints.
Don't take so much upon yourself, but let him
Possess what's his, at his own risk and peril;
Consider, it were better he misused it,
Than you should be accused of robbing him.
I am astounded that unblushingly
You could allow such offers to be made!
Tell me—has true religion any maxim
That teaches us to rob the lawful heir?
If Heaven has made it quite impossible
Damis and you should live together here,
Were it not better you should quietly
And honourably withdraw, than let the son
Be driven out for your sake, dead against
All reason? 'Twould be giving, sir, believe me,
Such an example of your probity . . .

Tartuffe

Sir, it is half-past three; certain devotions
Recall me to my closet; you'll forgive me
For leaving you so soon.

Cléante (alone)

Ah!

Scene II

ELMIRE, MARIANE, CLÉANTE, DORINE

Dorine (to CLÉANTE)

Sir, we beg you
To help us all vou can in her behalf;

She's suffering almost more than heart can bear;
This match her father means to make to-night
Drives her each moment to despair. He's coming.
Let us unite our efforts now, we beg you,
And try by strength or skill to change his purpose.

SCENE III

ORGON, ELMIRE, MARIANE, CLÉANTE, DORINI

Orgon

So ho! I'm glad to find you all together.

(*To* MARIANE)

Here is the contract that shall make you happy,
My dear. You know already what it means.

Mariane (*on her knees before* ORGON)

Father, I beg you, in the name of Heaven
That knows my grief, and by whate'er can move you,
Relax a little your paternal rights,
And free my love from this obedience!
Oh, do not make me, by your harsh command,
Complain to Heaven you ever were my father;
Do not make wretched this poor life you gave me.
If, crossing that fond hope which I had formed,
You'll not permit me to belong to one
Whom I have dared to love, at least, I beg you
Upon my knees, oh, save me from the torment
Of being possessed by one whom I abhor!
And do not drive me to some desperate act
By exercising all your rights upon me.

Orgon (*a little touched*)

Come, come, my heart, be firm! no human weakness!

Mariane

I am not jealous of your love for him;
Display it freely; give him your estate,

And if that's not enough, add all of mine;
I willingly agree, and give it up,
If only you'll not give him me, your daughter;
Oh, rather let a convent's rigid rule
Wear out the wretched days that Heaven allots me.

Orgon

These girls are ninnies!—always turning nuns
When fathers thwart their silly love-affairs.
Get on your feet! The more you hate to have him,
The more 'twill help you earn your soul's salvation.
So, mortify your senses by this marriage,
And don't vex me about it any more.

Dorine

But what . . . ?

Orgon

   You hold your tongue, before your betters.
Don't dare to say a single word, I tell you.

Cléante

If you will let me answer, and advise . . .

Orgon

Brother, I value your advice most highly;
'Tis well thought out; no better can be had;
But you'll allow me—not to follow it.

Elmire (to her husband)

I can't find words to cope with such a case;
Your blindness makes me quite astounded at you.
You are bewitched with him, to disbelieve
The things we tell you happened here to-day.

Orgon

I am your humble servant, and can see
Things, when they're plain as noses on folks' faces,

I know you're partial to my rascal son,
And didn't dare to disavow the trick
He tried to play on this poor man; besides,
You were too calm, to be believed; if that
Had happened, you'd have been far more disturbed.

Elmire

And must our honour always rush to arms
At the mere mention of illicit love?
Or can we answer no attack upon it
Except with blazing eyes and lips of scorn?
For my part, I just laugh away such nonsense;
I've no desire to make a loud to-do.
Our virtue should, I think, be gentle-natured;
Nor can I quite approve those savage prudes
Whose honour arms itself with teeth and claws
To tear men's eyes out at the slightest word.
Heaven preserve me from that kind of honour!
I like my virtue not to be a vixen,
And I believe a quiet cold rebuff
No less effective to repulse a lover.

Orgon

I know . . . and you can't throw me off the scent.

Elmire

Once more, I am astounded at your weakness;
I wonder what your unbelief would answer,
If I should let you see we've told the truth?

Orgon

See it?

Elmire

Yes.

Orgon

Nonsense.

Elmire

Come! If I should find
A way to make you see it clear as day?

Orgon

All rubbish.

Elmire

What a man! But answer me.
I'm not proposing now that you believe us;
But let's suppose that here, from proper hiding,
You should be made to see and hear all plainly;
What would you say then, to your man of virtue?

Orgon

Why, then, I'd say . . . say nothing. It can't be.

Elmire

Your error has endured too long already,
And quite too long you've branded me a liar.
I must at once, for my own satisfaction,
Make you a witness of the things we've told you.

Orgon

Amen! I take you at your word. We'll see
What tricks you have, and how you'll keep your promise.

Elmire (*to* DORINE)

Send him to me.

Dorine (*to* ELMIRE)

The man's a crafty codger,
Perhaps you'll find it difficult to catch him.

Elmire (*to* DORINE)

Oh no! A lover's never hard to cheat,

And self-conceit leads straight to self-deceit.
Bid him come down to me.

(*To* CLÉANTE *and* MARIANE)

And you, withdraw.

SCENE IV

ELMIRE, ORGON

Elmire

Bring up this table, and get under it.

Orgon

What?

Elmire

One essential is to hide you well.

Orgon

Why under there?

Elmire

Oh, dear! Do as I say;
I know what I'm about, as you shall see.
Get under, now, I tell you; and once there
Be careful no one either sees or hears you.

Orgon

I'm going a long way to humour you,
I must say; but I'll see you through your scheme.

Elmire

And then you'll have, I think, no more to say.

(*To her husband, who is now under the table.*)

But mind, I'm going to meddle with strange matters;
Prepare yourself to be in no wise shocked.
Whatever I may say must pass, because

'Tis only to convince you, as I promised.
By wheedling speeches, since I'm forced to do it,
I'll make this hypocrite put off his mask,
Flatter the longings of his shameless passion,
And give free play to all his impudence.
But, since 'tis for your sake, to prove to you
His guilt, that I shall feign to share his love,
I can leave off as soon as you're convinced,
And things shall go no farther than you choose.
So, when you think they've gone quite far enough,
It is for you to stop his mad pursuit,
To spare your wife, and not expose me farther
Than you shall need, yourself, to undeceive you.
It is your own affair, and you must end it
When . . . Here he comes. Keep still, don't show your-
     self.

Scene V

Tartuffe, Elmire; Orgon (*under the table*)

Tartuffe

They told me that you wished to see me here.

Elmire

Yes. I have secrets for your ear alone.
But shut the door first, and look everywhere
For fear of spies.

(Tartuffe *goes and closes the door, and comes back.*)

                    We surely can't afford
Another scene like that we had just now;
Was ever anyone so caught before!
Damis did frighten me most terribly
On your account; you saw I did my best
To baffle his design, and calm his anger.
But I was so confused, I never thought
To contradict his story; still, thank Heaven,
Things turned out all the better, as it happened,

And now we're on an even safer footing.
The high esteem you're held in, laid the storm;
My husband can have no suspicion of you,
And even insists, to spite the scandal-mongers,
That we shall be together constantly;
So that is how, without the risk of blame,
I can be here locked up with you alone,
And can reveal to you my heart, perhaps
Only too ready to allow your passion.

Tartuffe

Your words are somewhat hard to understand,
Madam; just now you used a different style.

Elmire

If that refusal has offended you,
How little do you know a woman's heart!
How ill you guess what it would have you know,
When it presents so feeble a defence!
Always, at first, our modesty resists
The tender feelings you inspire us with.
Whatever cause we find to justify
The love that masters us, we still must feel
Some little shame in owning it; and strive
To make as though we would not, when we would.
But from the very way we go about it
We let a lover know our heart surrenders,
The while our lips, for honour's sake, oppose
Our heart's desire, and in refusing promise.
I'm telling you my secret all too freely
And with too little heed to modesty.
But—now that I've made bold to speak—pray tell me.
Should I have tried to keep Damis from speaking,
Should I have heard the offer of your heart
So quietly, and suffered all your pleading,
And taken it just as I did—remember—
If such a declaration had not pleased me,

And, when I tried my utmost to persuade you
Not to accept the marriage that was talked of,
What should my earnestness have hinted to you
If not the interest that you've inspired,
And my chagrin, should such a match compel me
To share a heart I want all to myself?

Tartuffe

'Tis, past a doubt, the height of happiness,
To hear such words from lips we dote upon;
Their honeyed sweetness pours through all my senses
Long draughts of suavity ineffable.
My heart employs its utmost zeal to please you,
And counts your love its one beatitude;
And yet that heart must beg that you allow it
To doubt a little its felicity.
I well might think these words an honest trick
To make me break off this approaching marriage;
And if I may express myself quite plainly,
I cannot trust these too enchanting words
Until the granting of some little favour
I sigh for, shall assure me of their truth
And build within my soul, on firm foundations,
A lasting faith in your sweet charity.

Elmire (*coughing to draw her husband's attention*)

What! Must you go so fast?—and all at once
Exhaust the whole love of a woman's heart?
She does herself the violence to make
This dear confession of her love, and you
Are not yet satisfied, and will not be
Without the granting of her utmost favours?

Tartuffe

The less a blessing is deserved, the less
We dare to hope for it; and words alone
Can ill assuage our love's desires. A fate

Too full of happiness, seems doubtful still;
We must enjoy it ere we can believe it.
And I, who know how little I deserve
Your goodness, doubt the fortunes of my daring;
So I shall trust to nothing, madam, till
You have convinced my love by something real.

Elmire

Ah! How your love enacts the tyrant's rôle,
And throws my mind into a strange confusion!
With what fierce sway it rules a conquered heart,
And violently will have its wishes granted!
What! Is there no escape from your pursuit?
No respite even?—not a breathing space?
Nay, is it decent to be so exacting,
And so abuse by urgency the weakness
You may discover in a woman's heart?

Tartuffe

But if my worship wins your gracious favour,
Then why refuse me some sure proof thereof?

Elmire

But how can I consent to what you wish,
Without offending Heaven you talk so much of?

Tartuffe

If Heaven is all that stands now in my way,
I'll easily remove that little hindrance;
Your heart need not hold back for such a trifle.

Elmire

But they affright us so with Heaven's commands!

Tartuffe

I can dispel these foolish fears, dear madam;
I know the art of pacifying scruples

Heaven forbids, 'tis true, some satisfactions;
But we find means to make things right with Heaven.

('Tis a scoundrel speaking.)[5]

There is a science, madam, that instructs us
How to enlarge the limits of our conscience
According to our various occasions,
And rectify the evil of the deed
According to our purity of motive.
I'll duly teach you all these secrets, madam;
You only need to let yourself be guided.
Content my wishes, have no fear at all;
I answer for't, and take the sin upon me.
                    (Elmire coughs still louder.)
Your cough is very bad.

Elmire

Yes, I'm in torture.

Tartuffe

Would you accept this bit of licorice?

Elmire

The case is obstinate, I find; and all
The licorice in the world will do no good.

Tartuffe

'Tis very trying.

Elmire

More than words can say.

Tartuffe

In any case, your scruple's easily
Removed. With me you're sure of secrecy,

[5] Molière's note, in the original edition.

And there's no harm unless a thing is known.
The public scandal is what brings offence,
And secret sinning is not sin at all.

Elmire (*after coughing again*)

So then, I see I must resolve to yield;
I must consent to grant you everything,
And cannot hope to give full satisfaction
Or win full confidence, at lesser cost.
No doubt 'tis very hard to come to this;
'Tis quite against my will I go so far;
But since I must be forced to it, since nothing
That can be said suffices for belief,
Since more convincing proof is still demanded,
I must make up my mind to humour people.
If my consent give reason for offence,
So much the worse for him who forced me to it;
The fault can surely not be counted mine.

Tartuffe

It need not, madam; and the thing itself . . .

Elmire

Open the door, I pray you, and just see
Whether my husband's not there, in the hall.

Tartuffe

Why take such care for him? Between ourselves,
He is a man to lead round by the nose.
He's capable of glorying in our meetings;
I've fooled him so, he'd see all, and deny it.

Elmire

No matter; go, I beg you, look about,
And carefully examine every corner.

Scene VI

Orgon, Elmire

Orgon (crawling out from under the table)

That is, I own, a man . . . abominable!
I can't get over it; the whole thing floors me.

Elmire

What? You come out so soon? You cannot mean it!
Get back under the table; 'tis not time yet;
Wait till the end, to see, and make quite certain,
And don't believe a thing on mere conjecture.

Orgon

Nothing more wicked e'er came out of Hell.

Elmire

Dear me! Don't go and credit things too lightly.
No, let yourself be thoroughly convinced;
Don't yield too soon, for fear you'll be mistaken.
          (*As* Tartuffe *enters, she makes her husband
                    stand behind her.*)

Scene VII

Tartuffe, Elmire, Orgon

Tartuffe (not seeing Orgon)

All things conspire toward my satisfaction,
Madam, I've searched the whole apartment through.
There's no one here; and now my ravished soul . . .

Orgon (stopping him)

Softly! You are too eager in your amours;
You needn't be so passionate. Ah ha!
My holy man! You want to put it on me!
How is your soul abandoned to temptation!

Marry my daughter, eh?—and want my wife, too?
I doubted long enough if this was earnest,
Expecting all the time the tone would change;
But now the proof's been carried far enough;
I'm satisfied, and ask no more, for my part.

Elmire (*to* TARTUFFE)

'Twas quite against my character to play
This part; but I was forced to treat you so.

Tartuffe

What? You believe . . . ?

Orgon

     Come, now, no protestations.
Get out from here, and make no fuss about it.

Tartuffe

But my intent . . .

Orgon

    That talk is out of season.
You leave my house this instant.

Tartuffe

       You're the one
To leave it, you who play the master here!
This house belongs to me, I'll have you know,
And show you plainly it's no use to turn
To these low tricks, to pick a quarrel with me,
And that you can't insult me at your pleasure,
For I have wherewith to confound your lies,
Avenge offended Heaven, and compel
Those to repent who talk to me of leaving.

Scene VIII

Elmire, Orgon

Elmire

What sort of speech is this? What can it mean?

Orgon

My faith, I'm dazed. This is no laughing matter.

Elmire

What?

Orgon

From his words I see my great mistake;
The deed of gift is one thing troubles me.

Elmire

The deed of gift . . .

Orgon

Yes, that is past recall.
But I've another thing to make me anxious.

Elmire

What's that?

Orgon

You shall know all. Let's see at once
Whether a certain box is still upstairs.

ACT V

Scene I

Orgon, Cléante

Cléante

Whither away so fast?

Orgon

How should I know?

Cléante

Methinks we should begin by taking counsel
To see what can be done to meet the case.

Orgon

I'm all worked up about that wretched box.
More than all else it drives me to despair.

Cléante

That box must hide some mighty mystery?

Orgon

Argas, my friend who is in trouble, brought it
Himself, most secretly, and left it with me.
He chose me, in his exile, for this trust;
And on these documents, from what he said,
I judge his life and property depend.

Cléante

How could you trust them to another's hands?

Orgon

By reason of a conscientious scruple.
I went straight to my traitor, to confide
In him; his sophistry made me believe
That I must give the box to him to keep,
So that, in case of search, I might deny
My having it at all, and still, by favour
Of this evasion, keep my conscience clear
Even in taking oath against the truth.

Cléante

Your case is bad, so far as I can see;
This deed of gift, this trusting of the secret
To him, were both—to state my frank opinion—

Steps that you took too lightly; he can lead you
To any length, with these for hostages;
And since he holds you at such disadvantage,
You'd be still more imprudent, to provoke him;
So you must go some gentler way about.

Orgon

What! Can a soul so base, a heart so false,
Hide neath the semblance of such touching fervour?
I took him in, a vagabond, a beggar! . . .
'Tis too much! No more pious folk for me!
I shall abhor them utterly forever,
And henceforth treat them worse than any devil.

Cléante

So! There you go again, quite off the handle!
In nothing do you keep an even temper.
You never know what reason is, but always
Jump first to one extreme, and then the other.
You see your error, and you recognise
That you've been cozened by a feignèd zeal;
But to make up for't, in the name of reason,
Why should you plunge into a worse mistake,
And find no difference in character
Between a worthless scamp, and all good people?
What! Just because a rascal boldly duped you
With pompous show of false austerity,
Must you needs have it everybody's like him,
And no one's truly pious nowadays?
Leave such conclusions to mere infidels;
Distinguish virtue from its counterfeit,
Don't give esteem too quickly, at a venture,
But try to keep, in this, the golden mean.
If you can help it, don't uphold imposture;
But do not rail at true devoutness, either;
And if you must fall into one extreme,
Then rather err again the other way.

Scene II

Damis, Orgon, Cléante

Damis

What! father, can the scoundrel threaten you,
Forget the many benefits received,
And in his base abominable pride
Make of your very favours arms against you?

Orgon

Too true, my son. It tortures me to think on't.

Damis

Let me alone, I'll chop his ears off for him.
We must deal roundly with his insolence;
'Tis I must free you from him at a blow;
'Tis I, to set things right, must strike him down.

Cléante

Spoke like a true young man. Now just calm down,
And moderate your towering tantrums, will you?
We live in such an age, with such a king,
That violence can not advance our cause.

Scene III

Madame Pernelle, Orgon, Elmire, Cléante, Mariane, Damis, Dorine

Madame Pernelle

What's this? I hear of fearful mysteries!

Orgon

Strange things indeed, for my own eyes to witness;
You see how I'm requited for my kindness,
I zealously receive a wretched beggar,
I lodge him, entertain him like my brother,

Load him with benefactions every day,
Give him my daughter, give him all my fortune:
And he meanwhile, the villain, rascal, wretch,
Tries with black treason to suborn my wife,
And not content with such a foul design,
He dares to menace me with my own favours,
And would make use of those advantages
Which my too foolish kindness armed him with,
To ruin me, to take my fortune from me,
And leave me in the state I saved him from.

Dorine

Poor man!

Madame Pernelle

My son, I cannot possibly
Believe he could intend so black a deed.

Orgon

What?

Madame Pernelle

Worthy men are still the sport of envy.

Orgon

Mother, what do you mean by such a speech?

Madame Pernelle

There are strange goings-on about your house,
And everybody knows your people hate him.

Orgon

What's that to do with what I tell you now?

Madame Pernelle

I always said, my son, when you were little:
That virtue here below is hated ever;
The envious may die, but envy never.

Orgon

What's that fine speech to do with present facts?

Madame Pernelle

Be sure, they've forged a hundred silly lies . . .

Orgon

I've told you once, I saw it all myself.

Madame Pernelle

For slanderers abound in calumnies . . .

Orgon

Mother, you'd make me damn my soul. I tell you
I saw with my own eyes his shamelessness.

Madame Pernelle

Their tongues for spitting venom never lack,
There's nothing here below they'll not attack.

Orgon

Your speech has not a single grain of sense.
I saw it, harkee, saw it, with these eyes
I saw—d'ye know what *saw* means?—must I say it
A hundred times, and din it in your ears?

Madame Pernelle

My dear, appearances are oft deceiving,
And seeing shouldn't always be believing.

Orgon

I'll go mad.

Madame Pernelle

      False suspicions may delude,
And good to evil oft is misconstrued.

Orgon

Must I construe as Christian charity
The wish to kiss my wife!

Madame Pernelle

You must, at least,
Have just foundation for accusing people,
And wait until you see a thing for sure.

Orgon

The devil! How could I see any surer?
Should I have waited till, before my eyes,
He . . . No, you'll make me say things quite improper.

Madame Pernelle

In short, 'tis known too pure a zeal inflames him;
And so, I cannot possibly conceive
That he should try to do what's charged against him.

Orgon

If you were not my mother, I should say
Such things! . . . I know not what, I'm so enraged!

Dorine (*to* ORGON)

Fortune has paid you fair, to be so doubted;
You flouted our report, now yours is flouted.

Cléante

We're wasting time here in the merest trifling,
Which we should rather use in taking measures
To guard ourselves against the scoundrel's threats.

Damis

You think his impudence could go so far?

Elmire

For one, I can't believe it possible;
Why, his ingratitude would be too patent.

Cléante

Don't trust to that; he'll find abundant warrant
To give good colour to his acts against you;
And for less cause than this, a strong cabal
Can make one's life a labyrinth of troubles.
I tell you once again: armed as he is
You never should have pushed him quite so far.

Orgon

True; yet what could I do? The rascal's pride
Made me lose all control of my resentment.

Cléante

I wish with all my heart that some pretence
Of peace could be patched up between you two

Elmire

If I had known what weapons he was armed with,
I never should have raised such an alarm,
And my . . .

Orgon (*to* Dorine, *seeing* Mr. Loyal *come in*)

       Who's coming now? Go quick, find out.
I'm in a fine state to receive a visit!

Scene IV

Orgon, Madame Pernelle, Elmire, Mariane,
Cléante, Damis, Dorine, Mr. Loyal

Mr. Loyal (*to* Dorine, *at the back of the stage*)

Good day, good sister. Pray you, let me see
The master of the house.

Dorine

       He's occupied;
I think he can see nobody at present.

Mr. Loyal

I'm not by way of being unwelcome here.
My coming can, I think, nowise displease him;
My errand will be found to his advantage.

Dorine

Your name, then?

Mr. Loyal

      Tell him simply that his friend
Mr. Tartuffe has sent me, for his goods . . .

Dorine (*to* ORGON)

It is a man who comes, with civil manners,
Sent by Tartuffe, he says, upon an errand
That you'll be pleased with.

Cléante (*to* ORGON)

       Surely you must see him,
And find out who he is, and what he wants.

Orgon (*to* CLÉANTE)

Perhaps he's come to make it up between us:
How shall I treat him?

Cléante

       You must not get angry;
And if he talks of reconciliation
Accept it.

Mr. Loyal (*to* ORGON)

    Sir, good-day. And Heaven send
Harm to your enemies, favour to you.

Orgon (*aside to* CLÉANTE)

This mild beginning suits with my conjectures
And promises some compromise already.

Mr. Loyal

All of your house has long been dear to me;
I had the honour, sir, to serve your father.

Orgon

Sir, I am much ashamed, and ask your pardon
For not recalling now your face or name.

Mr. Loyal

My name is Loyal. I'm from Normandy.
My office is court-bailiff, in despite
Of envy; and for forty years, thank Heaven,
It's been my fortune to perform that office
With honour. So I've come, sir, by your leave
To render service of a certain writ . . .

Orgon

What, you are here to . . .

Mr. Loyal

　　　　　　　　Pray, sir, don't be angry.
'Tis nothing, sir, but just a little summons:—
Order to vacate, you and yours, this house,
Move out your furniture, make room for others,
And that without delay or putting off,
As needs must be . . .

Orgon

　　　　　　　I? Leave this house?

Mr. Loyal

　　　　　　　　　　Yes, please, sir
The house is now, as you well know, of course,
Mr. Tartuffe's. And he, beyond dispute,
Of all your goods is henceforth lord and master
By virtue of a contract here attached,
Drawn in due form, and unassailable.

Damis (to Mr. Loyal)
Your insolence is monstrous, and astounding!

Mr. Loyal (to Damis)
I have no business, sir, that touches you;

(Pointing to Orgon)
This is the gentleman. He's fair and courteous,
And knows too well a gentleman's behaviour
To wish in any wise to question justice.

Orgon
But . . .

Mr. Loyal
                    Sir, I know you would not for a million
Wish to rebel; like a good citizen
You'll let me put in force the court's decree.

Damis
Your long black gown may well, before you know it,
Mister Court-bailiff, get a thorough beating.

Mr. Loyal (to Orgon)
Sir, make your son be silent or withdraw.
I should be loath to have to set things down,
And see your names inscribed in my report.

Dorine (aside)
This Mr. Loyal's looks are most disloyal.

Mr. Loyal
I have much feeling for respectable
And honest folk like you, sir, and consented
To serve these papers, only to oblige you,
And thus prevent the choice of any other
Who, less possessed of zeal for you than I am
Might order matters in less gentle fashion.

Orgon

And how could one do worse than order people
Out of their house?

Mr. Loyal

               Why, we allow you time;
And even will suspend until to-morrow
The execution of the order, sir.
I'll merely, without scandal, quietly,
Come here and spend the night, with half a score
Of officers; and just for form's sake, please,
You'll bring your keys to me, before retiring.
I will take care not to disturb your rest,
And see there's no unseemly conduct here.
But by to-morrow, and at early morning,
You must make haste to move your least belongings;
My men will help you—I have chosen strong ones
To serve you, sir, in clearing out the house.
No one could act more generously, I fancy,
And, since I'm treating you with great indulgence,
I beg you'll do as well by me, and see
I'm not disturbed in my discharge of duty.

Orgon

I'd give this very minute, and not grudge it,
The hundred best gold louis I have left,
If I could just indulge myself, and land
My fist, for one good square one, on his snout.

Cléante (*aside to* ORGON)

Careful!—don't make things worse.

Damis

                   Such insolence!
I hardly can restrain myself. My hands
Are itching to be at him.

Dorine
By my faith,
With such a fine broad back, good Mr. Loyal,
A little beating would become you well.

Mr. Loyal

My girl, such infamous words are actionable.
And warrants can be issued against women.

Cléante (to Mr. Loyal)

Enough of this discussion, sir; have done.
Give us the paper, and then leave us, pray.

Mr. Loyal

Then *au revoir.* Heaven keep you from disaster!

Orgon

May Heaven confound you both, you and your master!

Scene V

ORGON, MADAME PERNELLE, ELMIRE, CLÉANTE,
MARIANE, DAMIS, DORINE

Orgon

Well, mother, am I right or am I not?
This writ may help you now to judge the matter.
Or don't you see his treason even yet?

Madame Pernelle

I'm all amazed, befuddled, and beflustered!

Dorine (to Orgon)

You are quite wrong, you have no right to blame him;
This action only proves his good intentions.
Love for his neighbour makes his virtue perfect;
And knowing money is a root of evil,

In Christian charity, he'd take away
Whatever things may hinder your salvation.

Orgon

Be still. You always need to have that told you.

Cléante (to ORGON)

Come, let us see what course you are to follow.

Elmire

Go and expose his bold ingratitude.
Such action must invalidate the contract;
His perfidy must now appear too black
To bring him the success that he expects.

SCENE VI

VALÈRE, ORGON, MADAME PERNELLE, ELMIRE, CLÉANTE,
MARIANE, DAMIS, DORINE

Valère

'Tis with regret, sir, that I bring bad news;
But urgent danger forces me to do so.
A close and intimate friend of mine, who knows
The interest I take in what concerns you,
Has gone so far, for my sake, as to break
The secrecy that's due to state affairs,
And sent me word but now, that leaves you only
The one expedient of sudden flight.
The villain who so long imposed upon you,
Found means, an hour ago, to see the prince,
And to accuse you (among other things)
By putting in his hands the private strong-box
Of a state-criminal, whose guilty secret,
You, failing in your duty as a subject,
(He says) have kept. I know no more of it
Save that a warrant's drawn against you, sir,
And for the greater surety, that same rascal
Comes with the officer who must arrest you.

Cléante

His rights are armed; and this is how the scoundrel
Seeks to secure the property he claims.

Orgon

Man is a wicked animal, I'll own it!

Valère

The least delay may still be fatal, sir.
I have my carriage, and a thousand louis,
Provided for your journey, at the door.
Let's lose no time; the bolt is swift to strike,
And such as only flight can save you from.
I'll be your guide to seek a place of safety,
And stay with you until you reach it, sir.

Orgon

How much I owe to your obliging care!
Another time must serve to thank you fitly;
And I pray Heaven to grant me so much favour
That I may some day recompense your service.
Good-bye; see to it, all of you . . .

Cléante

                         Come hurry;
We'll see to everything that's needful, brother.

Scene VII

TARTUFFE, AN OFFICER, MADAME PERNELLE, ORGON,
ELMIRE, CLÉANTE, MARIANE, VALÈRE, DAMIS, DORINE

Tartuffe (*stopping* ORGON)

Softly, sir, softly; do not run so fast;
You haven't far to go to find your lodging;
By order of the prince, we here arrest you.

Orgon

Traitor! You saved this worst stroke for the last;
This crowns your perfidies, and ruins me.

Tartuffe

I shall not be embittered by your insults,
For Heaven has taught me to endure all things.

Cléante

Your moderation, I must own, is great.

Damis

How shamelessly the wretch makes bold with Heaven!

Tartuffe

Your ravings cannot move me; all my thought
Is but to do my duty.

Mariane

　　　　　You must claim
Great glory from this honourable act.

Tartuffe

The act cannot be aught but honourable,
Coming from that high power which sends me here.

Orgon

Ungrateful wretch, do you forget 'twas I
That rescued you from utter misery?

Tartuffe

I've not forgot some help you may have given;
But my first duty now is toward my prince.
The higher power of that most sacred claim
Must stifle in my heart all gratitude;
And to such puissant ties I'd sacrifice
My friend, my wife, my kindred, and myself.

Elmire
The hypocrite!

Dorine
How well he knows the trick
Of cloaking him with what we most revere!

Cléante
But if the motive that you make parade of
Is perfect as you say, why should it wait
To show itself, until the day he caught you
Soliciting his wife? How happens it
You have not thought to go inform against him
Until his honour forces him to drive you
Out of his house? And though I need not mention
That he'd just given you his whole estate,
Still, if you meant to treat him now as guilty,
How could you then consent to take his gift?

Tartuffe (*to the* OFFICER)
Pray, sir, deliver me from all this clamour;
Be good enough to carry out your order.

The Officer
Yes, I've too long delayed its execution;
'Tis very fitting you should urge me to it;
So therefore, you must follow me at once
To prison, where you'll find your lodging ready.

Tartuffe
Who? I, sir?

The Officer
You.

Tartuffe
But why to prison?

The Officer
You
Are not the one to whom I owe account.

You, sir (*to* ORGON), recover from your hot alarm.
Our prince is not a friend to double dealing,
His eyes can read men's inmost hearts, and all
The art of hypocrites cannot deceive him.
His sharp discernment sees things clear and true;
His mind cannot too easily be swayed,
For reason always holds the balance even.
He honours and exalts true piety
But knows the false, and views it with disgust.
This fellow was by no means apt to fool him;
Far subtler snares have failed against his wisdom,
And his quick insight pierced immediately
The hidden baseness of this tortuous heart.
Accusing you, the knave betrayed himself,
And by true recompense of Heaven's justice
He stood revealed before our monarch's eyes
A scoundrel known before by other names,
Whose horrid crimes, detailed at length, might fill
A long-drawn history of many volumes.
Our monarch—to resolve you in a word—
Detesting his ingratitude and baseness,
Added this horror to his other crimes,
And sent me hither under his direction
To see his insolence out-top itself,
And force him then to give you satisfaction.
Your papers, which the traitor says are his,
I am to take from him, and give you back;
The deed of gift transferring your estate
Our monarch's sovereign will makes null and void;
And for the secret personal offence
Your friend involved you in, he pardons you:
Thus he rewards your recent zeal, displayed
In helping to maintain his rights, and shows
How well his heart, when it is least expected,
Knows how to recompense a noble deed,
And will not let true merit miss its due,
Remembering always rather good than evil.

Dorine

Now, Heaven be praised!

Madame Pernelle

At last I breathe again.

Elmire

A happy outcome!

Mariane

Who'd have dared to hope it?

Orgon (*to* TARTUFFE, *who is being led off by the officer*)
There, traitor! Now you're . . .

SCENE VIII

MADAME PERNELLE, ORGON, ELMIRE, MARIANE,
CLÉANTE, VALÈRE, DAMIS, DORINE

Cléante

Brother, hold!—and don't
Descend to such indignities, I beg you.
Leave the poor wretch to his unhappy fate,
And let remorse oppress him, but not you.
Hope rather that his heart may now return
To virtue, hate his vice, reform his ways,
And win the pardon of our glorious prince;
While you must straightway go, and on your knees
Repay with thanks his noble generous kindness.

Orgon

Well said! We'll go, and at his feet kneel down
With joy to thank him for his goodness shown;
And this first duty done, with honours due,
We'll then attend upon another, too.
With wedded happiness reward Valère,
And crown a lover noble and sincere.

MINNA VON BARNHELM

OR

THE SOLDIER'S FORTUNE

BY

GOTTHOLD EPHRAIM LESSING

TRANSLATED BY
ERNEST BELL

INTRODUCTORY NOTE

GOTTHOLD EPHRAIM LESSING was born at Kamenz, Germany, January 22, 1729, the son of a Lutheran minister. He was educated at Meissen and Leipzic, and began writing for the stage before he was twenty. In 1748 he went to Berlin, where he met Voltaire and for a time was powerfully influenced by him. The most important product of this period was his tragedy of "Miss Sara Samson," a modern version of the story of Medea, which began the vogue of the sentimental middle-class play in Germany. After a second sojourn in Leipzic (1755–1758), during which he wrote criticism, lyrics, and fables, Lessing returned to Berlin and began to publish his "Literary Letters," making himself by the vigor and candor of his criticism a real force in contemporary literature. From Berlin he went to Breslau, where he made the first sketches of two of his greatest works, "Laocoön" and "Minna von Barnhelm," both of which were issued after his return to the Prussian capital. Failing in his effort to be appointed Director of the Royal Library by Frederick the Great, Lessing went to Hamburg in 1767 as critic of a new national theatre, and in connection with this enterprise he issued twice a week the "Hamburgische Dramaturgie," the two volumes of which are a rich mine of dramatic criticism and theory.

His next residence was at Wolfenbüttel, where he had charge of the ducal library from 1770 till his death in 1781. Here he wrote his tragedy of "Emilia Galotti," founded on the story of Virginia, and engaged for a time in violent religious controversies, one important outcome of which was his "Education of the Human Race," to be found in another volume of the Harvard Classics. On being ordered by the Brunswick authorities to give up controversial writing, he found expression for his views in his play "Nathan the Wise," his last great production.

The importance of Lessing's masterpiece in comedy, "Minna von Barnhelm," it is difficult to exaggerate. It was the beginning of German national drama; and by the patriotic interest of its historical background, by its sympathetic treatment of the German soldier and the German woman, and by its happy blending of the amusing and the pathetic, it won a place in the national heart from which no succeeding comedy has been able to dislodge it.

MINNA VON BARNHELM

DRAMATIS PERSONÆ

MAJOR VON TELLHEIM, *a discharged officer.*
MINNA VON BARNHELM.
COUNT VON BRUCHSAL, *her uncle.*
FRANZISKA, *her lady's maid.*
JUST, *servant to the* MAJOR.
PAUL WERNER, *an old Sergeant of the* MAJOR's.
The LANDLORD *of an Inn.*
A Lady.
An Orderly.
RICCAUT DE LA MARLINIÈRE.

*The scene alternates between the Parlour of an Inn,
and a Room adjoining it.*

ACT I

SCENE I.—JUST

JUST (*sitting in a corner, and talking while asleep*)

ROGUE of a landlord! *You* treat *us* so? On, comrade! hit hard! (*He strikes with his fist, and wakes through the exertion*). Ha! there he is again! I cannot shut an eye without fighting with him. I wish he got but half the blows. Why, it is morning! I must just look for my poor master at once; if I can help it, he shall not set foot in the cursed house again. I wonder where he has passed the night?

SCENE II.—LANDLORD, JUST

Land. Good-morning, Herr Just; good-morning! What, up so early! Or shall I say—up so late?

Just. Say which you please.

Land. I say only—good-morning! and that deserves, I suppose, that Herr Just should answer, "Many thanks."

299

Just. Many thanks.

Land. One is peevish, if one can't have one's proper rest. What will you bet the Major has not returned home, and you have been keeping watch for him?

Just. How the man can guess everything!

Land. I surmise, I surmise.

Just. (*turns round to go*). Your servant!

Land. (*stops him*). Not so, Herr Just!

Just. Very well, then, not your servant!

Land. What, Herr Just, I do hope you are not still angry about yesterday's affair! Who would keep his anger over night?

Just. I; and over a good many nights.

Land. Is that like a Christian?

Just. As much so as to turn an honourable man who cannot pay to a day, out of doors, into the street.

Land. Fie! who would be so wicked?

Just. A Christian innkeeper.—My master! such a man! such an officer!

Land. I thrust him from the house into the streets? I have far too much respect for an officer to do that, and far too much pity for a discharged one! I was obliged to have another room prepared for him. Think no more about it, Herr Just. (*Calls*)—Hullo! I will make it good in another way. (*A lad comes.*) Bring a glass; Herr Just will have a drop; something good.

Just. Do not trouble yourself, Mr. Landlord. May the drop turn to poison, which . . . But I will not swear; I have not yet breakfasted.

Land. (*to the lad, who brings a bottle of spirits and a glass*). Give it here; go! Now, Herr Just; something quite excellent; strong, delicious, and wholesome. (*Fills, and holds it out to him.*) That can set an over-taxed stomach to rights again!

Just. I hardly ought!—And yet why should I let my health suffer on account of his incivility? (*Takes it, and drinks.*)

Land. May it do you good, Herr Just!

Just. (*giving the glass back*). Not bad! But, Landlord, you are nevertheless an ill-mannered brute!

Land. Not so, not so! . . . Come, another glass; one cannot stand upon one leg.

Just. (*after drinking*). I must say so much—it is good, very good! Made at home, Landlord?

Land. At home, indeed! True Dantzig, real double distilled!

Just. Look ye, Landlord; if I could play the hypocrite, I would do so for such stuff as that; but I cannot, so it must out.—You are an ill-mannered brute all the same.

Land. Nobody in my life ever told me that before . . . But another glass, Herr Just; three is the lucky number!

Just. With all my heart!—(*Drinks.*) Good stuff indeed, capital! But truth is good also, and indeed, Landlord, you are an ill-mannered brute all the same!

Land. If I was, do you think I should let you say so?

Just. Oh! yes; a brute seldom has spirit.

Land. One more, Herr Just: a four-stranded rope is the strongest.

Just. No, enough is as good as a feast! And what good will it do you, Landlord? I shall stick to my text till the last drop in the bottle. Shame, Landlord, to have such good Dantzig, and such bad manners! To turn out of his room, in his absence—a man like my master, who has lodged at your house above a year; from whom you have had already so many shining thalers; who never owed a heller in his life—because he let payment run for a couple of months, and because he does not spend quite so much as he used.

Land. But suppose I really wanted the room and saw beforehand that the Major would willingly have given it up if we could only have waited some time for his return! Should I let strange gentle-folk like them drive away again from my door? Should I wilfully send such a prize into the clutches of another innkeeper? Besides, I don't believe they could have got a lodging elsewhere. The inns are all now quite full. Could such a young, beautiful, amiable lady remain in the street? Your master is much too gallant for that. And what does he lose by the change? Have not I given him another room?

Just. By the pigeon-house at the back, with a view between a neighbour's chimneys.

Land. The view was uncommonly fine, before the confounded neighbour obstructed it. The room is otherwise very nice, and is papered—

Just. Has been!

Land. No, one side is so still. And the little room adjoining, what is the matter with that? It has a chimney which, perhaps, smokes somewhat in the winter—

Just. But does very nicely in the summer. I believe, Landlord, you are mocking us into the bargain!

Land. Come, come; Herr Just, Herr Just—

Just. Don't make Herr Just's head hot—

Land. I make his head hot? It is the Dantzig does that.

Just. An officer, like my master! Or do you think that a discharged officer is not an officer, who may break your neck for you? Why were you all, you Landlords, so civil during the war? Why was every officer an honourable man then and every soldier a worthy, brave fellow? Does this bit of a peace make you so bumptious?

Land. What makes you fly out so, Herr Just!

Just. I will fly out.

Scene III.—Major von Tellheim, Landlord, Just

Maj. T. (entering). Just!

Just. (supposing the Landlord *is still speaking).* Just? Are we so intimate?

Maj. T. Just!

Just. I thought I was "Herr Just" with you.

Land. (seeing the Major*).* Hist! hist! Herr Just, Herr Just, look round; your master—

Maj. T. Just, I think you are quarreling! What did I tell you?

Land. Quarrel, your honour? God forbid! Would your most humble servant dare to quarrel with one who has the honour of being in your service?

Just. If I could but give him a good whack on that cringing cat's back of his!

Land. It is true Herr Just speaks up for his master, and rather warmly; but in that he is right. I esteem him so much the more: I like him for it.

Just. I should like to knock his teeth out for him!

Land. It is only a pity that he puts himself in a passion for nothing. For I feel quite sure that your honour is not displeased with me in this matter, since—necessity—made it necessary—

Maj. T. More than enough, sir! I am in your debt; you turn out my room in my absence. You must be paid, I must seek a lodging elsewhere. Very natural.

Land. Elsewhere? You are going to quit, honoured sir? Oh, unfortunate stricken man that I am. No, never! Sooner shall the lady give up the apartments again. The Major cannot and will not let her have his room. It is his; she must go; I cannot help it. I will go, honoured sir—

Maj. T. My friend, do not make two foolish strokes instead of one. The lady must retain possession of the room—

Land. And your honour could suppose that from distrust, from fear of not being paid, I . . . As if I did not know that your honour could pay me as soon as you pleased. The sealed purse . . . five hundred thalers in louis d'ors marked on it—which your honour had in your writing-desk . . . is in good keeping.

Maj. T. I trust so; as the rest of my property. Just shall take them into his keeping, when he has paid your bill—

Land. Really, I was quite alarmed when I found the purse. I always considered your honour a methodical and prudent man, who never got quite out of money . . . but still, had I supposed there was ready money in the desk—

Maj. T. You would have treated me rather more civilly. I understand you. Go, sir; leave me. I wish to speak with my servant.

Land. But, honoured sir—

Maj. T. Come, Just; he does not wish to permit me to give my orders to you in his house.

Land. I am going, honoured sir! My whole house is at your service. (*Exit.*)

Scene IV.—Major von Tellheim, Just

Just. (*stamping with his foot and spitting after the* Landlord). Ugh!

Maj. T. What is the matter?

Just. I am choking with rage.

Maj. T. That is as bad as from plethora.

Just. And for you, sir, I hardly know you any longer. May I die before your eyes, if you do not encourage this malicious, unfeeling wretch. In spite of gallows, axe, and torture I could . . . yes, I could have throttled him with these hands, and torn him to pieces with these teeth!

Maj. T. You wild beast!

Just. Better a wild beast than such a man!

Maj. T. But what is it that you want?

Just. I want you to perceive how much he insults you.

Maj. T. And then—

Just. To take your revenge . . . No, the fellow is beneath your notice!

Maj. T. But to commission you to avenge me? That was my intention from the first. He should not have seen me again, but have received the amount of his bill from your hands. I know that you can throw down a handful of money with a tolerably contemptuous mien.

Just. Oh! a pretty sort of revenge!

Maj. T. Which, however, we must defer. I have not one heller of ready money, and I know not where to raise any.

Just. No money! What is that purse then with five hundred dollars' worth of louis d'ors, which the Landlord found in your desk?

Maj. T. That is money given into my charge.

Just. Not the hundred pistoles which your old sergeant brought you four or five weeks back?

Maj. T. The same. Paul Werner's; right.

Just. And you have not used them yet? Yet, sir, you may do what you please with them. I will answer for it that—

Maj. T. Indeed!

Just. Werner heard from me, how they had treated your claims upon the War Office. He heard—

Maj. T. That I should certainly be a beggar soon, if I was not one already. I am much obliged to you, Just. And the news induced Werner to offer to share his little all with me. I am very glad that I guessed this. Listen, Just; let me have your account, directly, too; we must part.

Just. How! what!

Maj. T. Not a word. There is someone coming.

SCENE V.—LADY *in mourning,* MAJOR VON TELLHEIM, JUST

Lady. I ask your pardon, sir.

Maj. T. Whom do you seek, Madam?

Lady. The worthy gentleman with whom I have the honour of speaking. You do not know me again. I am the widow of your late captain.

Maj. T. Good heavens, Madam, how you are changed!

Lady. I have just risen from a sick bed, to which grief on the loss of my husband brought me. I am troubling you at a very early hour, Major von Tellheim, but I am going into the country, where a kind, but also unfortunate friend, has for the present offered me an asylum.

Maj. T. (to Just). Leave us.

SCENE VI.—LADY, MAJOR VON TELLHEIM

Maj. T. Speak freely, Madam! You must not be ashamed of your bad fortune before me. Can I serve you in any way?

Lady. Major—

Maj. T. I pity you, Madam! How can I serve you? You know your husband was my friend; my friend, I say, and I have always been sparing of this title.

Lady. Who knows better than I do how worthy you were of his friendship—how worthy he was of yours? You would have been in his last thoughts, your name would have been the last sound on his dying lips, had not natural affection, stronger than friendship, demanded this sad prerogative for his unfortunate son, and his unhappy wife.

Maj. T. Cease, Madam! I could willingly weep with you; but I have no tears to-day. Spare me! You come to me at a time when I might easily be misled to murmur against Providence. Oh! honest Marloff! Quick, Madam, what have you to request? If it is in my power to assist you, if it is in my power—

Lady. I cannot depart without fulfilling his last wishes. He recollected, shortly before his death, that he was dying a debtor to you, and he conjured me to discharge his debt with the first ready money I should have. I have sold his carriage, and come to redeem his note.

Maj. T. What, Madam! Is that your object in coming?

Lady. It is. Permit me to count out the money to you.

Maj. T. No, Madam. Marloff a debtor to me! that can hardly be. Let us look, however. (*Takes out a pocketbook, and searches.*) I find nothing of the kind.

Lady. You have doubtless mislaid his note; besides, it is nothing to the purpose. Permit me—

Maj. T. No, Madam; I am careful not to mislay such documents. If I have not got it, it is a proof that I never had it, or that it has been honoured and already returned by me.

Lady. Major!

Maj. T. Without doubt, Madam; Marloff does not owe me anything—nor can I remember that he ever did owe me anything. This is so, Madam. He has much rather left me in his debt. I have never been able to do anything to repay a man who shared with me good and ill luck, honour and danger, for six years. I shall not forget that he has left a son. He shall be my son, as soon as I can be a father to him. The embarrassment in which I am at present—

Lady. Generous man! But do not think so meanly of me. Take the money, Major, and then at least I shall be at ease.

Maj. T. What more do you require to tranquillize you, than my assurance that the money does not belong to me? Or do you wish that I should rob the young orphan of my friend? Rob, Madam; for that it would be in the true meaning of the word. The money belongs to him; invest it for him.

Lady. I understand you; pardon me if I do not yet rightly know how to accept a kindness. Where have you learnt that a mother will do more for her child than for the preservation of her own life? I am going—

Maj. T. Go, Madam, and may you have a prosperous journey! I do not ask you to let me hear from you. Your news might come to me when it might be of little use to me. There is yet one thing, Madam; I had nearly forgotten that which is of most consequence. Marloff also had claims upon the chest of our old regiment. His claims are as good as mine. If my demands are paid, his must be paid also. I will be answerable for them.

Lady. Oh! Sir . . . but what can I say? Thus to purpose future good deeds is, in the eyes of heaven, to have performed them already. May you receive its reward, as well as my tears. (*Exit.*)

Scene VII.—Major von Tellheim

Maj. T. Poor, good woman! I must not forget to destroy the bill. (*Takes some papers from his pocketbook and destroys them.*) Who would guarantee that my own wants might not some day tempt me to make use of it?

Scene VIII.—Just, Major von Tellheim

Maj. T. Is that you, Just?

Just. (*wiping his eyes*). Yes.

Maj. T. You have been crying?

Just. I have been writing out my account in the kitchen, and the place is full of smoke. Here it is, sir.

Maj. T. Give it to me.

Just. Be merciful with me, sir. I know well that they have not been so with you; still—

Maj. T. What do you want?

Just. I should sooner have expected my death, than my discharge.

Maj. T. I cannot keep you any longer: I must learn to manage without servants. (*Opens the paper, and reads.*) "What my master, the Major, owes me:—Three months and a half wages, six thalers per month, is 21 thalers. During the first part of this month, laid out in sundries—1 thaler 7 groschen 9 pfennigs. Total, 22 thalers 7gr. 9pf." Right; and it is just that I also pay your wages, for the whole of the current month.

Just. Turn over, sir.

Maj. T. Oh! more? (*Reads.*) "What I owe my master, the Major:—Paid for me to the army-surgeon twenty-five thalers. Attendance and nurse during my cure, paid for me, thirty-nine thalers. Advanced, at my request, to my father—who was burnt out of his house and robbed—without reckoning the two horses of which he made him a present, fifty thalers. Total 114 thalers. Deduct the above

22 thalers, 7gr. 9pf.; I remain in debt to my master, the Major, 91 thalers, 16gr. 3pf." You are mad, my good fellow!

Just. I willingly grant that I owe you much more; but it would be wasting ink to write it down. I cannot pay you that: and if you take my livery from me too, which, by the way, I have not yet earned,—I would rather you had let me die in the workhouse.

Maj. T. For what do you take me? You owe me nothing; and I will recommend you to one of my friends, with whom you will fare better than with me.

Just. I do not owe you anything, and yet you turn me away!

Maj. T. Because I do not wish to owe you anything.

Just. On that account? Only on that account? As certain as I am in your debt, as certain as you can never be in mine, so certainly shall you not turn me away now. Do what you will, Major, I remain in your service; I must remain.

Maj. T. With your obstinacy, your insolence, your savage boisterous temper towards all who you think have no business to speak to you, your malicious pranks, your love of revenge,—

Just. Make me as bad as you will, I shall not think worse of myself than of my dog. Last winter I was walking one evening at dusk along the river, when I heard something whine. I stooped down, and reached in the direction whence the sound came, and when I thought I was saving a child, I pulled a dog out of the water. That is well, thought I. The dog followed me; but I am not fond of dogs, so I drove him away—in vain. I whipped him away—in vain. I shut him out of my room at night; he lay down before the door. If he came too near me, I kicked him; he yelped, looked up at me, and wagged his tail. I have never yet given him a bit of bread with my own hand; and yet I am the only person whom he will obey, or who dare touch him. He jumps about me, and shows off his tricks to me, without my asking for them. He is an ugly dog, but he is a good animal. If he carries it on much longer, I shall at last give over hating him.

Maj. T. (*aside*). As I do him. No, there is no one perfectly inhuman. Just, we will not part.

Just. Certainly not! And you wanted to manage without servants! You forget your wounds, and that you only have the use of one arm. Why, you are not able to dress alone. I am indispensable to you; and I am—without boasting, Major,—I am a servant who, if the worst comes to the worst, can beg and steal for his master.

Maj. T. Just, we will part.

Just. All right, Sir!

SCENE IX.—SERVANT, MAJOR VON TELLHEIM, JUST

Ser. I say, comrade!

Just. What is the matter?

Ser. Can you direct me to the officer who lodged yesterday in that room? (*pointing to the one out of which he is coming*).

Just. That I could easily do. What have you got for him?

Ser. What we always have, when we have nothing—compliments. My mistress hears that he has been turned out on her account. My mistress knows good manners, and I am therefore to beg his pardon.

Just. Well then, beg his pardon; there he stands.

Ser. What is he? What is his name?

Maj. T. I have already heard your message, my friend. It is unnecessary politeness on the part of your mistress, which I beg to acknowledge duly. Present my compliments to her. What is the name of your mistress?

Ser. Her name! We call her my lady.

Maj. T. The name of her family?

Ser. I have not heard that yet, and it is not my business to ask. I manage so that I generally get a new master every six weeks. Hang all their names!

Just. Bravo, comrade!

Ser. I was engaged by my present mistress a few days ago, in Dresden. I believe she has come here to look for her lover.

Maj. T. Enough, friend. I wished to know the name of your mistress, not her secrets. Go!

Ser. Comrade, he would not do for my master.

SCENE X.—MAJOR VON TELLHEIM, JUST

Maj. T. Just! see that we get out of this house directly! The politeness of this strange lady affects me more than the churlishness of the host. Here, take this ring—the only thing of value which I have left—of which I never thought of making such a use. Pawn it! get eighty louis d'ors for it: our host's bill can scarcely amount to thirty. Pay him, and remove my things. . . . Ah, where? Where you will. The cheaper the inn, the better. You will find me in the neighbouring coffee-house. I am going; you will see to it all properly?

Just. Have no fear, Major!

Maj. T. (*comes back*). Above all things, do not let my pistols be forgotten, which hang beside the bed.

Just. I will forget nothing.

Maj. T. (*comes back again*). Another thing: bring your dog with you too. Do you hear, Just?

Scene XI.—Just

Just. The dog will not stay behind, he will take care of that. Hem! My master still had this valuable ring and carried it in his pocket instead of on his finger! My good landlord, we are not yet so poor as we look. To him himself, I will pawn you, you beautiful little ring! I know he will be annoyed that you will not all be consumed in his house. Ah!—

Scene XII.—Paul Werner, Just

Just. Hullo, Werner! good-day to you, Werner. Welcome to the town.

Wer. The accursed village! I can't manage to get at home in it again. Merry, my boys, merry; I have got some more money! Where is the Major?

Just. He must have met you; he just went down stairs.

Wer. I came up the back stairs. How is he? I should have been with you last week, but—

Just. Well, what prevented you?

Wer. Just, did you ever hear of Prince Heraclius?

Just. Heraclius? Not that I know of.

Wer. Don't you know the great hero of the East?

Just. I know the wise men of the East well enough, who go about with the stars on New Year's Eve.[1]

Wer. Brother, I believe you read the newspapers as little as the Bible. You do not know Prince Heraclius. Not know the brave man who seized Persia, and will break into the Ottoman Porte in a few days? Thank God, there is still war somewhere in the world! I have long enough hoped it would break out here again. But there they sit and take care of their skins. No, a soldier I was, and a soldier I must be again! In short (*looking round carefully, to see if anyone is listening*), between ourselves, Just, I am going to Persia, to have a few campaigns against the Turks, under his Royal Highness Prince Heraclius.

Just. You?

Wer. I myself. Our ancestors fought bravely against the Turks; and so ought we too, if we would be honest men and good Christians. I allow that a campaign against the Turks cannot be half so pleasant as one against the French; but then it must be so much the more beneficial in this world and the next. The swords of the Turks are all set with diamonds.

Just. I would not walk a mile to have my head split with one of their sabres. You will not be so mad as to leave your comfortable little farm!

Wer. Oh! I take that with me. Do you see? The property is sold.

Just. Sold?

Wer. Hist! Here are a hundred ducats, which I received yesterday towards the payment: I am bringing them for the Major.

Just. What is he to do with them?

Wer. What is he to do with them? Spend them; play them, or drink them away, or whatever he pleases. He must have money, and it is bad enough that they have made his own so troublesome to him. But I know what I would do, were I in his place. I would say—"The deuce take you all here; I will go with Paul Werner to Persia!" Hang it! Prince Heraclius must have heard of Major von Tellheim, if he has not heard of Paul Werner, his late sergeant. Our affair at Katzenhäuser—

[1] This refers to an old German custom.

Just. Shall I give you an account of that?

Wer. You give me! I know well that a fine battle array is beyond your comprehension. I am not going to throw my pearls before swine. Here, take the hundred ducats; give them to the Major: tell him, he may keep these for me too. I am going to the market now. I have sent in a couple of loads of rye; what I get for them he can also have.

Just. Werner, you mean it well; but we don't want your money. Keep your ducats; and your hundred pistoles you can also have back safe, as soon as you please.

Wer. What, has the Major money still?

Just. No.

Wer. Has he borrowed any?

Just. No.

Wer. On what does he live, then?

Just. We have everything put down in the bill; and when they won't put anything more down, and turn us out of the house, we pledge anything we may happen to have, and go somewhere else. I say, Paul, we must play this landlord here a trick.

Wer. If he has annoyed the Major, I am ready.

Just. What if we watch for him in the evening, when he comes from his club, and give him a good thrashing?

Wer. In the dark! Watch for him! Two to one! No, that won't do.

Just. Or if we burn his house over his head?

Wer. Fire and burn! Why, Just, one hears that you have been baggage-boy and not soldier. Shame!

Just. Or if we ruin his daughter? But she is cursedly ugly.

Wer. She has probably been ruined long ago. At any rate you don't want any help there. But what is the matter with you? What has happened?

Just. Just come with me, and you shall hear something to make you stare.

Wer. The devil must be loose here, then?

Just. Just so; come along.

Wer. So much the better! To Persia, then; to Persia.

ACT II

Scene I.—*Minna's Room.* Minna, Franziska

Min. (*in morning dress, looking at her watch*). Franziska, we have risen very early. The time will hang heavy on our hands.

Fran. Who can sleep in these abominable large towns? The carriages, the watchmen, the drums, the cats, the soldiers, never cease to rattle, to call, to roll, to mew, and to swear; just as if the last thing the night is intended for was for sleep. Have a cup of tea, my lady!

Min. I don't care for tea.

Fran. I will have some chocolate made.

Min. For yourself, if you like.

Fran. For myself! I would as soon talk to myself as drink by myself. Then the time will indeed hang heavy. For very weariness we shall have to make our toilets, and try on the dress in which we intend to make the first attack!

Min. Why do you talk of attacks, when I have only come to require that the capitulation be ratified?

Fran. But the officer whom we have dislodged, and to whom we have apologized, cannot be the best bred man in the world, or he might at least have begged the honour of being allowed to wait upon you.

Min. All officers are not Tellheims. To tell you the truth, I only sent him the message in order to have an opportunity of inquiring from him about Tellheim. Franziska, my heart tells me my journey will be a successful one and that I shall find him.

Fran. The heart, my lady! One must not trust to that too much. The heart echoes to us the words of our tongues. If the tongue was as much inclined to speak the thoughts of the heart, the fashion of keeping mouths under lock and key would have come in long ago.

Min. Ha! ha! mouths under lock and key. That fashion would just suit me.

Fran. Rather not show the most beautiful set of teeth, than let the heart be seen through them every moment.

Min. What, are you so reserved?

Fran. No, my lady; but I would willingly be more so. People seldom talk of the virtue they possess, and all the more often of that which they do not possess.

Min. Franziska, you made a very just remark there.

Fran. Made! Does one make it, if it occurs to one?

Min. And do you know why I consider it so good? It applies to my Tellheim.

Fran. What would not, in your opinion, apply to him?

Min. Friend and foe say he is the bravest man in the world. But who ever heard him talk of bravery? He has the most upright mind; but uprightness and nobleness of mind are words never on his tongue.

Fran. Of what virtues does he talk then?

Min. He talks of none, for he is wanting in none.

Fran. That is just what I wished to hear.

Min. Wait, Franziska; I am wrong. He often talks of economy. Between ourselves, I believe he is extravagant.

Fran. One thing more, my lady. I have often heard him mention truth and constancy toward you. What, if he be inconstant?

Min. Miserable girl! But do you mean that seriously?

Fran. How long is it since he wrote to you?

Min. Alas! he has only written to me once since the peace.

Fran. What!—A sigh on account of the peace? Surprising! Peace ought only to make good the ill which war causes; but it seems to disturb the good which the latter, its opposite, may have occasioned. Peace should not be so capricious! . . . How long have we had peace? The time seems wonderfully long, when there is so little news. It is no use the post going regularly again; nobody writes, for nobody has anything to write about.

Min. "Peace has been made," he wrote to me, "and I am approaching the fulfilment of my wishes." But since he only wrote that to me once, only once—

Fran. And since he compels us to run after this fulfilment of his wishes ourselves. . . If we can but find him, he shall pay for this! Suppose, in the meantime, he may have accomplished his wishes, and we should learn here that—

Min. (*anxiously*). That he is dead?

Fran. To you, my lady; and married to another.

Min. You teaze, you! Wait, Franziska, I will pay you out for this! But talk to me, or I shall fall asleep. His regiment was disbanded after the peace. Who knows into what a confusion of bills and papers he may thereby have been brought? Who knows into what other regiment, or to what distant station, he may have been sent? Who knows what circumstances—There's a knock at the door.

Fran. Come in!

Scene II.—Landlord, Minna, Franziska

Land. (*putting his head in at the door*). Am I permitted, your ladyship?

Fran. Our landlord?—Come in!

Land. (*A pen behind his ear, a sheet of paper and an inkstand in his hand*). I am come, your ladyship, to wish you a most humble good-morning; (*to* Franziska) and the same to you, my pretty maid.

Fran. A polite man!

Min. We are obliged to you.

Fran. And wish you also a good-morning.

Land. May I venture to ask how your ladyship has passed the first night under my poor roof?

Fran. The roof is not so bad, sir; but the beds might have been better.

Land. What do I hear! Not slept well! Perhaps the over-fatigue of the journey—

Min. Perhaps.

Land. Certainly, certainly, for otherwise. . . . Yet, should there be anything not perfectly comfortable, my lady, I hope you will not fail to command me.

Fran. Very well, Mr. Landlord, very well! We are not bashful; and least of all should one be bashful at an inn. We shall not fail to say what we may wish.

Land. I next come to . . . (*taking the pen from behind his ear*).

Fran. Well?

Land. Without doubt, my lady, you are already acquainted with the wise regulations of our police.

Min. Not in the least, sir.

Land. We landlords are instructed not to take in any stranger, of whatever rank or sex he may be, for four-and-twenty hours, without delivering, in writing, his name, place of abode, occupation, object of his journey, probable stay, and so on, to the proper author-ities.

Min. Very well.

Land. Will your ladyship then be so good . . . (*going to the table, and making ready to write*).

Min. Willingly. My name is—

Land. One minute! (*He writes.*) "Date, 22nd August, A. D., &c.; arrived at the King of Spain hotel." Now your name, my lady.

Min. Fräulein von Barnhelm.

Land. (*writes*). "Von Barnhelm." Coming from. . . . where, your ladyship?

Min. From my estate in Saxony.

Land. (*writes*). "Estate in Saxony." Saxony! Indeed, indeed! In Saxony, your ladyship? Saxony?

Fran. Well, why not? I hope it is no sin in this country to come from Saxony!

Land. A sin? Heaven forbid! That would be quite a new sin! From Saxony then? Yes, yes, from Saxony, a delightful country, Saxony! But if I am right, your ladyship, Saxony is not small, and has several—how shall I call them?—districts, provinces. Our police are very particular, your ladyship.

Min. I understand. From my estate in Thuringia, then.

Land. From Thuringia! Yes, that is better, your ladyship; that is more exact. (*Writes and reads.*) "Fräulein von Barnhelm, coming from her estate in Thuringia, together with her lady in waiting and two men servants."

Fran. Lady in waiting! That means me, I suppose!

Land. Yes, my pretty maid.

Fran. Well, Mr. Landlord, instead of "lady in waiting," write "maid in waiting." You say, the police are very exact; it might cause a misunderstanding, which might give me trouble some day when my banns are read out. For I really am still unmarried, and my name is Franziska, with the family name of Willig: Franziska Willig. I also come from Thuringia. My father was a miller, on one of my lady's estates. It is called Little Rammsdorf. My brother has the mill now. I was taken very early to the manor, and educated with my lady. We are of the same age—one-and-twenty next Candlemas. I learnt everything my lady learnt. I should like the police to have a full account of me.

Land. Quite right, my pretty maid; I will bear that in mind, in case of future inquiries. But now, your ladyship, your business here?

Min. My business here?

Land. Have you any business with His Majesty the King?

Min. Oh! no.

Land. Or at our courts of justice?

Min. No.

Land. Or—

Min. No, no. I have come here solely on account of my own private affairs.

Land. Quite right, your ladyship; but what are those private affairs?

Min. They are . . . Franziska, I think we are undergoing an examination.

Fran. Mr. Landlord, the police surely do not ask to know a young lady's secrets!

Land. Certainly, my pretty maid; the police wish to know everything, and especially secrets.

Fran. What is to be done, my lady? . . . Well, listen, Mr. Landlord—but take care that it does not go beyond ourselves and the police.

Min. What is the simpleton going to tell him?

Fran. We come to carry off an officer from the king.

Land. How? What? My dear girl!

Fran. Or to let ourselves be carried off by the officer. It is all one.

Min. Franziska, are you mad? The saucy girl is laughing at you.

Land. I hope not! With your humble servant indeed she may jest as much as she pleases; but with the police—

Min. I tell you what; I do not understand how to act in this matter. Suppose you postpone the whole affair till my uncle's arrival. I told you yesterday why he did not come with me. He had an accident with his carriage ten miles from here, and did not wish that I should remain a night longer on the road, so I had to come on. I am sure he will not be more than four-and-twenty hours after us.

Land. Very well, madam, we will wait for him.

Min. He will be able to answer your questions better. He will know to whom, and to what extent, he must give an account of himself—what he must relate respecting his affairs, and what he may withhold.

Land. So much the better! Indeed one cannot expect a young girl (*looking at* FRANZISKA *in a marked manner*) to treat a serious matter with serious people in a serious manner.

Min. And his rooms are in readiness, I hope?

Land. Quite, your ladyship, quite; except the one—

Fran. Out of which, I suppose, you will have to turn some other honourable gentleman!

Land. The waiting maids of Saxony, your ladyship, seem to be very compassionate.

Min. In truth, sir, that was not well done. You ought rather to have refused us.

Land. Why so, your ladyship, why so?

Min. I understand that the officer who was driven out on our account—

Land. Is only a discharged officer, your ladyship.

Min. Well, what then?

Land. Who is almost done for.

Min. So much the worse! He is said to be a very deserving man.

Land. But I tell you he is discharged.

Min. The king cannot be acquainted with every deserving man.

Land. Oh! doubtless he knows them; he knows them all.

Min. But he cannot reward them all.

Land. They would have been rewarded if they had lived so as to deserve it. But they lived during the war as if it would last for ever; as if the words "yours" and "mine" were done away with altogether. Now all the hotels and inns are full of them, and a landlord has to be on his guard with them. I have come off pretty well with this one. If he had no more money, he had at any rate money's worth; and I might indeed have let him remain quiet two or three months longer. However, it is better as it is. By-the-by, your ladyship, you understand about jewels, I suppose?

Min. Not particularly.

Land. Of course your ladyship must. I must show you a ring, a valuable ring. I see you have a very beautiful one on your finger; and the more I look at it, the more I am astonished at the resemblance it bears to mine. There! just look, just look! (*taking the ring from its case, and handing it to her.*) What brilliancy! The diamond in the middle alone weighs more than five carats.

Min. (*looking at it*). Good heavens! What do I see? This ring—

Land. Is honestly worth fifteen hundred thalers.

Min. Franziska! look!

Land. I did not hesitate for a moment to advance eighty pistoles on it.

Min. Do not you recognize it, Franziska?

Fran. The same! Where did you get that ring, Mr. Landlord?

Land. Come, my girl! you surely have no claim to it?

Fran. We have no claim to this ring! My mistress's monogram must be on it, on the inner side of the setting. Look at it, my lady.

Min. It is! it is! How did you get this ring?

Land. I! In the most honourable way in the world. You do not wish to bring me into disgrace and trouble, your ladyship! How do I know where the ring properly belongs? During the war many a thing often changed masters, both with and without the knowledge of its owner. War was war. Other rings will have crossed the borders of Saxony. Give it me again, your ladyship; give it me again!

Fran. When you have said from whom you got it.

Land. From a man whom I cannot think capable of such things; in other respects a good man.

Min. From the best man under the sun, if you have it from its owner. Bring him here directly! It is himself, or at any rate he must know him.

Land. Who? who, your ladyship?

Fran. Are you deaf? Our Major!

Land. Major! Right! he is a Major, who had this room before you, and from whom I received it.

Min. Major von Tellheim!

Land. Yes, Tellheim. Do you know him?

Min. Do I know him! He is here! Tellheim here! He had this room! He! he pledged this ring with you! What has brought him into this embarrassment? Where is he? Does he owe you anything? Franziska, my desk here! Open it! (FRANZISKA *puts it on the table and opens it.*) What does he owe you? To whom else does he owe anything? Bring me all his creditors! Here is gold: here are notes. It is all his!

Land. What is this?

Min. Where is he? Where is he?

Land. An hour ago he was here.

Min. Detested man! how could you act so rudely, so hardly, so cruelly towards him?

Land. Your ladyship must pardon—

Min. Quick! Bring him to me.

Land. His servant is perhaps still here. Does your ladyship wish that he should look for him?

Min. Do I wish it? Begone, run. For this service alone I will forget how badly you have behaved to him.

Fran. Now then, quick, Mr. Landlord! Be off! fly! fly! (*Pushes him out.*)

SCENE III.—MINNA, FRANZISKA

Min. Now I have found him again, Franziska! Do you hear? Now I have found him again! I scarcely know where I am for joy! Rejoice with me, Franziska. But why should you? And yet you shall; you must rejoice with me. Come, I will make you a present, that you may be able to rejoice with me. Say, Franziska, what shall I give you? Which of my things would please you? What would you like? Take what you will; only rejoice with me. I see you will take nothing. Stop! (*Thrusts her hand into the desk.*) There, Franziska (*gives her money*), buy yourself what you like. Ask for more, if it be not sufficient; but rejoice with me you must. It is so melancholy to be happy alone. There, take it, then.

Fran. It is stealing it from you, my lady. You are intoxicated, quite intoxicated with joy.

Min. Girl, my intoxication is of a quarrelsome kind. Take it, or (*forcing money into her hand*) . . . and if you thank me . . . Stay, it is well that I think of it. (*Takes more money from the desk.*) Put that aside, Franziska, for the first poor wounded soldier who accosts us.

Scene IV.—Landlord, Minna, and Franziska

Min. Well, is he coming?

Land. The cross, unmannered fellow!

Min. Who?

Land. His servant. He refuses to go for him.

Fran. Bring the rascal here, then. I know all the Major's servants. Which one of them was it?

Min. Bring him here directly. When he sees us he will go fast enough. (*Exit* Landlord.)

Scene V.—Minna, Franziska

Min. I cannot bear this delay. But, Franziska, how cold you are still! Why will you not share my joy with me?

Fran. I would from my heart, if only—

Min. If only what?

Fran. We have found him again. But how have we found him? From all we hear, it must go badly with him. He must be unfortunate. That distresses me.

Min. Distresses you! Let me embrace you for that, my dear playmate! I shall never forget this of you. I am only in love, *you* are good.

Scene VI.—Landlord, Just, *and the above*

Land. With great difficulty I have brought him.

Fran. A strange face! I do not know him.

Min. Friend, do you live with Major von Tellheim?

Just. Yes.

Min. Where is your master?

Just. Not here.

Min. But you could find him?

Just. Yes.

Min. Will you fetch him quickly?

Just. No.

Min. You will be doing me a favour.

Just. Indeed!

Min. And your master a service.

Just. Perhaps not.

Min. Why do you suppose that?

Just. You are the strange lady who sent your compliments to him this morning, I think?

Min. Yes.

Just. Then I am right.

Min. Does your master know my name?

Just. No; but he likes over-civil ladies as little as over-uncivil landlords.

Land. That is meant for me, I suppose?

Just. Yes.

Land. Well, do not let the lady suffer for it then; but bring him here directly.

Min. (*to* FRANZISKA). Franziska, give him something—

Fran. (*trying to put some money into* JUST's *hand*). We do not require your services for nothing.

Just. Nor I your money without services.

Fran. One in return for the other.

Just. I cannot. My master has ordered me to pack up. That I am now about, and I beg you not to hinder me further. When I have finished, I will take care to tell him that he may come here. He is close by, at the coffee-house; and if he finds nothing better to do there, I suppose he will come. (*Going.*)

Fran. Wait a moment! My lady is the Major's . . . sister.

Min. Yes, yes, his sister.

Just. I know better; the Major has not a sister. He has sent me twice in six months to his family in Courland. It is true there are different sorts of sisters—

Fran. Insolent!

Just. One must be so to get the people to let one alone. (*Exit.*)

Fran. That is a rascal.

Land. So I said. But let him go! I know now where his master is. I will fetch him instantly myself. I only beg your ladyship, most humbly, that you will make an excuse for me to the Major, that I have been so unfortunate as to offend a man of his merit against my will.

Min. Pray go quickly. I will set all that right again. (*Exit the* LANDLORD.) Franziska, run after him, and tell him not to mention my name! (*Exit* FRANZISKA.)

SCENE VII.—MINNA, *and afterwards* FRANZISKA

Min. I have found him again!—Am I alone?—I will not be alone to no purpose.—(*Clasping her hands.*) Yet I am not alone! (*Looking upwards.*) One single grateful thought towards heaven, is the most perfect prayer! I have found him! I have found him! (*With outstretched arms.*) I am joyful and happy! What can please the Creator more than a joyful creature! (FRANZISKA *returns.*) Have you returned, Franziska? You pity him! I do not pity him. Misfortune too is useful. Perhaps heaven deprived him of everything—to give him all again, through me!

Fran. He may be here at any moment.—You are still in your morning dress, my lady. Ought you not to dress yourself quickly?

Min. Not at all. He will now see me more frequently so, than dressed out.

Fran. Oh! you know, my lady, how you look best.

Min. (*after a pause*). Truly, girl, you have hit it again.

Fran. I think women who are beautiful, are most so when unadorned.

Min. Must we then be beautiful? Perhaps it was necessary that we should think ourselves so. Enough for me, if only I am beautiful in his eyes. Franziska, if all women feel as I now feel, we are—strange things. Tender-hearted, yet proud; virtuous, yet vain; passionate, yet innocent. I dare say you do not understand me. I do not rightly understand myself. Joy turns my head.

Fran. Compose yourself, my lady, I hear footsteps.

Min. Compose myself! What! receive him composedly?

Scene VIII.—Major von Tellheim, Landlord, *and the above*

Maj. T. (*walks in, and the moment he sees* Minna *rushes towards her*). Ah! my Minna!

Min. (*springing towards him*). Ah! my Tellheim!

Maj. T. (*starts suddenly, and draws back*). I beg your pardon, Fräulein von Barnhelm; but to meet you here—

Min. Cannot surely be so unexpected! (*Approaching him, whilst he draws back still more.*) Am I to pardon you because I am still your Minna? Heaven pardon you, that I am still Fräulein von Barnhelm!

Maj. T. Fräulein . . . (*Looks fixedly at the* Landlord, *and shrugs his shoulders.*)

Min. (*sees the* Landlord, *and makes a sign to* Franziska). Sir—

Maj. T. If we are not both mistaken—

Fran. Why, Landlord, whom have you brought us here? Come, quick! let us go and look for the right man.

Land. Is he not the right one? Surely!

Fran. Surely not! Come, quick! I have not yet wished your daughter good morning.

Land. Oh! you are very good (*still does not stir*).

Fran. (*takes hold of him*). Come, and we will make the bill of fare. Let us see what we shall have.

Land. You shall have first of all—

Fran. Stop, I say, stop! If my mistress knows now what she is to have for dinner, it will be all over with her appetite. Come, we must talk that over in private. (*Drags him off.*)

Scene IX.—Minna, Major von Tellheim

Min. Well, are we still both mistaken?

Maj. T. Would to heaven it were so!—But there is only one Minna, and you are that one.

Min. What ceremony! The world might hear what we have to say to one another.

Maj. T. You here? What do you want here, Madam?

Min. Nothing now (*going to him with open arms*). I have found all that I wanted.

Maj. T. (*drawing back*). You seek a prosperous man, and one worthy of your love; and you find—a wretched one.

Min. Then do you love me no longer? Do you love another?

Maj. T. Ah! he never loved you, who could love another afterwards.

Min. You draw but one dagger from my breast; for if I have lost your heart, what matters whether indifference or more powerful charms than mine have robbed me of it? You love me no longer; neither do you love another? Wretched man indeed, if you love nothing!

Maj. T. Right; the wretched must love nothing. He merits his misfortunes, if he cannot achieve this victory over himself—if he can allow the woman he loves to take part in his misfortune . . . Oh! how difficult is this victory! . . . Since reason and necessity have commanded me to forget Minna von Barnhelm, what pains have I taken! I was just beginning to hope that my trouble would not for ever be in vain—and you appear.

Min. Do I understand you right? Stop, sir; let us see what we mean before we make further mistakes. Will you answer me one question?

Maj. T. Any one.

Min. But will you answer me without shift or subterfuge? With nothing but a plain "Yes," or "No?"

Maj. T. I will—if I can.

Min. You can. Well, notwithstanding the pains which you have taken to forget me, do you love me still, Tellheim?

Maj. T. Madam, that question—

Min. You have promised to answer Yes, or No.

Maj. T. And added, If I can.

Min. You can. You must know what passes in your heart. Do you love me still, Tellheim? Yes, or No?

Maj. T. If my heart—

Min. Yes, or No?

Maj. T. Well, Yes!

Min. Yes?

Maj. T. Yes, yes! Yet—

Min. Patience! You love me still; that is enough for me. Into what a mood have we fallen! an unpleasant, melancholy, infectious mood! I assume my own again. Now, my dear unfortunate, you love me still, and have your Minna still, and are unhappy? Hear what a conceited, foolish thing your Minna was—is. She allowed—allows herself, to imagine that she makes your whole happiness. Declare all your misery at once. She would like to try how far she can outweigh it.—Well?

Maj. T. Madam, I am not accustomed to complain.

Min. Very well. I know nothing in a soldier, after boasting, that pleases me less than complaining. But there is a certain cold, careless way of speaking of bravery and misfortune—

Maj. T. Which at the bottom is still boasting and complaining.

Min. You disputant! You should not have called yourself unhappy at all then. You should have told the whole, or kept quiet. Reason and necessity commanded you to forget me? I am a great stickler for reason; I have a great respect for necessity. But let me hear how reasonable this reason, and how necessary this necessity may be.

Maj. T. Listen then, Madam. You call me Tellheim; the name is correct. But suppose I am not that Tellheim whom you knew at home; the prosperous man, full of just pretensions, with a thirst for glory; the master of all his faculties, both of body and mind; before whom the lists of honour and prosperity stood open; who, if he was not then worthy of your heart and your hand, dared to hope that he might daily become more nearly so. This Tellheim I am now, as little as I am my own father. They both have been. Now I am Tellheim the discharged, the suspected, the cripple, the beggar. To the former, Madam, you promised your hand; do you wish to keep your word?

Min. That sounds very tragic . . . Yet, Major Tellheim, until I find the former one again—I am quite foolish about the Tellheims—the latter will have to help me in my dilemma. Your hand, dear beggar! (*taking his hand*).

Maj. T. (*holding his hat before his face with the other hand, and turning away from her*). This is too much! . . . What am I? . . . Let me go, Madam. Your kindness tortures me! Let me go.

Min. What is the matter? Where would you go?

Maj. T. From you!

Min. From me (*drawing his hand to her heart*)? Dreamer!

Maj. T. Despair will lay me dead at your feet.

Min. From me?

Maj. T. From you. Never, never to see you again. Or at least determined, fully determined, never to be guilty of a mean action; never to cause you to commit an imprudent one. Let me go, Minna!

(*Tears himself away, and Exit.*)

Min. (*calling after him*). Let you go, Minna? Minna, let **you** go? Tellheim! Tellheim!

ACT III

Scene I.—*The Parlour. Enter* Just (*with a letter in his hand*)

Just. Must I come again into this cursed house! A note from my master to her ladyship that would be his sister. I hope nothing will come of this, or else there will be no end to letter carrying. I should like to be rid of it; but yet I don't wish to go into the room. The women ask so many questions, and I hate answering—Ah! the door opens. Just what I wanted, the waiting puss!

Scene II.—Franziska and Just

Fran. (*calling through the door by which she has just entered*). Fear not; I will watch. See! (*observing* Just) I have met with something immediately. But nothing is to be done with that brute.

Just. Your servant.

Fran. I should not like such a servant.

Just. Well, well, pardon the expression! There is a note from my master to your mistress—her ladyship—his sister, wasn't it?—sister.

Fran. Give it me! (*Snatches it from his hand.*)

Just. You will be so good, my master begs, as to deliver it. Afterwards you will be so good, my master begs, as not to think I ask for anything!

Fran. Well?

Just. My master understands how to manage the affair. He knows that the way to the young lady is through her maid, methinks. The maid will therefore be so good, my master begs, as to let him know whether he may not have the pleasure of speaking with the maid for a quarter of an hour.

Fran. With me?

Just. Pardon me, if I do not give you your right title. Yes, with you. Only for one quarter of an hour; but alone, quite alone, in private tête-à-tête. He has something very particular to say to you.

Fran. Very well! I have also much to say to him. He may come; I shall be at his service.

Just. But when can he come? When is it most convenient for you, young woman? In the evening?

Fran. What do you mean? Your master can come when he pleases; and now be off.

Just. Most willingly! (*Going.*)

Fran. I say! one word more! Where are the rest of the Major's servants?

Just. The rest? Here, there, and everywhere.

Fran. Where is William?

Just. The valet? He has let him go for a trip.

Fran. Oh! and Philip, where is he?

Just. The huntsman? Master has found him a good place.

Fran. Because he does not hunt now, of course. But Martin?

Just. The coachman? He is off on a ride.

Fran. And Fritz?

Just. The footman? He is promoted.

Fran. Where were you then, when the Major was quartered in Thuringia with us that winter? You were not with him, I suppose!

Just. Oh! yes, I was groom; but I was in the hospital.

Fran. Groom! and now you are—

Just. All in all; valet and huntsman, footman and groom.

Fran. Well, I never! To turn away so many good, excellent servants, and to keep the very worst of all! I should like to know what your master finds in you!

Just. Perhaps he finds that I am an honest fellow.

Fran. Oh! one is precious little if one is nothing more than honest. William was another sort of a man! So your master has let him go for a trip!

Just. Yes, he . . . let him—because he could not prevent him.

Fran. How so?

Just. Oh! William will do well on his travels. He took master's wardrobe with him.

Fran. What! he did not run away with it?

Just. I cannot say that exactly; but when we left Nürnberg, he did not follow us with it.

Fran. Oh! the rascal!

Just. He was the right sort! he could curl hair and shave—and chatter—and flirt—couldn't he?

Fran. At any rate, I would not have turned away the huntsman, had I been in the Major's place. If he did not want him any longer as huntsman, he was still a useful fellow. Where has he found him a place?

Just. With the Commandant of Spandau.

Fran. The fortress! There cannot be much hunting within the walls either.

Just. Oh! Philip does not hunt there.

Fran. What does he do, then?

Just. He rides—on the treadmill.

Fran. The treadmill!

Just. But only for three years. He made a bit of a plot amongst master's company, to get six men through the outposts.

Fran. I am astonished; the knave!

Just. Ah! he was a useful fellow; a huntsman who knew all the foot-paths and by-ways for fifty miles round, through forests and bogs. And he could shoot!

Fran. It is lucky the Major has still got the honest coachman.

Just. Has he got him still?

Fran. I thought you said Martin was off on a ride: of course he will come back!

Just. Do you think so?

Fran. Well, where has he ridden to?

Just. It is now going on for ten weeks since he rode master's last and only horse—to water.

Fran. And has not he come back yet? Oh! the rascal!

Just. The water may have washed the honest coachman away. Oh! he was a famous coachman! He had driven ten years in Vienna.

My master will never get such another again. When the horses were in full gallop, he only had to say "Wo!" and there they stood, like a wall. Moreover, he was a finished horse-doctor!

Fran. I begin now to be anxious about the footman's promotion.

Just. No, no; there is no occasion for that. He has become a drummer in a garrison regiment.

Fran. I thought as much!

Just. Fritz chummed up with a scamp, never came home at night, made debts everywhere in master's name, and a thousand rascally tricks. In short, the Major saw that he was determined to rise in the world (*pantomimically imitating the act of hanging*), so he put him in the right road.

Fran. Oh! the stupid!

Just. Yet a perfect footman, there is no doubt of that. In running, my master could not catch him on his best horse if he gave him fifty paces; but on the other hand, Fritz could give the gallows a thousand paces, and, I bet my life, he would overhaul it. They were all great friends of yours, eh, young woman? . . . William and Philip, Martin and Fritz! Now, Just wishes you good-day. (*Exit.*)

SCENE III.—FRANZISKA, *and afterwards the* LANDLORD

Fran. (*looking after him seriously*). I deserve the hit! Thank you, Just. I undervalued honesty. I will not forget the lesson. Ah! our unfortunate Major! (*Turns round to enter her mistress's room, when the* LANDLORD *comes.*)

Land. Wait a bit, my pretty maid.

Fran. I have not time now, Mr. Landlord.

Land. Only half a moment! No further tidings of the Major? That surely could not possibly be his leave-taking!

Fran. What could not?

Land. Has not your ladyship told you? When I left you, my pretty maid, below in the kitchen, I returned accidentally into this room—

Fran. Accidentally—with a view to listen a little.

Land. What, girl! how can you suspect me of that? There is nothing so bad in a landlord as curiosity. I had not been here long, when suddenly her ladyship's door burst open: the Major dashed out; the lady after him; both in such a state of excitement; with looks— in attitudes—that must be seen to be understood. She seized hold of him; he tore himself away; she seized him again—"Tellheim." "Let me go, Madam." "Where?" Thus he drew her as far as the stair-case. I was really afraid he would drag her down; but he got away. The lady remained on the top step; looked after him; called after him; wrung her hands. Suddenly she turned round; ran to the win-dow; from the window to the staircase again; from the staircase into the room, backwards and forwards. There I stood; she passed me three times without seeing me. At length it seemed as if she saw me; but heaven defend us! I believe the lady took me for you. "Fran-ziska," she cried, with her eyes fixed upon me, "am I happy now?" Then she looked straight up to the ceiling, and said again—"Am I happy now?" Then she wiped the tears from her eyes, and smiled, and asked me again—"Franziska, am I happy now?" I really felt, I know not how. Then she ran to the door of her room, and turned round again towards me, saying—"Come, Franziska, whom do you pity now?" and with that she went in.

Fran. Oh! Mr. Landlord, you dreamt that.

Land. Dreamt! No, my pretty maid; one does not dream so minutely. Yes, what would not I give—I am not curious: but what would not I give—to have the key to it!

Fran. The key? Of our door? Mr. Landlord, that is inside; we took it in at night; we are timid.

Land. Not that sort of key; I mean, my dear girl, the key—the explanation, as it were; the precise connexion of all that I have seen.

Fran. Indeed! Well, good-bye, Mr. Landlord. Shall we have din-ner soon?

Land. My dear girl, not to forget what I came to say—

Fran. Well? In as few words as possible.

Land. Her ladyship has my ring still. I call it mine—

Fran. You shall not lose it.

Land. I have no fear on that account: I merely put you in mind. Do you see, I do not wish to have it again at all. I can guess pretty well how she knew the ring, and why it was so like her own. It is best in her hands. I do not want it any more; and I can put them down—the hundred pistoles which I advanced for it, to the lady's bill. Will not that do, my pretty maid?

Scene IV.—Paul Werner, Landlord, Franziska

Wer. There he is!

Fran. A hundred pistoles? I thought it was only eighty.

Land. True, only ninety, only ninety. I will do so, my pretty maid, I will do so.

Fran. All that will come right, Mr. Landlord.

Wer. (*coming from behind, and tapping* Franziska *on the shoulder*). Little woman—Little woman.

Fran. (*frightened*). Oh! dear!

Wer. Don't be alarmed! I see you are pretty, and a stranger, too. And strangers who are pretty must be warned. Little woman! little woman! I advise you to beware of that fellow! (*pointing to the* Landlord).

Land. Ah! What an unexpected pleasure! Herr Werner! Welcome, welcome! Yes, you are just the same jovial, joking, honest Werner! So you are to beware of me, my pretty maid. Ha! ha! ha!

Wer. Keep out of his way everywhere!

Land. My way? Am I such a dangerous man? Ha! ha! ha! Hear him, my pretty maid! A good joke, isn't it?

Wer. People like him always call it a joke, if one tells them the truth.

Land. The truth. Ha! ha! ha! Better and better, my pretty maid, isn't it? He knows how to joke! I dangerous? I? Twenty years ago there might have been something in it. Yes, yes, my pretty maid, then I was a dangerous man: many a one knew it; but now—

Wer. Oh! the old fool!

Land. There it is! When we get old, danger is at an end! It will be so with you too, Herr Werner!

Wer. You utter old fool!—Little woman, you will give me credit for enough common sense not to speak of danger from him. That one devil has left him, but seven others have entered into him.

Land. Oh! hear him! How cleverly he can turn things about. Joke upon joke, and always something new! Ah! he is an excellent man, Paul Werner is. (*To* FRANZISKA, *as if whispering.*) A well-to-do man, and a bachelor still. He has a nice little freehold three miles from here. He made prize-money in the war, and was a sergeant to the Major. Yes, he is a real friend of the Major's; he is a friend who would give his life for him.

Wer. Yes; and that is a friend of the Major's—that is a friend . . . whose life the Major ought to take (*pointing to the* LANDLORD).

Land. How! What! No, Herr Werner, that is not a good joke. I no friend to the Major! I don't understand that joke.

Wer. Just has told me pretty things.

Land. Just! Ah! I thought Just was speaking through you. Just is a nasty, ill-natured man. But here on the spot stands a pretty maid —she can speak, she can say if I am no friend of the Major's—if I have not done him good service. And why should not I be his friend? Is not he a deserving man? It is true, he has had the misfortune to be discharged; but what of that? The king cannot be acquainted with all deserving officers; and if he knew them, he could not reward them all.

Wer. Heaven put those words into your mouth. But Just . . . certainly there is nothing remarkable about Just, but still Just is no liar; and if that what he has told me be true—

Land. I don't want to hear anything about Just. As I said, this pretty maid here can speak. (*Whispering to her.*) You know, my dear; the ring! Tell Herr Werner about it. Then he will learn better what I am. And that it may not appear as if she only said what I wish, I will not even be present. I will go; but you shall tell me after, Herr Werner, you shall tell me, whether Just is not a foul slanderer. (*Exit.*)

SCENE V.—WERNER, FRANZISKA

Wer. Little woman, do you know my Major?

Fran. Major von Tellheim? Yes, indeed, I do know that good man.

Wer. Is he not a good man? Do you like him?

Fran. From the bottom of my heart.

Wer. Indeed! I tell you what, little woman, you are twice as pretty now as you were before. But what are the services, which the landlord says he has rendered our Major?

Fran. That is what I don't know; unless he wished to take credit to himself for the good result which fortunately has arisen from his knavish conduct.

Wer. Then what Just told me is true? (*Towards the side where the* LANDLORD *went off.*) A lucky thing for you that you are gone! He did really turn him out of his room?—To treat such a man so, because the donkey fancied that he had no more money! The Major no money!

Fran. What! Has the Major any money?

Wer. By the load. He doesn't know how much he has. He doesn't know who is in his debt. I am his debtor, and have brought him some old arrears. Look, little woman, in this purse (*drawing it out of one pocket*) are a hundred louis d'ors; and in this packet (*drawing it out of another pocket*) a hundred ducats. All his money!

Fran. Really! Why then does the Major pawn his things? He pledged a ring, you know—

Wer. Pledged! Don't you believe it. Perhaps he wanted to get rid of the rubbish.

Fran. It is no rubbish; it is a very valuable ring; which, moreover, I suspect, he received from a loving hand.

Wer. That will be the reason. From a loving hand! Yes, yes; such a thing often puts one in mind of what one does not wish to remember, and therefore one gets rid of it.

Fran. What!

Wer. Odd things happen to the soldier in winter quarters. He has nothing to do then, so he amuses himself, and to pass the time he makes acquaintances, which he only intends for the winter, but which the good soul with whom he makes them, looks upon for life. Then, presto! a ring is suddenly conjured on to his finger; he hardly knows himself how it gets there; and very often he would willingly give the finger with it, if he could only get free from it again.

Fran. Oh! and do you think this has happened to the Major?

Wer. Undoubtedly. Especially in Saxony. If he had had ten fingers on each hand, he might have had all twenty full of rings.

Fran. (*aside*). That sounds important, and deserves to be inquired into. Mr. Freeholder, or Mr. Sergeant—

Wer. Little woman, if it makes no difference to you, I like "Mr. Sergeant" best.

Fran. Well, Mr. Sergeant, I have a note from the Major to my mistress. I will just carry it in, and be here again in a moment. Will you be so good as to wait? I should like very much to have a little talk with you.

Wer. Are you fond of talking, little woman? Well, with all my heart. Go quickly. I am fond of talking too: I will wait.

Fran. Yes, please wait. (*Exit.*)

Scene VI.—Paul Werner

Wer. That is not at all a bad little woman. But I ought not to have promised her that I would wait, for it would be most to the purpose, I suppose, to find the Major. He will not have my money, but rather pawns his property. That is just his way. A little trick occurs to me. When I was in the town, a fortnight back, I paid a visit to Captain Marloff's widow. The poor woman was ill, and was lamenting that her husband had died in debt to the Major for four hundred thalers, which she did not know how to pay. I went to see her again to-day; I intended to tell her that I could lend her five hundred thalers, when I had received the money for my property; for I must put some of it by, if I do not go to Persia. But she was gone; and no doubt she has not been able to pay the Major. Yes, I'll do that; and the sooner the better. The little woman must not take it ill of me; I cannot wait.

(*Is going in thought, and almost runs against the* Major, *who meets him.*)

Scene VII.—Major von Tellheim, Paul Werner

Maj. T. Why so thoughtful, Werner?

Wer. Oh! that is you. I was just going to pay you a visit in your new quarters, Major.

Maj. T. To fill my ears with curses against the Landlord of my old one. Do not remind me of it.

Wer. I should have done that by the way: yes. But more particularly, I wish to thank you for having been so good as to take care of my hundred louis d'ors. Just has given them to me again. I should have been very glad if you would have kept them longer for me. But you have got into new quarters, which neither you nor I know much about. Who knows what sort of place it is? They might be stolen, and you would have to make them good to me; there would be no help for it. So I cannot ask you to take them again.

Maj. T. (*smiling*). When did you begin to be so careful, Werner?

Wer. One learns to be so. One cannot now be careful enough of one's money. I have also a commission for you, Major, from Frau Marloff; I have just come from her. Her husband died four hundred thalers in your debt; she sends you a hundred ducats here, in part payment. She will forward you the rest next week. I believe I am the cause that she has not sent you the whole sum. For she also owed me about eighty thalers, and she thought I was come to dun her for them—which, perhaps, was the fact—so she gave them me out of the roll which she had put aside for you. You can spare your hundred thalers for a week longer, better than I can spare my few groschens. There, take it! (*Hands him the ducats.*)

Maj. T. Werner!

Wer. Well! Why do you stare at me so? Take it, Major!

Maj. T. Werner!

Wer. What is the matter with you? What annoys you?

Maj. T. (*angrily striking his forehead, and stamping with his foot.*) That . . . the four hundred thalers are not all there.

Wer. Come! Major, did not you understand me?

Maj. T. It is just because I did understand you! Alas, that the best men should to-day distress me most!

Wer. What do you say?

Maj. T. This only applies partly to you. Go, Werner! (*Pushing back* WERNER's *hand with the money in it.*)

Wer. As soon as I have got rid of this.

Maj. T. Werner, suppose I tell you that Frau Marloff was here herself early this morning—

Wer. Indeed?

Maj. T. That she owes me nothing now—

Wer. Really?

Maj. T. That she has paid me every penny—What will you say then?

Wer. (*thinks for a minute*). I shall say that I have told a lie, and that lying is a low thing, because one may be caught at it.

Maj. T. And you will be ashamed of yourself?

Wer. And what of him who compels me to lie? Should not he be ashamed too? Look ye, Major; if I was to say that your conduct has not vexed me, I should tell another lie, and I won't lie any more.

Maj. T. Do not be annoyed, Werner. I know your heart, and your affection for me. But I do not require your money.

Wer. Not require it! Rather sell, rather pawn, and get talked about!

Maj. T. Oh! people may know that I have nothing more. One must not wish to appear richer than one is.

Wer. But why poorer? A man has something as long as his friend has.

Maj. T. It is not proper that I should be your debtor.

Wer. Not proper! On that summer day which the sun and the enemy made hot for us, when your groom, who had your canteen, was not to be found, and you came to me and said—"Werner, have you nothing to drink?" and I gave you my flask, you took it and drank, did you not? Was that proper? Upon my life, a mouthful of dirty water at that time was often worth more than such filth (*taking the purse also out of his pocket, and holding out both to him*). Take them, dear Major! Fancy it is water. God has made this, too, for all.

Maj. T. You torment me: don't you hear, I will not be your debtor.

Wer. At first, it was not proper; now, you will not. Ah! that is a different thing. (*Rather angrily.*) You will not be my debtor? But suppose you are already, Major? Or, are you not a debtor to the man who once warded off the blow that was meant to split your head; and, at another time, knocked off the arm which was just going to pull and send a ball through your breast? How can you become a greater debtor to that man? Or, is my neck of less consequence than my money? If that is a noble way of thinking, by my soul it is a very silly one too.

Maj. T. To whom do you say that, Werner? We are alone, and therefore I may speak; if a third person heard us, it might sound like boasting. I acknowledge with pleasure, that I have to thank you for twice saving my life. Do you not think, friend, that if an opportunity occurred I would have done as much for you, eh?

Wer. If an opportunity occurred! Who doubts it, Major? Have I not seen you risk your life a hundred times for the lowest soldier, when he was in danger?

Maj. T. Well!

Wer. But—

Maj. T. Why cannot you understand me? I say, it is not proper that I should be your debtor; I will not be your debtor. That is, not in the circumstances in which I now am.

Wer. Oh! so you would wait till better times. You will borrow money from me another time, when you do not want any: when you have some yourself, and I perhaps none.

Maj. T. A man ought not to borrow, when he has not the means of repaying.

Wer. A man like yourself cannot always be in want.

Maj. T. You know the world . . . Least of all should a man borrow from one who wants his money himself.

Wer. Oh! yes; I am such a one! Pray, what do I want it for? When they want a sergeant, they give him enough to live on.

Maj. T. You want it, to become something more than a sergeant— to be able to get forward in that path in which even the most deserving, without money, may remain behind.

Wer. To become something more than a sergeant! I do not think of that. I am a good sergeant; I might easily make a bad captain, and certainly a worse general.

Maj. T. Do not force me to think ill of you, Werner! I was very sorry to hear what Just has told me. You have sold your farm, and wish to rove about again. Do not let me suppose that you do not love the profession of arms so much as the wild dissolute way of living which is unfortunately connected with it. A man should be a soldier for his own country, or from love of the cause for which he fights. To serve without any purpose—to-day here, to-morrow there —is only travelling about like a butcher's apprentice, nothing more.

Wer. Well, then, Major, I will do as you say. You know better what is right. I will remain with you. But, dear Major, do take my money in the meantime. Sooner or later your affairs must be settled. You will get money in plenty then; and then you shall repay me with interest. I only do it for the sake of the interest.

Maj. T. Do not talk of it.

Wer. Upon my life, I only do it for the sake of the interest. Many a time I have thought to myself—"Werner, what will become of you in your old age? when you are crippled? when you will have nothing in the world? when you will be obliged to go and beg!" And then I thought again—"No, you will not be obliged to beg: you will go to Major Tellheim; he will share his last penny with you; he will feed you till you die; and with him you can die like an honest fellow."

Maj. T. (taking WERNER's *hand).* And, comrade, you do not think so still?

Wer. No, I do not think so any longer. He who will not take anything from me, when he is in want, and I have to give, will not give me anything when he has to give, and I am in want. So be it. *(Is going.)*

Maj. T. Man, do not drive me mad! Where are you going? *(Detains him.)* If I assure you now, upon my honour, that I still have money—If I assure you, upon my honour, that I will tell you when I have no more—that you shall be the first and only person from whom I will borrow anything—will that content you?

Wer. I suppose it must. Give me your hand on it, Major.

Maj. T. There, Paul! And now enough of that. I came here to speak with a certain young woman.

SCENE VIII.—FRANZISKA *(coming out of* MINNA's *room)*, MAJOR VON TELLHEIM, PAUL WERNER

Fran. (entering). Are you there still, Mr. Sergeant? *(Seeing* TELLHEIM.) And you there too, Major? I will be at your service instantly. *(Goes back quickly into the room.)*

SCENE IX.—MAJOR VON TELLHEIM, PAUL WERNER

Maj. T. That was she! But it seems you know her, Werner.

Wer. Yes, I know her.

Maj. T. Yet, if I remember rightly, when I was in Thuringia you were not with me.

Wer. No; I was seeing after the uniforms in Leipsic.

Maj. T. Where did you make her acquaintance, then?

Wer. Our acquaintance is very young. Not a day old. But young friendship is warm.

Maj. T. Have you seen her mistress, too?

Wer. Is her mistress a young lady? She told me you are acquainted with her mistress.

Maj. T. Did not you hear? She comes from Thuringia.

Wer. Is the lady young?

Maj. T. Yes.

Wer. Pretty?

Maj. T. Very pretty.

Wer. Rich?

Maj. T. Very rich.

Wer. Is the mistress as fond of you as the maid is? That would be capital!

Maj. T. What do you mean?

SCENE X.—FRANZISKA (*with a letter in her hand*), MAJOR VON TELLHEIM, PAUL WERNER

Fran. Major—

Maj. T. Franziska, I have not yet been able to give you a "Welcome" here.

Fran. In thought, I am sure that you have done it. I know you are friendly to me; so am I to you. But it is not at all kind to vex those who are friendly to you so much.

Wer. (*aside*). Ah! now I see it. It is so!

Maj. T. My destiny, Franziska! Did you give her the letter?

Fran. Yes; and here I bring you . . . (*holding out a letter*).

Maj. T. An answer!

Fran. No, your own letter again.

Maj. T. What! She will not read it!

Fran. She would have liked, but—we can't read writing well.

Maj. T. You are joking!

Fran. And we think that writing was not invented for those who can converse with their lips whenever they please.

Maj. T. What an excuse! She must read it. It contains my justification—all the grounds and reasons—

Fran. My mistress wishes to hear them all from you yourself, not to read them.

Maj. T. Hear them from me myself! That every look, every word of hers, may embarrass me; that I may feel in every glance the greatness of my loss.

Fran. Without any pity! Take it. (*Giving him his letter.*) She expects you at three o'clock. She wishes to drive out and see the town; you must accompany her.

Maj. T. Accompany her!

Fran. And what will you give me to let you drive out by yourselves? I shall remain at home.

Maj. T. By ourselves!

Fran. In a nice close carriage.

Maj. T. Impossible!

Fran. Yes, yes, in the carriage, Major. You will have to submit quietly; you cannot escape there! And that is the reason. In short, you will come, Major, and punctually at three. . . . Well, you wanted to speak to me too alone. What have you to say to me? Oh! we are not alone. (*Looking at* WERNER.)

Maj. T. Yes, Franziska; as good as alone. But as your mistress has not read my letter, I have nothing now to say to you.

Fran. As good as alone! Then you have no secrets from the Sergeant?

Maj. T. No, none.

Fran. And yet I think you should have some from him.

Maj. T. Why so?

Wer. How so, little woman?

Fran. Particularly secrets of a certain kind. . . . All twenty, Mr. Sergeant! (*Holding up both her hands, with open fingers.*)

Wer. Hist! hist! girl.

Maj. T. What is the meaning of that?

Fran. Presto! conjured on to his finger, Mr. Sergeant (*as if she was putting a ring on her fingers*).

Maj. T. What are you talking about?

Wer. Little woman, little woman, don't you understand a joke?

Maj. T. Werner, you have not forgotten, I hope, what I have often told you; that one should not jest beyond a certain point with a young woman!

Wer. Upon my life I may have forgotten it! Little woman, I beg—

Fran. Well, if it was a joke, I will forgive you this once.

Maj. T. Well, if I must come, Franziska, just see that your mistress reads my letter beforehand? That will spare me the pain of thinking again—of talking again, of things which I would willingly forget. There, give it to her! (*He turns the letter in giving it to her, and sees that it has been opened.*) But do I see aright? Why it has been opened.

Fran. That may be. (*Looks at it.*) True, it is open. Who can have opened it? But really we have not read it, Major; really not. And we do not wish to read it, because the writer is coming himself. Come; and I tell you what, Major! don't come as you are now—in boots, and with such a head. You are excusable, you do not expect us. Come in shoes, and have your hair fresh dressed. You look too soldierlike, too Prussian for me as you are.

Maj. T. Thank you, Franziska.

Fran. You look as if you had been bivouacking last night.

Maj. T. You may have guessed right.

Fran. We are going to dress, directly too, and then have dinner. We would willingly ask you to dinner, but your presence might hinder our eating; and observe, we are not so much in love that we have lost our appetites.

Maj. T. I will go. Prepare her somewhat, Franziska, beforehand, that I may not become contemptible in her eyes, and in my own. Come, Werner, you shall dine with me.

Wer. At the table d'hôte here in the house? I could not eat a bit there.

Maj. T. With me, in my room.

Wer. I will follow you directly. One word first with the little woman.

Maj. T. I have no objection to that. (*Exit.*)

SCENE XI.—PAUL WERNER, FRANZISKA

Fran. Well, Mr. Sergeant!

Wer. Little woman, if I come again, shall I too come smartened up a bit?

Fran. Come as you please: my eyes will find no fault with you. But my ears will have to be so much the more on their guard. Twenty fingers, all full of rings. Ah! ah! Mr. Sergeant!

Wer. No, little woman; that is just what I wished to say to you. I only rattled on a little. There is nothing in it. One ring is quite enough for a man. Hundreds and hundreds of times I have heard the Major say—"He must be a rascally soldier, who can mislead a young girl." So think I too, little woman. You may trust to that! I must be quick and follow him. A good appetite to you. (*Exit.*)

Fran. The same to you! I really believe, I like that man! (*Going in, she meets* MINNA *coming out.*)

SCENE XII.—MINNA, FRANZISKA

Min. Has the Major gone already, Franziska? I believe I should have been sufficiently composed again now to have detained him here.

Fran. And I will make you still more composed.

Min. So much the better! His letter! oh! his letter! Each line spoke the honourable noble man. Each refusal to accept my hand declared his love for me. I suppose he noticed that we had read his letter. I don't mind that, if he does but come. But are you sure he will come? There only seems to me to be a little too much pride in his conduct. For not to be willing to be indebted for his good fortune, even to the woman he loves, is pride, unpardonable pride! If he shows me too much of this, Franziska—

Fran. You will discard him!

Min. See there! Do you begin to pity him again already! No, silly girl, a man is never discarded for a single fault. No; but I have thought of a trick—to pay him off a little for this pride, with pride of the same kind.

Fran. Indeed, you must be very composed, my lady, if you are thinking of tricks again.

Min. I am so; come. You will have a part to play in my plot. (*Exeunt.*)

ACT IV

SCENE I.—MINNA's *Room.* MINNA (*dressed handsomely and richly, but in good taste*), FRANZISKA

(*They have just risen from a table, which a servant is clearing.*)

Fran. You cannot possibly have eaten enough, my lady.

Min. Don't you think so, Franziska? Perhaps I had no appetite when I sat down.

Fran. We had agreed not to mention him during dinner. We should have resolved likewise, not to think of him.

Min. Indeed, I have thought of nothing but him.

Fran. So I perceived. I began to speak of a hundred different things, and you made wrong answers to each. (*Another servant brings coffee.*) Here comes a beverage more suited to fancies—sweet, melancholy coffee.

Min. Fancies! I have none. I am only thinking of the lesson I will give him. Did you understand my plan, Franziska?

Fran. Oh! yes; but it would be better if he spared us the putting it in execution.

Min. You will see that I know him thoroughly. He who refuses me now with all my wealth, will contend for me against the whole world, as soon as he hears that I am unfortunate and friendless.

Fran. (*seriously*). That must tickle the most refined self-love.

Min. You moralist! First you convict me of vanity—now of self-love. Let me do as I please, Franziska. You, too, shall do as you please with your Sergeant.

Fran. With my Sergeant?

Min. Yes. If you deny it altogether, then it is true. I have not seen him yet; but from all you have said respecting him, I foretell your husband for you.

SCENE II.—RICCAUT DE LA MARLINIÈRE, MINNA, FRANZISKA

Ric. (*before he enters*). Est-il permis, Monsieur le Major?

Fran. Who is that? Any one for us? (*going to the door*).

Ric. Parbleu! I am wrong. Mais non—I am not wrong. C'est la chambre—

Fran. Without doubt, my lady, this gentleman expects to find Major von Tellheim here still.

Ric. Oui, dat is it! Le Major de Tellheim; juste, ma belle enfant, c'est lui que je cherche. Où est-il?

Fran. He does not lodge here any longer.

Ric. Comment? Dere is four-and-twenty hour ago he did lodge here, and not lodge here any more? Where lodge he den?

Min. (*going up to him*). Sir—

Ric. Ah! Madame, Mademoiselle, pardon, lady.

Min. Sir, your mistake is quite excusable, and your astonishment very natural. Major von Tellheim has had the kindness to give up his apartments to me, as a stranger, who was not able to get them elsewhere.

Ric. Ah! voilà de ses politesses! C'est un très-galant homme que ce Major!

Min. Where has he gone now?—truly I am ashamed that I do not know.

Ric. Madame not know? C'est dommage; j'en suis fâché.

Min. I certainly ought to have inquired. Of course his friends will seek him here.

Ric. I am vary great his friend, Madame.

Min. Franziska, do you not know?

Fran. No, my lady.

Ric. It is vary nécessaire dat I speak him. I come and bring him a nouvelle, of which he will be vary much at ease.

Min. I regret it so much the more. But I hope to see him perhaps shortly. If it is a matter of indifference from whom he hears this good news, I would offer, sir—

Ric. I comprehend. Mademoiselle parle français? Mais sans doute; telle que je la vois! La demande était bien impolie; vous me pardonnerez, Mademoiselle.

Min. Sir—

Ric. No! You not speak French, Madame?

Min. Sir, in France I would endeavour to do so; but why here? I perceive that you understand me, sir; and I, sir, shall doubtless understand you; speak as you please.

Ric. Good, good! I can also explain me in your langue. Sachez

donc, Mademoiselle, you must know, Madame, dat I come from de
table of de ministre, ministre de, ministre de . . . What is le ministre
out dere, in de long street, on de broad place?

Min. I am a perfect stranger here.

Ric. Si, le ministre of de war departement. Dere I have eat my
dinner; I ordinary dine dere, and de conversation did fall on Major
Tellheim; et le ministre m'a dit en confidence, car Son Excellence
est de mes amis, et il n'y a point de mystères entre nous; Son Excellence, I say, has trust to me, dat l'affaire from our Major is on de
point to end, and to end good. He has made a rapport to de king,
and de king has resolved et tout à fait en faveur du Major. "Monsieur," m'a dit Son Excellence, "vous comprenez bien, que tout dé-
pend de la manière, dont on fait envisager les choses au roi, et vous
me connaissez. Cela fait un très-joli garçon que ce Tellheim, et ne
sais-je pas que vous l'aimez? Les amis de mes amis sont aussi les
miens. Il coûte un peu cher au Roi ce Tellheim, mais est-ce que
l'on sert les rois pour rien? Il faut s'entr'aider en ce monde; et
quand il s'agit de pertes, que ce soit le Roi qui en fasse, et non pas
un honnête homme de nous autres. Voilà le principe, dont je ne me
dépars jamais." But what say Madame to it? N'est pas, dat is a
fine fellow! Ah! que Son Excellence a le cœur bien placé! He
assure me au reste, if de Major has not reçu already une lettre de
la main—a royal letter, dat to-day infailliblement must he receive
one.

Min. Certainly, sir, this news will be most welcome to Major von
Tellheim. I should like to be able to name the friend to him, who
takes such an interest in his welfare.

Ric. Madame, you wish my name? Vous voyez en moi—you see,
lady, in me, le Chevalier Riccaut de la Marlinière, Seigneur de Prêt-
au-val, de la branche de Prens d'or. You remain astonished to hear
me from so great, great a family, qui est véritablement du sang
royal. Il faut le dire; je suis sans doute le cadet le plus aventureux
que la maison n'a jamais eu. I serve from my eleven year. Une
affaire d'honneur make me flee. Den I serve de holy Papa of Rome,
den de Republic St. Marino, den de Poles, den de States General, till
enfin I am brought here. Ah! Mademoiselle, que je voudrais n'avoir
jamais vu ce pays-ci! Had one left me in de service of de States Gen-

eral, should I be now at least colonel. But here always to remain capitaine, and now also a discharged capitaine.

Min. That is ill luck.

Ric. Oui, Mademoiselle, me voilà réformé, et par là mis sur le pavé!

Min. I am very sorry for you.

Ric. Vous êtes bien bonne, Mademoiselle. . . . No, merit have n. reward here. Réformer a man, like me! A man who also have ruin himself in dis service! I have lost in it so much as twenty thousand livres. What have I now? Tranchons le mot; je n'ai pas le sou, et me voilà exactement vis-à-vis de rien.

Min. I am exceedingly sorry.

Ric. Vous êtes bien bonne, Mademoiselle. But as one say—misfortune never come alone! qu'un malheur ne vient jamais seul: so it arrive with me. What ressource rests for an honnête homme of my extraction, but play? Now, I always played with luck, so long I not need her. Now I very much need her, je joue avec un guignon, Mademoiselle, qui surpasse toute croyance. For fifteen days, not one is passed, dat I always am broke. Yesterday, I was broke dree times. Je sais bien, qu'il y avait quelque chose de plus que le jeu. Car parmi mes pontes se trouvaient certaines dames. I will not speak more. One must be very galant to les dames. Dey have invite me again to-day, to give me revanche; mais—vous m'entendez, Mademoiselle, —one must first have to live, before one can have to play.

Min. I hope, sir—

Ric. Vous êtes bien bonne, Mademoiselle.

Min. (*Takes* FRANZISKA *aside.*) Franziska, I really feel for the man. Would he take it ill, if I offer him something?

Fran. He does not look to me like a man who would.

Min. Very well! Sir, I perceive that—you play, that you keep the bank; doubtless in places where something is to be won. I must also confess that I . . . am very fond of play.

Ric. Tant mieux, Mademoiselle, tant mieux! Tous les gens d'esprit aiment le jeu à la fureur.

Min. That I am very fond of winning; that I like to trust my money to a man, who—knows how to play. Are you inclined, sir, to let me join you? To let me have a share in your bank?

Ric. Comment, Mademoiselle, vous voulez être de moitié avec moi? De tout mon cœur.

Min. At first, only with a trifle. (*Opens her desk and takes out some money.*)

Ric. Ah! Mademoiselle, que vous êtes charmante!

Min. Here is what I won a short time back; only ten pistoles. I am ashamed, so little—

Ric. Donnez toujours, Mademoiselle, donnez. (*Takes it.*)

Min. Without doubt, your bank, sir, is very considerable.

Ric. Oh! yes, vary considerable. Ten pistoles! You shall have, Madame, an interest in my bank for one third, pour le tiers. Yes, one third part it shall be—something more. With a beautiful lady one must not be too exac. I rejoice myself, to make by that a liaison with Madame, et de ce moment je recommence à bien augurer de ma fortune.

Min. But I cannot be present, sir, when you play.

Ric. For why it nécessaire dat you be present? We other players are honourable people between us.

Min. If we are fortunate, sir, you will of course bring me my share. If we are unfortunate—

Ric. I come to bring recruits, n'est pas, Madame?

Min. In time recruits might fail. Manage our money well, sir.

Ric. What does Madame think me? A simpleton, a stupid devil?

Min. I beg your pardon.

Ric. Je suis des bons, Mademoiselle. Savez vous ce que cela veut dire? I am of the quite practised—

Min. But still, sir,—

Ric. Je sais monter un coup—

Min. (*amazed*). Could you?

Ric. Je file la carte avec une adresse.

Min. Never!

Ric. Je fais sauter la coupe avec une dextérité.

Min. You surely would not, sir!—

Ric. What not, Madame; what not? Donnez moi un pigeonneau à plumer, et—

Min. Play false! Cheat!

Ric. Comment, Mademoiselle? Vous appelez cela cheat? Corriger

la fortune, l'enchaîner sous ses doigts, être sûr de son fait, dat you
call cheat? Cheat! Oh! what a poor tongue is your tongue! what
an awkward tongue!

Min. No, sir, if you think so—

Ric. Laissez-moi faire, Mademoiselle, and be tranquille! What
matter to you how I play! Enough! to-morrow, Madame, you see me
again or with hundred pistol, or you see no more. Votre très-humble,
Mademoiselle, votre très-humble. (*Exit quickly.*)

Min. (*looking after him with astonishment and displeasure*). I
hope the latter, sir.

SCENE III.—MINNA AND FRANZISKA

Fran. (*angrily*). What can I say? Oh! how grand! how grand!

Min. Laugh at me; I deserve it. (*After reflecting, more calmly.*)
No, do not laugh; I do not deserve it.

Fran. Excellent! You have done a charming act—set a knave upon
his legs again.

Min. It was intended for an unfortunate man.

Fran. And what is the best part of it, the fellow considers you like
himself. Oh! I must follow him, and take the money from him.
(*Going.*)

Min. Franziska, do not let the coffee get quite cold; pour it out.

Fran. He must return it to you; you have thought better of it;
you will not play in partnership with him. Ten pistoles! You heard,
my lady, that he was a beggar! (MINNA *pours out the coffee herself.*)
Who would give such a sum to a beggar? And to endeavour, into
the bargain, to save him the humiliation of having begged for it!
The charitable woman who, out of generosity, mistakes the beggar, is
in return mistaken by the beggar. It serves you right, my lady, if
he considers your gift as—I know not what. (MINNA *hands a cup
of coffee to* FRANZISKA.) Do you wish to make my blood boil still
more? I do not want any. (MINNA *puts it down again.*) "Parbleu,
Madame, merit have no reward here" (*imitating the Frenchman*).
I think not, when such rogues are allowed to walk about unhanged.

Min. (*coldly and slowly, while sipping her coffee*). Girl, you understand good men very well; but when will you learn to bear with
the bad? And yet they are also men; and frequently not so bad as

they seem. One should look for their good side. I fancy this French-man is nothing worse than vain. Through mere vanity he gives himself out as a false player; he does not wish to appear under an obligation to one; he wishes to save himself the thanks. Perhaps he may now go, pay his small debts, live quietly and frugally on the rest as far as it will go, and think no more of play. If that be so, Franziska, let him come for recruits whenever he pleases. (*Gives her cup to* FRANZISKA.) There, put it down! But, tell me, should not Tellheim be here by this time?

Fran. No, my lady, I can neither find out the bad side in a good man, nor the good side in a bad man.

Min. Surely he will come!

Fran. He ought to remain away! You remark in him—in him, the best of men—a little pride; and therefore you intend to tease him so cruelly!

Min. Are you at it again? Be silent! I will have it so. Woe to you if you spoil this fun of mine . . . if you do not say and do all, as we have agreed. I will leave you with him alone; and then—but here he comes.

SCENE IV.—PAUL WERNER (*comes in, carrying himself very erect as if on duty*), MINNA, FRANZISKA

Fran. No, it is only his dear Sergeant.

Min. Dear Sergeant! Whom does the "dear" refer to?

Fran. Pray, my lady, do not make the man embarrassed. Your servant, Mr. Sergeant; what news do you bring us?

Wer. (*goes up to* MINNA, *without noticing* FRANZISKA). Major von Tellheim begs to present, through me, Sergeant Werner, his most respectful compliments to Fräulein von Barnhelm, and to inform her that he will be here directly.

Min. Where is he then?

Wer. Your ladyship will pardon him; we left our quarters before it began to strike three; but the paymaster met us on the way; and because conversation with those gentlemen has no end, the Major made me a sign to report the case to your ladyship.

Min. Very well, Mr. Sergeant. I only hope the paymaster may have good news for him.

Wer. Such gentlemen seldom have good news for officers.—Has your ladyship any orders? (*Going.*)

Fran. Why, where are you going again, Mr. Sergeant? Had not we something to say to each other?

Wer. (*In a whisper to* Franziska, *and seriously*). Not here, little woman; it is against respect, against discipline. . . . Your ladyship—

Min. Thank you for your trouble. I am glad to have made your acquaintance. Franziska has spoken in high praise of you to me. (Werner *makes a stiff bow, and goes.*)

Scene V.—Minna, Franziska

Min. So that is your Sergeant, Franziska?

Fran. (*aside*). I have not time to reproach her for that jeering *your.* (*Aloud.*) Yes, my lady, that is my Sergeant. You think him, no doubt, somewhat stiff and wooden. He also appeared so to me just now; but I observed, he thought he must march past you as if on parade. And when soldiers are on parade, they certainly look more like wooden dolls than men. You should see and hear him when he is himself.

Min. So I should, indeed!

Fran. He must still be in the next room; may I go and talk with him a little?

Min. I refuse you this pleasure unwillingly: but you must remain here, Franziska. You must be present at our conversation. Another thing occurs to me. (*Takes her ring from her finger.*) There, take my ring; keep it for me, and give me the Major's in the place of it.

Fran. Why so?

Min. (*whilst Franziska is fetching the ring*). I scarcely know, myself; but I fancy I see, beforehand, how I may make use of it. Some one is knocking. Give it to me, quickly. (*Puts the ring on.*) It is he.

Scene VI.—Major von Tellheim (*in the same coat, but otherwise as* Franziska *advised*), Minna, Franziska

Maj. T. Madam, you will excuse the delay.

Min. Oh! Major, we will not treat each other in quite such a military fashion. You are here now; and to await a pleasure, is itself a pleasure. Well (*looking at him and smiling*) dear Tellheim, have we not been like children?

Maj. T. Yes, Madam; like children, who resist when they ought to obey quietly.

Min. We will drive out, dear Major, to see a little of the town, and afterwards to meet my uncle.

Maj. T. What!

Min. You see, we have not yet had an opportunity of mentioning the most important matters even. He is coming here to-day. It was accident that brought me here without him, a day sooner.

Maj. T. Count von Bruchsal! Has he returned?

Min. The troubles of the war drove him into Italy: peace has brought him back again. Do not be uneasy, Tellheim; if we formerly feared on his part the greatest obstacle to our union—

Maj. T. To our union!

Min. He is now your friend. He has heard too much good of you from too many people, not to become so. He longs to become personally acquainted with the man whom his heiress has chosen. He comes as uncle, as guardian, as father, to give me to you.

Maj. T. Ah! dear lady, why did you not read my letter? Why would you not read it?

Min. Your letter! Oh! yes, I remember you sent me one. What did you do with that letter, Franziska? Did we, or did we not read it? What was it you wrote to me, dear Tellheim?

Maj. T. Nothing but what honour commands me.

Min. That is, not to desert an honourable woman who loves you. Certainly that is what honour commands. Indeed, I ought to have read your letter. But what I have not read, I shall hear, shall not I?

Maj. T. Yes, you shall hear it.

Min. No, I need not even hear it. It speaks for itself. As if you could be guilty of such an unworthy act, as not to take me! Do you know that I should be pointed at for the rest of my life? My countrywomen would talk about me, and say, "That is she, that is the Fräulein von Barnhelm, who fancied that because she was rich she could marry the noble Tellheim; as if such men were to be caught with money." That is what they would say, for they are all

envious of me. That I am rich, they cannot deny; but they do not
wish to acknowledge that I am also a tolerably good girl, who
would prove herself worthy of her husband. Is that not so, Tellheim?

Maj. T. Yes, yes, Madam, that is like your countrywomen. They
will envy you exceedingly a discharged officer, with sullied honour,
a cripple, and a beggar.

Min. And are you all that? If I mistake not, you told me some-
thing of the kind this forenoon. Therein is good and evil mixed.
Let us examine each charge more closely. You are discharged?
So you say. I thought your regiment was only drafted into another.
How did it happen that a man of your merit was not retained?

Maj. T. It has happened, as it must happen. The great ones are
convinced that a soldier does very little through regard for them,
not much more from a sense of duty, but everything for his own
advantage. What then can they think they owe him? Peace has
made a great many, like myself, superfluous to them; and at last
we shall all be superfluous.

Min. You talk as a man must talk, to whom in return the great
are quite superfluous. And never were they more so than now.
I return my best thanks to the great ones that they have given up
their claims to a man whom I would very unwillingly have shared
with them. I am your sovereign, Tellheim; you want no other
master. To find you discharged, is a piece of good fortune I dared
scarcely dream of! But you are not only discharged; you are more.
And what are you more? A cripple, you say! Well! (*looking at him
from head to foot*), the cripple is tolerably whole and upright—
appears still to be pretty well, and strong. Dear Tellheim, if you
expect to go begging on the strength of your limbs, I prophesy that
you will be relieved at very few doors; except at the door of a good-
natured girl like myself.

Maj. T. I only hear the joking girl now, dear Minna.

Min. And I only hear the "dear Minna" in your chiding. I will
not joke any longer; for I recollect that after all you are something
of a cripple. You are wounded by a shot in the right arm; but all
things considered, I do not find much fault with that. I am so
much the more secure from your blows.

Maj. T. Madam!

Min. You would say, "You are so much the less secure from mine." Well, well, dear Tellheim, I hope you will not drive me to that.

Maj. T. You laugh, Madam. I only lament that I cannot laugh with you.

Min. Why not? What have you to say against laughing? Cannot one be very serious even whilst laughing? Dear Major, laughter keeps us more rational than vexation. The proof is before us. Your laughing friend judges of your circumstances more correctly than you do yourself. Because you are discharged, you say your honour is sullied; because you are wounded in the arm, you call yourself a cripple. Is that right? Is that no exaggeration? And is it my doing that all exaggerations are so open to ridicule? I dare say, if I examine your beggary that it will also be as little able to stand the test. You may have lost your equipage once, twice, or thrice; your deposits in the hands of this or that banker may have disappeared together with those of other people; you may have no hope of seeing this or that money again which you may have advanced in the service; but are you a beggar on that account? If nothing else remained to you but what my uncle is bringing for you—

Maj. T. Your uncle, Madam, will bring nothing for me.

Min. Nothing but the two thousand pistoles which you so generously advanced to our government.

Maj. T. If you had but read my letter, Madam!

Min. Well, I did read it. But what I read in it, on this point, is a perfect riddle. It is impossible that any one should wish to turn a noble action into a crime. But explain to me, dear Major.

Maj. T. You remember, Madam, that I had orders to collect the contribution for the war most strictly in cash in all the districts in your neighbourhood. I wished to forego this severity, and advanced the money that was deficient myself.

Min. I remember it well. I loved you for that deed before I had seen you.

Maj. T. The government gave me their bill, and I wished, at the signing of the peace, to have the sum entered amongst the debts to be repaid by them. The bill was acknowledged as good, but my ownership of the same was disputed. People looked incredulous, when I declared that I had myself advanced the amount in cash. It was considered as bribery, as a *douceur* from the government, because I at once agreed to take the smallest sum with which I could have been satisfied in a case of the greatest exigency. Thus the bill went from my possession, and if it be paid, will certainly not be paid to me. Hence, Madam, I consider my honour to be suspected! not on account of my discharge, which, if I had not received, I should have applied for. You look serious, Madam! Why do you not laugh? Ha! ha! ha! I am laughing.

Min. Oh! stifle that laugh, Tellheim, I implore you! It is the terrible laugh of misanthropy. No, you are not the man to repent of a good deed, because it may have had a bad result for yourself. Nor can these consequences possibly be of long duration. The truth must come to light. The testimony of my uncle, of our government—

Maj. T. Of your uncle! Of your government! Ha! ha! ha!

Min. That laugh will kill me, Tellheim. If you believe in virtue and Providence, Tellheim, do not laugh so! I never heard a curse more terrible than that laugh! But, viewing the matter in the worst light, if they are determined to mistake your character here, with us you will not be misunderstood. No, we cannot, we will not, misunderstand you, Tellheim. And if our government has the least sentiment of honour, I know what it must do. But I am foolish; what would that matter? Imagine, Tellheim, that you have lost the two thousand pistoles on some gay evening. The king was an unfortunate card for you: the queen (*pointing to herself*) will be so much the more favourable. Providence, believe me, always indemnifies a man of honour—often even beforehand. The action which was to cost you two thousand pistoles, gained you me. Without that action, I never should have been desirous of making your acquaintance. You know I went uninvited to the first party where I thought I should meet you. I went entirely on your account. I went with a fixed determination to love you—I loved you already! with the fixed determination to make you mine, if I should find you as dark and ugly as the Moor of Venice. So dark and ugly you are not; nor will you be so jealous. But, Tellheim, Tellheim, you are yet very like him! Oh! the unmanageable, stubborn man, who always keeps his eye fixed upon the phantom of honour, and becomes hardened against every other sentiment! Your eyes this way! Upon me,—me, Tellheim! (*He remains thoughtful and immovable, with his eyes fixed on one spot.*) Of what are you thinking? Do you not hear me?

Maj. T. (*absent*). Oh, yes; but tell me, how came the Moor into the service of Venice? Had the Moor no country of his own? Why did he hire his arm and his blood to a foreign land?

Min. (*alarmed*). Of what are you thinking, Tellheim? It is time to break off. Come! (*taking him by the hand*). Franziska, let the carriage be brought round.

Maj. T. (*disengaging his hand, and following* Franziska). No, Franziska; I cannot have the honour of accompanying your mistress—Madam, let me still retain my senses unimpaired for to-day, and give me leave to go. You are on the right way to deprive me of them. I resist it as much as I can. But hear, whilst I am still myself, what I have firmly determined, and from which nothing in the world shall turn me. If I have not better luck in the game of life; if a complete change in my fortune does not take place; if—

Min. I must interrupt you, Major. We ought to have told him that at first, Franziska.—You remind me of nothing.—Our conversation would have taken quite a different turn, Tellheim, if I had commenced with the good news which the Chevalier de la Marlinière brought just now.

Maj. T. The Chevalier de la Marlinière! Who is he?

Fran. He may be a very honest man, Major von Tellheim, except that—

Min. Silence, Franziska! Also a discharged officer from the Dutch service, who—

Maj. T. Ah! Lieutenant Riccaut!

Min. He assured us he was a friend of yours.

Maj. T. I assure you that I am not his.

Min. And that some minister or other had told him, in confidence, that your business was likely to have the very best termination. A letter from the king must now be on its way to you.

Maj. T. How came Riccaut and a minister in company? Something certainly must have happened concerning my affair; for just now the paymaster of the forces told me that the king had set aside all the evidence offered against me, and that I might take back my promise, which I had given in writing, not to depart from here until acquitted. But that will be all. They wish to give me an opportunity of getting away. But they are wrong, I shall not go. Sooner shall the utmost distress waste me away before the eyes of my calumniators, than—

Min. Obstinate man!

Maj. T. I require no favour; I want justice. My honour—

Min. The honour of such a man—

Maj. T. (*warmly*). No, Madam, you may be able to judge of any other subject, but not of this. Honour is not the voice of conscience, not the evidence of a few honourable men—

Min. No, no, I know it well. Honour is . . . honour.

Maj. T. In short, Madam . . . You did not let me finish.—I was going to say, if they keep from me so shamefully what is my own; if my honour be not perfectly righted—I cannot, Madam, ever be yours, for I am not worthy, in the eyes of the world, of being yours. Minna von Barnhelm deserves an irreproachable husband. It is a worthless love which does not scruple to expose its object to scorn. He is a worthless man, who is not ashamed to owe a woman all his good fortune; whose blind tenderness—

Min. And is that really your feeling, Major? (*turning her back suddenly*). Franziska!

Maj. T. Do not be angry.

Min. (*aside to* FRANZISKA). Now is the time! What do you advise me, Franziska?

Fran. I advise nothing. But certainly he goes rather too far.

Maj. T. (*approaching to interrupt them*). You are angry, Madam.

Min. (*ironically*). I? Not in the least.

Maj. T. If I loved you less—

Min. (*still in the same tone*). Oh! certainly, it would be a misfortune for me. And hear, Major, I also will not be the cause of your unhappiness. One should love with perfect disinterestedness. It is as well that I have not been more open! Perhaps your pity might have granted to me what your love refuses. (*Drawing the ring slowly from her finger.*)

Maj. T. What does this mean, Madam?

Min. No, neither of us must make the other either more or less happy. True love demands it. I believe you, Major; and you have too much honour to mistake love.

Maj. T. Are you jesting, Madam?

Min. Here! take back the ring with which you plighted your troth to me. (*Gives him the ring.*) Let it be so! We will suppose we have never met.

Maj. T. What do I hear?

Min. Does it surprise you? Take it, sir. You surely have not been pretending only!

Maj. T. (*takes the ring from her*). Heavens! can Minna speak thus?

Min. In one case you cannot be mine; in no case can I be yours. Your misfortune is probable; mine is certain. Farewell! (*Is going.*)

Maj. T. Where are you going, dearest Minna?

Min. Sir, you insult me now by that term of endearment.

Maj. T. What is the matter, Madam? Where are you going?

Min. Leave me. I go to hide my tears from you, deceiver! (*Exit.*)

SCENE VII.—MAJOR VON TELLHEIM, FRANZISKA

Maj. T. Her tears? And I am to leave her. (*Is about to follow her.*)

Fran. (*holding him back*). Surely not, Major. You would not follow her into her own room!

Maj. T. Her misfortune? Did she not speak of misfortune?

Fran. Yes, truly; the misfortune of losing you, after—

Maj. T. After? After what? There is more in this. What is it, Franziska? Tell me! Speak!

Fran. After, I mean, she has made such sacrifices on your account.

Maj. T. Sacrifices for me!

Fran. Well, listen. It is a good thing for you, Major, that you are freed from your engagement with her in this manner.—Why should I not tell you? It cannot remain a secret long. We have fled from home. Count von Bruchsal has disinherited my mistress, because she would not accept a husband of his choice. On that every one deserted and slighted her. What could we do? We determined to seek him, whom—

Maj. T. Enough! Come, and let me throw myself at her feet.

Fran. What are you thinking about! Rather go, and thank your good fortune.

Maj. T. Pitiful creature! For what do you take me? Yet no, my dear Franziska, the advice did not come from your heart. Forgive my anger!

Fran. Do not detain me any longer. I must see what she is about. How easily something might happen to her. Go now, and come again, if you like. (*Follows* MINNA.)

SCENE VIII.—MAJOR VON TELLHEIM

Maj. T. But, Franziska! Oh! I will wait your return here.—No, that is more torturing!—If she is in earnest, she will not refuse to forgive me.—Now I want your aid, honest Werner!—No, Minna, I am no deceiver! (*Rushes off.*)

ACT V

SCENE I.—MAJOR VON TELLHEIM (*from one side*), WERNER (*from the other*)

Maj. T. Ah! Werner! I have been looking for you everywhere. Where have you been?

Wer. And I have been looking for you, Major; that is always the way.—I bring you good news.

Maj. T. I do not want your news now; I want your money. Quick, Werner, give me all you have; and then raise as much more as you can.

Wer. Major! Now, upon my life, that is just what I said—"He will borrow money from me, when he has got it himself to lend."

Maj. T. You surely are not seeking excuses!

Wer. That I may have nothing to upbraid you with, take it with your right hand, and give it me again with your left.

Maj. T. Do not detain me, Werner. It is my intention to repay you; but when and how, God knows!

Wer. Then you do not know yet that the treasury has received an order to pay you your money? I just heard it at—

Maj. T. What are you talking about? What nonsense have you let them palm off on you? Do you not see that if it were true

I should be the first person to know it? In short, Werner, money! money!

Wer. Very well, with pleasure. Here is some! A hundred louis d'ors there, and a hundred ducats there. (*Gives him both.*)

Maj. T. Werner, go and give Just the hundred louis d'ors. Let him redeem the ring again, on which he raised the money this morning. But whence will you get some more, Werner? I want a good deal more.

Wer. Leave that to me. The man who bought my farm lives in the town. The date for payment is a fortnight hence, certainly; but the money is ready, and by a reduction of one half per cent—

Maj. T. Very well, my dear Werner! You see that I have had recourse to you alone—I must also confide all to you. The young lady you have seen is in distress—

Wer. That is bad!

Maj. T. But to-morrow she shall be my wife.

Wer. That is good!

Maj. T. And the day after, I leave this place with her. I can go; I will go. I would sooner throw over everything here! Who knows where some good luck may be in store for me? If you will, Werner, come with us. We will serve again.

Wer. Really? But where there is war, Major!

Maj. T. To be sure. Go, Werner, we will speak of this again.

Wer. Oh! my dear Major! The day after to-morrow! Why not to-morrow? I will get everything ready. In Persia, Major, there is a famous war; what do you say?

Maj. T. We will think of it. Only go, Werner!

Wer. Hurrah! Long live Prince Heraclius! (*Exit.*)

Scene II.—Major von Tellheim

Maj. T. How do I feel! . . . My whole soul has acquired a new impulse. My own unhappiness bowed me to the ground; made me fretful, short-sighted, shy, careless: her unhappiness raises me. I see clearly again, and feel myself ready and capable of undertaking anything for her sake. Why do I tarry? (*Is going towards* Minna's *room, when* Franziska *comes out of it.*)

Scene III.—Franziska, Major von Tellheim

Fran. Is it you? I thought I heard your voice. What do you want, Major?

Maj. T. What do I want? What is she doing? Come!

Fran. She is just going out for a drive.

Maj. T. And alone? Without me? Where to?

Fran. Have you forgotten, Major?

Maj. T. How silly you are, Franziska! I irritated her, and she was angry. I will beg her pardon, and she will forgive me.

Fran. What! After you have taken the ring back, Major!

Maj. T. Ah! I did that in my confusion. I had forgotten about the ring. Where did I put it? (*Searches for it.*) Here it is.

Fran. Is that it? (*Aside, as he puts it again in his pocket.*) If he would only look at it closer!

Maj. T. She pressed it upon me so bitterly. But I have forgotten that. A full heart cannot weigh words. She will not for one moment refuse to take it again. And have I not hers?

Fran. She is now waiting for it in return. Where is it, Major? Show it to me, do!

Maj. T. (*embarrassed*). I have . . . forgotten to put it on. Just —Just will bring it directly.

Fran. They are something alike, I suppose; let me look at that one. I am very fond of such things.

Maj. T. Another time, Franziska. Come now.

Fran. (*aside*). He is determined not to be drawn out of his mistake.

Maj. T. What do you say? Mistake!

Fran. It is a mistake, I say, if you think my mistress is still a good match. Her own fortune is far from considerable; by a few calculations in their own favour her guardians may reduce it to nothing. She expected everything from her uncle; but this cruel uncle—

Maj. T. Let him go! Am I not man enough to make it all good to her again!

Fran. Do you hear? She is ringing; I must go in again.

Maj. T. I will accompany you.

Fran. For heaven's sake, no! She forbade me expressly to speak with you. Come in at any rate a little time after me. *(Goes in.)*

Scene IV.—Major von Tellheim

Maj. T. (calling after her). Announce me! Speak for me, Franziska! I shall follow you directly. What shall I say to her? Yet where the heart can speak, no preparation is necessary. There is one thing only which may need a studied turn . . . this reserve, this scrupulousness of throwing herself, unfortunate as she is, into my arms; this anxiety to make a false show of still possessing that happiness which she has lost through me. How she is to exculpate herself to herself—for by me it is already forgiven—for this distrust in my honour, in her own worth . . . Ah! here she comes.

Scene V.—Minna, Franziska, Major von Tellheim

Min. (speaking as she comes out, as if not aware of the Major's *presence).* The carriage is at the door, Franziska, is it not? My fan!

Maj. T. (advancing to her). Where are you going, Madam?

Min. (with forced coldness). I am going out, Major. I guess why you have given yourself the trouble of coming back: to return me my ring.—Very well, Major von Tellheim, have the goodness to give it to Franziska.—Franziska, take the ring from Major von Tellheim!—I have no time to lose. *(Is going.)*

Maj. T. (stepping before her). Madam! Ah! what have I heard? I was unworthy of such love.

Min. So, Franziska, you have—

Fran. Told him all.

Maj. T. Do not be angry with me, Madam. I am no deceiver. You have, on my account, lost much in the eyes of the world, but not in mine. In my eyes you have gained beyond measure by this loss. It was too sudden. You feared it might make an unfavourable impression on me; at first you wished to hide it from me. I do not complain of this mistrust. It arose from the desire to retain my affection. That desire is my pride. You found me in distress; and you did not wish to add distress to distress. You could not divine how far your distress would raise me above any thoughts of my own.

Min. That is all very well, Major, but it is now over. I have released you from your engagement; you have, by taking back the ring—

Maj. T. Consented to nothing! On the contrary, I now consider myself bound more firmly than ever. You are mine, Minna, mine for ever. (*Takes off the ring.*) Here, take it for the second time—the pledge of my fidelity.

Min. I take that ring again! That ring?

Maj. T. Yes, dearest Minna, yes.

Min. What are you asking me? that ring?

Maj. T. You received it for the first time from my hand, when our positions were similar and the circumstances propitious. They are no longer propitious, but are again similar. Equality is always the strongest tie of love. Permit me, dearest Minna! (*Seizes her hand to put on the ring.*)

Min. What! by force, Major! No, there is no power in the world which shall compel me to take back that ring! Do you think that I am in want of a ring? Oh! you may see (*pointing to her ring*) that I have another here which is in no way inferior to yours.

Fran. (*aside*). Well, if he does not see it now!

Maj. T. (*letting fall her hand*). What is this? I see Fräulein von Barnhelm, but I do not hear her.—You are pretending.—Pardon me, that I use your own words.

Min. (*in her natural tone*). Did those words offend you, Major?

Maj. T. They grieved me much.

Min. (*affected*). They were not meant to do that, Tellheim. Forgive me, Tellheim.

Maj. T. Ah! that friendly tone tells me you are yourself again, Minna: that you still love me.

Fran. (*exclaims*). The joke would soon have gone a little too far.

Min. (*in a commanding tone*). Franziska, you will not interfere in our affairs, I beg.

Fran. (*aside, in a surprised tone*). Not enough yet!

Min. Yes, sir, it would only be womanish vanity in me to pretend to be cold and scornful. No! Never! You deserve to find me as sincere as yourself. I do love you still, Tellheim, I love you still; but notwithstanding—

Maj. T. No more, dearest Minna, no more! (*Seizes her hand again, to put on the ring.*)

Min. (*drawing back her hand*). Notwithstanding, so much the more am I determined that that shall never be,—never!—Of what are you thinking, Major?—I thought your own distress was sufficient. You must remain here; you must obtain by obstinacy—no better phrase occurs to me at the moment—the most perfect satisfaction, obtain it by obstinacy. . . . And that even though the utmost distress should waste you away before the eyes of your calumniators—

Maj. T. So I thought, so I said, when I knew not what I thought or said. Chagrin and stifling rage had enveloped my whole soul; love itself, in the full blaze of happiness, could not illumine it. But it has sent its daughter, Pity, more familiar with gloomy misfortune, and she has dispelled the cloud, and opened again all the avenues of my soul to sensations of tenderness. The impulse of self-preservation awakes, when I have something more precious than myself to support, and to support through my own exertions. Do not let the word "pity" offend you. From the innocent cause of our distress we may hear the term without humiliation. I am this cause; through me, Minna, have you lost friends and relations, fortune and country. Through me, in me, must you find them all again, or I shall have the destruction of the most lovely of her sex upon my soul. Let me not think of a future in which I must detest myself.—No, nothing shall detain me here longer. From this moment I will oppose nothing but contempt to the injustice which I suffer. Is this country the world? Does the sun rise here alone? Where can I not go? In what service shall I be refused? And should I be obliged to seek it in the most distant clime, only follow me with confidence, dearest Minna—we shall want for nothing. I have a friend who will assist me with pleasure.

SCENE VI.—*An* ORDERLY, MAJOR VON TELLHEIM, MINNA, FRANZISKA

Fran. (*seeing the* ORDERLY). Hist, Major!

Maj. T. (*to the* ORDERLY). Who do you want?

Ord. I am looking for Major von Tellheim. Ah! you are the

Major, I see. I have to give you this letter from His Majesty the King *(taking one out of his bag)*.

Maj. T. To me?

Ord. According to the direction.

Min. Franziska, do you hear? The Chevalier spoke the truth after all.

Ord. (whilst TELLHEIM *takes the letter).* I beg your pardon, Major; you should properly have had it yesterday, but I could not find you out. I learnt your address this morning only from Lieutenant Riccaut, on parade.

Fran. Do you hear, my lady?—That is the Chevalier's minister. "What is the name of de ministre out dere, on de broad place?"

Maj. T. I am extremely obliged to you for your trouble.

Ord. It is my duty, Major. *(Exit.)*

SCENE VII.—MAJOR VON TELLHEIM, MINNA, FRANZISKA

Maj. T. Ah! Minna, what is this? What does this contain?

Min. I am not entitled to extend my curiosity so far.

Maj. T. What! You would still separate my fate from yours?— But why do I hesitate to open it? It cannot make me more unhappy than I am: no, dearest Minna, it cannot make us more unhappy— but perhaps more happy! Permit me. *(While he opens and reads the letter, the* LANDLORD *comes stealthily on the stage.)*

SCENE VIII.—LANDLORD, *the rest as before*

Land. (to FRANZISKA). Hist! my pretty maid! A word!

Fran. (to the LANDLORD). Mr. Landlord, we do not yet know ourselves what is in the letter.

Land. Who wants to know about the letter! I come about the ring. The lady must give it to me again, directly. Just is there, and wants to redeem it.

Min. (who in the meantime has approached the LANDLORD). Tell Just that it is already redeemed; and tell him by whom—by me.

Land. But—

Min. I take it upon myself. Go! *(Exit* LANDLORD.)

SCENE IX.—MAJOR VON TELLHEIM, MINNA, FRANZISKA

Fran. And now, my lady, make it up with the poor Major.

Min. Oh! kind intercessor! As if the difficulties must not soon explain themselves.

Maj. T. (after reading the letter, with much emotion.) Ah! nor has he herein belied himself! Oh! Minna, what justice! what clemency! This is more than I expected; more than I deserved!—My fortune, my honour, all is reestablished!—Do I dream? *(Looking at the letter, as if to convince himself.)* No, no delusion born of my own desires! Read it yourself, Minna; read it yourself!

Min. I would not presume, Major.

Maj. T. Presume! The letter is to me; to your Tellheim, Minna. It contains—what your uncle cannot take from you. You must read it! Do read it.

Min. If it affords you pleasure, Major. *(Takes the letter and reads.)* "My dear Major von Tellheim,

"I hereby inform you, that the business which caused me some anxiety on account of your honour, has been cleared up in your favour. My brother had a more detailed knowledge of it, and his testimony has more than proved your innocence. The Treasury has received orders to deliver again to you the bill in question, and to reimburse the sum advanced. I have also ordered that all claims which the Paymaster's Office brings forward against your accounts be nullified. Please to inform me whether your health will allow of your taking active service again. I can ill spare a man of your courage and sentiments. I am your gracious King," &c.

Maj. T. Now, what do you say to that, Minna?

Min. (folding up and returning the letter). I? Nothing.

Maj. T. Nothing?

Min. Stay—yes. That your king, who is a great man, can also be a good man.—But what is that to me! He is not my king.

Maj. T. And do you say nothing more? Nothing about ourselves?

Min. You are going to serve again. From Major, you will become Lieutenant-Colonel, perhaps Colonel. I congratulate you with all my heart.

Maj. T. And you do not know me better? No, since fortune restores me sufficient to satisfy the wishes of a reasonable man, it shall depend upon my Minna alone, whether for the future I shall belong to any one else but her. To her service alone my whole life shall be devoted! The service of the great is dangerous, and does not repay the trouble, the restraint, the humiliation which it costs. Minna is not amongst those vain people who love nothing in their husbands beyond their titles and positions. She will love me for myself; and for her sake I will forget the whole world. I became a soldier from party feeling—I do not myself know on what political principles—and from the whim that it is good for every honourable man to try the profession of arms for a time, to make himself familiar with danger, and to learn coolness and determination. Extreme necessity alone could have compelled me to make this trial a fixed mode of life, this temporary occupation a profession. But now that nothing compels me, my whole and sole ambition is to be a peaceful and a contented man. This with you, dearest Minna, I shall infallibly become; this in your society I shall unchangeably remain. Let the holy bond unite us to-morrow; and then we will look round us, and in the whole wide habitable world seek out the most peaceful, the brightest, most smiling nook which wants but a happy couple to be a Paradise. There we will dwell; there shall each day. . . . What is the matter, Minna? (MINNA *turns away uneasily, and endeavours to hide her emotion.*)

Min. (*regaining her composure*). It is cruel of you, Tellheim, to paint such happiness to me, when I am forced to renounce it. My loss—

Maj. T. Your loss! Why name your loss? All that Minna could lose is not Minna. You are still the sweetest, dearest, loveliest, best creature under the sun; all goodness and generosity, innocence and bliss! Now and then a little petulant; at times somewhat wilful—so much the better! So much the better! Minna would otherwise be an angel, whom I should honour with trepidation, but not dare to love. (*Takes her hand to kiss it.*)

Min. (*drawing away her hand*). Not so, sir. Why this sudden change? Is this flattering impetuous lover, the cold Tellheim!— Could his returning good fortune alone create this ardour in him? He will permit me during his passionate excitement to retain the power of reflection for us both. When he could himself reflect, I heard him say—"it is a worthless love which does not scruple to expose its object to scorn."—True; and I aspire to as pure and noble a love as he himself. Now, when honour calls him, when a great monarch solicits his services, shall I consent that he shall give himself up to love-sick dreams with me? that the illustrious warrior shall degenerate into a toying swain? No, Major, follow the call of your higher destiny.

Maj. T. Well! if the busy world has greater charms for you, Minna, let us remain in the busy world! How mean, how poor is this busy world; you now only know its gilded surface. Yet certainly, Minna, you will. . . . But let it be so! until then! Your charms shall not want admirers, nor will my happiness lack enviers.

Min. No, Tellheim, I do not mean that! I send you back into the busy world, on the road of honour, without wishing to accompany you. Tellheim will there require an irreproachable wife! A fugitive Saxon girl who has thrown herself upon him—

Maj. T. (*starting up, and looking fiercely about him*). Who dare say that! Ah! Minna, I feel afraid of myself, when I imagine that any one but yourself could have spoken so. My anger against him would know no bounds.

Min. Exactly! That is just what I fear. You would not endure one word of calumny against me, and yet you would have to put up with the very bitterest every day. In short, Tellheim, hear what I have firmly determined, and from which nothing in the world shall turn me—

Maj. T. Before you proceed, I implore you, Minna, reflect for one moment, that you are about to pronounce a sentence of life or death upon me!

Min. Without a moment's reflection! . . . As certainly as I have given you back the ring with which you formerly pledged your troth to me, as certainly as you have taken back that same ring, so certainly shall the unfortunate Minna never be the wife of the fortunate Tellheim!

Maj. T. And herewith you pronounce my sentence.

Min. Equality is the only sure bond of love. The happy Minna only wished to live for the happy Tellheim. Even Minna in misfortune would have allowed herself to be persuaded either to increase or to assuage the misfortune of her friend through herself. . . . He must have seen, before the arrival of that letter, which has again destroyed all equality between us, that in appearance only I refused.

Maj. T. Is that true? I thank you, Minna, that you have not yet pronounced the sentence. You will only marry Tellheim when unfortunate? You may have him. (*Coolly.*) I perceive now that it would be indecorous in me to accept this tardy justice; that it will be better if I do not seek again that of which I have been deprived by such shameful suspicion. Yes; I will suppose that I have not received the letter. Behold my only answer to it! (*About to tear it up.*)

Min. (*stopping him*). What are you going to do, Tellheim?

Maj. T. Obtain your hand.

Min. Stop!

Maj. T. Madam, it is torn without fail if you do not quickly recall your words.—Then we will see what else you may have to object to in me.

Min. What! In such a tone? Shall I, must I, thus become contemptible in my own eyes? Never! She is a worthless creature, who is not ashamed to owe her whole happiness to the blind tenderness of a man!

Maj. T. False! utterly false!

Min. Can you venture to find fault with your own words when coming from my lips?

Maj. T. Sophistry! Does the weaker sex dishonour itself by every action which does not become the stronger? Or can a man do everything which is proper in a woman? Which is appointed by nature to be the support of the other?

Min. Be not alarmed, Tellheim! . . . I shall not be quite unprotected, if I must decline the honour of your protection. I shall still have as much as is absolutely necessary. I have announced my arrival to our ambassador. I am to see him to-day. I hope he will assist me. Time is flying. Permit me, Major—

Maj. T. I will accompany you, Madam.

Min. No, Major; leave me.

Maj. T. Sooner shall your shadow desert you! Come Madam, where you will, to whom you will everywhere, to friends and strangers, will I repeat in your presence—repeat a hundred times each day—what a bond binds you to me, and with what cruel caprice you wish to break it—

Scene X.—Just, *the rest as before*

Just. (*impetuously*). Major! Major!

Maj. T. Well!

Just. Here quick! quick!

Maj. T. Why? Come to me. Speak, what is the matter?

Just. What do you think? (*Whispers to him.*)

Min. (*aside to* Franziska). Do you notice anything, Franziska?

Fran. Oh! you merciless creature! I have stood here on thorns!

Maj . T. (*to* Just). What do you say? . . . That is not possible! . . . You? (*Looking fiercely at* Minna.) Speak it out; tell it to her face. Listen, Madam.

Just. The Landlord says, that Fräulein von Barnhelm has taken the ring which I pledged to him; she recognised it as her own, and would not return it.

Maj. T. Is that true, Madam? No, that cannot be true!

Min. (*smiling*). And why not, Tellheim? Why can it not be true?

Maj. T. (*vehemently*). Then it is true! . . . What terrible light suddenly breaks in upon me! . . . Now I know you—false, faithless one!

Min. (*alarmed*). Who, who is faithless?

Maj. T. You, whom I will never more name!

Min. Tellheim!

Maj. T. Forget my name . . . You came here with the intention of breaking with me . . . It is evident! . . . Oh, that chance should thus delight to assist the faithless! It brought your ring into your possession. Your craftiness contrived to get my own back into mine!

Min. Tellheim, what visions are you conjuring up! Be calm, and listen to me.

Fran. (*aside*). Now she will catch it!

Scene XI.—Werner (*with a purse full of gold*), *the rest as before*

Wer. Here I am already, Major!

Maj. T. (*without looking at him*). Who wants you?

Wer. I have brought more money! A thousand pistoles!

Maj. T. I do not want them!

Wer. And to-morrow, Major, you can have as many more.

Maj. T. Keep your money!

Wer. It is your money, Major . . . I do not think you see whom you are speaking to!

Maj. T. Take it away! I say.

Wer. What is the matter with you?—I am Werner.

Maj. T. All goodness is dissimulation; all kindness deceit.

Wer. Is that meant for me?

Maj. T. As you please!

Wer. Why I have only obeyed your commands.

Maj. T. Obey once more, and be off!

Wer. Major (*vexed*). I am a man—

Maj. T. So much the better!

Wer. Who can also be angry.

Maj. T. Anger is the best thing we possess.

Wer. I beg you, Major.

Maj. T. How often must I tell you? I do not want your money!

Wer. (*in a rage*). Then take it, who will! (*Throws the purse on the ground, and goes to the side*).

Min. (*to* FRANZISKA). Ah! Franziska, I ought to have followed your advice. I have carried the jest too far.—Still, when he hears me . . . (*going to him*).

Fran. (*without answering* MINNA, *goes up to* WERNER). Mr. Sergeant—

Wer. (*pettishly*). Go along!

Fran. Ah! what men these are.

Min. Tellheim! Tellheim! (TELLHEIM, *biting his fingers with rage, turns away his face, without listening.*) No, this is too bad . . . Only listen! . . . You are mistaken! . . . A mere misunderstanding. Tellheim, will you not hear your Minna? Can you have such a suspicion? . . . I break my engagement with you? I came here for that purpose? . . . Tellheim!

SCENE XII.—TWO SERVANTS (*running into the room from different sides*), *the rest as before*

First Ser. Your ladyship, his excellency the Count!

Second Ser. He is coming, your ladyship!

Fran. (*running to the window*). It is! it is he!

Min. Is it? Now, Tellheim, quick!

Maj. T. (*suddenly recovering himself*). Who, who comes? Your uncle, Madam! this cruel uncle! . . . Let him come; just let him come! . . . Fear not! . . . He shall not hurt you even by a look. He shall have to deal with me . . . You do not indeed deserve it of me.

Min. Quick, Tellheim! one embrace and forget all.

Maj. T. Ah! did I but know that you could regret—

Min. No, I can never regret having obtained a sight of your whole heart! . . . Ah! what a man you are! . . . Embrace your Minna, your happy Minna: and in nothing more happy than in the possession of you. (*Embracing.*) And now to meet him!

Maj. T. To meet whom?

Min. The best of your unknown friends.

Maj. T. What!

Min. The Count, my uncle, my father, your father . . . My flight, his displeasure, my loss of property—do you not see that all is a fiction, credulous knight?

Maj. T. Fiction! But the ring? the ring?

Min. Where is the ring that I gave back to you?

Maj. T. You will take it again? Ah! now I am happy . . . Here, Minna (*taking it from his pocket*).

Min. Look at it first! Oh! how blind are those who will not see! . . . What ring is that? the one you gave me? or the one I gave to you? Is it not the one which I did not like to leave in the land-lord's possession?

Maj. T. Heavens! what do I see! What do I hear!

Min. Shall I take it again now? Shall I? Give it to me! give it! (*Takes it from him, and then puts it on his finger herself.*) There, now all is right!

Maj. T. Where am I? (*Kissing her hand.*) Oh! malicious angel, to torture me so!

Min. As a proof, my dear husband, that you shall never play me a trick without my playing you one in return. . . . Do you suppose that you did not torture me also?

Maj. T. Oh you actresses! But I ought to have known you.

Fran. Not I, indeed; I am spoilt for acting. I trembled and shook, and was obliged to hold my lips together with my hand.

Min. Nor was mine an easy part.—But come now—

Maj. T. I have not recovered myself yet. How happy, yet how anxious, I feel. It is like awaking suddenly from a frightful dream.

Min. We are losing time . . . I hear him coming now.

SCENE XIII.—COUNT VON BRUCHSAL (*accompanied by several servants and the* LANDLORD). *The rest as before*

Count. (*entering*). She arrived in safety, I hope?

Min. (*running to meet him*). Ah! my father!

Count. Here I am, dear Minna (*embracing her*). But what, girl (*seeing* TELLHEIM), only four-and-twenty hours here, and friends —company already!

Min. Guess who it is?

Count. Not your Tellheim, surely!

Min. Who else!—Come, Tellheim (*introducing him*).

Count. Sir, we have never met; but at the first glance I fancied I recognised you. I wished it might be Major von Tellheim.—Your hand, sir; you have my highest esteem; I ask for your friendship. My niece, my daughter loves you.

Min. You know that, my father!—And was my love blind?

Count. No, Minna, your love was not blind; but your lover—is dumb.

Maj. T. (*throwing himself in the* COUNT'S *arms*). Let me recover myself, my father!

Count. Right, my son. I see your heart can speak, though your lips cannot. I do not usually care for those who wear this uniform. But you are an honourable man, Tellheim; and one must love an honourable man, in whatever garb he may be.

Min. Ah! did you but know all!

Count. Why should I not hear all?—Which are my apartments, landlord?

Land. Will your Excellency have the goodness to walk this way?

Count. Come, Minna! Pray come, Major! (*Exit with the* LAND-LORD *and servants.*)

Min. Come, Tellheim!

Maj. T. I will follow you in an instant, Minna. One word first with this man (*turning to* WERNER).

Min. And a good word, methinks, it should be. Should it not, Franziska? (*Exit.*)

SCENE XIV.—MAJOR VON TELLHEIM, WERNER, JUST, FRANZISKA

Maj. T. (*pointing to the purse which* WERNER *had thrown down*). Here, Just, pick up the purse and carry it home. Go! (JUST *takes it up and goes.*)

Wer. (*still standing, out of humour, in a corner, and absent till he hears the last words*). Well, what now?

Maj. T. (*in a friendly tone while going up to him*). Werner, when can I have the other two thousand pistoles?

Wer. (*in a good humour again instantly*). To-morrow, Major, to-morrow.

Maj. T. I do not need to become your debtor; but I will be your banker. All you good-natured people ought to have guardians. You are in a manner spendthrifts.—I irritated you just now, Werner.

Wer. Upon my life you did! But I ought not to have been such a dolt. Now I see it all clearly. I deserve a hundred lashes. You may give them to me, if you will, Major. Only no more ill will, dear Major!

Maj. T. Ill will! (*shaking him by the hand*). Read in my eyes all that I cannot say to you—Ah! let me see the man with a better wife and a more trusty friend than I shall have.—Eh! Franziska? (*Exit.*)

SCENE XV.—WERNER, FRANZISKA

Fran. (*aside*). Yes, indeed, he is more than good!—Such a man will never fall in my way again.—It must come out. (*Approaching* WERNER *bashfully.*) Mr. Sergeant!

Wer. (*wiping his eyes*). Well!

Fran. Mr. Sergeant—

Wer. What do you want, little woman?

Fran. Look at me, Mr. Sergeant.

Wer. I can't yet; there is something, I don't know what, in **my** eyes.

Fran. Now do look at me!

Wer. I am afraid I have looked at you too much already, little woman!—There, now I can see you. What then?

Fran. Mr. Sergeant—don't you want a Mrs. Sergeant?

Wer. Do you really mean it, little woman?

Fran. Really I do.

Wer. And would you go with me to Persia even?

Fran. Wherever you please.

Wer. You will! Hullo, Major, no boasting! At any rate I have got as good a wife, and as trusty a friend, as you.—Give me your hand, my little woman! It's a match!—In ten years' time you shall be a general's wife, or a widow!

WILLIAM TELL

BY

JOHANN CHRISTOPH FRIEDRICH VON SCHILLER

TRANSLATED BY

SIR THEODORE MARTIN, K.C.B., LL.D.

INTRODUCTORY NOTE

JOHANN CHRISTOPH FRIEDRICH VON SCHILLER was born at Marbach, Würtemberg, Germany, November 10, 1759. His father had served both as surgeon and soldier in the War of the Austrian Succession, and at the time of the poet's birth held an appointment under the Duke of Würtemberg. Friedrich's education was begun with a view to holy orders, but this idea was given up when he was placed in a military academy established by the Duke. He tried the study of law and then of medicine, but his tastes were literary; and, while holding a position as regimental surgeon, he wrote his revolutionary drama, "The Robbers," which brought down on him the displeasure of his ducal master. Finding the interference with his personal liberty intolerable, he finally fled from the Duchy, and in various retreats went on with his dramatic work. Later he turned to philosophy and history and through his book on "The Revolt of the Netherlands" he was appointed professor extraordinarius at Jena, in 1789. His "History of the Thirty Years' War" appeared in 1790–93, and in 1794 began his intimate relation with Goethe, beside whom he lived in Weimar from 1799 till his death in 1805. His lyrical poems were produced throughout his career, but his last period was most prolific both in these and in dramatic composition, and includes such great works as his "Wallenstein," "Marie Stuart," "The Maid of Orleans," "The Bride of Messina," and "William Tell" (1804). His life was a continual struggle against ill-health and unfavorable circumstances; but he maintained to the end the spirit of independence and love of liberty which are the characteristic mark of his writings.

This enthusiasm for freedom is well illustrated in "William Tell," the most widely popular of his plays. Based upon a world-wide legend which became localized in Switzerland in the fifteenth century and was incorporated into the history of the struggle of the Forest Cantons for deliverance from Austrian domination, it unites with the theme of liberty that of the beauty of life in primitive natural conditions, and both in its likenesses and differences illustrates Schiller's attitude toward the principles of the French Revolution.

WILLIAM TELL

DRAMATIS PERSONÆ

HERMANN GESSLER, *Governor of Schwytz, and Uri.*
WERNER, *Baron of Attinghausen, free noble of Switzerland.*
ULRICH VON RUDENZ, *his Nephew.*

WERNER STAUFFACHER,
CONRAD HUNN,
HANS AUF DER MAUER,
JORG IM HOFE,
ULRICH DER SCHMIDT,
JOST VON WEILER,
ITEL REDING, } *people of Schwytz.*

WALTER FÜRST,
WILLIAM TELL,
RÖSSELMANN, *the Priest,*
PETERMANN, *Sacristan,*
KUONI, *herdsman,*
WERNI, *huntsman,*
RUODI, *fisherman,* } *of Uri.*

ARNOLD OF MELCHTHAL,
CONRAD BAUMGARTEN,
MEYER VON SARNEN,
STRUTH VON WINKELRIED,
KLAUS VON DER FLUE,
BURKHART AM BUHEL.
ARNOLD VON SEWA, } *of Unterwald.*

PFEIFFER OF LUCERNE.
KUNZ OF GERSAU.

JENNI, *fisherman's son.*
SEPPI, *herdsman's son.*
GERTRUDE, *Stauffacher's wife.*
HEDWIG, *wife of Tell, daughter of Fürst.*
BERTHA OF BRUNECK, *a rich heiress.*

ARMGART,
MECHTHILD,
ELSBETH,
HILDEGARD, } *peasant women.*

WALTER,
WILLIAM, } *Tell's sons.*

FRIESSHARDT,
LEUTHOLD, } *soldiers.*

RUDOLPH DER HARRAS, *Gessler's master of the horse.*
JOHANNES PARRICIDA, *Duke of Suabia.*
STUSSI, *Overseer.*
The Mayor of Uri.
A Courier.
Master Stonemason, Companions, and Workmen.
Taskmaster.
A Crier.
Monks of the Order of Charity.
Horsemen of Gessler and Landenberg.
Many Peasants—Men and Women from the Waldstetten.

ACT I

SCENE I.—*A high rocky shore of the Lake of Lucerne opposite Schwytz. The lake makes a bend into the land; a hut stands at a short distance from the shore; the fisher boy is rowing about in his boat. Beyond the lake are seen the green meadows, the hamlets and farms of Schwytz, lying in the clear sunshine. On the left are observed the peaks of The Hacken, surrounded with clouds; to the right, and in the remote distance, appear the Glaciers. The Ranz des Vaches, and the tinkling of cattle bells, continue for some time after the rising of the curtain.*

379

Fisher Boy (*sings in his boat*)
Melody of the Ranz des Vaches

The smile-dimpled lake woo'd to bathe in its deep,
A boy on its green shore had laid him to sleep;
　　Then heard he a melody
　　　　Floating along,
　　　　Sweet as the notes
　　　　Of an angel's song.
And as thrilling with pleasure he wakes from his rest,
The waters are rippling over his breast;
　　　　And a voice from the deep cries,
　　　　"With me thou must go,
　　　I charm the young shepherd,
　　　I lure him below."

Herdsman (*on the mountains*)
Air.—Variation of the Ranz des Vaches

Farewell, ye green meadows,
　　Farewell, sunny shore,
The herdsman must leave you,
　　The summer is o'er.
We go to the hills, but you'll see us again,
　When the cuckoo calls, and the merry birds sing,
When the flowers bloom afresh in glade and in glen,
　And the brooks sparkle bright in the sunshine of spring.
　　Farewell, ye green meadows,
　　Farewell, sunny shore,
　　The herdsman must leave you,
　　The summer is o'er.

Chamois Hunter (*appearing on the top of a cliff*)
Second Variation of the Ranz des Vaches

On the heights peals the thunder, and trembles the bridge,
The huntsman bounds on by the dizzying ridge.
　　　Undaunted he hies him
　　　O'er ice-covered wild,

Where leaf never budded,
Nor Spring ever smiled;
And beneath him an ocean of mist, where his eye
No longer the dwellings of man can espy;
Through the parting clouds only
The earth can be seen,
Far down 'neath the vapour
The meadows of green.

[*A change comes over the landscape. A rumbling, cracking noise is heard among the mountains. Shadows of clouds sweep across the scene.*

[RUODI, *the fisherman, comes out of his cottage.* WERNI, *the huntsman, descends from the rocks.* KUONI, *the shepherd, enters, with a milkpail on his shoulders, followed by* SEPPI, *his assistant.*

Ruodi. Come, Jenni, bustle; get the boat on shore.
The grizzly Vale-King[1] comes, the Glaciers moan,
The Mytenstein[2] is drawing on his hood,
And from the Stormcleft chilly blows the wind;
The storm will burst before we know what's what.
Kuoni. 'Twill rain ere long; my sheep browse eagerly,
And Watcher there is scraping up the earth.
Werni. The fish are leaping, and the water-hen
Keeps diving up and down. A storm is brewing.
Kuoni (to his boy).
Look, Seppi, if the beasts be all in sight.
Seppi. There goes brown Liesel, I can hear her bells.
Kuoni. Then all are safe; she ever ranges farthest.
Ruodi. You've a fine chime of bells there, master herdsman.
Werni. And likely cattle, too. Are they your own?
Kuoni. I'm not so rich. They are the noble lord's
Of Attinghaus, and told off to my care.
Ruodi. How gracefully yon heifer bears her ribbon!

[1] The German is, Thalvogt, Ruler of the Valley—the name given figuratively to a dense grey mist which the south wind sweeps into the valleys from the mountain tops. It is well known as the precursor of stormy weather.
[2] A steep rock, standing on the north of Rütli, and nearly opposite to Brumen.

Kuoni. Ay, well she knows she's leader of the herd,
And, take it from her, she'd refuse to feed.

Ruodi. You're joking now. A beast devoid of reason—

Werni. Easily said. But beasts have reason, too,—
And that we know, we chamois-hunters, well.
They never turn to feed—sagacious creatures!
Till they have placed a sentinel ahead,
Who pricks his ears whenever we approach,
And gives alarm with clear and piercing pipe.

Ruodi (*to the shepherd*). Are you for home?

Kuoni.   The Alp is grazed quite bare.

Werni. A safe return, my friend!

Kuoni.   The same to you!
Men come not always back from tracks like yours.

Ruodi. But who comes here, running at topmost speed?

Werni. I know the man; 'tis Baumgart of Alzellen.

Konrad Baumgarten (*rushing in breathless*). For God's sake,
    ferryman, your boat!

Ruodi.   How now?
Why all this haste?

Baum.   Cast off! My life's at stake!
Set me across!

Kuoni.   Why, what's the matter, friend?

Werni. Who are pursuing you? First tell us that.

Baum. (*to the fisherman*). Quick, quick, man, quick! they're
    close upon my heels!
It is the Viceroy's men are after me;
If they should overtake me, I am lost.

Ruodi. Why are the troopers in pursuit of you?

Baum. First make me safe and then I'll tell you all.

Werni. There's blood upon your garments—how is this?

Baum. The Imperial Seneschal, who dwelt at Rossberg—

Kuoni. How! What! The Wolfshot?[3] Is it he pursues you?

Baum. He'll ne'er hurt man again; I've settled him.

[3] In German, Wolfenschiessen—a young man of noble family, and a native of Unterwalden, who attached himself to the House of Austria, and was appointed Burvogt, or Seneschal, of the Castle of Rossberg. He was killed by Baumgarten in the manner, and for the cause, mentioned in the text.

All (*starting back*). Now, God forgive you, what is this you've
 done!

Baum. What every free man in my place had done.
Mine own good household right I have enforced
'Gainst him that would have wrong'd my wife—my honour.

Kuoni. How? Wronged you in your honour, did he so?

Baum. That he did not fulfil his foul desire,
Is due to God, and to my trusty axe.

Werni. And you have cleft his skull then with your axe?

Kuoni. O, tell us all! You've time enough, and more,
While he is getting out the boat there from the beach.

Baum. When I was in the forest felling timber,
My wife came running out in mortal fear.
"The Seneschal," she said, "was in my house,
Had ordered her to get a bath prepared,
And thereupon had ta'en unseemly freedoms,
From which she rid herself, and flew to me."
Arm'd as I was, I sought him, and my axe
Has given his bath a bloody benison.

Werni. And you did well; no man can blame the deed.

Kuoni. The tyrant! Now he has his just reward!
We men of Unterwald have owed it long.

Baum. The deed got wind, and now they're in pursuit.
Heavens! whilst we speak, the time is flying fast.

          [*It begins to thunder*

Kuoni. Quick, ferryman, and set the good man over.

Ruodi. Impossible! a storm is close at hand,
Wait till it pass! You must.

Baum.   Almighty heavens!
I cannot wait; the least delay is death.

Kuoni. (*to the fisherman*). Push out—God with you! We should
 help our neighbours;
The like misfortune may betide us all.

      [*Thunder and the roaring of the wind.*

Ruodi. The South-wind's up![4] See how the lake is rising!

---

[4] Literally, The Föhn is loose! "When," says Müller, in his History of Switzerland,
"the wind called the Föhn is high, the navigation of the lake becomes extremely
dangerous. Such is its vehemence, that the laws of the country require that the fires

I cannot steer against both wind and wave.

Baum. (*clasping him by the knees*). God so help you as now
you pity me!

Werni. His life's at stake. Have pity on him, man!

Kuoni. He is a father: has a wife and children.

[*Repeated peals of thunder.*

Ruodi. What! and have I not, then, a life to lose,
A wife and child at home as well as he?
See how the breakers foam, and toss, and whirl,
And the lake eddies up from all its depths!
Right gladly would I save the worthy man,
But 'tis impossible, as you must see.

Baum. (*still kneeling*). Then must I fall into the tyrant's hands.
And with the shore of safety close in sight!
Yonder it lies! My eyes can see it clear,
My very voice can echo to its shores.
There is the boat to carry me across,
Yet must I lie here helpless and forlorn.

Kuoni. Look! who comes here?

Ruodi. 'Tis Tell, ay, Tell, of Bürglen.[5]

[*Enter* TELL *with a crossbar.*

Tell. What man is he that here implores for aid?

Kuoni. He is from Alzellen, and to guard his honour
From touch of foulest shame, has slain the Wolfshot,
The Imperial Seneschal, who dwelt at Rossberg.
The Viceroy's troopers are upon his heels;
He begs the ferryman to take him over,
But frightened at the storm he says he won't.

Ruodi. Well, there is Tell can steer as well as I.
He'll be my judge, if it be possible.

[*Violent peals of thunder—the lake becomes more tempestuous.*
Am I to plunge into the jaws of hell?
I should be mad to dare the desperate act.

---

shall be extinguished in the houses while it lasts, and the night watches are doubled.
The inhabitants lay heavy stones upon the roofs of their houses, to prevent their
being blown away."

[5] Bürglen, the birthplace and residence of Tell. A chapel, erected in 1522, remains
on the spot formerly occupied by his house.

Tell. The brave man thinks upon himself the last.
Put trust in God, and help him in his need!

Ruodi. Safe in the port, 'tis easy to advise.
There is the boat, and there the lake! Try you!

Tell. The lake may pity, but the Viceroy never.
Come, risk it, man!

Shepherd and Huntsman. O save him! save him! save him!

Ruodi. Though 'twere my brother, or my darling child,
I would not go. 'Tis Simon and Jude's day,
The lake is up, and calling for its victim.

Tell. Nought's to be done with idle talking here.
Each moment's precious; the man must be help'd,
Say, boatman, will you venture?

Ruodi.   No; not I.

Tell. In God's name, then, give me the boat! I will,
With my poor strength, see what is to be done!

Kuoni. Ha, gallant Tell!

Werni.   That's like a huntsman true.

Baum. You are my angel, my preserver, Tell.

Tell. I may preserve you from the Viceroy's power,
But from the tempest's rage another must.
Yet better 'tis you fall into God's hands,
Than into those of men.   [*To the herdsman.*
                    Herdsman, do thou
Console my wife if I should come to grief.
I could not choose but do as I have done.

                    [*He leaps into the boat.*

Kuoni (*to the fisherman*). A pretty man to keep a ferry, truly!
What Tell could risk, you dared not venture on.

Ruodi. Far better men would never cope with Tell.
There's no two such as he 'mong all our hills.

Werni (*who has ascended a rock*). Now he is off. God help thee,
    gallant sailor!
Look how the little boat reels on the waves!
There! they have swept clean over it. And now

Kuoni (*on the shore*).
'Tis out of sight. Yet stay, there 'tis again!

Stoutly he stems the breakers, noble fellow!

Seppi. Here come the troopers hard as they can ride!

Kuoni. Heavens! so they do! Why, that was help, indeed.

[*Enter a troop of horsemen.*

1st H. Give up the murderer! You have him here!

2nd H. This way he came! 'Tis useless to conceal him!

Ruodi and Kuoni. Whom do you mean?

1st H. (*discovering the boat*). The devil! What do I see?

Werni. (*from above*). Isn't he in yonder boat ye seek? Ride on,
If you lay to, you may o'ertake him yet.

2nd H. Curse on you, he's escaped!

1st H. (*to the shepherd and fisherman*). You help'd him off,
And you shall pay for it! Fall on their herds!
Down with the cottage! burn it! beat it down!

[*They rush off.*

Seppi (*hurrying after them*). Oh, my poor lambs!

Kuoni (*following him*).   Unhappy me, my herds!

Werni. The tyrants!

Ruodi. (*wringing his hands*). Righteous Heaven! Oh, when
     will come
Deliverance to this doom-devoted land?   [*Exeunt severally.*

SCENE II.—*A lime tree in front of* STAUFFACHER'S *house at Steinen, in
     Schwytz, upon the public road, near a bridge*

WERNER STAUFFACHER *and* PFEIFFER, *of Lucerne, enter
     into conversation*

Pfeiff. Ay, ay, friend Stauffacher, as I have said,
Swear not to Austria, if you can help it.
Hold by the Empire stoutly as of yore,
And God preserve you in your ancient freedom!

[*Presses his hand warmly, and is going.*

Stauff. Wait till my mistress comes. Now do! You are
My guest in Schwytz—I in Lucerne am yours.

Pfeiff. Thanks! thanks! But I must reach Gersau to-day.
Whatever grievances your rulers' pride
And grasping avarice may yet inflict,

Bear them in patience—soon a change may come.
Another emperor may mount the throne.
But Austria's once, and you are hers for ever.   [*Exit.*

> [STAUFFACHER *sits down sorrowfully upon a bench under the lime tree. Gertrude, his wife, enters, and finds him in this posture. She places herself near him, and looks at him for some time in silence.*

  Gert. So sad, my love! I scarcely know thee now.
For many a day in silence I have mark'd
A moody sorrow furrowing thy brow.
Some silent grief is weighing on thy heart.
Trust it to me. I am thy faithful wife,
And I demand my half of all thy cares.

> [STAUFFACHER *gives her his hand and is silent.*

Tell me what can oppress thy spirits thus?
Thy toil is blest—the world goes well with thee—
Our barns are full—our cattle, many a score;
Our handsome team of well-fed horses, too,
Brought from the mountain pastures safely home,
To winter in their comfortable stalls.
There stands thy house—no nobleman's more fair!
'Tis newly built with timber of the best,
All grooved and fitted with the nicest skill;
Its many glistening windows tell of comfort!
'Tis quarter'd o'er with 'scutcheons of all hues,
And proverbs sage, which passing travellers
Linger to read, and ponder o'er their meaning.

  Stauff. The house is strongly built, and handsomely,
But, ah! the ground on which we built it quakes.

  Gert. Tell me, dear Werner, what you mean by that?

  Stauff. No later gone than yesterday, I sat
Beneath this linden, thinking with delight,
How fairly all was finished, when from Küssnacht
The Viceroy and his men came riding by.
Before this house he halted in surprise:
At once I rose, and, as beseemed his rank,
Advanced respectfully to greet the lord,

To whom the Emperor delegates his power,
As judge supreme within our Canton here.
"Who is the owner of this house?" he asked,
With mischief in his thoughts, for well he knew.
With prompt decision, thus I answered him:
"The Emperor, your grace—my lord and yours,
And held by me in fief." On this he answered,
"I am the Emperor's viceregent here,
And will not that each peasant churl should build
At his own pleasure, bearing him as freely
As though he were the master in the land.
I shall make bold to put a stop to this!"
So saying, he, with menaces, rode off,
And left me musing with a heavy heart
On the fell purpose that his words betray'd.

   Gert. My own dear lord and husband! Wilt thou take
A word of honest counsel from thy wife?
I boast to be the noble Iberg's child,
A man of wide experience. Many a time,
As we sat spinning in the winter nights,
My sisters and myself, the people's chiefs
Were wont to gather round our father's hearth,
To read the old imperial charters, and
To hold sage converse on the country's weal.
Then heedfully I listened, marking well
What now the wise man thought, the good man wished,
And garner'd up their wisdom in my heart.
Hear then, and mark me well; for thou wilt see,
I long have known the grief that weighs thee down.
The Viceroy hates thee, fain would injure thee,
For thou hast cross'd his wish to bend the Swiss
In homage to this upstart house of princes,
And kept them staunch, like their good sires of old,
In true allegiance to the Empire. Say,
Is't not so, Werner? Tell me, am I wrong?

   Stauff. 'Tis even so. For this doth Gessler hate me.

   Gert. He burns with envy, too, to see thee living

Happy and free on thine ancestral soil,
For he is landless. From the Emperor's self
Thou hold'st in fief the lands thy fathers left thee.
There's not a prince i' the Empire that can show
A better title to his heritage;
For thou hast over thee no lord but one,
And he the mightiest of all Christian kings.
Gessler, we know, is but a younger son,
His only wealth the knightly cloak he wears;
He therefore views an honest man's good fortune
With a malignant and a jealous eye.
Long has he sworn to compass thy destruction.
As yet thou art uninjured. Wilt thou wait
Till he may safely give his malice vent?
A wise man would anticipate the blow.
   Stauff. What's to be done?
   Gert.   Now hear what I advise.
Thou knowest well, how here with us in Schwytz
All worthy men are groaning underneath
This Gessler's grasping, grinding tyranny.
Doubt not the men of Unterwald as well,
And Uri, too, are chafing like ourselves,
At this oppressive and heart-wearying yoke.
For there, across the lake, the Landenberg
Wields the same iron rule as Gessler here—
No fishing-boat comes over to our side,
But brings the tidings of some new encroachment,
Some fresh outrage, more grievous than the last.
Then it were well, that some of you—true men—
Men sound at heart, should secretly devise,
How best to shake this hateful thraldom off.
Full sure I am that God would not desert you,
But lend His favour to the righteous cause.
Hast thou no friend in Uri, one to whom
Thou frankly may'st unbosom all thy thoughts?
   Stauff. I know full many a gallant fellow there,
And nobles, too,—great men, of high repute,

In whom I can repose unbounded trust.   [*Rising.*
Wife! What a storm of wild and perilous thoughts
Hast thou stirr'd up within my tranquil breast!
The darkest musings of my bosom thou
Hast dragg'd to light, and placed them full before me;
And what I scarce dared harbour e'en in thought,
Thou speakest plainly out with fearless tongue.
But hast thou weigh'd well what thou urgest thus?
Discord will come, and the fierce clang of arms,
To scare this valley's long unbroken peace,
If we, a feeble shepherd race, shall dare
Him to the fight, that lords it o'er the world.
Ev'n now they only wait some fair pretext
For setting loose their savage warrior hordes,
To scourge and ravage this devoted land,
To lord it o'er us with the victor's rights,
And, 'neath the show of lawful chastisement,
Despoil us of our chartered liberties.

   Gert. You, too, are men; can wield a battle axe
As well as they. God ne'er deserts the brave.

   Stauff. Oh wife! a horrid, ruthless fiend is war,
That smites at once the shepherd and his flock.

   Gert. Whate'er great Heaven inflicts, we must endure;
But wrong is what no noble heart will bear.

   Stauff. This house—thy pride—war, unrelenting war
Will burn it down.

   Gert.   And did I think this heart
Enslaved and fettered to the things of earth,
With my own hand I'd hurl the kindling torch.

   Stauff. Thou hast faith in human kindness, wife; but war
Spares not the tender infant in its cradle.

   Gert. There is a Friend to innocence in heaven.
Send your gaze forward, Werner—not behind.

   Stauff. We men may die like men, with sword in hand;
But oh, what fate, my Gertrude, may be thine?

   Gert. None are so weak, but one last choice is left
A spring from yonder bridge and I am free!

Stauff. (*embracing her*). Well may he fight for hearth and home,
   that clasps
A heart so rare as thine against his own!
What are the host of emperors to him?
Gertrude, farewell! I will to Uri straight.
There lives my worthy comrade, Walter Fürst;
His thoughts and mine upon these times are one.
There, too, resides the noble Banneret
Of Attinghaus. High though of blood he be,
He loves the people, honours their old customs.
With both of these I will take counsel, how
To rid us bravely of our country's foe.
Farewell! and while I am away, bear thou
A watchful eye in management at home.
The pilgrim journeying to the house of God,
And holy friar, collecting for his cloister,
To these give liberally from purse and garner.
Stauffacher's house would not be hid. Right out
Upon the public way it stands, and offers
To all that pass a hospitable roof.
            [*While they are retiring,* TELL *enters with* BAUMGARTEN.
Tell. Now, then, you have no further need of me.
Enter yon house. 'Tis Werner Stauffacher's,
A man that is a father to distress.
See, there he is, himself! Come, follow me.
                       [*They retire up. Scene changes.*

SCENE III.—*A common near Altdorf. On an eminence in the background a castle in progress of erection, and so far advanced that the
   outline of the whole may be distinguished. The back part is finished:
   men are working at the front. Scaffolding, on which the workmen
   are going up and down. A slater is seen upon the highest part of the
   roof. All is bustle and activity.*

TASKMASTER, MASON, WORKMEN *and* LABOURERS

Task. (*with a stick, urging on the workmen*). Up, up! You've
   rested long enough. To work!
The stones here! Now the mortar, and the lime!

And let his lordship see the work advanced,
When next he comes. These fellows crawl like snails!

[*To two labourers, with loads.*

What! call ye that a load? Go, double it.
Is this the way ye earn your wages, laggards?

1st W. 'Tis very hard that we must bear the stones,
To make a keep and dungeon for ourselves!

Task. What's that you mutter? 'Tis a worthless race,
For nothing fit but just to milk their cows,
And saunter idly up and down the hills.

Old Man (sinks down exhausted). I can no more.

Task. (shaking him).   Up, up, old man, to work!

1st W. Have you no bowels of compassion, thus
To press so hard upon a poor old man,
That scarce can drag his feeble limbs along?

Master Mason and Workmen. Shame, shame upon you—shame!
    It cries to heaven.

Task. Mind your own business. I but do my duty.

1st W. Pray, master, what's to be the name of this
Same castle, when 'tis built?

Task.   The Keep of Uri;
For by it we shall keep you in subjection.

Work. The Keep of Uri?

Task.   Well, why laugh at that?

2nd W. Keep Uri, will you, with this paltry place!

1st W. How many molehills such as that must first
Be piled up each on each, ere you make
A mountain equal to the least in Uri?

[*Taskmaster retires up the stage.*

Mas. M. I'll drown the mallet in the deepest lake,
That served my hand on this accursed pile.

[*Enter* TELL *and* STAUFFACHER.

Stauff. O, that I had not lived to see this sight!

Tell. Here 'tis not good to be. Let us proceed.

Stauff. Am I in Uri,—Uri, freedom's home?

Mas. M. O, sir, if you could only see the vaults
Beneath these towers. The man that tenants them

Will ne'er hear cock crow more.

   Stauff.   O God! O God!

   Mason. Look at these ramparts and these buttresses,

That seem as they were built to last for ever.

   Tell. What hands have built, my friend, hands can destroy.

                            [Pointing to the mountains.

That home of freedom God hath built for us.

       [A drum is heard. People enter bearing a cap upon a pole,
        followed by a crier. Women and children thronging
        tumultuously after them.

   1st W. What means the drum? Give heed!

   Mason.   Why, here's a mumming!

And look, the cap—what can they mean by that?

   Crier. In the Emperor's name, give ear!

   Work.   Hush! silence! hush!

   Crier. Ye men of Uri, ye do see this cap!

It will be set upon a lofty pole

In Altdorf, in the market place: and this

Is the Lord Governor's good will and pleasure;

The cap shall have like honour as himself,

All do it reverence with bended knee,

And head uncovered; thus the king will know

Who are his true and loyal subjects here;

His life and goods are forfeit to the crown

That shall refuse obedience to the order.

     [The people burst out into laughter. The drum beats and the
       procession passes on.

   1st W. A strange device to fall upon indeed:

Do reverence to a cap! A pretty farce!

Heard ever mortal anything like this?

   Mas. M. Down to a cap on bended knee, forsooth!

Rare jesting this with men of sober sense!

   1st W. Nay, an it were the imperial crown! A cap!

Merely the cap of Austria! I've seen it

Hanging above the throne in Gessler's hall.

   Mason. The cap of Austria? Mark that! A snare

To get us into Austria's power, by Heaven!

Work. No freeborn man will stoop to such disgrace.

Mas. M. Come—to our comrades, and advise with them!

[*They retire up.*

Tell (*to* STAUFFACHER). You see how matters stand. Farewell, my
   friend;

Stauff. Whither away? Oh, leave us not so soon.

Tell. They look for me at home. So fare ye well.

Stauff. My heart's so full, and has so much to tell you.

Tell. Words will not make a heart that's heavy light.

Stauff. Yet words may possibly conduct to deeds.

Tell. Endure in silence! We can do no more.

Stauff. But shall we bear what is not to be borne?

Tell. Impetuous rulers have the shortest reigns.

When the fierce Southwind rises from its chasms,

Men cover up their fires, the ships in haste

Make for the harbour, and the mighty spirit

Sweeps o'er the earth, and leaves no trace behind.

Let every man live quietly at home;

Peace to the peaceful rarely is denied.

Stauff. And is it thus you view our grievances?

Tell. The serpent stings not till it is provoked.

Let them alone; they'll weary of themselves,

When they shall see we are not to be roused.

Stauff. Much might be done—did we stand fast together.

Tell. When the ship founders, he will best escape,

Who seeks no other's safety but his own.

Stauff. And you desert the common cause so coldly?

Tell. A man can safely count but on himself!

Stauff. Nay, even the weak grow strong by union.

Tell. But the strong man is strongest when alone.

Stauff. So, then, your country cannot count on you,

If in despair she rise against her foes.

Tell. Tell rescues the lost sheep from yawning gulphs:

Is he a man, then, to desert his friends?

Yet, whatsoe'er you do, spare me from council!

I was not born to ponder and select;

But when your course of action is resolved,

Then call on Tell: you shall not find him fail.

[*Exeunt severally. A sudden tumult is heard around the scaffolding.*

    Mason (running in). What's wrong?

    First Workman (running forward). The slater's fallen from the roof.

    Bertha (rushing in). Heavens! Is he dashed to pieces? Save him, help!

If help be possible, save him! Here is gold.

                        [*Throws her trinkets among the people.*

    Mason. Hence with your gold,—your universal charm,

And remedy for ill! When you have torn

Fathers from children, husbands from their wives,

And scattered woe and wail throughout the land,

You think with gold to compensate for all.

Hence! Till we saw you, we were happy men;

With you came misery and dark despair.

    Bertha (to the TASKMASTER, *who has returned)*.

Lives he?   [TASKMASTER *shakes his head.*

           Ill-omened towers, with curses built,

And doomed with curses to be tenanted!   [*Exit.*

SCENE IV.—*The House of* WALTER FÜRST. WALTER FÜRST *and* ARNOLD
    VON MELCHTHAL *enter simultaneously at different sides.*

    Melch. Good Walter Fürst.

    Fürst.   If we should be surprised!

Stay where you are. We are beset with spies.

    Melch. Have you no news for me from Unterwald?

What of my father? 'Tis not to be borne,

Thus to be pent up like a felon here!

What have I done so heinous that I must

Skulk here in hiding, like a murderer?

I only laid my staff across the fists

Of the pert varlet, when before my eyes,

By order of the governor, he tried

To drive away my handsome team of oxen.

    Fürst. You are too rash by far. He did no more

Than what the Governor had ordered him.
You had transgress'd, and therefore should have paid
The penalty, however hard, in silence.

Melch. Was I to brook the fellow's saucy gibe,
"That if the peasant must have bread to eat,
Why, let him go and draw the plough himself!"
It cut me to the very soul to see
My oxen, noble creatures, when the knave
Unyoked them from the plough. As though they felt
The wrong, they lowed and butted with their horns.
On this I could contain myself no longer,
And, overcome by passion, struck him down.

Fürst. O, we old men can scarce command ourselves!
And can we wonder youth breaks out of bounds?

Melch. I'm only sorry for my father's sake!
To be away from him, that needs so much
My fostering care! The Governor detests him,
Because, whene'er occasion served, he has
Stood stoutly up for right and liberty.
Therefore they'll bear him hard—the poor old man!
And there is none to shield him from their gripe.
Come what come may, I must go home again.

Fürst. Compose yourself, and wait in patience till
We get some tidings o'er from Unterwald.
Away! away! I hear a knock! Perhaps
A message from the Viceroy! Get thee in!
You are not safe from Landenberger's[6] arm
In Uri, for these tyrants pull together.

Melch. They teach us Switzers what *we* ought to do.

Fürst. Away! I'll call you when the coast is clear.

[MELCHTHAL *retires.*

Unhappy youth! I dare not tell him all
The evil that my boding heart predicts!
Who's there? The door ne'er opens, but I look

---

[6] Berenger von Landenberg, a man of noble family in Thurgau, and Governor of Unterwald, infamous for his cruelties to the Swiss, and particularly to the venerable Henry of the Halden. He was slain at the battle of Morgarten, in 1315.

For tidings of mishap. Suspicion lurks
With darkling treachery in every nook.
Even to our inmost rooms they force their way,
These myrmidons of power; and soon we'll need
To fasten bolts and bars upon our doors.

[*He opens the door, and steps back in surprise as* WERNER
STAUFFACHER *enters.*

What do I see? You, Werner? Now, by Heaven!
A valued guest, indeed. No man e'er set
His foot across this threshold, more esteem'd,
Welcome! thrice welcome, Werner, to my roof!
What brings you here? What seek you here in Uri?

Stauff. (*shakes* FÜRST *by the hand*). The olden times and olden
Switzerland.

Fürst. You bring them with you. See how glad I am,
My heart leaps at the very sight of you.
Sit down—sit down, and tell me how you left
Your charming wife, fair Gertrude? Iberg's child,
And clever as her father. Not a man,
That wends from Germany, by Meinrad's Cell,[7]
To Italy, but praises far and wide
Your house's hospitality. But say,
Have you come here direct from Flüelen,
And have you noticed nothing on your way,
Before you halted at my door?

Stauff. (*sits down*).   I saw
A work in progress, as I came along,
I little thought to see—that likes me ill.

Fürst. O friend! you've lighted on my thought at once.

Stauff. Such things in Uri ne'er were known before.
Never was prison here in man's remembrance,
Nor ever any stronghold but the grave.

Fürst. You name it well. It is the grave of freedom.

Stauff. Friend, Walter Fürst, I will be plain with you.
No idle curiosity it is

---

[7] A cell built in the 9th century, by Meinrad, Count of Hohenzollern, the founder
of the Convent of Einsiedeln, subsequently alluded to in the text.

That brings me here, but heavy cares. I left
Thraldom at home, and thraldom meets me here.
Our wrongs, e'en now, are more than we can bear
And who shall tell us where they are to end?
From eldest time the Switzer has been free,
Accustom'd only to the mildest rule.
Such things as now we suffer ne'er were known,
Since herdsman first drove cattle to the hills.

Fürst. Yes, our oppressions are unparallel'd!
Why, even our own good lord of Attinghaus,
Who lived in olden times, himself declares
They are no longer to be tamely borne.

Stauff. In Unterwalden yonder 'tis the same;
And bloody has the retribution been.
The imperial Seneschal, the Wolfshot, who
At Rossberg dwelt, long'd for forbidden fruit—
Baumgarten's wife, that lives at Alzellen,
He tried to make a victim to his lust,
On which the husband slew him with his axe.

Fürst. O, Heaven is just in all its judgments still!
Baumgarten, say you? A most worthy man.
Has he escaped, and is he safely hid?

Stauff. Your son-in-law conveyed him o'er the lake,
And he lies hidden in my house at Steinen.
He brought the tidings with him of a thing
That has been done at Sarnen, worse than all,
A thing to make the very heart run blood!

Fürst. (*attentively*). Say on. What is it?

Stauff.   There dwells in Melchthal, then,
Just as you enter by the road from Kerns,
An upright man, named Henry of the Halden,
A man of weight and influence in the Diet.

Fürst. Who knows him not? But what of him? Proceed.

Stauff. The Landenberg, to punish some offence
Committed by the old man's son, it seems,
Had given command to take the youth's best pair
Of oxen from his plough; on which the lad

Struck down the messenger and took to flight.

Fürst. But the old father—tell me, what of him?

Stauff. The Landenberg sent for him, and required
He should produce his son upon the spot;
And when the old man protested, and with truth,
That he knew nothing of the fugitive,
The tyrant call'd his torturers.

Fürst. (*springs up and tries to lead him to the other side*).
                                   Hush, no more!

Stauff. (*with increasing warmth*). "And though thy son," he
    cried, "has 'scaped me now,
I have thee fast, and thou shalt feel my vengeance."
With that they flung the old man to the ground,
And plunged the pointed steel into his eyes.

Fürst. Merciful Heaven!

Melch. (*rushing out*). Into his eyes, his eyes?

Stauff. (*addresses himself in astonishment to* WALTER FÜRST). Who
    is this youth?

Melch. (*grasping him convulsively*). Into his eyes? Speak, speak!

Fürst. Oh, miserable hour!

Stauff.   Who is it, tell me?
             [STAUFFACHER *makes a sign to him.*
It is his son! All-righteous Heaven!

Melch.   And I
Must be from thence! What! Into both his eyes?

Fürst. Be calm, be calm; and bear it like a man!

Melch. And all for me—for my mad willful folly!
Blind, did you say? Quite blind—and both his eyes?

Stauff. Ev'n so. The fountain of his sight is quench'd,
He ne'er will see the blessed sunshine more.

Fürst. Oh, spare his anguish!

Melch.   Never, never more!
        [*Presses his hands upon his eyes and is silent for some
            moments: then turning from one to the other, speaks
            in a subdued tone, broken by sobs.*
O, the eye's light, of all the gifts of Heaven,
The dearest, best! From light all beings live—

Each fair created thing—the very plants
Turn with a joyful transport to the light,
And he—he must drag on through all his days
In endless darkness! Never more for him
The sunny meads shall glow, the flow'rets bloom;
Nor shall he more behold the roseate tints
Of the iced mountain top! To die is nothing.
But to have life, and not have sight,—oh that
Is misery, indeed! Why do you look
So piteously at me? I have two eyes,
Yet to my poor blind father can give neither!
No, not one gleam of that great sea of light,
That with its dazzling splendour floods my gaze.

   Stauff. Ah, I must swell the measure of your grief,
Instead of soothing it. The worst, alas!
Remains to tell. They've stripp'd him of his all;
Nought have they left him, save his staff, on which,
Blind, and in rags, he moves from door to door.

   Melch. Nought but his staff to the old eyeless man!
Stripp'd of his all—even of the light of day,
The common blessing of the meanest wretch?
Tell me no more of patience, of concealment!
Oh, what a base and coward thing am I,
That on mine own security I thought,
And took no care of thine! Thy precious head
Left as a pledge within the tyrant's grasp!
Hence, craven-hearted prudence, hence! And all
My thoughts be vengeance, and the despot's blood!
I'll seek him straight—no power shall stay me now—
And at his hands demand my father's eyes.
I'll beard him 'mid a thousand myrmidons!
What's life to me, if in his heart's best blood
I cool the fever of this mighty anguish?   [*He is going.*

   Fürst. Stay, this is madness, Melchthal! What avails
Your single arm against his power? He sits
At Sarnen high within his lordly keep,

And, safe within its battlemented walls,
May laugh to scorn your unavailing rage.

   Melch. And though he sat within the icy domes
Of yon far Schreckhorn—ay, or higher, where,
Veil'd since eternity, the Jungfrau soars,
Still to the tyrant would I make my way;
With twenty comrades minded like myself,
I'd lay his fastness level with the earth!
And if none follow me, and if you all,
In terror for your homesteads and your herds,
Bow in submission to the tyrant's yoke,
Round me I'll call the herdsmen on the hills,
And there beneath heaven's free and boundless roof,
Where men still feel as men, and hearts are true,
Proclaim aloud this foul enormity!

   Stauff. (*to* FÜRST.)
The measure's full—and we are then to wait
Till some extremity—

   Melch.   Peace! What extremity
Remains for us to dread? What, when our eyes
No longer in their sockets are secure?
Heavens! Are we helpless? Wherefore did we learn
To bend the cross-bow,—wield the battle-axe?
What living creature but in its despair,
Finds for itself a weapon of defence?
The baited stag will turn, and with the show
Of his dread antlers hold the hounds at bay;
The chamois drags the huntsman down th' abyss,
The very ox, the partner of man's toil,
The sharer of his roof, that meekly bends
The strength of his huge neck beneath the yoke,
Springs up, if he's provoked, whets his strong horn,
And tosses his tormentor to the clouds.

   Fürst. If the three Cantons thought as we three do,
Something might then be done, with good effect.

   Stauff. When Uri calls, when Unterwald replies,

Schwytz will be mindful of her ancient league.[8]

Melch. I've many friends in Unterwald, and none
That would not gladly venture life and limb,
If fairly back'd and aided by the rest.
Oh! sage and reverend fathers of this land,
Heie do I stand before your riper years,
An unskill'd youth, who in the Diet must
Into respectful silence hush his voice.
Yet do not, for that I am young, and want
Experience, slight my counsel and my words.
'Tis not the wantonness of youthful blood
That fires my spirit; but a pang so deep
That e'en the flinty rocks must pity me.

---

[8] The League, or Bond, of the Three Cantons was of very ancient origin. They met and renewed it from time to time, especially when their liberties were threatened with danger. A remarkable instance of this occurred in the end of the 13th century, when Albert of Austria became Emperor, and when, possibly, for the first time, the Bond was reduced to writing. As it is important to the understanding of many passages of the play, a translation is subjoined of the oldest known document relating to it. The original, which is in Latin and German, is dated in August, 1291, and is under the seals of the whole of the men of Schwytz, the commonalty of the vale of Uri, and the whole of the men of the upper and lower vales of Stanz.

THE BOND

Be it known to every one, that the men of the Dale of Uri, the Community of Schwytz, as also the men of the mountains of Unterwald, in consideration of the evil times, have full confidently bound themselves, and sworn to help each other with all their power and might, property and people, against all who shall do violence to them, or any of them. That is our Ancient Bond.

Whoever hath a Seignior, let him obey according to the conditions of his service.

We are agreed to receive into these dales no Judge, who is not a countryman and indweller, or who hath bought his place.

Every controversy amongst the sworn confederates shall be determined by some of the sagest of their number, and if any one shall challenge their judgment, then shall he be constrained to obey it by the rest.

Whoever intentionally or deceitfully kills another, shall be executed, and whoever shelters him shall be banished.

Whoever burns the property of another shall no longer be regarded as a countryman, and whoever shelters him shall make good the damage done.

Whoever injures another, or robs him, and hath property in our country, shall make satisfaction out of the same.

No one shall distrain a debtor without a judge, nor any one who is not his debtor, or the surety for such debtor.

Every one in these dales shall submit to the judge, or we, the sworn confederates, all will take satisfaction for all the injury occasioned by his contumacy. And if in any internal division the one party will not accept justice, all the rest shall help the other party. These decrees shall, God willing, endure eternally for our general advantage.

You, too, are fathers, heads of families,
And you must wish to have a virtuous son,
To reverence your grey hairs, and shield your eyes
With pious and affectionate regard.
Do not, I pray, because in limb and fortune
You still are unassailed, and still your eyes
Revolve undimm'd and sparkling in their spheres;
Oh, do not, therefore, disregard our wrongs!
Above you, also, hangs the tyrant's sword.
You, too, have striven to alienate the land
From Austria. This was all my father's crime:
You share his guilt, and may his punishment.
    Stauff. (*to* FÜRST).
Do thou resolve! I am prepared to follow.
    Fürst. First let us learn what steps the noble lords
Von Sillinen and Attinghaus propose.
Their names would rally thousands to the cause.
    Melch. Is there a name within the Forest Mountains
That carries more respect than yours—and yours?
On names like these the people build their trust
In time of need—such names are household words.
Rich was your heritage of manly worth,
And richly have you added to its stores.
What need of nobles? Let us do the work
Ourselves. Yes, though we have to stand alone,
We shall be able to maintain our rights.
    Stauff. The nobles' wrongs are not so great as ours.
The torrent, that lays waste the lower grounds,
Hath not ascended to the uplands yet.
But let them see the country once in arms,
They'll not refuse to lend a helping hand.
    Fürst. Were there an umpire 'twixt ourselves and Austria,
Justice and law might then decide our quarrel.
But our oppressor is our Emperor too,
And judge supreme. 'Tis God must help us, then,
And our own arm! Be yours the task to rouse
The men of Schwytz; I'll rally friends in Uri.

But whom are we to send to Unterwald?

Melch. Thither send me. Whom should it more concern!

Fürst. No, Melchthal, no; you are my guest, and I
Must answer for your safety.

Melch.   Let me go.
I know each forest-track and mountain-path;
Friends too, I'll find, be sure, on every hand,
To give me willing shelter from the foe.

Stauff. Nay, let him go; no traitors harbour there:
For tyranny is so abhorred in Unterwald,
No tools can there be found to work her will.
In the low valleys, too, the Alzeller
Will gain confederates, and rouse the country.

Melch. But how shall we communicate, and not
Awaken the suspicion of the tyrants?

Stauff. Might we not meet at Brunnen or at Treib,
Where merchant vessels with their cargoes come?

Fürst. We must not go so openly to work.
Hear my opinion. On the lake's left bank,
As we sail hence to Brunnen, right against
The Mytenstein, deep-hidden in the wood
A meadow lies, by shepherds called the Rootli,
Because the wood has been uprooted there.
(*To* MELCHTHAL.) 'Tis where our Canton bound'ries verge on
        yours;—
(*To* STAUFFACHER.) Your boat will carry you across from Schwytz.
Thither by lonely bypaths let us wend
At midnight, and deliberate o'er our plans.
Let each bring with him there ten trusty men,
All one at heart with us; and then we may
Consult together for the general weal,
And, with God's guidance, fix what next to do.

Stauff. So let it be. And now your true right hand!—
Yours, too, young man!—and as we now three men
Among ourselves thus knit our hands together
In all sincerity and truth, e'en so
Shall we three cantons, too, together stand

In victory and defeat, in life and death.

   Fürst and Melch. In life and death!

    [*They hold their hands clasped together for some moments
in silence.*

   Melch.   Alas, my old blind father!

The day of freedom, that thou canst not see,

But thou shalt hear it, when from Alp to Alp

The beacon fires throw up their flaming signs,

And the proud castles of the tyrants fall,

Into thy cottage shall the Switzer burst,

Bear the glad tidings to thine ear, and o'er

Thy darken'd way shall Freedom's radiance pour.

ACT II

Scene I.—*The mansion of the* Baron of Attinghausen. *A Gothic Hall,
decorated with escutcheons and helmets. The* Baron, *a grey-headed
man, eighty-five years old, tall and of a commanding mien, clad in a
furred pelisse, and leaning on a staff tipped with chamois horn.*
Kuoni *and six hinds standing round him with rakes and scythes.*
Ulrich of Rudenz *enters in the costume of a knight.*

   Rud. Uncle, I'm here! Your will?

   Atting.   First let me share,

After the ancient custom of our house,

The morning cup, with these my faithful servants!

    [*He drinks from a cup, which is then passed round.*

Time was, I stood myself in field and wood,

With mine own eyes directing all their toil,

Even as my banner led them in the fight,

Now I am only fit to play the steward:

And, if the genial sun come not to me,

I can no longer seek it on the hills.

Thus slowly, in an ever-narrowing sphere,

I move on to the narrowest and the last,

Where all life's pulses cease. I now am but

The shadow of my former self, and that

Is fading fast—'twill soon be but a name.

Kuoni (*offering* Rudenz *the cup*). A pledge, young master!

[Rudenz *hesitates to take the cup.*

Nay, Sir, drink it off!

One cup, one heart! You know our proverb, Sir?

Atting. Go, children, and at eve, when work is done,
We'll meet and talk the country's business over.

[*Exeunt servants.*

Belted and plumed, and all thy bravery on!
Thou art for Altdorf—for the castle, boy?

Rud. Yes, uncle. Longer may I not delay—

Atting. (*sitting down*). Why in such haste? Say, are thy youthful
   hours
Doled in such niggard measure, that thou must
Be chary of them to thy aged uncle?

Rud. I see my presence is not needed here,
I am but as a stranger in this house.

Atting. (*gazes fixedly at him for a considerable time*).
Ay, pity 'tis thou art! Alas, that home
To thee has grown so strange! Oh, Uly! Uly!
I scarce do know thee now, thus deck'd in silks,
The peacock's feather[9] flaunting in thy cap,
And purple mantle round thy shoulders flung;
Thou look'st upon the peasant with disdain;
And tak'st his honest greeting with a blush.

Rud. All honour due to him I gladly pay,
But must deny the right he would usurp.

Atting. The sore displeasure of its monarch rests
Upon our land, and every true man's heart,
Is full of sadness for the grievous wrongs
We suffer from our tyrants. Thou alone
Art all unmoved amid the general grief.
Abandoning thy friends, thou tak'st thy stand
Beside thy country's foes, and, as in scorn
Of our distress, pursuest giddy joys,

---

[9] The Austrian knights were in the habit of wearing a plume of peacock's feathers
in their helmets. After the overthrow of the Austrian dominion in Switzerland, it
was made highly penal to wear the peacock's feather at any public assembly there.

Courting the smiles of princes all the while
Thy country bleeds beneath their cruel scourge.

Rud. The land is sore oppress'd, I know it, uncle.
But why? Who plunged it into this distress?
A word, one little easy word, might buy
Instant deliverance from all our ills,
And win the good will of the Emperor.
Woe unto those who seal the people's eyes.
And make them adverse to their country's good—
The men who, for their own vile, selfish ends,
Are seeking to prevent the Forest States
From swearing fealty to Austria's House,
As all the countries round about have done.
It fits their humour well, to take their seats
Amid the nobles on the Herrenbank;[10]
They'll have the Kaiser for their lord, forsooth,—
That is to say, they'll have no lord at all.

Atting. Must I hear this, and from thy lips, rash boy!

Rud. You urged me to this answer. Hear me out.
What, uncle, is the character you've stoop'd
To fill contentedly through life? Have you
No higher pride, than in these lonely wilds
To be the Landamman or Banneret,[11]
The petty chieftain of a shepherd race?
How! Were it not a far more glorious choice,
To bend in homage to our royal lord,
And swell the princely splendours of his court,
Than sit at home, the peer of your own vassals,
And share the judgment-seat with vulgar clowns?

Atting. Ah, Uly, Uly; all too well I see,
The tempter's voice has caught thy willing ear,
And pour'd its subtle poison in thy heart.

Rud. Yes, I conceal it not. It doth offend
My inmost soul, to hear the stranger's gibes,

[10] The bench reserved for the nobility.

[11] The Landamman was an officer chosen by the Swiss Gemeinde, or Diet, to preside over them. The Banneret was an officer entrusted with the keeping of the State Banner, and such others as were taken in battle.

That taunt us with the name of "Peasant Nobles!"
Think you the heart that's stirring here can brook,
While all the young nobility around
Are reaping honour under Hapsburg's banner,
That I should loiter, in inglorious ease,
Here on the heritage my fathers left,
And, in the dull routine of vulgar toil,
Lose all life's glorious spring? In other lands
Great deeds are done. A world of fair renown
Beyond these mountains stirs in martial pomp.
My helm and shield are rusting in the hall;
The martial trumpet's spirit-stirring blast,
The herald's call, inviting to the lists,
Rouse not the echoes of these vales, where nought
Save cowherd's horn and cattle bell is heard,
In one unvarying dull monotony.
    Atting. Deluded boy, seduced by empty show!
Despise the land that gave thee birth! Ashamed
Of the good ancient customs of thy sires!
The day will come, when thou, with burning tears,
Wilt long for home, and for thy native hills,
And that dear melody of tuneful herds,
Which now, in proud disgust, thou dost despise!
A day when wistful pangs shall shake thy heart,
Hearing their music in a foreign land.
Oh! potent is the spell that binds to home!
No, no, the cold, false world is not for thee.
At the proud court, with thy true heart, thou wilt
For ever feel a stranger among strangers.
The world asks virtues of far other stamp
Than thou hast learned within these simple vales.
But go—go thither,—barter thy free soul,
Take land in fief, be minion to a prince,
Where thou might'st be lord paramount, and prince
Of all thine own unburden'd heritage!
O, Uly, Uly, stay among thy people!
Go not to Altdorf. Oh. abandon not

The sacred cause of thy wrong'd native land!
I am the last of all my race. My name
Ends with me. Yonder hang my helm and shield;
They will be buried with me in the grave.[12]
And must I think, when yielding up my breath,
That thou but wait'st the closing of mine eyes,
To stoop thy knee to this new feudal court,
And take in vassalage from Austria's hands
The noble lands, which I from God received,
Free and unfetter'd as the mountain air!

   Rud. 'Tis vain for us to strive against the King.
The world pertains to him:—shall we alone,
In mad presumptuous obstinacy, strive
To break that mighty chain of lands, which he
Hath drawn around us with his giant grasp?
His are the markets, his the courts,—his, too,
The highways; nay, the very carrier's horse,
That traffics on the Gotthardt, pays him toll.
By his dominions, as within a net,
We are enclosed, and girded round about.
—And will the Empire shield us? Say, can it
Protect itself 'gainst Austria's growing power?
To God, and not to emperors must we look!
What store can on their promises be placed,
When they, to meet their own necessities,
Can pawn, and even alienate the towns
That flee for shelter 'neath the Eagle's wings?[13]
No, uncle! It is wise and wholesome prudence,
In times like these, when faction's all abroad,
To vow attachment to some mighty chief.
The imperial crown's transferred from line to line.[14]
It has no memory for faithful service:

---

[12] According to the custom, by which, when the last male descendant of a noble family died, his sword, helmet, and shield were buried with him.

[13] This frequently occurred. But in the event of an imperial city being mortgaged for the purpose of raising money, it lost its freedom, and was considered as put out of the realm.

[14] An allusion to the circumstance of the Imperial Crown not being hereditary, but conferred by election on one of the Counts of the Empire.

But to secure the favour of these great
Hereditary masters, were to sow
Seed for a future harvest.

    Atting.   Art so wise?
Wilt thou see clearer than thy noble sires,
Who battled for fair freedom's priceless gem,
With life, and fortune, and heroic arm?
Sail down the lake to Lucerne, there inquire,
How Austria's thraldom weighs the Cantons down.
Soon she will come to count our sheep, our cattle,
To portion out the Alps, e'en to their peaks,
And in our own free woods to hinder us
From striking down the eagle or the stag;
To set her tolls on every bridge and gate,
Impoverish us, to swell her lust of sway,
And drain our dearest blood to feed her wars.
No, if our blood must flow, let it be shed
In our own cause! We purchase liberty
More cheaply far than bondage.

    Rudenz.   What can we,
A shepherd race, against great Albert's hosts?

    Atting. Learn, foolish boy, to know this shepherd race!
I know them, I have led them on in fight,—
I saw them in the battle at Favenz.
What! Austria try, forsooth, to force on us
A yoke we are determined not to bear!
Oh, learn to feel from what a stock thou'rt sprung;
Cast not, for tinsel trash and idle show,
The precious jewel of thy worth away,
To be the chieftain of a free-born race,
Bound to thee only by their unbought love,
Ready to stand—to fight—to die with thee,
Be that thy pride, be that thy noblest boast!
Knit to thy heart the ties of kindred—home—
Cling to the land, the dear land of thy sires,
Grapple to that with thy whole heart and soul!
Thy power is rooted deep and strongly here,

But in yon stranger world thou'lt stand alone,
A trembling reed beat down by every blast.
Oh come! 'tis long since we have seen thee, Uly!
Tarry but this one day. Only to-day!
Go not to Altdorf. Wilt thou? Not to-day!
For this one day, bestow thee on thy friends.

[Takes his hand.

   Rud. I gave my word. Unhand me! I am bound.
   Atting. (drops his hand and says sternly).
Bound, didst thou say? Oh yes, unhappy boy,
Thou art indeed. But not by word or oath.
'Tis by the silken mesh of love thou'rt bound.

[R<small>UDENZ</small> turns away.

Ah, hide thee, as thou wilt. 'Tis she, I know,
Bertha of Bruneck, draws thee to the court;
'Tis she that chains thee to the Emperor's service.
Thou think'st to win the noble knightly maid
By thy apostasy. Be not deceived.
She is held out before thee as a lure;
But never meant for innocence like thine.

   Rud. No more, I've heard enough. So fare you well.   [Exit.
   Atting. Stay, Uly! Stay! Rash boy, he's gone! I can
Nor hold him back, nor save him from destruction.
And so the Wolfshot has deserted us;—
Others will follow his example soon.
This foreign witchery, sweeping o'er our hills,
Tears with its potent spell our youth away.
O luckless hour, when men and manners strange
Into these calm and happy valleys came,
To warp our primitive and guileless ways!
The new is pressing on with might. The old,
The good, the simple, all fleet fast away.
New times come on. A race is springing up,
That think not as their fathers thought before!
What do I hear? All, all are in the grave
With whom erewhile I moved, and held converse;
My age has long been laid beneath the sod;

Happy the man, who may not live to see
What shall be done by those that follow me!

SCENE II.—*A meadow surrounded by high rocks and wooded ground.
On the rocks are tracks, with rails and ladders, by which the peasants
are afterwards seen descending. In the back-ground the lake is
observed, and over it a moon rainbow in the early part of the scene.
The prospect is closed by lofty mountains, with glaciers rising behind
them. The stage is dark, but the lake and glaciers glisten in the
moonlight.*

MELCHTHAL, BAUMGARTEN, WINKELRIED, MEYER VON SARNEN, BURK-
HART AM BUHEL, ARNOLD VON SEWA, KLAUS VON DER FLUE, *and
four other peasants, all armed.*

Melchthal (behind the scenes).
The mountain pass is open. Follow me!
I see the rock, and little cross upon it:
This is the spot; here is the Rootli.　　　　[*They enter with torches.*
　Wink.　　　　　　　　　　Hark!
　Sewa. The coast is clear.
　Meyer.　　　　　　　None of our comrades come?
We are the first, we Unterwaldeners.
　Melch. How far is't i' the night?
　Baum.　　　　　　　　　The beacon watch
Upon the Selisberg has just called two.
　　　　　　　　　　[*A bell is heard at a distance.*
　Meyer. Hush! Hark!
　Buhel.　　　　　　　The forest chapel's matin bell
Chimes clearly o'er the lake from Switzerland.
　Von F. The air is clear, and bears the sound so far.
　Melch. Go, you and you, and light some broken boughs,
Let's bid them welcome with a cheerful blaze.
　　　　　　　　　　[*Two peasants exeunt.*
　Sewa. The moon shines fair to-night. Beneath its beams
The lake reposes, bright as burnish'd steel.
　Buhel. They'll have an easy passage.
　Wink. (pointing to the lake).　　　　Ha! look there!
Do you see nothing?

Meyer.   Ay, indeed, I do!
A rainbow in the middle of the night.

Melch. Formed by the bright reflection of the moon!

Von F. A sign most strange and wonderful, indeed!
Many there be, who ne'er have seen the like.

Sewa. 'Tis doubled, see, a paler one above!

Baum. A boat is gliding yonder right beneath it.

Melch. That must be Werner Stauffacher! I knew
The worthy patriot would not tarry long.

> [*Goes with* BAUMGARTEN *towards the shore.*

Meyer. The Uri men are like to be the last.

Buhel. They're forced to take a winding circuit through
The mountains; for the Viceroy's spies are out.

> [*In the meanwhile the two peasants have kindled a fire in the centre of the stage.*

Melch. (*on the shore*). Who's there? The word?

Stauff. (*from below*).   Friends of the country.

> [*All retire up the stage, towards the party landing from the boat. Enter* STAUFFACHER, ITEL REDING, HANS AUF DER MAUER, JORG IM HOFE, CONRAD HUNN, ULRICH DER SCHMIDT, JOST VON WEILER, *and three other peasants, armed.*

All.   Welcome!

> [*While the rest remain behind exchanging greetings,* MELCHTHAL *comes forward with* STAUFFACHER.

Melch. Oh, worthy Stauffacher, I've look'd but now
On him, who could not look on me again;
I've laid my hands upon his rayless eyes,
And on their vacant orbits sworn a vow
Of vengeance, only to be cool'd in blood.

Stauff. Speak not of vengeance. We are here, to meet
The threatened evil, not to avenge the past.
Now tell me what you've done, and what secured,
To aid the common cause in Unterwald.
How stand the peasantry disposed, and how
Yourself escaped the wiles of treachery?

Melch. Through the Surenen's fearful mountain chain,

Where dreary ice-fields stretch on every side,
And sound is none, save the hoarse vulture's cry,
I reach'd the Alpine pasture, where the herds
From Uri and from Engelberg resort,
And turn their cattle forth to graze in common.
Still as I went along, I slaked my thirst
With the coarse oozings of the glacier heights
That thro' the crevices come foaming down,
And turned to rest me in the herdsmen's cots,[15]
Where I was host and guest, until I gain'd
The cheerful homes and social haunts of men.
Already through these distant vales had spread
The rumour of this last atrocity;
And wheresoe'er I went, at every door,
Kind words saluted me and gentle looks.
I found these simple spirits all in arms
Against our ruler's tyrannous encroachments
For as their Alps through each succeeding year
Yield the same roots,—their streams flow ever on
In the same channels,—nay, the clouds and winds
The selfsame course unalterably pursue,
So have old customs there, from sire to son,
Been handed down, unchanging and unchanged;
Nor will they brook to swerve or turn aside
From the fixed even tenor of their life.
With grasp of their hard hands they welcomed me,—
Took from the walls their rusty falchions down,—
And from their eyes the soul of valour flash'd
With joyful lustre, as I spoke those names,
Sacred to every peasant in the mountains,
Your own and Walter Fürst's. Whate'er your voice
Should dictate as the right, they swore to do;
And you they swore to follow e'en to death.
—So sped I on from house to house, secure

---

[15] These are the cots, or shealings, erected by the herdsmen for shelter, while pasturing their herds on the mountains during the summer. These are left deserted in winter, during which period Melchthal's journey was taken.

In the guest's sacred privilege;—and when
I reached at last the valley of my home,
Where dwell my kinsmen, scatter'd far and near—
And when I found my father, stript and blind,
Upon the stranger's straw, fed by the alms
Of charity—
    Stauff.   Great Heaven!
    Melch.   Yet wept I not!
No—not in weak and unavailing tears
Spent I the force of my fierce burning anguish;
Deep in my bosom, like some precious treasure,
I lock'd it fast, and thought on deeds alone.
Through every winding of the hills I crept,—
No valley so remote but I explored it;
Nay, at the very glacier's ice-clad base,
I sought and found the homes of living men;
And still, where'er my wandering footsteps turn'd,
The selfsame hatred of these tyrants met me.
For even there, at vegetation's verge,
Where the numb'd earth is barren of all fruits,
Their grasping hands had been for plunder thrust.
Into the hearts of all this honest race,
The story of my wrongs struck deep, and now
They, to a man, are ours; both heart and hand.
    Stauff. Great things, indeed, you've wrought in little time.
    Melch. I did still more than this. The fortresses,
Rossberg and Sarnen, are the country's dread;
For from behind their adamantine walls
The foe, like eagle from his eyrie, swoops,
And, safe himself, spreads havoc o'er the land.
With my own eyes I wish'd to weigh its strength,
So went to Sarnen, and explored the castle.
    Stauff. How! Venture even into the tiger's den?
    Melch. Disguised in pilgrim's weeds I entered it;
I saw the Viceroy feasting at his board—
Judge if I'm master of myself or no!
I saw the tyrant, and I slew him not!

Stauff. Fortune, indeed, upon your boldness smiled.

[*Meanwhile the others have arrived and join* MELCHTHAL
and STAUFFACHER.

Yet tell me now, I pray, who are the friends,
The worthy men, who came along with you?
Make me acquainted with them, that we may
Speak frankly, man to man, and heart to heart.

Meyer. In the three Cantons, who, sir, knows not you?
Meyer of Sarnen is my name; and this
Is Struth of Winkelried, my sister's son.

Stauff. No unknown name. A Winkelried it was,
Who slew the dragon in the fen at Weiler,
And lost his life in the encounter, too.

Wink. That, Master Stauffacher, was my grandfather.

Melch. (*pointing to two peasants*).
These two are men who till the cloister lands
Of Engelberg, and live behind the forest.
You'll not think ill of them, because they're serfs,
And sit not free upon the soil, like us.
They love the land, and bear a good repute.

Stauff. (*to them*). Give me your hands. He has good cause for
    thanks,
That to no man his body's service owes.
But worth is worth, no matter where 'tis found.

Hun. That is Herr Reding, sir, our old Landamman.

Meyer. I know him well. I am at law with him
About a piece of ancient heritage.
Herr Reding, we are enemies in court,
Here we are one.   [*Shakes his hand.*

Stauff.   That's well and bravely said.

Wink. Listen! They come. The horn of Uri! Hark!

[*On the right and left armed men are seen descending the rocks
    with torches.*

Mauer. Look, is not that the holy man of God?
A worthy priest! The terrors of the night,
And the way's pains and perils scare not him,
A faithful shepherd caring for his flock.

Baum. The Sacrist follows him, and Walter Fürst.
But where is Tell? I do not see him there.

> [WALTER FÜRST, RÖSSELMANN *the Pastor*, PETERMANN *the*
> *Sacrist*, KUONI *the Shepherd*, WERNI *the Huntsman*,
> RUODI *the Fisherman, and five other countrymen, thirty-*
> *three in all, advance and take their places round the fire.*

Fürst. Thus must we, on the soil our fathers left us,
Creep forth by stealth to meet like murderers,
And in the night, that should her mantle lend
Only to crime and black conspiracy,
Assert our own good rights, which yet are clear
As is the radiance of the noonday sun.

Melch. So be it. What is hatch'd in gloom of night
Shall free and boldly meet the morning light.

Rössel. Confederates! Listen to the words which God
Inspires my heart withal. Here we are met,
To represent the general weal. In us
Are all the people of the land convened.
Then let us hold the Diet, as of old,
And as we're wont in peaceful times to do.
The time's necessity be our excuse,
If there be aught informal in this meeting.
Still, wheresoe'er men strike for justice, there
Is God, and now beneath His heav'n we stand.

Stauff. 'Tis well advised.—Let us, then, hold the Diet,
According to our ancient usages.—
Though it be night, there's sunshine in our cause.

Melch. Few though our numbers be, the hearts are here
Of the whole people; here the BEST are met.

Hunn. The ancient books may not be near at hand,
Yet are they graven in our inmost hearts.

Rössel. 'Tis well. And now, then, let a ring be formed,
And plant the swords of power within the ground.[16]

Mauer. Let the Landamman step into his place,
And by his side his secretaries stand.

---

[16] It was the custom at the Meetings of the Landes Gemeinde, or Diet, to set swords
upright in the ground as emblems of authority.

Sacrist. There are three Cantons here. Which hath the right
To give the head to the united Council?
Schwytz may contest that dignity with Uri,
We Unterwald'ners enter not the field.

Melch. We stand aside. We are but suppliants here,
Invoking aid from our more potent friends.

Stauff. Let Uri have the sword. Her banner takes,
In battle, the precedence of our own.

Fürst. Schwytz, then, must share the honour of the sword;
For she's the honoured ancestor of all.

Rössel. Let me arrange this generous controversy.
Uri shall lead in battle—Schwytz in Council.

Fürst. (*gives* STAUFFACHER *his hand*).
Then take your place.

Stauff.   Not I. Some older man.

Hofe. Ulrich, the smith, is the most aged here.

Mauer. A worthy man, but not a freeman; no!
—No bondman can be judge in Switzerland.

Stauff. Is not Herr Reding here, our old Landamman?
Where can we find a worthier man than he?

Fürst. Let him be Amman and the Diet's chief!
You that agree with me, hold up your hands!
                    [*All hold up their right hands.*

Reding. (*stepping into the centre*). I cannot lay my hands upon
  the books;
But by yon everlasting stars I swear,
Never to swerve from justice and the right.
            [*The two swords are placed before him, and a circle formed;
                Schwytz in the centre, Uri on his right, Unterwald
                on his left.*

Reding. (*resting on his battle-sword*). Why, at the hour when
  spirits walk the earth,
Meet the three Cantons of the mountains here,
Upon the lake's inhospitable shore?
What may the purport be of this new league
We here contract beneath the starry heaven?

Stauff. (*entering the circle*).

'Tis no new league that here we now contract,
But one our fathers framed, in ancient times,
We purpose to renew! For know, confederates,
Though mountain ridge and lake divide our bounds,
And each Canton by its own laws is ruled,
Yet are we but one race, born of one blood,
And all are children of one common home.

   Wink. Is then the burden of our legends true,
That we came hither from a distant land?
Oh, tell us what you know, that our new league
May reap fresh vigour from the leagues of old.

   Stauff. Hear, then, what aged herdsmen tell. There dwelt
A mighty people in the land that lies
Back to the north. The scourge of famine came;
And in this strait 'twas publicly resolved,
That each tenth man, on whom the lot might fall,
Should leave the country. They obey'd—and forth,
With loud lamentings, men and women went,
A mighty host; and to the south moved on.
Cutting their way through Germany by the sword,
Until they gained these pine-clad hills of ours;
Nor stopp'd they ever on their forward course,
Till at the shaggy dell they halted, where
The Müta flows through its luxuriant meads.
No trace of human creature met their eye,
Save one poor hut upon the desert shore,
Where dwelt a lonely man, and kept the ferry.
A tempest raged—the lake rose mountains high
And barr'd their further progress. Thereupon
They view'd the country—found it rich in wood,
Discover'd goodly springs, and felt as they
Were in their own dear native land once more.
Then they resolved to settle on the spot;
Erected there the ancient town of Schwytz;
And many a day of toil had they to clear
The tangled brake and forest's spreading roots.
Meanwhile their numbers grew, the soil became

Unequal to sustain them, and they cross'd
To the black mountain, far as Weissland, where,
Conceal'd behind eternal walls of ice,
Another people speak another tongue.
They built the village Stanz, beside the Kernwald;
The village Altdorf, in the vale of Reuss;
Yet, ever mindful of their parent stem,
The men of Schwytz, from all the stranger race,
That since that time have settled in the land,
Each other recognize. Their hearts still know,
And beat fraternally to kindred blood.
              [*Extends his hand right and left.*
  Mauer. Ay, we are all one heart, one blood, one race!
  All (joining hands). We are one people, and will act as one.
  Stauff. The nations round us bear a foreign yoke;
For they have to the conqueror succumbed.
Nay, e'en within our frontiers may be found
Some, that owe villein service to a lord,
A race of bonded serfs from sire to son.
But we, the genuine race of ancient Swiss,
Have kept our freedom from the first till now.
Never to princes have we bow'd the knee;
Freely we sought protection of the Empire.
  Rössel. Freely we sought it—freely it was given.
'Tis so set down in Emperor Frederick's charter.
  Stauff. For the most free have still some feudal lord
There must be still a chief, a judge supreme,
To whom appeal may lie, in case of strife.
And therefore was it, that our sires allow'd,
For what they had recover'd from the waste
This honour to the Emperor, the lord
Of all the German and Italian soil;
And, like the other free men of his realm,
Engaged to aid him with their swords in war;
The free man's duty this alone should be,
To guard the Empire that keeps guard for him.
  Melch. He's but a slave that would acknowledge more.

Stauff. They followed, when the Heribann[17] went forth,
The imperial standard, and they fought its battles!
To Italy they march'd in arms, to place
The Cæsars' crown upon the Emperor's head.
But still at home they ruled themselves in peace,
By their own laws and ancient usages.
The Emperor's only right was to adjudge
The penalty of death; he therefore named
Some mighty noble as his delegate,
That had no stake or interest in the land,
Who was call'd in, when doom was to be pass'd,
And, in the face of day, pronounced decree,
Clear and distinctly, fearing no man's hate.
What traces here, that we are bondsmen? Speak,
If there be any can gainsay my words!
  Hofe. No! You have spoken but the simple truth;
We never stoop'd beneath a tyrant's yoke.
  Stauff. Even to the Emperor we did not submit,
When he gave judgment 'gainst us for the church;
For when the Abbey of Einsiedlen claimed
The Alp our fathers and ourselves had grazed,
And showed an ancient charter, which bestowed
The land on them as being ownerless—
For our existence there had been concealed—
What was our answer? This: "The grant is void.
No Emperor can bestow what is our own:
And if the Empire shall deny our rights,
We can, within our mountains, right ourselves!"
Thus spake our fathers! And shall we endure
The shame and infamy of this new yoke,
And from the vassal brook what never king
Dared, in his plenitude of power, attempt?
This soil we have created for ourselves,
By the hard labour of our hands; we've changed
The giant forest, that was erst the haunt
Of savage bears, into a home for man;

[17] The Heribann was a muster of warriors similar to the *arrière ban* of France.

Extirpated the dragon's brood, that wont
To rise, distent with venom, from the swamps;
Rent the thick misty canopy that hung
Its blighting vapours on the dreary waste;
Blasted the solid rock; across the chasm
Thrown the firm bridge for the wayfaring man.
By the possession of a thousand years
The soil is ours. And shall an alien lord,
Himself a vassal, dare to venture here,
Insult us by our own hearth fires,—attempt
To forge the chains of bondage for our hands,
And do us shame on our own proper soil?
Is there no help against such wrong as this?
                    [*Great sensation among the people.*
Yes! there's a limit to the despot's power!
When the oppress'd for justice looks in vain,
When his sore burden may no more be borne,
With fearless heart he makes appeal to Heaven,
And thence brings down his everlasting rights,
Which there abide, inalienably his,
And indestructible as are the stars.
Nature's primæval state returns again,
Where man stands hostile to his fellow man;
And if all other means shall fail his need,
One last resource remains—his own good sword.
Our dearest treasures call to us for aid,
Against the oppressor's violence; we stand
For country, home, for wives, for children here!
   All (*clashing their swords*). Here stand we for our homes, our
      wives, and children.
   Rössel. (*stepping into the circle*). Bethink ye well, before ye draw
      the sword.
Some peaceful compromise may yet be made;
Speak but one word, and at your feet you'll see
The men who now oppress you. Take the terms
That have been often tendered you; renounce
The Empire, and to Austria swear allegiance!

Mauer. What says the priest? To Austria allegiance?

Buhel. Hearken not to him!

Winkelreid.   'Tis a traitor's counsel,
His country's foe!

Reding.   Peace, peace, confederates!

Sewa. Homage to Austria, after wrongs like these!

Flue. Shall Austria extort from us by force
What we denied to kindness and entreaty?

Meyer. Then should we all be slaves, deservedly.

Mauer. Yes! Let him forfeit all a Switzer's rights,
Who talks of yielding thus to Austria's yoke!
I stand on this, Landamman. Let this be
The foremost of our laws!

Melch.   Even so! Whoe'er
Shall talk of bearing Austria's yoke, let him
Of all his rights and honours be despoiled,
No man thenceforth receive him at his hearth!

All (*raising their right hands.*) Agreed! Be this the law!

Reding. (*After a pause*). The law it is.

Rössel. Now you are free—this law hath made you free.
Never shall Austria obtain by force
What she has fail'd to gain by friendly suit.

Weil. On with the order of the day! Proceed!

Reding. Confederates! Have all gentler means been tried?
Perchance the Emp'ror knows not of our wrongs,
It may not be his will we suffer thus:
Were it not well to make one last attempt,
And lay our grievances before the throne,
Ere we unsheath the sword? Force is at best
A fearful thing e'en in a righteous cause;
God only helps, when man can help no more.

Stauff. (*to* Conrad Hunn).
Here you can give us information. Speak!

Hunn. I was at Rheinfeld, at the Emperor's Court,
Deputed by the Cantons to complain
Of the oppressions of these governors,
And of our liberties the charter claim,

Which each new king till now has ratified.
I found the envoys there of many a town,
From Suabia and the valley of the Rhine,
Who all received their parchments as they wish'd,
And straight went home again with merry heart.
But me, your envoy, they to the Council sent,
Where I with empty cheer was soon dismiss'd:
"The Emperor at present was engaged;
Some other time he would attend to us!"
I turn'd away, and passing through the hall,
With heavy heart, in a recess I saw
The Grand Duke John[18] in tears, and by his side
The noble lords of Wart and Tegerfeld,
Who beckon'd me, and said, "Redress yourselves.
Expect not justice from the Emperor.
Does he not plunder his own brother's child,
And keep from him his just inheritance?"
The Duke claims his maternal property,
Urging he's now of age, and 'tis full time,
That he should rule his people and estates;
What is the answer made to him? The King
Places a chaplet on his head; "Behold
The fitting ornament," he cries, "of youth!"

Mauer. You hear. Expect not from the Emperor
Or right or justice! Then redress yourselves!

Reding. No other course is left us. Now, advise
What plan most likely to ensure success.

Fürst. To shake a thraldom off that we abhor,
To keep our ancient rights inviolate,
As we received them from our fathers,—this,
Not lawless innovation, is our aim.
Let Cæsar still retain what is his due;
And he that is a vassal, let him pay
The service he is sworn to faithfully.

Meyer. I hold my land of Austria in fief.

---

[18] The Duke of Suabia, who soon afterwards assassinated his uncle, for withholding his patrimony from him.

Fürst. Continue, then, to pay your feudal dues.

Weil. I'm tenant of the lords of Rappersweil.

Fürst. Continue, then, to pay them rent and tithe.

Rössel. Of Zurich's abbess humble vassal I.

Fürst. Give to the cloister, what the cloister claims.

Stauff. The Empire only is my feudal lord.

Fürst. What needs must be, we'll do, but nothing more.
We'll drive these tyrants and their minions hence,
And raze their towering strongholds to the ground,
Yet shed, if possible, no drop of blood,
Let the Emperor see that we were driven to cast
The sacred duties of respect away;
And when he finds we keep within our bounds,
His wrath, belike, may yield to policy;
For truly is that nation to be fear'd,
That, arms in hand, is temperate in its wrath.

Reding. But prithee tell us how may this be done?
The enemy is arm'd as well as we,
And, rest assured, he will not yield in peace.

Stauff. He will, whene'er he sees us up in arms;
We shall surprise him, ere he is prepared.

Meyer. Easily said, but not so easily done.
Two strongholds dominate the country—they
Protect the foe, and should the King invade us,
Our task would then be dangerous, indeed.
Rossberg and Sarnen both must be secured,
Before a sword is drawn in either Canton.

Stauff. Should we delay, the foe would soon be warned;
We are too numerous for secrecy.

Meyer. There is no traitor in the Forest States.

Rössel. But even zeal may heedlessly betray.

Fürst. Delay it longer, and the keep at Altdorf
Will be complete,—the governor secure.

Meyer. You think but of yourselves.

Sacris.   You are unjust!

Meyer. Unjust! said you? Dares Uri taunt us so?

Reding. Peace, on your oath!

Sacris.   If Schwytz be leagued with Uri,
Why, then, indeed, we must perforce be dumb.
    Reding. And let me tell you, in the Diet's name,
Your hasty spirit much disturbs the peace.
Stand we not all for the same common cause?
    Wink. What, if till Christmas we delay? 'Tis then
The custom for the serfs to throng the castle,
Bringing the Governor their annual gifts.
Thus may some ten or twelve selected men
Assemble unobserved, within its walls.
Bearing about their persons pikes of steel,
Which may be quickly mounted upon staves,
For arms are not admitted to the fort.
The rest can fill the neighb'ring wood, prepared
To sally forth upon a trumpet's blast,
Soon as their comrades have secured the gate;
And thus the castle will with ease be ours.
    Melch. The Rossberg I will undertake to scale.
I have a sweetheart in the garrison,
Whom with some tender words I could persuade
To lower me at night a hempen ladder.
Once up, my friends will not be long behind.
    Reding. Are all resolved in favor of delay?
                         [*The majority raise their hands.*
    Stauff. (*counting them*). Twenty to twelve is the majority.
    Fürst. If on the appointed day the castles fall,
From mountain on to mountain we shall speed
The fiery signal: in the capital
Of every Canton quickly rouse the Landsturm.[19]
Then, when these tyrants see our martial front,
Believe me, they will never make so bold
As risk the conflict, but will gladly take
Safe conduct forth beyond our boundaries.
    Stauff. Not so with Gessler. He will make a stand.
Surrounded with his dread array of horse,
Blood will be shed before he quits the field,

----

[19] A sort of national militia.

And even expell'd he'd still be terrible.
'Tis hard, nay, dangerous, to spare his life.
   Baum. Place me where'er a life is to be lost;
I owe my life to Tell, and cheerfully
Will pledge it for my country. I have clear'd
My honour, and my heart is now at rest.
   Reding. Counsel will come with circumstance. Be patient!
Something must still be to the moment left.
Yet, while by night we hold our Diet here,
The morning, see, has on the mountain tops
Kindled her glowing beacon. Let us part,
Ere the broad sun surprise us.
   Fürst.   **Do not fear.**
The night wanes slowly from these vales of ours.
      [*All have involuntarily taken off their caps, and contemplate
        the breaking of day, absorbed in silence.*
   Rössel. By this fair light which greeteth us, before
Those other nations, that, beneath us far,
In noisome cities pent, draw painful breath,
Swear we the oath of our confederacy!
A band of brothers true we swear to be,
Never to part in danger or in death!
          [*They repeat his words with three fingers raised.*
We swear we will be free as were our sires,
And sooner die than live in slavery!   [*All repeat as before.*
We swear, to put our trust in God Most High,
And not to quail before the might of man!
        [*All repeat as before, and embrace each other.*
   Stauff. Now every man pursue his several way
Back to his friends, his kindred, and his home.
Let the herd winter up his flock, and gain
In secret friends for this great league of ours!
What for a time must be endured, endure,
And let the reckoning of the tyrants grow,
Till the great day arrive when they shall pay
The general and particular debt at once.
Let every man control his own just rage,

And nurse his vengeance for the public wrongs:
For he whom selfish interests now engage
Defrauds the general weal of what to it belongs.

> [*As they are going off in profound silence, in three different
> directions, the orchestra plays a solemn air. The empty
> scene remains open for some time showing the rays of the
> sun rising over the Glaciers.*

ACT III

SCENE I.—*Court before* TELL'S *house.* TELL *with an axe.* HEDWIG *engaged in her domestic duties.* WALTER *and* WILLIAM *in the background, playing with a little cross-bow.*

(WALTER *sings*)

With his cross-bow, and his quiver,
 The huntsman speeds his way,
Over mountain, dale and river,
 At the dawning of the day.
As the eagle, on wild pinion,
 Is the king in realms of air,
So the hunter claims dominion
 Over crag and forest lair.
Far as ever bow can carry,
 Thro' the trackless airy space,
All he sees he makes his quarry,
 Soaring bird and beast of chase.

Will. (*runs forward*). My string has snapped! Oh, father, mend it, do!

Tell. Not I; a true-born archer helps himself. [*Boys retire.*

Hedw. The boys begin to use the bow betimes.

Tell. 'Tis early practice only makes the master.

Hedw. Ah! Would to heaven they never learned the art!

Tell. But they shall learn it, wife, in all its points.
Whoe'er would carve an independent way
Through life, must learn to ward or plant a blow.

Hedw. Alas, alas! and they will never rest

Contentedly at home.

Tell.   No more can I!
I was not framed by nature for a shepherd.
My restless spirit ever yearns for change;
I only feel the flush and joy of life,
If I can start fresh quarry every day.

Hedw. Heedless the while of all your wife's alarms,
As she sits watching through long hours at home.
For my soul sinks with terror at the tales
The servants tell about the risks you run,
Whene'er we part, my trembling heart forebodes,
That you will ne'er come back to me again.
I see you on the frozen mountain steeps,
Missing, perchance, your leap from crag to crag.
I see the chamois, with a wild rebound,
Drag you down with him o'er the precipice.
I see the avalanche close o'er your head,—
The treacherous ice give way, and you sink down
Intombed alive within its hideous gulf.
Ah! in a hundred varying forms does death
Pursue the Alpine huntsman on his course.
That way of life can surely ne'er be blessed,
Where life and limb are perill'd every hour.

Tell. The man that bears a quick and steady eye,
And trusts in God, and his own lusty thews,
Passes, with scarce a scar, through every danger.
The mountain cannot awe the mountain child.

          [*Having finished his work, he lays aside his tools.*
And now, methinks, the door will hold awhile,—
Axe in the house oft saves the carpenter.   [*Takes his cap.*

Hedw. Whither away?

Tell.   To Altdorf, to your father.

Hedw. You have some dangerous enterprise in view?
Confess!

Tell. Why think you so?

Hedw.   Some scheme's on foot
Against the governors. There was a Diet

Held on the Rootli—that I know—and you
Are one of the confederacy, I'm sure.

Tell. I was not there. Yet will I not hold back,
Whene'er my country calls me to her aid.

Hedw. Wherever danger is, will you be placed.
On you, as ever, will the burden fall.

Tell. Each man shall have the post that fits his powers.

Hedw. You took—ay, 'mid the thickest of the storm—
The man of Unterwald across the lake.
'Tis marvel you escaped. Had you no thought
Of wife and children, then?

Tell.   Dear wife, I had;
And therefore saved the father for his children.

Hedw. To brave the lake in all its wrath! 'Twas not
To put your trust in God! 'Twas tempting Him.

Tell. Little will he that's over cautious do.

Hedw. Yes, you've a kind and helping hand for all;
But be in straits, and who will lend you aid?

Tell. God grant I ne'er may stand in need of it!

                          [*Takes up his crossbow and arrows.*
Hedw. Why take your cross-bow with you? leave it here.

Tell. I want my right hand, when I want my bow.

                          [*The boys return.*
Walt. Where, father, are you going?

Tell.   To grand-dad, boy—
To Altdorf. Will you go?

Walt.   Ay, that I will!

Hedw. The Viceroy's there just now. Go not to Altdorf!

Tell. He leaves to-day.

Hedw.   Then let him first be gone,
Cross not his path.—You know he bears us grudge.

Tell. His ill-will cannot greatly injure me.
I do what's right, and care for no man's hate.

Hedw. 'Tis those who do what's right, whom most he hates.

Tell. Because he cannot reach them. Me, I ween,
His knightship will be glad to leave in peace.

Hedw. Ay!—Are you sure of that?

Tell.   Not long ago,
As I was hunting through the wild ravines
Of Shechenthal, untrod by mortal foot,—
There, as I took my solitary way
Along a shelving ledge of rocks, where 'twas
Impossible to step on either side;
For high above rose, like a giant wall,
The precipice's side, and far below
The Shechen thunder'd o'er its rifted bed;—

> [*The boys press towards him, looking upon him with excited*
> *curiosity.*

There, face to face, I met the Viceroy. He
Alone with me—and I myself alone—
Mere man to man, and near us the abyss;
And when his lordship had perused my face,
And knew the man he had severely fined
On some most trivial ground, not long before,
And saw me, with my sturdy bow in hand,
Come striding towards him, his cheek grew pale,
His knees refused their office, and I thought
He would have sunk against the mountain side.
Then, touch'd with pity for him, I advanced,
Respectfully, and said, " 'Tis I, my lord."
But ne'er a sound could he compel his lips
To frame in answer. Only with his hand
He beckoned me in silence to proceed.
So I pass'd on, and sent his train to seek him.

Hedw. He trembled, then, before you? Woe the while
You saw his weakness; that he'll ne'er forgive.

Tell. I shun him, therefore, and he'll not seek me.

Hedw. But stay away to-day. Go hunt instead!

Tell. What do you fear?

Hedw.   I am uneasy. Stay!

Tell. Why thus distress yourself without a cause?

Hedw. Because there is no cause. Tell, Tell! stay here!

Tell. Dear wife, I gave my promise I would go.

Hedw. Must you,—then go. But leave the boys with me.

Walt. No, mother dear, I go with father, I.

Hedw. How, Walter! Will you leave your mother then?

Walt. I'll bring you pretty things from grandpapa.

[*Exit with his father.*

Will. Mother, I'll stay with you!

Hedw. (*embracing him*).   Yes, yes! thou art
My own dear child. Thou'rt all that's left to me.

[*She goes to the gate of the court and looks anxiously after*
Tell *and her son for a considerable time.*

Scene II.—*A retired part of the forest—brooks dashing in spray over
the rocks.*

Enter Bertha *in a hunting dress. Immediately afterwards* Rudenz

Berth. He follows me. Now, then, to speak my mind!

Rud. (*entering hastily*).
At length, dear lady, we have met alone
In this wild dell, with rocks on every side,
No jealous eye can watch our interview.
Now let my heart throw off this weary silence.

Berth. But are you sure they will not follow us?

Rud. See, yonder goes the chase! Now, then, or never!
I must avail me of this precious chance,—
Must hear my doom decided by thy lips,
Though it should part me from thy side forever.
Oh, do not arm that gentle face of thine
With looks so stern and harsh! Who—who am I,
That dare aspire so high, as unto thee?
Fame hath not stamp'd me yet; nor may I take
My place amid the courtly throng of knights,
That, crown'd with glory's lustre, woo thy smiles.
Nothing have I to offer, but a heart
That overflows with truth and love for thee.

Berth. (*sternly and with severity*). And dare you speak to me of
love—of truth?
You, that are faithless to your nearest ties!
You, that are Austria's slave—bartered and sold

To her—an alien, and your country's tyrant!

Rud. How! This reproach from thee! Whom do I seek,
On Austria's side, my own beloved, but thee?

Berth. Think you to find me in the traitor's ranks?
Now, as I live, I'd rather give my hand
To Gessler's self, all despot though he be,
Than to the Switzer who forgets his birth,
And stoops to be a tyrant's servile tool.

Rud. Oh Heaven, what words are these?

Berth.   Say! What can lie
Nearer the good man's heart than friends and kindred?
What dearer duty to a noble soul,
Than to protect weak, suffering innocence,
And vindicate the rights of the oppress'd?
My very soul bleeds for your countrymen.
I suffer with them, for I needs must love them;
They are so gentle, yet so full of power;
They draw my whole heart to them. Every day
I look upon them with increased esteem.
But you, whom nature and your knightly vow,
Have given them as their natural protector,
Yet who desert them and abet their foes
In forging shackles for your native land,
You—you incense and wound me to the core.
It tries me to the utmost not to hate you.

Rud. Is not my country's welfare all my wish?
What seek I for her, but to purchase peace
'Neath Austria's potent sceptre?

Berth.   Bondage, rather!
You would drive Freedom from the last stronghold
That yet remains for her upon the earth.
The people know their own true int'rests better: .
Their simple natures are not warp'd by show.
But round your head a tangling net is wound.

Rud. Bertha, you hate me—you despise me!

Berth.   Nay!
And if I did, 'twere better for my peace.

But to see him despised and despicable,—
The man whom one might love—

   Rud.   Oh, Bertha! You
Show me the pinnacle of heavenly bliss,
Then, in a moment, hurl me to despair!

   Berth. No, no! the noble is not all extinct
Within you. It but slumbers,—I will rouse it.
It must have cost you many a fiery struggle
To crush the virtues of your race within you.
But, Heaven be praised, 'tis mightier than yourself,
And you are noble in your own despite!

   Rud. You trust me, then? Oh, Bertha, with thy love
What might I not become!

   Berth.   Be only that
For which your own high nature destin'd you.
Fill the position you were born to fill;—
Stand by your people and your native land—
And battle for your sacred rights!

   Rud.   Alas!
How can I win you—how can you be mine,
If I take arms against the Emperor?
Will not your potent kinsmen interpose,
To dictate the disposal of your hand?

   Berth. All my estates lie in the Forest Cantons;
And I am free, when Switzerland is free.

   Rud. Oh! what a prospect, Bertha, hast thou shown me!

   Berth. Hope not to win my hand by Austria's grace;
Fain would they lay their grasp on my estates,
To swell the vast domains which now they hold.
The selfsame lust of conquest, that would rob
You of your liberty, endangers mine.
Oh, friend, I'm mark'd for sacrifice;—to be
The guerdon of some parasite, perchance!
They'll drag me hence to the Imperial court,
That hateful haunt of falsehood and intrigue,
And marriage bonds I loathe await me there.
Love, love alone—your love,—can rescue me.

Rud. And thou couldst be content, love, to live here;
In my own native land to be my own?
Oh, Bertha, all the yearnings of my soul
For this great world and its tumultuous strife,
What were they, but a yearning after thee?
In glory's path I sought for thee alone,
And all my thirst of fame was only love.
But if in this calm vale thou canst abide
With me, and bid earth's pomps and pride adieu,
Then is the goal of my ambition won;
And the rough tide of the tempestuous world
May dash and rave around these firm-set hills!
No wandering wishes more have I to send
Forth to the busy scene that stirs beyond.
Then may these rocks, that girdle us, extend
Their giant walls impenetrably round,
And this sequestered happy vale alone
Look up to heaven, and be my paradise!
   Berth. Now art thou all my fancy dream'd of thee.
My trust has not been given to thee in vain.
   Rud. Away, ye idle phantoms of my folly;
In mine own home I'll find my happiness.
Here, where the gladsome boy to manhood grew,
Where ev'ry brook, and tree, and mountain peak,
Teems with remembrances of happy hours,
In mine own native land thou wilt be mine.
Ah, I have ever loved it well, I feel
How poor without it were all earthly joys.
   Berth. Where should we look for happiness on earth,
If not in this dear land of innocence?
Here, where old truth hath its familiar home.
Where fraud and guile are strangers, envy ne'er
Shall dim the sparkling fountain of our bliss,
And ever bright the hours shall o'er us glide.
There do I see thee, in true manly worth,
The foremost of the free and of thy peers,
Revered with homage pure and unconstrain'd.

Wielding a power that kings might envy thee.

   Rud. And thee I see, thy sex's crowning gem,
With thy sweet woman's grace and wakeful love,
Building a heaven for me within my home,
And, as the spring-time scatters forth her flowers,
Adorning with thy charms my path of life,
And spreading joy and sunshine all around.

   Berth. And this it was, dear friend, that caused my grief,
To see thee blast this life's supremest bliss
With thine own hand. Ah! what had been my fate,
Had I been forced to follow some proud lord,
Some ruthless despot, to his gloomy keep!
Here are no keeps, here are no bastion'd walls
To part me from a people I can bless.

   Rud. Yet, how to free myself; to loose the coils
Which I have madly twined around my head?

   Berth. Tear them asunder with a man's resolve.
Whate'er ensue, firm by thy people stand!
It is thy post by birth.

                [*Hunting horns are heard in the distance.*
                But hark! The chase!
Farewell,—'tis needful we should part—away!
Fight for thy land; thou fightest for thy love.
One foe fills all our souls with dread; the blow
That makes one free, emancipates us all.

                     [*Exeunt severally.*

Scene III.—*A meadow near Altdorf. Trees in the foreground. At the
back of the stage a cap upon a pole. The prospect is bounded by the
Bannberg, which is surmounted by a snow-capped mountain.*

        Friesshardt *and* Leuthold *on guard*

   Friess. We keep our watch in vain. Zounds! not a soul
Will pass, and do obeisance to the cap.
But yesterday the place swarm'd like a fair;
Now the old green looks like a desert, quite,
Since yonder scarecrow hung upon the pole.

Leuth. Only the vilest rabble show themselves,
And wave their tattered caps in mockery at us.
All honest citizens would sooner make
A weary circuit over half the town,
Than bend their backs before our master's cap.
 Friess. They were obliged to pass this way at noon,
As they were coming from the Council House.
I counted then upon a famous catch,
For no one thought of bowing to the cap,
But Rösselmann, the priest, was even with me:
Coming just then from some sick man, he takes
His stand before the pole,—lifts up the Host—
The Sacrist, too, must tinkle with his bell,—
When down they dropp'd on knee—myself and all—
In reverence to the Host, but not the cap.
 Leuth. Hark ye, companion, I've a shrewd suspicion,
Our post's no better than the pillory.
It is a burning shame, a trooper should
Stand sentinel before an empty cap,
And every honest fellow must despise us.
To do obeisance to a cap, too! Faith,
I never heard an order so absurd!
 Friess. Why not, an't please you, to an empty cap?
You've duck'd, I'm sure, to many an empty sconce.

> [Hildegard, Mechthild, *and* Elsbeth *enter with their
> children, and station themselves around the pole.*

 Leuth. And you are a time-serving sneak, that takes
Delight in bringing honest folks to harm.
For my part, he that likes may pass the cap:—
I'll shut my eyes and take no note of him.
 Mech. There hangs the Viceroy! Your obeisance, children!
 Els. I would to God he'd go, and leave his cap!
The country would be none the worse for it.
 Friess. (*driving them away*). Out of the way! Confounded pack
  of gossips!
Who sent for you? Go, send your husbands here,
If they have courage to defy the order.

[TELL *enters with his cross-bow, leading his son* WALTER *by the hand. They pass the hat without noticing it, and advance to the front of the stage.*

Walt. (*pointing to the Bannberg*). Father, is't true, that on the mountain there
The trees, if wounded with a hatchet, bleed?

Tell. Who says so, boy?

Walt.   The master herdsman, father!
He tells us there's a charm upon the trees,
And if a man shall injure them, the hand
That struck the blow will grow from out the grave.

Tell. There is a charm about them—that's the truth.
Dost see those glaciers yonder—those white horns—
That seem to melt away into the sky?

Walt. They are the peaks that thunder so at night,
And send the avalanches down upon us.

Tell. They are; and Altdorf long ago had been
Submerged beneath these avalanches' weight,
Did not the forest there above the town
Stand like a bulwark to arrest their fall.

Walt. (*after musing a little*). And are there countries with no mountains, father?

Tell. Yes, if we travel downwards from our heights,
And keep descending where the rivers go,
We reach a wide and level country, where
Our mountain torrents brawl and foam no more,
And fair large rivers glide serenely on.
All quarters of the heaven may there be scann'd
Without impediment. The corn grows there
In broad and lovely fields, and all the land
Is like a garden fair to look upon.

Walt. But, father, tell me, wherefore haste we not
Away to this delightful land, instead
Of toiling here, and struggling as we do?

Tell. The land is fair and bountiful as Heaven;
But they who till it never may enjoy
The fruits of what they sow.

Walt.   Live they not free,
As you do, on the land their fathers left them?
Tell. The fields are all the bishop's or the king's.
Walt. But they may freely hunt among the woods?
Tell. The game is all the monarch's—bird and beast.
Walt. But they, at least, may surely fish the streams?
Tell. Stream, lake, and sea, all to the king belong.
Walt. Who is this king, of whom they're so afraid?
Tell. He is the man who fosters and protects them.
Walt. Have they not courage to protect themselves?
Tell. The neighbour there dare not his neighbour trust.
Walt. I should want breathing room in such a land.
I'd rather dwell beneath the avalanches.
Tell. 'Tis better, child, to have these glacier peaks
Behind one's back, than evil-minded men!

                                    [*They are about to pass on.*
Walt. See, father, see the cap on yonder pole!
Tell. What is the cap to us? Come, let's begone.

      [*As he is going,* FRIESSHARDT, *presenting his pike, stops him.*
Friess. Stand, I command you, in the Emperor's name!
Tell. (*seizing the pike*). What would ye? Wherefore do ye stop
   me thus?
Friess. You've broke the mandate, and with us must go.
Leuth. You have not done obeisance to the cap.
Tell. Friend, let me go.
Friess.   Away, away to prison!
Walt. Father to prison. Help!   [*Calling to the side scene.*
                              This way, you men!
Good people, help! They're dragging him to prison!

      [RÖSSELMANN *the priest and the* SACRISTAN, *with three other
         men, enter.*
Sacris. What's here amiss?
Rössel.   Why do you seize this man?
Friess. He is an enemy of the King—a traitor.
Tell. (*seizing him with violence*). A traitor, I!
Rössel.   Friend, thou art wrong. 'Tis Tell,
An honest man, and worthy citizen.

Wali. (*descries* FÜRST, *and runs up to him*). Grandfather, help;
they want to seize my father!

Friess. Away to prison!

Fürst (*running in*).   Stay, I offer bail.
For God's sake, Tell, what is the matter here?

[MELCHTHAL *and* STAUFFACHER *enter.*

Leuth. He has contemn'd the Viceroy's sovereign power,
Refusing flatly to acknowledge it.

Stauff. Has Tell done this?

Melch.   Villain, you know 'tis false!

Leuth. He has not made obeisance to the cap.

Fürst. And shall for this to prison? Come, my friend,
Take my security, and let him go.

Friess. Keep your security for yourself—you'll need it.
We only do our duty. Hence with him.

Melch. (*to the country people*). This is too bad—shall we stand
by and see
Him dragged away before our very eyes?

Sacris. We are the strongest. Friends, endure it not,
Our countrymen will back us to a man.

Friess. Who dares resist the governor's commands?

Other Three Peasants (*running in*). We'll help you. What's the
matter? Down with them!

[HILDEGARD, MECHTHILD *and* ELSBETH *return.*

Tell. Go, go, good people, I can help myself.
Think you, had I a mind to use my strength,
These pikes of theirs should daunt me?

Melch. (*to* FRIESSHARDT).   Only try—
Try from our midst to force him, if you dare.

Fürst and Stauff. Peace, peace, friends!

Friess. (*loudly*).   Riot! Insurrection, ho!

[*Hunting horns without.*

Women. The Governor!

Friess. (*raising his voice*). Rebellion! Mutiny!

Stauff. Roar till you burst, knave!

Rössel. and Melch. Will you hold your tongue?

Friess. (*calling still louder*). Help, help, I say, the servants of
the law!

Fürst. The Viceroy here! Then we shall smart for this!

[*Enter* GESSLER *on horseback, with a falcon on his wrist:*
RUDOLPH DER HARRAS, BERTHA, *and* RUDENZ, *and a*
numerous train of armed attendants, who form a
circle of lances round the whole stage.

Har. Room for the Viceroy!

Gessl.   Drive the clowns apart.
Why throng the people thus? Who calls for help?

[*General silence.*

Who was it? I *will* know.   [FRIESSHARDT *steps forward.*
                        And who art thou?
And why hast thou this man in custody?

[*Gives his falcon to an attendant.*

Friess. Dread sir, I am a soldier of your guard,
And station'd sentinel beside the cap;
This man I apprehended in the act
Of passing it without obeisance due,
So as you ordered, I arrested him,
Whereon to rescue him the people tried.

Gessl. (*after a pause*). And do you, Tell, so lightly hold your
    King,
And me, who act as his viceregent here,
That you refuse obeisance to the cap,
I hung aloft to test your loyalty?
I read in this a disaffected spirit.

Tell. Pardon me, good my lord! The action sprung
From inadvertence,—not from disrespect.
Were I discreet, I were not William Tell.
Forgive me now—I'll not offend again.

Gessl. (*after a pause*). I hear, Tell, you're a master with the bow,—
From every rival bear the palm away.

Walt. That's very truth, sir! At a hundred yards
He'll shoot an apple for you off the tree.

Gessl. Is that boy thine, Tell?

Tell.   Yes, my gracious lord.

Gessl. Hast any more of them?

Tell.   Two boys, my lord.

Gessl. And, of the two, which dost thou love the most?

Tell. Sir, both the boys are dear to me alike.

Gessl. Then, Tell, since at a hundred yards thou canst
Bring down the apple from the tree, thou shalt
Approve thy skill before me. Take thy bow—
Thou hast it there at hand—make ready, then,
To shoot an apple from the stripling's head!
But take this counsel,—look well to thine aim,
See, that thou hit'st the apple at the first,
For, shouldst thou miss, thy head shall pay the forfeit.

> [*All give signs of horror.*

Tell. What monstrous thing, my lord, is this you ask?
What! from the head of mine own child!—No, no!
It cannot be, kind sir, you meant not that—
God, in His grace, forbid! You could not ask
A father seriously to do that thing!

Gessl. Thou art to shoot an apple from his head!
I do desire—command it so.

Tell.   What, I!
Level my crossbow at the darling head
Of mine own child? No—rather let me die!

Gessl. Or thou must shoot, or with thee dies the boy.

Tell. Shall I become the murderer of my child!
You have no children, sir—you do not know
The tender throbbings of a father's heart.

Gessl. How now, Tell, on a sudden so discreet?
I had been told thou wert a visionary,—
A wanderer from the paths of common men.
Thou lov'st the marvellous. So have I now
Cull'd out for thee a task of special daring.
Another man might pause and hesitate;—
Thou dashest at it, heart and soul, at once.

Berth. Oh, do not jest, my lord, with these poor souls!
See, how they tremble, and how pale they look,
So little used are they to hear thee jest.

Gessl. Who tells thee that I jest?

> [*Grasping a branch above his head.*
> Here is the apple.

Room there, I say! And let him take his distance—
Just eighty paces,—as the custom is,—
Not an inch more or less! It was his boast,
That at a hundred he could hit his man.
Now, archer, to your task, and look you miss not!

Har. Heavens! this grows serious—down, boy, on your knees,
And beg the governor to spare your life.

Fürst (*aside to* MELCHTHAL, *who can scarcely restrain his indignation*). Command yourself,—be calm, I beg of you!

Bertha (*to the Governor*). Let this suffice you, sir! It is inhuman
To trifle with a father's anguish thus.
Although this wretched man had forfeited
Both life and limb for such a slight offence,
Already has he suffer'd tenfold death.
Send him away uninjured to his home;
He'll know thee well in future; and this hour
He and his children's children will remember.

Gessl. Open a way there—quick! Why this delay?
Thy life is forfeited; I might dispatch thee,
And see, I graciously repose thy fate
Upon the skill of thine own practised hand.
No cause has he to say his doom is harsh,
Who's made the master of his destiny.
Thou boastest thine unerring aim. 'Tis well!
Now is the fitting time to show thy skill;
The mark is worthy and the prize is great.
To hit the bull's eye in the target;—that
Can many another do as well as thou;
But he, methinks, is master of his craft,
Who can at all times on his skill rely,
Nor lets his heart disturb or eye or hand.

Fürst. My lord, we bow to your authority;
But oh, let justice yield to mercy here.
Take half my property, nay, take it all,
But spare a father this unnatural doom!

Walt. Grandfather, do not kneel to that bad man!
Say, where am I to stand? I do not fear;

My father strikes the bird upon the wing,
And will not miss now when 'twould harm his boy!
   Stauff. Does the child's innocence not touch your heart?
   Rössel. Bethink you, sir, there is a God in heaven,
To whom you must account for all your deeds.
   Gessl. (*pointing to the boy*). Bind him to yonder lime tree!
   Walter. What! Bind me?
No, I will not be bound! I will be still.
Still as a lamb—nor even draw my breath!
But if you bind me, I can not be still.
Then I shall writhe and struggle with my bonds.
   Har. But let your eyes at least be bandaged, boy!
   Walt. And why my eyes? No! Do you think I fear
An arrow from my father's hand? Not I!
I'll wait it firmly, nor so much as wink!
Quick, father, show them what thy bow can do.
He doubts thy skill—he thinks to ruin us.
Shoot then and hit, though but to spite the tyrant!
     [*He goes to the lime tree, and an apple is placed on his head.*
   Melch. (*to the country people*). What! Is this outrage to be per-
    petrated
Before our very eyes? Where is our oath?
   Stauff. Resist we cannot! Weapons we have none.
And see the wood of lances round us! See!
   Melch. Oh! would to heaven that we had struck at once!
God pardon those who counsell'd the delay!
   Gessl. (*to* TELL). Now to your task! Men bear not arms for
    naught.
To carry deadly tools is dangerous,
And on the archer oft his shaft recoils.
This right, these haughty peasant churls assume,
Trenches upon their master's privileges:
None should be armed, but those who bear command.
It pleases you to carry bow and bolt;—
Well,—be it so. I will prescribe the mark.
   Tell. (*bends the bow, and fixes the arrow*). A lane there! Room!
   Stauff.   What. Tell? You would—no, no!

You shake—your hand's unsteady—your knees tremble.

Tell (letting the bow sink down). There's something swims
  before mine eyes!

Women.   Great Heaven!

Tell. Release me from this shot! Here is my heart!

                    [*Tears open his breast.*

Summon your troopers—let them strike me down!

Gessl. 'Tis not thy life I want—I want the shot,
Thy talent's universal! Nothing daunts thee!
The rudder thou canst handle like the bow!
No storms affright thee, when a life's at stake.
Now, saviour, help thyself,—thou savest all!

      [TELL *stands fearfully agitated by contending emotions, his
      hands moving convulsively, and his eyes turning alter-
      nately to the Governor and Heaven. Suddenly he takes
      a second arrow from his quiver, and sticks it in his belt.
      The Governor notes all he does.*

Walter (beneath the lime tree). Shoot, father, shoot! fear not!

Tell.   It must be!

                    [*Collects himself and levels the bow.*

*Rud. (who all the while has been standing in a state of violent ex-
    citement, and has with difficulty restrained himself, advances).*

    My lord, you will not urge this matter further;
You will not. It was surely but a test.
You've gained your object. Rigour push'd too far
Is sure to miss its aim, however good,
As snaps the bow that's all too straitly bent.

Gessl. Peace, till your counsel's ask'd for!

Rud.   I will speak!
Ay, and I dare! I reverence my King;
But acts like these must make his name abhorr'd.
He sanctions not this cruelty. I dare
Avouch the fact. And you outstep your powers
In handling thus my harmless countrymen.

Gessl. Ha! thou grow'st bold, methinks!

Rud.   I have been dumb
To all the oppressions I was doomed to see.

I've closed mine eyes to shut them from my view,
Bade my rebellious, swelling heart be still,
And pent its struggles down within my breast.
But to be silent longer, were to be
A traitor to my King and country both.

    Berth. (*casting herself between him and the Governor*).
Oh, Heavens! you but exasperate his rage!

    Rud. My people I forsook—renounced my kindred—
Broke all the ties of nature, that I might
Attach myself to you. I madly thought
That I should best advance the general weal
By adding sinews to the Emperor's power.
The scales have fallen from mine eyes—I see
The fearful precipice on which I stand.
You've led my youthful judgment far astray,—
Deceived my honest heart. With best intent,
I had well-nigh achiev'd my country's ruin.

    Gessl. Audacious boy, this language to thy lord?

    Rud. The Emperor is my lord, not you! I'm free.
As you by birth, and I can cope with you
In every virtue that beseems a knight.
And if you stood not here in that King's name,
Which I respect e'en where 'tis most abused,
I'd throw my gauntlet down, and you should give
An answer to my gage in knightly sort.
Ay, beckon to your troopers! Here I stand;
But not like these   [*Pointing to the people.*
           —unarmed. I have a sword,
And he that stirs one step—

    Stauff. (*exclaims*).   The apple's down!
    [*While the attention of the crowd has been directed to the
      spot where* BERTHA *had cast herself between* RUDENZ *and*
      GESSLER, TELL *has shot.*

    Rössel. The boy's alive!

    Many Voices.   The apple has been struck!
    [WALTER FÜRST *staggers and is about to fall.* BERTHA *sup-
      ports him.*

Gessl. (*astonished*). How? Has he shot? The madman!
Berth.   Worthy father!
Pray you, compose yourself. The boy's alive.
Walter (*runs in with the apple*). Here is the apple, father! Well
I knew
You would not harm your boy
> [TELL *stands with his body bent forwards, as if still following
> the arrow. His bow drops from his hand. When he sees
> the boy advancing, he hastens to meet him with open
> arms, and, embracing him passionately, sinks down with
> him quite exhausted. All crowd round them deeply
> affected.*

Berth.   Oh, ye kind Heavens!
Fürst (*to father and son*). My children, my dear children!
Stauff.   God be praised!
Leuth. Almighty powers! That was a shot indeed!
It will be talked of to the end of time.
Har. This feat of Tell, the archer, will be told
Long as these mountains stand upon their base.
> [*Hands the apple to* GESSLER.
Gessl. By Heaven! the apple's cleft right through the core.
It was a master shot, I must allow.
Rössel. The shot was good. But woe to him who drove
The man to tempt his God by such a feat!
Stauff. Cheer up, Tell, rise! You've nobly freed yourself,
And now may go in quiet to your home.
Rössel. Come, to the mother let us bear her son!
> [*They are about to lead him off.*
Gessl. A word, Tell.
Tell.   Sir, your pleasure?
Gessl.   Thou didst place
A second arrow in thy belt—nay, nay!
I saw it well. Thy purpose with it? Speak!
Tell (*confused*). It is a custom with all archers, sir.
Gessl. No, Tell, I cannot let that answer pass.
There was some other motive, well I know.
Frankly and cheerfully confess the truth;—

Whate'er it be, I promise thee thy life.
Wherefore the second arrow?

Tell.   Well, my lord,
Since you have promised not to take my life,
I will, without reserve, declare the truth.

> [*He draws the arrow from his belt, and fixes his eyes sternly upon the governor.*

If that my hand had struck my darling child,
This second arrow I had aimed at you,
And, be assured, I should not then have miss'd.

Gessl. Well, Tell, I promised thou shouldst have thy life;
I gave my knightly word, and I will keep it.
Yet, as I know the malice of thy thoughts,
I'll have thee carried hence, and safely penn'd,
Where neither sun nor moon shall reach thine eyes.
Thus from thy arrows I shall be secure.
Seize on him, guards, and bind him!   [*They bind him.*

Stauff.   How, my lord—
How can you treat in such a way a man
On whom God's hand has plainly been reveal'd?

Gessl. Well, let us see if it will save him twice!
Remove him to my ship; I'll follow straight,
At Küssnacht I will see him safely lodged.

Rössel. You dare not do't. Nor durst the Emperor's self
So violate our dearest chartered rights.

Gessl. Where are they? Has the Emp'ror confirm'd them?
He never has. And only by obedience
May you that favour hope to win from him.
You are all rebels 'gainst the Emp'ror's power,—
And bear a desperate and rebellious spirit.
I know you all—I see you through and through.
Him do I single from amongst you now,
But in his guilt you all participate.
If you are wise, be silent and obey!

> [*Exit, followed by* BERTHA, RUDENZ, HARRAS, *and attendants.*
> FRIESSHARDT *and* LEUTHOLD *remain.*

Fürst (*in violent anguish*). All's over now! He is resolved to bring
Destruction on myself and all my house.
    Stauff. (*to* TELL). Oh, why did you provoke the tyrant's rage?
    Tell. Let him be calm who feels the pangs I felt.
    Stauff. Alas! alas! Our every hope is gone.
With you we all are fettered and enchain'd.
    Country People (*surrounding* TELL). Our last remaining comfort goes with you!
    Leuth. (*approaching him*). I'm sorry for you, Tell, but must obey.
    Tell. Farewell!
    Walter Tell (*clinging to him in great agony*). Oh, father, father, father dear!
    Tell (*pointing to Heaven*). Thy father is on high—appeal to Him!
    Stauff. Have you no message, Tell, to send your wife?
    Tell. (*clasping the boy passionately to his breast*). The boy's uninjured; God will succour me!
        [*Tears himself suddenly away, and follows the soldiers of the guard.*

ACT IV

SCENE I.—*Eastern shore of the Lake of Lucerne; rugged and singularly shaped rocks close the prospect to the west. The lake is agitated, violent roaring and rushing of wind, with thunder and lightning at intervals.*

KUNZ OF GERSAU, Fisherman *and* Boy

Kunz. I saw it with these eyes! Believe me, friend,
It happen'd all precisely as I've said.
    Fisher. How! Tell a prisoner, and to Küssnacht borne?
The best man in the land, the bravest arm,
Had we for liberty to strike a blow!
    Kunz. The Viceroy takes him up the lake in person:
They were about to go on board, as I
Started from Flüelen; but the gathering storm,

That drove me here to land so suddenly,
May well have hindered them from setting out.

Fisher. Our Tell in chains, and in the Viceroy's power!
O, trust me, Gessler will entomb him, where
He never more shall see the light of day;
For Tell once free, the tyrant well might dread
The just revenge of one so deeply wrong'd.

Kunz. The old Landamman, too—von Attinghaus—
They say, is lying at the point of death.

Fisher. Then the last anchor of our hopes gives way!
He was the only man that dared to raise
His voice in favour of the people's rights.

Kunz. The storm grows worse and worse. So, fare ye well!
I'll go and seek out quarters in the village.
There's not a chance of getting off to-day.   [*Exit.*

Fisher. Tell dragg'd to prison, and the Baron dead!
Now, tyranny, exalt thy brazen front,—
Throw every shame aside! Truth's voice is dumb!
The eye that watch'd for us, in darkness closed,
The arm that should have stuck thee down, in chains!

Boy. 'Tis hailing hard—come, let us to the hut!
This is no weather to be out in, father!

Fisher. Rage on, ye winds! Ye lightnings, flash your fires!
Burst, ye swollen clouds! Ye cataracts of Heaven
Descend, and drown the country! In the germ
Destroy the generations yet unborn!
Ye savage elements, be lords of all!
Return, ye bears: ye ancient wolves, return
To this wide howling waste! The land is yours.
Who would live here, when liberty is gone?

Boy. Hark! How the wind whistles, and the whirlpool roars.
I never saw a storm so fierce as this!

Fisher. To level at the head of his own child!
Never had father such command before.
And shall not Nature, rising in wild wrath,
Revolt against the deed? I should not marvel,
Though to the lake these rocks should bow their heads,

Though yonder pinnacles, yon towers of ice,
That, since creation's dawn, have known no thaw,
Should, from their lofty summits, melt away,—
Though yonder mountains, yon primeval cliffs,
Should topple down, and a new deluge whelm
Beneath its waves all living men's abodes!

[Bells heard.

Boy. Hark, they are ringing on the mountain, yonder!
They surely see some vessel in distress.
And toll the bell that we may pray for it. *[Ascends a rock.*

Fisher. Woe to the bark that now pursues its course,
Rock'd in the cradle of these storm-tost waves!
Nor helm nor steersman here can aught avail;
The storm is master. Man is like a ball,
Toss'd 'twixt the winds and billows. Far or near,
No haven offers him its friendly shelter!
Without one ledge to grasp, the sheer smooth rocks
Look down inhospitably on his despair,
And only tender him their flinty breasts.

Boy (calling from above). Father, a ship: from Flüelen bearing
down.

Fisher. Heaven pity the poor wretches! When the storm
Is once entangled in this strait of ours,
It rages like some savage beast of prey,
Struggling against its cage's iron bars!
Howling, it seeks an outlet—all in vain;
For the rocks hedge it round on every side,
Walling the narrow gorge as high as Heaven.

[He ascends a cliff.

Boy. It is the Governor of Uri's ship;
By its red poop I know it, and the flag.

Fisher. Judgments of Heaven! Yes, it is he himself,
It is the Governor! Yonder he sails,
And with him bears the burden of his crimes.
The avenger's arm has not been slow to strike!
Now over him he knows a mightier lord.
These waves yield no obedience to his voice.

These rocks bow not their heads before his cap.
Boy, do not pray; stay not the Judge's arm!
  Boy. I pray not for the Governor, I pray
For Tell, who's with him there on board the ship.
  Fisher. Alas, ye blind, unreasoning elements!
Must ye, in punishing one guilty head,
Destroy the vessel and the pilot too?
  Boy. See, see, they've clear'd the Buggisgrat;[20] but now
The blast, rebounding from the Devil's Minster,[20]
Has driven them back on the Great Axenberg.[20]
I cannot see them now.
  Fisher.   The Hakmesser[20]
Is there, that's founder'd many a gallant ship.
If they should fail to double that with skill,
Their bark will go to pieces on the rocks,
That hide their jagged peaks below the lake.
The best of pilots, boy, they have on board.
If man could save them, Tell is just the man,
But he is manacled both hand and foot.
      [*Enter* WILLIAM TELL, *with his cross-bow. He enters precipi-*
        tately, looks wildly round, and testifies the most violent
        agitation. When he reaches the centre of the stage, he
        throws himself upon his knees, and stretches out his
        hands, first towards the earth, then towards Heaven.
  Boy (*observing him*). See, father! A man on's knees; who can
    it be?
  Fisher. He clutches at the earth with both his hands,
And looks as though he were beside himself.
  Boy (*advancing*). What do I see? Come father, come and look!
  Fisher. (*approaches*). Who is it? God in Heaven! What! William
    Tell!
How came you hither? Speak, Tell!
  Boy.   Were you not
In yonder ship, a prisoner, and in chains?
  Fisher. Were they not carrying you to Küssnacht, Tell?
        [20] Rocks on the shore of the Lake of Lucerne.

Tell (*rising*). I am released.

Fisher. and Boy. Released, oh miracle!

Boy. Whence came you here?

Tell. From yonder vessel!

Fisher. What?

Boy. Where is the Viceroy?

Tell. Drifting on the waves.

Fisher. Is't possible? But you! How are you here?
How 'scaped you from your fetters and the storm?

Tell. By God's most gracious providence. Attend.

Fisher. and Boy. Say on, say on!

Tell. You know what passed at Altdorf.

Fisher. I do—say on!

Tell. How I was seized and bound,
And order'd by the governor to Küssnacht.

Fisher. And how at Flüelen he embarked with you.
All this we know. Say, how have you escaped?

Tell. I lay on deck, fast bound with cords, disarm'd,
In utter hopelessness. I did not think
Again to see the gladsome light of day,
Nor the dear faces of my wife and boys,
And eyed disconsolate the waste of waters.—

Fisher. Oh, wretched man!

Tell. Then we put forth; the Viceroy,
Rudolph der Harras, and their suite. My bow
And quiver lay astern beside the helm;
And just as we had reached the corner, near
The little Axen,[21] Heaven ordain'd it so,
That from the Gotthardt's gorge, a hurricane
Swept down upon us with such headlong force,
That every oarsman's heart within him sank,
And all on board look'd for a watery grave.
Then heard I one of the attendant train,
Turning to Gessler, in this wise accost him:
"You see our danger, and your own, my lord,

---

[21] A rock on the shore of the Lake of Lucerne.

And that we hover on the verge of death.
The boatmen there are powerless from fear,
Nor are they confident what course to take;—
Now, here is Tell, a stout and fearless man,
And knows to steer with more than common skill,
How if we should avail ourselves of him
In this emergency?" The Viceroy then
Address'd me thus: "If thou wilt undertake
To bring us through this tempest safely, Tell,
I might consent to free thee from thy bonds."
I answer'd, "Yes, my lord; so help me God,
I'll see what can be done." On this they loosed
The cords that bound me, and I took my place
Beside the helm, and steered as best I could,
Yet ever eyed my shooting gear askance,
And kept a watchful eye upon the shore,
To find some point where I might leap to land;
And when I had descried a shelving crag,
That jutted, smooth atop, into the lake—

   Fisher. I know it. At the foot of the Great Axen;
So steep it looks, I never could have dreamt
That from a boat a man could leap to it.

   Tell. I bade the men to row with all their force
Until we came before the shelving ledge.
For there, I said, the danger will be past!
Stoutly they pull'd, and soon we near'd the point;
One prayer to God for His assisting grace,
And, straining every muscle, I brought round
The vessel's stern close to the rocky wall;
Then snatching up my weapons, with a bound
I swung myself upon the flattened shelf,
And with my feet thrust off, with all my might,
The puny bark into the watery hell.
There left it drift about, as Heaven ordains!
Thus am I here, deliver'd from the might
Of the dread storm, and man's more dreadful still.

Fisher. Tell, Tell, the Lord has manifestly wrought
A miracle in thy behalf! I scarce
Can credit my own eyes. But tell me, now,
Whither you purpose to betake yourself?
For you will be in peril, should perchance
The Viceroy 'scape this tempest with his life.

Tell. I heard him say, as I lay bound on board,
At Brunnen he proposed to disembark,
And, crossing Schwytz, convey me to his castle.

Fisher. Means he to go by land?

Tell. So he intends.

Fisher. Oh, then conceal yourself without delay!
Not twice will Heaven release you from his grasp.

Tell. Which is the nearest way to Arth and Küssnacht?

Fisher. The public road leads by the way of Steinen,
But there's a nearer road, and more retired,
That goes by Lowerz, which my boy can show you.

Tell (*gives him his hand*). May Heaven reward your kindness!
Fare ye well. [*As he is going, he comes back.*
Did not you also take the oath at Rootli?
I heard your name, methinks.

Fisher. Yes, I was there,
And took the oath of the confederacy.

Tell. Then do me this one favour; speed to Bürglen—
My wife is anxious at my absence—tell her
That I am free, and in secure concealment.

Fisher. But whither shall I tell her you have fled?

Tell. You'll find her father with her, and some more,
Who took the oath with you upon the Rootli;
Bid them be resolute, and strong of heart,—
For Tell is free and master of his arm;
They shall hear further news of me ere long.

Fisher. What have you, then, in view? Come, tell me frankly!

Tell. When once 'tis *done*, 'twill be in every mouth. [*Exit.*

Fisher. Show him the way, boy. Heaven be his support!
Whate'er he has resolved, he'll execute. [*Exit.*

SCENE II.—*Baronial mansion of Attinghausen. The* BARON *upon a couch dying.* WALTER FÜRST, STAUFFACHER, MELCHTHAL, *and* BAUMGARTEN *attending round him.* WALTER TELL *kneeling before the dying man.*

Fürst. All now is over with him. He is gone.

Stauff. He lies not like one dead. The feather, see,
Moves on his lips! His sleep is very calm,
And on his features plays a placid smile.

    [BAUMGARTEN *goes to the door and speaks with some one.*

Fürst. Who's there?

Baum. (*returning*). Tell's wife, your daughter, she insists
That she must speak with you, and see her boy.

    [WALTER TELL *rises.*

Fürst. I who need comfort—can I comfort her?
Does every sorrow centre on my head?

Hedw. (*forcing her way in*). Where is my child? unhand me!
I must see him.

Stauff. Be calm! Reflect, you're in the house of death!

Hedw. (*falling upon her boy's neck*). My Walter! Oh, he yet
is mine!

Walt.   Dear mother!

Hedw. And is it surely so? Art thou unhurt?

    [*Gazing at him with anxious tenderness.*

And is it possible he aim'd at thee?
How could he do it? Oh, he has no heart—
And he could wing an arrow at his child!

Fürst. His soul was rack'd with anguish when he did it.
No choice was left him, but to shoot or die!

Hedw. Oh, if he had a father's heart, he would
Have sooner perish'd by a thousand deaths!

Stauff. You should be grateful for God's gracious care,
That ordered things so well.

Hedw.   Can I forget
What might have been the issue? God of Heaven.
Were I to live for centuries, I still
Should see my boy tied up,—his father's mark,-
And still the shaft would quiver in my heart.

Melch. You know not how the Viceroy taunted him!

Hedw. Oh, ruthless heart of man! Offend his pride,
And reason in his breast forsakes her seat;
In his blind wrath he'll stake upon a cast
A child's existence, and a mother's heart!

Baum. Is then your husband's fate not hard enough,
That you embitter it by such reproaches?
Have you not feeling for his sufferings?

Hedw. (turning to him and gazing full upon him).
Hast thou tears only for thy friend's distress?
Say, where were you when he—my noble Tell—
Was bound in chains? Where was your friendship then?
The shameful wrong was done before your eyes;
Patient you stood, and let your friend be dragg'd,
Ay, from your very hands. Did ever Tell
Act thus to you? Did he stand whining by,
When on your heels the Viceroy's horsemen press'd,
And full before you roared the storm-toss'd lake?
Oh, not with idle tears his pity show'd;
Into the boat he sprang, forgot his home,
His wife, his children, and delivered thee!

Fürst. It had been madness to attempt his rescue,
Unarm'd and few in numbers as we were!

Hedw. (casting herself upon his bosom).
Oh, father, and thou, too, hast lost my Tell!
The country—all have lost him! All lament
His loss; and, oh, how he must pine for us!
Heaven keep his soul from sinking to despair!
No friend's consoling voice can penetrate
His dreary dungeon walls. Should he fall sick!
Ah! In the vapours of the murky vault
He must fall sick. Even as the Alpine rose
Grows pale and withers in the swampy air,
There is no life for him, but in the sun,
And in the breath of Heaven's fresh-blowing airs.
Imprison'd! Liberty to him is breath;
He cannot live in the rank dungeon air!

Stauff. Pray you be calm! And hand in hand we'll all
Combine to burst his prison doors.

Hedw.   He gone,
What have you power to do? While Tell was free,
There still, indeed, was hope—weak innocence
Had still a friend, and the oppress'd a stay.
Tell saved you all! You cannot all combined
Release him from his cruel prison bonds.

[*The* BARON *wakes.*

Baum. Hush, hush! He starts!
Atting. (*sitting up*).   Where is he?
Stauff.   Who?
Atting.   He leaves me,—
In my last moments he abandons me.
Stauff. He means his nephew. Have they sent for him?
Fürst. He has been summoned. Cheerly, sir! Take comfort!
He has found his heart at last, and is our own.
Atting. Say, has he spoken for his native land?
Stauff. Ay, like a hero!
Atting.   Wherefore comes he not,
That he may take my blessing ere I die?
I feel my life fast ebbing to a close.
Stauff. Nay, talk not thus, dear sir! This last short sleep
Has much refresh'd you, and your eye is bright.
Atting. Life is but pain, and that has left me now;
My sufferings, like my hopes, have pass'd away.

[*Observing the boy.*
What boy is that?
Fürst.   Bless him. Oh, good my lord!
He is my grandson, and is fatherless.

[HEDWIG *kneels with the boy before the dying man.*
Atting. And fatherless—I leave you all, ay, all!
Oh wretched fate, that these old eyes should see
My country's ruin, as they close in death!
Must I attain the utmost verge of life,
To feel my hopes go with me to the grave?
Stauff. (*to* FÜRST). Shall he depart 'mid grief and gloom like this?

Shall not his parting moments be illumed
By hope's inspiring beams? My noble lord,
Raise up your drooping spirit! We are not
Forsaken quite—past all deliverance.
    Atting. Who shall deliver you?
    Fürst.   Ourselves. For know,
The Cantons three are to each other pledged,
To hunt the tyrants from the land. The league
Has been concluded, and a sacred oath
Confirms our union. Ere another year
Begins its circling course—the blow shall fall.
In a free land your ashes shall repose.
    Atting. The league concluded! Is it really so?
    Melch. On one day shall the Cantons rise together.
All is prepared to strike—and to this hour
The secret closely kept, though hundreds share it;
The ground is hollow 'neath the tyrants' feet;
Their days of rule are number'd, and ere long
No trace will of their hateful sway be left.
    Atting. Ay, but their castles, how to master them?
    Melch. On the same day they, too, are doom'd to fall.
    Atting. And are the nobles parties to this league?
    Stauff. We trust to their assistance, should we need it;
As yet the peasantry alone have sworn.
    Atting. (*raising himself up in great astonishment*). And have the
        peasantry dared such a deed
On their own charge, without the nobles' aid—
Relied so much on their own proper strength?
Nay then, indeed, they want our help no more;
We may go down to death cheer'd by the thought,
That after us the majesty of man
Will live, and be maintain'd by other hands.
    [*He lays his hand upon the head of the child who is kneeling
        before him.*
From this boy's head, whereon the apple lay,
Your new and better liberty shall spring;
The old is crumbling down—the times are changing—

And from the ruins blooms a fairer life.

Stauff. (*to Fürst*). See, see, what splendour streams around his
    eye!
This is not Nature's last expiring flame,
It is the beam of renovated life.

Atting. From their old towers the nobles are descending,
And swearing in the towns the civic oath.
In Uechtland and Thurgau the work's begun;
The noble Berne lifts her commanding head,
And Freyburg is a stronghold of the free;
The stirring Zurich calls her guilds to arms;—
And now, behold!—the ancient might of kings
Is shiver'd 'gainst her everlasting walls.

[*He speaks what follows with a prophetic tone; his utterance
    rising into enthusiasm.*

I see the princes and their haughty peers,
Clad all in steel, come striding on to crush
A harmless shepherd race with mailèd hand.
Desp'rate the conflict; 'tis for life or death;
And many a pass will tell to after years
Of glorious victories sealed in foeman's blood.[22]
The peasant throws himself with naked breast,
A willing victim on their serried spears;
They yield—the flower of chivalry's cut down,
And Freedom waves her conquering banner high.

[*Grasps the hands of* WALTER FÜRST *and* STAUFFACHER.

Hold fast together, then,—forever fast!
Let freedom's haunts be one in heart and mind!
Set watches on your mountain tops, that league
May answer league, when comes the hour to strike.
Be one—be one—be one—

---

[22] An allusion to the gallant self-devotion of Arnold Struthan of Winkelried, at the
battle of Sempach [9th July, 1386], who broke the Austrian phalanx by rushing on
their lances, grasping as many of them as he could reach, and concentrating them
upon his breast. The confederates rushed forward through the gap thus opened by
the sacrifice of their comrade, broke and cut down their enemy's ranks, and soon
became the masters of the field. "Dear and faithful confederates, I will open you
a passage. Protect my wife and children," were the words of Winkelried, as he
rushed to death.

[*He falls back upon the cushion. His lifeless hands continue to grasp those of* FÜRST *and* STAUFFACHER, *who regard him for some moments in silence, and then retire, over-come with sorrow. Meanwhile the servants have quietly pressed into the chamber, testifying different degrees of grief. Some kneel down beside him and weep on his body: while this scene is passing, the castle bell tolls.*

Rud. (*entering hurriedly*). Lives he? Oh say, can he still hear my voice?

Fürst. (*averting his face*). You are our seignior and protector now;

Henceforth this castle bears another name.

Rud. (*gazing at the body with deep emotion*). Oh, God! Is my repentance, then, too late?

Could he not live some few brief moments more,
To see the change that has come o'er my heart?
Oh, I was deaf to his true counselling voice,
While yet he walked on earth. Now he is gone,—
Gone, and forever,—leaving me the debt—
The heavy debt I owe him—undischarged!
Oh, tell me! did he part in anger with me?

Stauff. When dying, he was told what you had done,
And bless'd the valour that inspired your words!

Rud. (*kneeling down beside the dead body*). Yes, sacred relics of a man beloved!

Thou lifeless corpse! Here, on thy death-cold hand
Do I abjure all foreign ties for ever!
And to my country's cause devote myself.
I am a Switzer, and will act as one,
With my whole heart and soul.   [*Rises.*

                    Mourn for our friend,
Our common parent, yet be not dismay'd!
'Tis not alone his lands that I inherit,—
His heart—his spirit have devolved on me;
And my young arm shall execute the task,
Which in his hoary age he could not pay.
Give me your hands, ye venerable sires!

Thine, Melchthal, too! Nay, do not hesitate,
Nor from me turn distrustfully away.
Accept my plighted vow—my knightly oath!
   Fürst. Give him your hands, my friends! A heart like his,
That sees and owns its error, claims our trust.
   Melch. You ever held the peasantry in scorn,
What surety have we, that you mean us fair?
   Rud. Oh, think not of the error of my youth!
   Stauff. (*to* Melch.). Be one! They were our father's latest words.
See they be not forgotten!
   Melch.   Take my hand,—
A peasant's hand,—and with it, noble sir,
The gage and the assurance of a man!
Without us, sir, what would the nobles be?
Our order is more ancient, too, than yours!
   Rud. I honour it—will shield it with my sword!
   Melch. The arm, my lord, that tames the stubborn earth,
And makes its bosom blossom with increase,
Can also shield its owner's breast at need.
   Rud. Then you shall shield my breast, and I will yours,
Thus each be strengthen'd by the other's strength.
Yet wherefore talk ye, while our native land
Is still to alien tyranny a prey?
First let us sweep the foemen from the soil,
Then reconcile our difference in peace!
                             [*After a moment's pause.*
How! You are silent! Not a word for me?
And have I yet no title to your trust?—
Then must I force my way, despite your will,
Into the League you secretly have form'd.
You've held a Diet on the Rootli,—I
Know this,—know all that was transacted there;
And though not trusted with your secret, I
Have kept it closely like a sacred pledge.
Trust me—I never was my country's foe,
Nor would I ever have against you stood!
Yet you did wrong—to put your rising off.

Time presses! We must strike, and swiftly too!
Already Tell is lost through your delay.

   Stauff. We swore that we should wait till Christmastide.

   Rud. I was not there,—I did not take the oath.
If you delay, I will not!

   Melch.   What! You would—

   Rud. I count me now among the country's chiefs,
And my first duty is to guard your rights.

   Fürst. Your nearest and holiest duty is
Within the earth to lay these dear remains.

   Rud. When we have set the country free, we'll place
Our fresh victorious wreaths upon his bier.
Oh, my dear friends, 'tis not your cause alone!—
I with the tyrants have a cause to fight,
That more concerns myself. My Bertha's gone,
Has disappear'd,—been carried off by stealth,—
Stolen from amongst us by their ruffian hands!

   Stauff. So fell an outrage has the tyrant dared
Against a lady free and nobly born!

   Rud. Alas! my friends, I promised help to you,
And I must first implore it for myself!
She that I love, is stolen—is forced away,
And who knows where she's by the tyrant hid,
Or with what outrages his ruffian crew
May force her into nuptials she detests?
Forsake me not!—Oh, help me to her rescue!
She loves you! Well, oh well, has she deserved,
That all should rush to arms in her behalf!

   Stauff. What course do you propose?

   Rud.   Alas! I know not.
In the dark mystery that shrouds her fate,—
In the dread agony of this suspense,—
Where I can grasp at nought of certainty,—
One single ray of comfort beams upon me.
From out the ruins of the tyrant's power
Alone can she be rescued from the grave.
Their strongholds must be levell'd, every one,

Ere we can penetrate her dungeon walls.

    Melch. Come, lead us on! We follow! Why defer
Until to-morrow, what to-day may do?
Tell's arm was free when we at Rootli swore.
This foul enormity was yet undone.
And change of circumstance brings change of vow;
Who such a coward as to waver still?

    Rud. (*to* WALTER FÜRST). Meanwhile to arms, and wait in readiness
The fiery signal on the mountain tops!
For swifter than a boat can scour the lake
Shall you have tidings of our victory;
And when you see the welcome flames ascend
Then, like the lightning, swoop upon the foe,
And lay the despots and their creatures low!

SCENE III.—*The pass near Küssnacht, sloping down from behind, with
rocks on either side. The travellers are visible upon the heights,
before they appear on the stage. Rocks all round the stage. Upon one
of the foremost a projecting cliff overgrown with brushwood.*

    Tell. (*enters with his crossbow*). Through this ravine he needs
    must come. There is
No other way to Küssnacht. Here I'll do it!
The ground is everything I could desire.
Yon elder bush will hide me from his view,
And from that point my shaft is sure to hit.
The straitness of the gorge forbids pursuit.
Now, Gessler, balance thine account with Heaven!
Thou must away from earth,—thy sand is run.

    Quiet and harmless was the life I led,
My bow was bent on forest game alone;
No thoughts of murder rested on my soul.
But thou hast scared me from my dream of peace;
The milk of human kindness thou hast turn'd
To rankling poison in my breast; and made
Appalling deeds familiar to my soul.

He who could make his own child's head his mark,
Can speed his arrow to his foeman's heart.

My boys, poor innocents, my loyal wife,
Must be protected, tyrant, from thy rage!
When last I drew my bow—with trembling hand—
And thou, with fiendishly remorseless glee
Forced me to level at my own boy's head,
When I, imploring pity, writhed before thee,
Then in the anguish of my soul, I vow'd
A fearful oath, which met God's ear alone,
That when my bow next wing'd an arrow's flight,
Its aim should be thy heart. The vow I made,
Amid the hellish torments of that moment,
I hold a sacred debt, and I will pay it.

Thou art my lord, my Emperor's delegate;
Yet would the Emperor not have stretch'd his power,
So far as thou hast done. He sent thee here
To deal forth law—stern law—for he is wroth;
But not to wanton with unbridled will
In every cruelty, with fiend-like joy:—
There lives a God to punish and avenge.

Come forth, thou bringer once of bitter pangs,
My precious jewel now,—my chiefest treasure—
A mark I'll set thee, which the cry of grief
Could never penetrate,—but thou shalt pierce it,—
And thou, my trusty bowstring, that so oft
For sport has served me faithfully and well,
Desert me not in this dread hour of need,—
Only be true this once, my own good cord,
That hast so often wing'd the biting shaft:—
For shouldst thou fly successless from my hand,
I have no second to send after thee.

[*Travellers pass over the stage.*

I'll sit me down upon this bench of stone,
Hewn for the way-worn traveller's brief repose—
For here there is no home. Men hurry past
Each other, with quick step and careless look,
Nor stay to question of their grief. Here goes
The merchant, all anxiety,—the pilgrim,
With scanty furnished scrip,—the pious monk,
The scowling robber, and the jovial player,
The carrier with his heavy-laden horse,
That comes to us from the far haunts of men;
For every road conducts to the world's end.
They all push onwards—every man intent
On his own several business—mine is murder!   *[Sits down.*

Time was, my dearest children, when with joy
You hail'd your father's safe return to home
From his long mountain toils; for, when he came,
He ever brought with him some little gift,—
A lovely Alpine flower—a curious bird—
Or elf-bolt such as on the hills are found.
But now he goes in quest of other game,
Sits in this gorge, with murder in his thoughts,
And for his enemy's life-blood lies in wait.
But still it is of you alone he thinks,
Dear children. 'Tis to guard your innocence,
To shield you from the tyrant's fell revenge,
He bends his bow to do a deed of blood!   *[Rises.*

Well—I am watching for a noble prey—
Does not the huntsman, with unflinching heart,
Roam for whole days, when winter frosts are keen,
Leap at the risk of death from rock to rock,—
And climb the jagged, slippery steeps, to which
His limbs are glued by his own streaming blood—
And all to hunt a wretched chamois down?
A far more precious prize is now my aim—
The heart of that dire foe, who seeks my life.

[*Sprightly music heard in the distance, which comes grad-
ually nearer.*

From my first years of boyhood I have used
The bow—been practised in the archer's feats;
The bull's eye many a time my shafts have hit,
And many a goodly prize have I brought home
From competitions. But this day I'll make
My master-shot, and win what's best to win
In the whole circuit of our mountain range.

[*A bridal party passes over the stage, and goes up the pass.
TELL gazes at it, leaning on his bow. He is joined by
STUSSI, the Ranger.*

Stussi. There goes the cloister bailiff's bridal train
Of Mörlischachen. A rich fellow he!
And has some half score pastures on the Alps.
He goes to fetch his bride from Imisee.
At Küssnacht there will be high feast to-night—
Come with us—ev'ry honest man is asked.

Tell. A gloomy guest fits not a wedding feast.

Stussi. If you've a trouble, dash it from your heart!
Take what Heaven sends! The times are heavy now,
And we must snatch at pleasure as it flies.
Here 'tis a bridal, there a burial.

Tell. And oft the one close on the other treads.

Stussi. So runs the world we live in. Everywhere
Mischance befalls and misery enough.
In Glarus there has been a landslip, and
A whole side of the Glärnisch has fallen in.

Tell. How! Do the very hills begin to quake?
There is stability for nought on earth.

Stussi. Of strange things, too, we hear from other parts.
I spoke with one but now, from Baden come,
Who said a knight was on his way to court,
And, as he rode along, a swarm of wasps
Surrounded him, and settling on his horse,
So fiercely stung the beast, that it fell dead,

And he proceeded to the court on foot.

   Tell. The weak are also furnish'd with a sting.

(ARMGART *enters with several children, and places herself at the entrance of the pass.*)

   Stussi. 'Tis thought to bode disaster to the land,—
Some horrid deeds against the course of nature.

   Tell. Why, every day brings forth such fearful deeds;
There needs no prodigy to herald them.

   Stussi. Ay, happy he who tills his field in peace,
And sits at home untroubled with his kin.

   Tell. The very meekest cannot be at peace
If his ill neighbour will not let him rest.

> [TELL *looks frequently with restless expectation towards the top of the pass.*

   Stussi. So fare you well! You're waiting some one here?

   Tell. I am.

   Stussi.   God speed you safely to your home!
You are from Uri, are you not? His grace
The Governor's expected thence to-day.

   Traveller (*entering*). Look not to see the Governor to-day.
The streams are flooded by the heavy rains,
And all the bridges have been swept away.   [TELL *rises.*

   Arm. (*coming forward*).   Gessler not coming?

   Stussi.   Want you aught with him?

   Arm. Alas, I do!

   Stussi.   Why, then, thus place yourself
Where you obstruct his passage down the pass?

   Arm. Here he cannot escape me. He *must* hear me.

   Friess. (*coming hastily down the pass and calls upon the stage*).
Make way, make way! My lord, the Governor,
Is close behind me, riding down the pass.   [*Exit* TELL.

   Arm. (*excitedly*).   The Viceroy comes!

> [*She goes towards the pass with her children,* GESSLER *and*
> RUDOLPH DER HARRAS *appear on horseback at the upper
> end of the pass.*

   Stussi. (*to* FRIESS.). How got ye through the stream,
When all the bridges have been carried down?

Friess. We've fought, friend, with the tempest on the lake;
An Alpine torrent's nothing after that.

   Stussi. How! Were you out, then, in that dreadful storm?

   Friess. We were! I'll not forget it while I live.

   Stussi. Stay, speak—

   Friess.   I can't—must to the castle haste,
And tell them, that the Governor's at hand.   [*Exit.*

   Stussi. If honest men, now, had been in the ship,
It had gone down with every soul on board:—
Some folks are proof 'gainst fire and water both.   [*Looking round.*
Where has the huntsman gone with whom I spoke?   [*Exit.*

   Enter GESSLER *and* RUDOLPH DER HARRAS *on horseback.*

   Gessl. Say what you will; I am the Emperor's liege,
And how to please him my first thought must be.
He did not send me here to fawn and cringe,
And coax these boors into good humour. No!
Obedience he must have. The struggle's this:
Is king or peasant to be sovereign here?

   Arm. Now is the moment! Now for my petition!

   Gessl. 'Twas not in sport that I set up the cap
In Altdorf—or to try the people's hearts—
All this I knew before. I set it up
That they might learn to bend those stubborn necks
They carry far too proudly—and I placed
What well I knew their pride could never brook
Full in the road, which they perforce must pass,
That, when their eye fell on it, they might call
That lord to mind whom they too much forget.

   Har. But surely, sir, the people have some rights—

   Gessl. This is no time to settle what they are.
Great projects are at work, and hatching now.
The imperial house seeks to extend its power.
Those vast designs of conquest which the sire
Has gloriously begun, the son will end.
This petty nation is a stumbling-block—
One way or other, it must be put down.

[*They are about to pass on.* Armgart *throws herself down before* Gessler.

Arm. Mercy, Lord Governor! Oh, pardon, pardon!

Gessl. Why do you cross me on the public road?
Stand back, I say.

    Arm. My husband lies in prison;
My wretched orphans cry for bread. Have pity,
Pity, my lord, upon our sore distress!

    Har. Who are you? and your husband, what is he?

    Arm. A poor wild hay-man of the Rigiberg,
Kind sir, who on the brow of the abyss,
Mows the unowner'd grass from craggy shelves,
To which the very cattle dare not climb.

    Har. (*to* Gessl.).
By Heaven! a sad and pitiable life!
I pray you set the wretched fellow free.
How great soever may be his offence,
His horrid trade is punishment enough.

[*To* Armgart.

You shall have justice. To the castle bring
Your suit. This is no place to deal with it.

    Arm. No, no, I will not stir from where I stand,
Until your grace gives me my husband back.
Six months already has he been shut up,
And waits the sentence of a judge in vain.

    Gessl. How! would you force me, woman? Hence! Begone!

    Arm. Justice, my lord! Ay, justice! Thou art judge:
Vice-regent of the Emperor—of Heaven.
Then do thy duty,—as thou hopest for justice
From Him who rules above, show it to us!

    Gessl. Hence! Drive this insolent rabble from my sight!

    Arm. (*seizing his horse's reins*).
No, no, by Heaven, I've nothing more to lose—
Thou stir'st not, Viceroy, from this spot, until
Thou dost me fullest justice. Knit thy brows,
And roll thine eyes—I fear not. Our distress
Is so extreme, so boundless, that we care

No longer for thine anger.

Gessl.   Woman, hence!

Give way, or else my horse shall ride you down.

   Arm. Well, let it!—there—

      [Throws her children and herself upon the ground before him.

                    Here on the ground I lie,

I and my children. Let the wretched orphans

Be trodden by thy horse into the dust!

It will not be the worst that thou hast done.

   Har. Are you mad, woman?

   Arm. (continuing with vehemence). Many a day thou hast

Trampled the Emperor's lands beneath thy feet.

Oh, I am but a woman! Were I man,

I'd find some better thing to do, than here

Lie grovelling in the dust.

      [The music of the bridal party is again heard from the top

        of the pass, but more softly.

   Gessl.   Where are **my** knaves?

Drag her away, lest I forget myself,

And do some deed I may repent me of.

   Har. My lord, the servants cannot force their way;

The pass is block'd up by a bridal train.

   Gessl. Too mild a ruler am I to this people,

Their tongues are all too bold—nor have they yet

Been tamed to due submission, as they shall be.

I must take order for the remedy;

I will subdue this stubborn mood of theirs,

This braggart spirit of freedom I will crush,

I will proclaim a new law through the land;

I will—

      [An arrow pierces him,—he puts his hand on his heart and

        is about to sink—with a feeble voice.

           Oh God, have mercy on my soul!

   Har. My lord! my lord! Oh God! What's this? Whence came it?

   Arm. (starts up). Dead, dead! He reels, he falls! 'Tis in his heart!

   Har. (springs from his horse). Horror of horrors! Heavenly

   powers! Sir Knight,

Address yourself for mercy to your God!
You are a dying man.
    Gessl.   That shot was Tell's.

> [*He slides from his horse into the arms of* RUDOLPH DER
> HARRAS, *who lays him down upon the bench.* TELL
> *appears above upon the rocks.*

Tell. Thou know'st the marksman—I, and I alone.
Now are our homesteads free, and innocence
From thee is safe: thou'lt be our curse no more.

>   [TELL *disappears. People rush in.*

Stussi. What is the matter? Tell me what has happen'd?
Arm. The Viceroy's shot,—pierced by a crossbow bolt!
People (*running in*). Who has been shot?

> [*While the foremost of the marriage party are coming on the
> stage, the hindmost are still upon the heights. The music
> continues.*

Har.   He's bleeding fast to death.
Away, for help—pursue the murderer!
Unhappy man, is this to be your end?
You would not listen to my warning words.
Stussi. By Heaven, his cheek is pale! Life's ebbing fast.
Many Voices. Who did the deed?
Har.   What! Are the people mad,
That they make music to a murder? Silence!

> [*Music breaks off suddenly. People continue to flock in.*

Speak, if you can, my lord. Have you no charge
To trust me with?

> [GESSLER *makes signs with his hand, which he repeats with
> vehemence, when he finds they are not understood.*

                  Where shall I take you to?
To Küssnacht? What you say I can't make out.
Oh, do not grow impatient! Leave all thought
Of earthly things and make your peace with Heaven.

> [*The whole marriage party gather round the dying man.*

Stussi. See there! how pale he grows! Death's gathering now
About his heart;—his eyes grow dim and glazed.
Arm. (*holds up a child*). Look, children, how a tyrant dies!

Har.   Mad hag!
Have you no touch of feeling, that your eyes
Gloat on a sight so horrible as this?
Help me—take hold. What, will not one assist
To pull the torturing arrow from his breast?
  Women. What! touch the man whom God's own hand has
    struck!
  Har. All curses light on you!   [*Draws his sword.*
  Stussi (seizes his arm).   Gently, Sir Knight!
Your power is at end. 'Twere best forbear.
Our country's foe has fallen. We will brook
No further violence. We are free men.
  All. The country's free.
  Har.   And is it come to this?
Fear and obedience at an end so soon?
        [*To the soldiers of the guard who are thronging in.*
You see, my friends, the bloody piece of work
Has here been done. 'Tis now too late for help,
And to pursue the murderer were vain.
We've other things to think of. On to Küssnacht.
And let us save that fortress for the King!
For in a moment such as this, all ties
Of order, fealty and faith, are rent.
And we can trust to no man's loyalty.
        [*As he is going out with the soldiers, six* FRATRES MISERICORDIÆ
          appear.
  Arm. Here comes the brotherhood of mercy. Room!
  Stussi. The victim's slain, and now the ravens stoop.
  *Brothers of Mercy (form a semicircle round the body, and sing in
      solemn tones).*

            Death hurries on with hasty stride,
              No respite man from him may gain,
            He cuts him down, when life's full tide
              Is throbbing strong in every vein.
            Prepared or not the call to hear,
            He must before his Judge appear.
      [*While they are repeating the two last lines, the curtain falls.*

ACT V

SCENE I.—*A common near Altdorf. In the background to the right the keep of Uri, with the scaffold still standing, as in the third scene of the first Act. To the left, the view opens upon numerous mountains, on all of which signal fires are burning. Day is breaking, and distant bells are heard ringing in several directions.*

RUODI, KUONI, WERNI, MASTER MASON, *and many other country people, also women and children.*

Ruodi. See there! The beacons on the mountain heights!
Mason. Hark how the bells above the forest toll!
Ruodi. The enemy's routed.
Mason.   And the forts are storm'd.
Ruodi. And we of Uri, do we still endure
Upon our native soil the tyrant's keep?
Are we the last to strike for liberty?
Mason. Shall the yoke stand, that was to curb our necks?
Up! Tear it to the ground!
All.   Down, down with it!
Ruodi. Where is the Stier of Uri?
Uri.   Here. What would ye?
Ruodi. Up to your tower, and wind us such a blast,
As shall resound afar, from peak to peak;
Rousing the echoes of each glen and hill,
To rally swiftly all the mountain men!

                          [*Exit* STIER OF URI—*Enter* WALTER FÜRST.
Fürst. Stay, stay, my friends! As yet we have not learn'd
What has been done in Unterwald and Schwytz.
Let's wait till we receive intelligence!
Ruodi. Wait, wait for what? The accursed tyrant's dead
And on us freedom's glorious day has dawn'd!
Mason. How! Are these flaming signals not enough,
That blaze on every mountain-top around?
Ruodi. Come all, fall to—come, men and women, all!
Destroy the scaffold! Burst the arches! Down,
Down with the walls, let not a stone remain!

Mason. Come, comrades, come! We built it, and we know
How best to hurl it down.

All. Come! Down with it!

[*They fall upon the building on every side.*

Fürst. The floodgate's burst. They're not to be restrained.

[*Enter* MELCHTHAL *and* BAUMGARTEN.

Melch. What! Stands the fortress still, when Sarnen lies
In ashes, and the Rossberg's in our hands?

Fürst. You, Melchthal, here? D'ye bring us liberty?
Are all the Cantons from our tyrants freed?

Melch. We've swept them from the soil. Rejoice, my friend,
Now, at this very moment, while we speak,
There's not one tyrant left in Switzerland!

Fürst. How did you get the forts into your power?

Melch. Rudenz it was who by a bold assault
With manly valour mastered Sarnen's keep.
The Rossberg I had storm'd the night before.
But hear, what chanced. Scarce had we driven the foe
Forth from the keep, and given it to the flames,
That now rose crackling upwards to the skies,
When from the blaze rush'd Diethelm, Gessler's page,
Exclaiming, "Lady Bertha will be burnt!"

Fürst. Good heavens!

[*The beams of the scaffold are heard falling.*

Melch. 'Twas she herself. Here had she been
By Gessler's orders secretly immured.
Up sprang Rudenz in frenzy. For even now
The beams and massive posts were crashing down,
And through the stifling smoke the piteous shrieks
Of the unhappy lady.

Fürst. Is she saved?

Melch. 'Twas not a time to hesitate or pause!
Had he been but our baron, and no more,
We should have been most chary of our lives;
But he was our confederate, and Bertha
Honour'd the people. So, without a thought,
We risk'd the worst, and rush'd into the flames.

Fürst. But is she saved?

Melch.   She is. Rudenz and I
Bore her between us from the blazing pile.
With crashing timbers toppling all around.
And when she had revived, the danger past,
And raised her eyes to look upon the sun,
The baron fell upon my breast; and then
A silent vow between us two was sworn,
A vow that, welded in yon furnace heat,
Will last through ev'ry shock of time and fate.

Fürst. Where is the Landenberg?

Melch.   Across the Brünig.
'Twas not my fault he bore his sight away;
He who had robb'd my father of his eyes!
He fled—I followed—overtook him soon,
And dragg'd him to my father's feet. The sword
Already quiver'd o'er the caitiff's head,
When from the pity of the blind old man,
He wrung the life which, craven-like, he begged.
He swore URPHEDE,[23] never to return:
He'll keep his oath, for he has felt our arm.

Fürst. Oh, well for you, you have not stain'd with blood
Our spotless victory!

Children (*running across the stage with fragments of wood*).
We're free! we're free!

Fürst. Oh! what a joyous scene! These children will
Remember it when all their heads are grey.

> [*Girls bring in the cap upon a pole. The whole stage is filled
> with people.*

Ruodi. Here is the cap, to which we were to bow!

Baum. What shall we do with it? Do you decide!

Fürst. Heavens! 'Twas beneath this cap my grandson stood!

Several Voices. Destroy the emblem of the tyrant's power!
Let it be burnt!

---

[23] The URPHEDE was an oath of peculiar force. When a man, who was at feud
with another, invaded his lands and was worsted, he often made terms with his
enemy by swearing the *Urphede,* by which he bound himself to depart, and never
to return with a hostile intention.

Fürst.　　　　　No. Rather be preserved;
'Twas once the instrument of despots—now
'Twill of our freedom be a lasting sign.

> [*Peasants, men, women, and children, some standing, others
> sitting upon the beams of the shattered scaffold, all pic-
> turesquely grouped, in a large semicircle.*

Melch. Thus now, my friends, with light and merry hearts,
We stand upon the wreck of tyranny;
And gloriously the work has been fulfilled,
Which we at Rootli pledged ourselves to do.

Fürst. No, not fulfilled. The work is but begun:
Courage and concord firm, we need them both;
For, be assured, the king will make all speed,
To avenge his Viceroy's death, and reinstate,
By force of arms, the tyrant we've expelled.

Melch. Why let him come, with all his armaments!
The foe's expelled, that press'd us from within.
The foe without we are prepared to meet!

Ruodi. The passes to our Cantons are but few;
These with our bodies we will block, we will!

Baum. Knit are we by a league will ne'er be rent,
And all his armies shall not make us quail.

> [*Enter* RÖSSELMANN *and* STAUFFACHER.

Rössel. (*speaking as he enters*). These are the awful judgments
of the Lord!

Peas. What is the matter?

Rössel.　　　　　　　In what times we live!

Fürst. Say on, what is't? Ha, Werner, is it you?
What tidings?

Peas.　　　　　What's the matter?

Rössel.　　　　　　　Hear and wonder!

Stauff. We are released from one great cause of dread.

Rössel. The Emperor is murdered.

Fürst.　　　　　　　Gracious Heaven!

> [PEASANTS *rise up and throng round* STAUFFACHER.

All. Murder'd!—the Emp'ror? What! The Emp'ror! Hear!

Melch. Impossible! How came you by the news?

Stauff. 'Tis true! Near Bruck, by the assassin's hand,
King Albert fell. A most trustworthy man,
John Müller, from Schaffhausen, brought the news.
　　Fürst. Who dared commit so horrible a deed?
　　Stauff. The doer makes the deed more dreadful still;
It was his nephew, his own brother's son,
Duke John of Austria, who struck the blow.
　　Melch. What drove him to so dire a parricide?
　　Stauff. The Emp'ror kept his patrimony back,
Despite his urgent importunities;
'Twas said, he meant to keep it for himself,
And with a mitre to appease the duke.
However this may be, the duke gave ear
To the ill counsel of his friends in arms:
And with the noble lords, Von Eschenbach,
Von Tegerfeld, Von Wart and Palm, resolved,
Since his demands for justice were despised,
With his own hands to take revenge at least.
　　Fürst. But say—the dreadful deed, how was it done?
　　Stauff. The king was riding down from Stein to Baden,
Upon his way to join the court at Rheinfeld,—
With him a train of high-born gentlemen,
And the young Princes John and Leopold;
And when they'd reach'd the ferry of the Reuss,
The assassins forced their way into the boat,
To separate the Emperor from his suite.
His highness landed, and was riding on
Across a fresh plough'd field—where once, they say,
A mighty city stood in Pagan times—
With Hapsburg's ancient turrets full in sight,
That was the cradle of his princely race.
When Duke John plunged a dagger in his throat,
Palm ran him thro' the body with his lance,
And Eschenbach, to end him, clove his skull;
So down he sank, all weltering in his blood,
On his own soil, by his own kinsmen slain.
Those on the opposite bank beheld the deed,

But, parted by the stream, could only raise
An unavailing cry of loud lament.
A poor old woman, sitting by the way,
Raised him, and on her breast he bled to death.

Melch. Thus has he dug his own untimely grave,
Who sought insatiably to grasp it all.

Stauff. The country round is fill'd with dire alarm,
The passes are blockaded everywhere,
And sentinels on ev'ry frontier set;
E'en ancient Zurich barricades her gates,
That have stood open for these thirty years,
Dreading the murd'rers and th' avengers more.
For cruel Agnes comes, the Hungarian Queen,
By all her sex's tenderness untouch'd,
Arm'd with the thunders of the ban, to wreak
Dire vengeance for her parent's royal blood,
On the whole race of those that murder'd him,—
Their servants, children, children's children,—yea,
Upon the stones that built their castle walls.
Deep has she sworn a vow to immolate
Whole generations on her father's tomb,
And bathe in blood as in the dew of May.

Melch. Is't known which way the murderers have fled?

Stauff. No sooner had they done the deed, than they
Took flight, each following a different route,
And parted ne'er to see each other more.
Duke John must still be wand'ring in the mountains.

Fürst. And thus their crime has borne no fruit for them.
Revenge bears never fruit. Itself, it is
The dreadful food it feeds on; its delight
Is murder—its satiety despair.

Stauff. The assassins reap no profit by their crime;
But we shall pluck with unpolluted hands
The teeming fruits of their most bloody deed.
For we are ransomed from our heaviest fear;
The direst foe of liberty has fallen,
And, 'tis reported, that the crown will pass

From Hapsburg's house into another line;
The Empire is determined to assert
Its old prerogative of choice, I hear.

Fürst (and several others). Is any named?

Stauff.   The Count of Luxembourg's
Already chosen by the general voice.

Fürst. 'Tis well we stood so staunchly by the Empire!
Now we may hope for justice, and with cause.

Stauff. The Emperor will need some valiant friends.
He will 'gainst Austria's vengeance be our shield.

> [*The peasantry embrace. Enter* SACRISTAN *with Imperial
> messenger.*

Sacris. Here are the worthy chiefs of Switzerland!

Rössel. (and several others). Sacrist, what news?

Sacris.   A courier brings this letter.

All (to WALTER FÜRST). Open and read it.

Fürst (reading).   "To the worthy men
Of Uri, Schwytz, and Unterwald, the Queen
Elizabeth sends grace and all good wishes."

Many Voices. What wants the queen with us? Her reign is done.

Fürst (reading). "In the great grief and doleful widowhood,
In which the bloody exit of her lord
Has plunged the queen, still in her mind she bears
The ancient faith and love of Switzerland."

Melch. She ne'er did that in her prosperity.

Rössel. Hush, let us hear!

Fürst (reading).   "And she is well assured,
Her people will in due abhorrence hold
The perpetrators of this damned deed.
On the three Cantons, therefore, she relies,
That they in nowise lend the murderers aid;
But rather, that they loyally assist,
To give them up to the avenger's hand,
Remembering the love and grace which they
Of old received from Rudolph's royal house."

> [*Symptoms of dissatisfaction among the peasantry.*

Many Voices. The love and grace!

Stauff. Grace from the father we, indeed, received,
But what have we to boast of from the son?
Did he confirm the charter of our freedom,
As all preceding emperors had done?
Did he judge righteous judgment, or afford
Shelter, or stay, to innocence oppress'd?
Nay, did he e'en give audience to the men
We sent to lay our grievances before him?
Not one of all these things did the king do,
And had we not ourselves achieved our rights
By our own stalwart hands, the wrongs we bore
Had never touch'd him. Gratitude to him!
Within these vales he sowed no seeds of that;
He stood upon an eminence—he might
Have been a very father to his people,
But all his aim and pleasure was to raise
Himself and his own house: and now may those
Whom he has aggrandized, lament for him.

Fürst. We will not triumph in his fall, nor now
Recall to mind the wrongs that we endured.
Far be't from us! Yet, that we should avenge
The sovereign's death, who never did us good,
And hunt down those who ne'er molested us,
Becomes us not, nor is our duty. Love
Must be a tribute free, and unconstrain'd;
From all enforced duties death absolves,
And unto him we owe no further debt.

Melch. And if the queen laments within her bower,
Accusing Heaven in sorrow's wild despair;
Here see a people, from its anguish freed,
To that same Heav'n send up its thankful praise.
Who would reap tears, must sow the seeds of love.

                                          [*Exit the Imperial courier.*

Stauff. (*to the people*). But where is Tell? Shall he, our freedom's
    founder,
Alone be absent from our festival?
He did the most—endured the worst of all.

Come—to his dwelling let us all repair,
And bid the Saviour of our country hail!   [*Exeunt omnes.*

SCENE II.—*Interior of* TELL's *cottage. A fire burning on the hearth. The open door shows the scene outside*

HEDWIG, WALTER, *and* WILLIAM

Hedw. My own dear boys! your father comes to-day;
He lives, is free, and we and all are free;
The country owes its liberty to him!
Walt. And I, too, mother, bore my part in it!
I must be named with him. My father's shaft
Ran my life close, but yet I never flinch'd.
Hedw. (*embracing him*). Yes, yes, thou art restored to me again!
Twice have I seen thee given to my sad eyes,
Twice suffered all a mother's pangs for thee!
But this is past—I have you both, boys, both!
And your dear father will be back to-day.
               [*A monk appears at the door.*
Will. See, mother, yonder stands a holy friar;
He comes for alms, no doubt.
Hedw.   Go lead him in,
That we may give him cheer, and make him feel
That he has come into the house of joy.
         [*Exit, and returns immediately with a cup.*
Will. (*to the monk*). Come in, good man. Mother will give
    you food!
Walt. Come in and rest, then go refresh'd away!
Monk (*glancing round in terror, with unquiet looks*).
    Where am I? In what country? Tell me.
Walt.   How!
Are you bewildered, that you know not where?
You are at Bürglen, in the land of Uri,
Just at the entrance of the Shechenthal.
Monk (*to* HEDWIG). Are you alone? Your husband, is he here?
Hedw. I am expecting him. But what ails you, man?
There's something in your looks, that omens ill!

Whoe'er you be, you are in want—take that.

> [*Offers him the cup.*

    Monk. Howe'er my sinking heart may yearn for food,
Nought will I taste till you have promised first—
    Hedw. Touch not my garments, come not near me, monk!
You must stand farther back, if I'm to hear you.
    Monk. Oh, by this hearth's bright, hospitable blaze,
By your dear children's heads, which I embrace—

> [*Grasps the boys.*

    Hedw. Stand back, I say! What is your purpose, man?
Back from my boys! You are no monk,—no, no,
Beneath the robe you wear peace should abide,
But peace abides not in such looks as yours.
    Monk. I am the wretchedest of living men.
    Hedw. The heart is never deaf to wretchedness;
But your look freezes up my inmost soul.
    Walt. (*springs up*). Mother, here's father!
    Hedw.   Oh, my God!

> [*Is about to follow, trembles and stops.*

    Will. (*running after his brother*). My father!
    Walt. (*without*). Here, here once more!
    Will. (*without*).   My father, my dear father!
    Tell (*without*). Yes, here once more! Where is your
    mother, boys?   [*They enter.*
    Walt. There at the door she stands, and can no further,
She trembles so with terror and with joy.
    Tell. Oh Hedwig, Hedwig, mother of my children!
God has been kind and helpful in our woes.
No tyrant's hand shall e'er divide us more.
    Hedw. (*falling on his neck*). Oh, Tell, what anguish have I borne
    for thee!   [*Monk becomes attentive.*
    Tell. Forget it, now, and live for joy alone!
I'm here again with you! This is my cot!
I stand again upon mine own hearthstone!
    Will. But, father, where's your crossbow? Not with you?
    Tell. Thou shalt not ever see it more, my boy.
Within a holy shrine it has been placed,

And in the chase shall ne'er be used again.

 Hedw. Oh, Tell! Tell!   [*Steps back, dropping his hand.*

 Tell.   What alarms thee, dearest wife?

 Hedw. How—how doest thou return to me? This hand—

Dare I take hold of it? This hand—Oh, God!

 Tell (*with firmness and animation*). Has shielded you and set

  my country free;

Freely I raise it in the face of Heaven.

      [*Monk gives a sudden start—he looks at him.*

Who is this friar here?

 Hedw.   Ah, I forgot him;

Speak thou with him; I shudder at his presence.

 Monk (*stepping nearer*). Are you the Tell who slew the Gover-

  nor?

 Tell. Yes, I am he. I hide the fact from no man.

 Monk. And you are Tell! Ah! it is God's own hand,

That hath conducted me beneath your roof.

 Tell (*examining him closely*).

You are no monk. Who are you?

 Monk.   You have slain

The Governor, who did you wrong. I, too,

Have slain a foe, who robb'd me of my rights.

He was no less your enemy than mine.

I've rid the land of him.

 Tell (*drawing back*). You are—oh, horror!

In—children, children—in, without a word,

Go, my dear wife! Go! Go! Unhappy man,

You should be—

 Hedw.   Heav'ns, who is it?

 Tell.   Do not ask.

Away! away! the children must not hear it.

Out of the house—away! You must not rest

'Neath the same roof with this unhappy man!

 Hedw. Alas! What is it? Come.   [*Exit with the children.*

 Tell (*to the* MONK).   You are the Duke

Of Austria—I know it. You have slain

The Emperor, your uncle and liege lord.

John. He robb'd me of my patrimony.
Tell.   How!
Slain him—your King, your uncle! And the earth
Still bears you! And the sun still shines on you!
John. Tell, hear me; are you—
Tell.   Reeking, with the blood
Of him that was your Emperor, your kinsman,
Dare you set foot within my spotless house,
Dare to an honest man to show your face,
And claim the rights of hospitality?
John. I hoped to find compassion at your hands.
You took, like me, revenge upon your foe!
Tell. Unhappy man! Dare you confound the crime
Of blood-imbrued ambition with the act
Forced on a father in mere self-defence?
Had you to shield your children's darling heads,
To guard your fireside's sanctuary—ward off
The last, the direst doom from all you loved?
To Heaven I raise my unpolluted hands,
To curse your act and you! I have avenged
That holy nature which you have profaned.
I have no part with you. You murdered, I
Have shielded all that was most dear to me.
John. You cast me off to comfortless despair!
Tell. I shrink with horror while I talk with you.
Hence, on the dread career you have begun!
Cease to pollute the home of innocence!
                              [JOHN *turns to depart.*
John. I cannot and I will not live this life!
Tell. And yet my soul bleeds for you. Gracious Heaven,
So young, of such a noble line, the grandson
Of Rudolph, once my lord and Emperor,
An outcast—murderer—standing at my door,
The poor man's door—a suppliant, in despair!   [*Covers his face.*
John. If you have power to weep, oh let my fate
Move your compassion—it is horrible!
I am—say, rather was—a prince. I might

Have been most happy, had I only curb'd
The impatience of my passionate desires:
But envy gnaw'd my heart—I saw the youth
Of mine own cousin Leopold endow'd
With honour, and enrich'd with broad domains,
The while myself, of equal age with him,
In abject slavish nonage was kept back.

    Tell. Unhappy man, your uncle knew you well,
When from you land and subjects he withheld!
You, by your mad and desperate act have set
A fearful seal upon his wise resolve.
Where are the bloody partners of your crime?

    John. Where'er the avenging furies may have borne them;
I have not seen them since the luckless deed.

    Tell. Know you the Empire's ban is out,—that you
Are interdicted to your friends, and given
An outlaw'd victim to your enemies!

    John. Therefore I shun all public thoroughfares,
And venture not to knock at any door—
I turn my footsteps to the wilds, and through
The mountains roam, a terror to myself!
From mine own self I shrink with horror back,
If in a brook I see my ill-starr'd form!
If you have pity or a human heart—

                        [*Falls down before him.*

    Tell. Stand up, stand up! I say.

    John.   Not till you give
Your hand in promise of assistance to me.

    Tell. Can I assist you? Can a sinful man?
Yet get ye up—how black soe'er your crime—
You are a man. I, too, am one. From Tell
Shall no one part uncomforted. I will
Do all that lies within my power.

    John (*springs up and grasps him ardently by the hand*). Oh, Tell,
You save me from the terrors of despair.

    Tell. Let go my hand! You must away. You can not
Remain here undiscover'd, and, discover'd,

You cannot count on succour. Which way, then,
Would you be going? Where do you hope to find
A place of rest?

    John.   Alas! I know not where.

    Tell. Hear, then, what Heaven unto my heart suggests.
You must to Italy,—to Saint Peter's City—
There cast yourself at the Pope's feet,—confess
Your guilt to him, and ease your laden soul!

    John. Will he not to the avengers yield me up?

    Tell. Whate'er he does, accept it as from God.

    John. But how am I to reach that unknown land?
I have no knowledge of the way, and dare not
Attach myself to other travellers.

    Tell. I will describe the road, so mark me well!
You must ascend, keeping along the Reuss,
Which from the mountains dashes wildly down.

    John (in alarm). What! See the Reuss? The witness of my deed!

    Tell. The road you take lies through the river's gorge,
And many a cross proclaims where travellers
Have been by avalanches done to death.

    John. I have no fear for nature's terrors, so
I can appease the torments of my soul.

    Tell. At every cross, kneel down and expiate
Your crime with burning penitential tears—
And if you 'scape the perils of the pass,
And are not whelm'd beneath the drifted snows,
That from the frozen peaks come sweeping down,
You'll reach the bridge that's drench'd with drizzling spray.
Then if it give not way beneath your guilt,
When you have left it safely in your rear,
Before you frowns the gloomy Gate of Rocks,
Where never sun did shine. Proceed through this,
And you will reach a bright and gladsome vale.
Yet must you hurry on with hasty steps,
You must not linger in the haunts of peace.

    John. O, Rudolph, Rudolph, royal grandsire! Thus
Thy grandson first sets foot within thy realms!

Tell. Ascending still, you gain the Gotthardt's heights,
Where are the tarns, the everlasting tarns,
That from the streams of Heaven itself are fed,
There to the German soil you bid farewell;
And thence, with swift descent, another stream
Leads you to Italy, your promised land.

    [*Ranz des Vaches sounded on Alp-horns is heard without.*
But I hear voices! Hence!

    Hedw. (*hurrying in*).   Where art thou, Tell?
My father comes, and in exulting bands
All the confederates approach.

    Duke John (*covering himself*). Woe's me!
I dare not tarry 'mong these happy men!

    Tell. Go, dearest wife, and give this man to eat.
Spare not your bounty; for his road is long.
And one where shelter will be hard to find.
Quick—they approach!

    Hedw.   Who is he?

    Tell.   Do not ask!
And when he quits you, turn your eyes away,
So that you do not see which way he goes.

    [Duke John *advances hastily towards* Tell, *but he beckons*
        him aside and exit. When both have left the stage, the
        scene changes, and discloses in

    Scene III.—*The whole valley before* Tell's *house, the heights which*
enclose it occupied by peasants, grouped into tableaux. Some are seen
crossing a lofty bridge, which crosses the Shechen. Walter Fürst
with the two boys. Walter Fürst *with the two boys,* Werner, *and*
Stauffacher *come forward. Others throng after them. When* Tell
appears, all receive him with loud cheers.

    All. Long live brave Tell, our shield, our saviour!

    [*While those in front are crowding round* Tell, *and embrac-*
        ing him, Rudenz *and* Bertha *appear. The former salutes*
        the peasantry, the latter embraces Hedwig. *The music*
        from the mountains continues to play. When it has
        stopped, Bertha *steps into the centre of the crowd.*

Berth. Peasants! Confederates! Into your league
Receive me, who was happily the first
That found deliverance in the land of freedom.
To your brave hands I now entrust my rights.
Will you protect me as your citizen?
   Peas. Ay, that we will, with life and goods!
   Berth.   'Tis well!
And now to him (*turning to* RUDENZ). I frankly give my hand,
A free Swiss maiden to a free Swiss man!
   Rud. And from this moment all my serfs are free!
                        [*Music, and the curtain falls.*

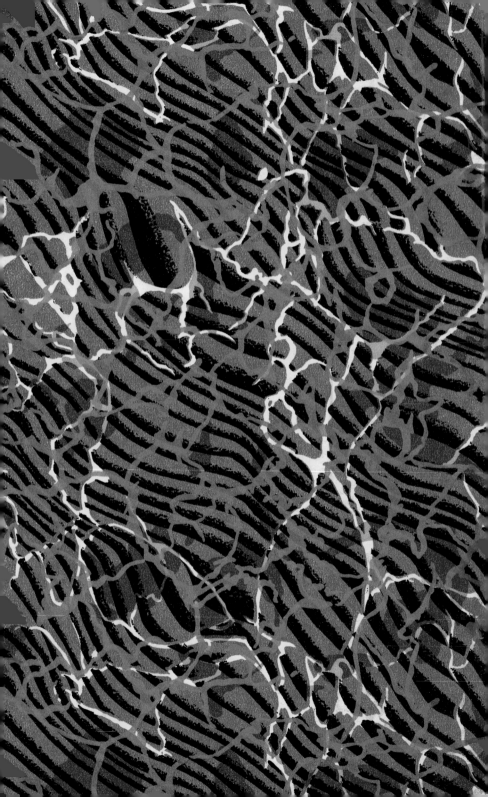